Praise for *Choosing Emotions*

"It is really good. It's a book I can enjoy not only as an overall book to read at a sitting, but one I can pick up when I have an emotional emergency."
—**Hon. Susan Patterson, JD, MBA,** SVRA Champion and 2016 Rookie of the Year Magistrate Judge

"This is a world-class conversation starter, and it is one of the most helpful references for writers and public speakers ever put together."
—**Bradford T. Lefton, Esq.,** Seattle

"If you find that brilliant emotional quotes and street phrases help you connect and resonate with your clients, patients, and audience, here is your gold mine."
—**Dr. Peter Lindquist, DNP, RN, NEA-BC,** and Healthcare CEO, Nashville

"Choosing Emotions is a great resource for finding how the greatest minds in history have approached and handled emotional problems in their lives."
—**Joseph J. Hessel, MD,** Cardiovascular and Thoracic Surgery, Phoenix

"I love the manuscript. I keep it nearby."
—**Nick Christensen,** Father, Husband, Commercial Real Estate Executive, and Former #1-ranked U.S. Amateur Surfer, Manhattan Beach

"Fun and provocative. Ten minutes spent with this book will change your life for the better. I think you will also find it is a platform for serious introspection."
—**H. Hill McAlister,** Former President of the Rotary Club of Nashville, and Former President of the Middle Tennessee Council of the Boy Scouts of America

"Choosing Emotions is a go-to resource, providing expert emotional quotes and back-stories, plus powerful 'street' usages to help connect better with your audience in any paper, talk, or presentation. You'll be really moved by the book's precise and powerful life insights."
—**David Gow,** Chairman, Gow Media, Inc.
CEO, The Center for Houston's Future

"Choosing Emotions is a modern sacred masterpiece. This book is a tool that will transform the heart of every reader. I call it my Emotional Bible."
—**Jan Goss,** Executive Consultant, Speaker, and #1 Best-Selling Author, Austin Presidential Lifetime Achievement Award (2025)

"Choosing Emotions *is a fun and welcome resource for knowing ourselves more deeply and a pathway to wisdom. The more we can define and understand emotions the closer we come to wisdom. With deep research and zinger quotes, D. Earl Johnston gives us those definitions and a deep well of wise sayings.*"

— **Lois Farfel Stark,** Emmy-awarded global documentary filmmaker with NBC News and multiple award-winning author of *The Telling Image: Shapes of Changing Times.* Her TEDx talk is *Shape: Hiding in Plain Sight.*

"*D. Earl Johnston has brilliantly and methodically gathered thousands of timely quotes from a wide variety of authors, spanning centuries, to help all of us navigate these difficult days in which we find ourselves. This outstanding book of helpful quotes will benefit us when we simply need some encouraging words to lift our spirits or assist us in facing a challenge.*"

— **Sayres Dudley,** Dudley & Associates, Dallas

"*Moving beyond mere dictionary definitions of emotions to how many of the world's greatest minds have actually lived them out,* Choosing Emotions *adds both depth and richness to how we can improve our lives. From Bullying to Bravery, from Calm to Charisma, from Fear to Friendship, and from Parenting to Prayer, this book delivers.*"

— **J. Pittman McGehee, DD,** Episcopal priest and Jungian analyst in private practice in Austin, Texas, and widely known as a lecturer and educator in the field of analytical psychology and religion, as well as a poet and essayist. He is the author of *The Invisible Church: Finding Spirituality Where You Are, Raising Lazarus: The Science of Healing the Soul, Words Made Flesh, The Paradox of Love,* and *Growing Down.*

"*Emotions can be toxic, particularly in our current fractured world. They can also be glorious. By using famous quotes along with 'street' phrases from the heart,* Choosing Emotions *has created an innovative new 'Emotionary.' It's fun too and sets a break-through standard for explaining emotions. As a frequent speaker, I find it to be a guideline for successful communication with whatever audience I'm addressing. It's a must read.*"

— **The Honorable Rodney Mims Cook, Jr.**
CEO, National Monuments Foundation
President, Millennium Gate Museum
President, Shin Dae-yong Global Peace Institute
Former United States Commissioner of Fine Arts
Atlanta, Seoul, Washington

CHOOSING EMOTIONS

Thinking with Your Head and Acting with Your Heart

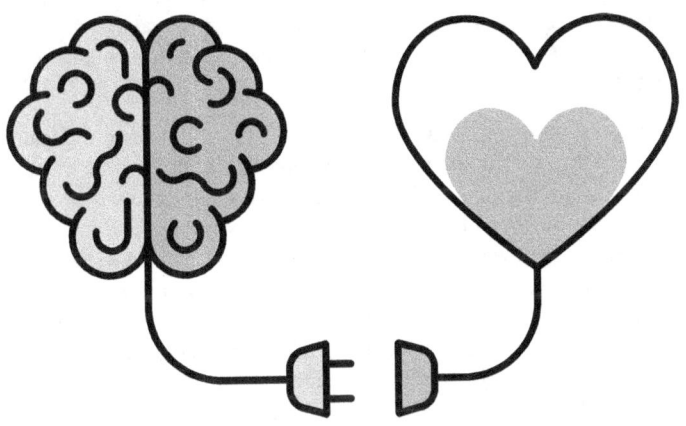

*Life Insights from the Street to the Stratosphere
Anxiety, Depression, OCD, Belief, Wisdom, Joy,
and 272 Emotions*

D. EARL JOHNSTON
EDITED BY PAUL HIGGINS, PHD

WESTERN GOLD
PUBLISHING
NEW YORK•LOS ANGELES

Editorial services by Paul Higgins, Ph.D.
Design by TLC Book Design, *TLCBookDesign.com*
Cover: Marisa Jackson | Interior: Monica Thomas
Cover image: © istockphoto.com | Anastasiia_New

To David, John, Buddy, Ernie, Albert, Jay, Nick, Brad,
Bob, Marc, Rodney, Whitney, Larry, Jim, Hy, Shelly,
Debbie, Robin, Jackie, Carrie, Betty, Maureen,
Lois, and Catherine;

To Scooter and all of the Smith, Glasgow,
and McMurrey families;
Thank you for teaching me about life.
To paraphrase Walt Whitman:
"No doubt I have deserved my enemies, but I don't
really think I deserved friends as special as you."

To Hill, whose modest brilliance, depth, and wisdom
set me on the right path;

To my family, whose love of words and happy stories
are always part of me;

To Kamri Belle, my loyal, joyful companion
and four-footed Muse;

and

To my exceptional and inspiring daughter
Lexi, Always in My Heart.

TABLE OF CONTENTS

WHO WILL REALLY LIKE THIS BOOK

Where would you turn quickly to bring yourself up to speed about an emotional issue? What if you were addressing a surprising new emotional scene at home, school, or work? How about if you were looking for ways to resonate with your audience in a presentation, paper, or talk? Chatting with friends over coffee or at the gym? Or just wanting to know "how to say it" about new trends on the web or in the media? By developing an innovative format which consolidates the best elements of the dictionary, encyclopedia, thesaurus, "street" expressions, world-class quotes, and best-sellers into one place, we have created a state-of-the-art full concept briefing (our new 'emotionary' format) to answer the call.

Choosing Emotions is a compact self-help research gem for students, teachers, writers, speechmakers, presenters, podcasters, influencers, editors, researchers, artists, parents, and anyone in a relationship. By introducing a concise and original format which is far more useful than prior desk references, the book defines over 250 emotions and emotional conditions, with entertaining and enlightening perspectives presented through a pioneering compilation of popular, heart-based, and even "street"-level uses of each word. We then build out each emotion with 12–25 supporting quotes from the world's top experts. Our quotes are deeply researched, inclusive, and draw on thousands of time-tested and state-of-the-art insights from 1,800 thought leaders across three thousand years of history. All are presented to help solve today's issues. Importantly, we reduce volumes of research data into a *brief* of only a page or two per emotion, each of which identifies key life insights and top professional references at a glance.

The book especially shares heartfelt humor and cutting-edge terms and phrases from world-class experts in their own words. Our layout is innovative, combining both popular usages and academic insights in helping to frame an advanced understanding of each emotion. The curated quotes have been selected to be widely inclusive and apolitical, and they are designed to provide you with a meaningful *Who's Who* introduction to leading professional voices in each field.

We are aware of no comparable book which references even a third as many emotional conditions, or which includes even a tenth as many expert contributors, and we do not know of a faster, more informative, or more entertaining way to gain an elite orientation to over 250 emotional conditions than from these pages.

From *Addiction, Bullying, Anxiety, Depression, Procrastination, Trauma,* and *OCD,* to *Attitude, Belief, Charisma, Determination, Love, Joy, Patience,* and *Wisdom,* your resource is here.

PREFACE

Emotions uniquely connect our body, spirit, and mind. From this, it emerges that virtually every memory, thought, and vision incorporates at least one basic emotional component or theme. Yet we navigate our lives from birth with limited instruction or a 'guidebook on emotions.' We learn through trial and error, the behaviors we observe in our families and friends, what we absorb from religious and spiritual texts, and in school. In many ways we are thrown into the pool of daily living to figure it out on our own. As we mature, we steadily refine our own insights about how best to navigate issues through our emotional reactions and choices. Academia and the latest news in psychology clearly help, and yet the sciences can easily get overburdened by technical talk and dense acronyms understood by relatively few experts. Very notably, the frequently dry, short, and *objective* technical references found in classic reference dictionaries and self-help books often fall far short in explaining the *subjective* emotional realities we feel in our daily lives.

Choosing Emotions was developed to bridge the gap between advances known to "the sciences" with the equally helpful but more practical *heart-based* viewpoints of "the humanities" (including music, drama, literature, and the arts). Emotions operate in the twin worlds of both science and spirituality, and our goal was to expand on classic objective definitions by adding subjective, idiomatic, popular, and heart-based phrases and meaningful expert quotes to provide truly enlightening breadth and depth.

This book began nine years ago as a self-help research project intended to help unpack the troubling gateway emotions of anxiety, depression, shame, and obsessive-compulsive disorder (OCD), among others. But gaining any quick clarity was blunted by dense or lengthier books and also limited by single-author viewpoints. There had to be a faster and broader way to get up to speed and to "brief" ourselves. In trying to be practical in getting our heads around what was needed, a radically streamlined format began to take shape.

A familiar approach in modern literature—as seen in both the arts and sciences—has been for the author to import a quote or reference from another known expert in order to support his or her viewpoint. Highlighting a supporting "expert" quote can often be both memorable and on-point, and this technique is widely used. *But what happens if we turn the current paradigm upside down, and make **multiple** imported expert quotes the actual **core** substance of the discussion about an emotional condition? That is, why not make a broad variety of expert quotes the "cake" instead of merely the "icing"? And what happens if we also add still further breadth and depth through a rich survey of popular, heart-based, and "street" usages of the emotions as used in everyday conversation?*

Was Shakespeare the First to Use Subjective or Slang Emotional Phrases?

Up to now, so-called slang and "experiential" phrases have been dismissed by virtually all traditional reference works, usually because they have been regarded as too trendy or as potentially offensive. Yet emotional phrases need not be overly trendy or offensive at all. They simply need to add lasting value through precision and usefulness. Why not build out our understanding of emotions with selected subjective *popular and heart-based usages*? As we will see, these uses often resonate, and so they are remembered. Where they are remembered, they truly enter the language. After all, didn't Shakespeare reset the world of literature by being first to introduce unpublished, colorful, and popular emotional phrases and words into his works? Over four centuries years later—

it's Greek to me	*swagger*
star-crossed lovers	*bedazzled*
wearing your heart on your sleeve	*cold-blooded*
wild goose chase	*good riddance*
break the ice	*brave new world*

—plus scores of Shakespeare's vivid and colorful phrases are examples of heart-based emotional resonance at its enduring best. Remarkably, he was even first to introduce the word "lonely" in his drama *Coriolanus*. As a grandmaster of innovation, impact, and resonance in language, Shakespeare may have been first to make emotional wording *cool*.

This book took first form as a compendium of 'zinger' emotional quotes—as introduced by classic *objective* definitions—and then it mushroomed by adding in popular and heart-based *subjective* phrases. Emotional phrases and quotes added valuable impact because of their conversational relevance and usefulness. If we can say that standard definitions provided the "black-and-white" basics, then heart-based emotional phrases added the quantum leap of "color" and relevance into daily life. In the worlds of both music and poetry, the words which stay with us longest are often where the emotions ring truest to our hearts. Stated simply, heart-based phrases add power because they are how *friends* talk to each other, and because they *resonate*.

Our end goal is the promotion of **emotional coherence**. That is, to help define, inform, enlighten, and inspire both your head *and* your heart through resonant popular phrases *and* expert quotes covering over 250 emotional conditions. Overall, we present the latest in scientific, literary, and professional interpretations in a concise format which includes an effective *Who's Who* survey of experts, along with top *phrases of art* used in each field.

Before moving ahead, a short personal note. While researching this book, a few of my own scribblings came to mind for inclusion here until I overheard a guest bantering on a TV talk show: "You know, everyone has a good book in them, and that is probably where it should stay." The audience laughed. I had second thoughts, and then quietly abandoned any inklings of including my own thoughts. But days later a few surprise quotes surfaced, and each of them helped me gain the nerve to incorporate a few observations of my own:

TONI MORRISON, LITT.D, PULITZER, NOBEL: *"If there's a book you really want to read, but it isn't written yet, then you must write it."*

WALT WHITMAN, POET LAUREATE: *"That the powerful play goes on and you may contribute a verse."*

SIR ISAAC NEWTON, FRS: *"If I have seen further, it is by standing on the shoulders of giants."*

Thank you—to each of you reading and to all who contributed—for joining me in this improbable step forward, and for being here. May you find your own trove of phrases and quotes in these pages which truly turn your head and move your world. The heart of emotion is relatability, and my wish is that you find your own inspiration about emotional coherence in this realization which emerged during the writing of the book, and which later became part of the title:

"Think with your head, and act with your heart."

INTRODUCTION

Growing up in a rough-and-tumble household in west Houston of four boys, I was born into a well-established brotherly pecking order. I could go along with what my brothers wanted *willingly*, or I could go along with what they wanted *the hard way*. There was rarely any shortage of direction about what I should be doing. Once, at age 8, when I bravely dared to reach over from the back seat to change the car radio to a different station and song, I was quickly met with a flurry of elbow-jab push backs and memorable warnings never to try anything like *that* again under any circumstances. So my days were usually the same—go with the flow and do as instructed—*or else*. This unfortunately meant my being delegated a lot of odd errands and "run and get me this" chores which seemed always to fall to the pesky littlest brother. (Years later at a laughter-filled holiday family reunion, my brothers generously explained that they had actually been doing me a very *big favor* at the time by *not letting me get spoiled*.)

A minor miracle emerged at age 10 which rescued me from the brotherly-favors drudgery at home. My elementary science teacher, Mr. Caldwell, asked me to join a handful of kids to assist him after school. He was both very popular and knowledgeable about a lot of things beyond science, and he became our much-loved tutor. The library became ours, and we quickly learned how to use the dictionaries, encyclopedias, and all library space and references to investigate our projects. He made it fun, we studied and built things, and the hours and days began to fly by. And by the time I arrived home late afternoons closer to dinner, my brothers had barely noticed I was gone. What had developed was a win-win kid euphoria. From that point on, books, libraries, and bookstores became my 'go-to' destinations on several levels, and the foundation for this book began to take shape. I had always loved to read, and books and research adventures soon became my best friends.

Much later, following my career as a corporate finance and 'due diligence' executive, I had morphed into a professional researcher, hired by law firms to pore over case disputes and to assist them with their clients' business lawsuits. One night at dinner with a childhood friend, I was asked what I knew about *depression*. Hoping I had misunderstood him, and quickly trying to re-direct the discussion toward my finance background, I rattled off an 'economic' answer about economic cycles, interest rates, and slowdowns in business activity, until he gently raised his hand: "No... Not that kind of depression... My wife is back on her feet from her car accident, but she just isn't herself... She says she feels lost and doesn't recognize her life... So far what we have is acronyms that don't help... I don't know what to do..." He understood that I was not credentialed in emotional studies, but he trusted me to give it a fresh look, and I offered to spend a few days digging in to help.

The project started out as a long shot, and I barely knew where to begin. But I rushed to become a student again, surrounding myself with self-help books, articles, and computer screens describing depression, trauma, and related emotions, and in sifting through the professional literature. While reading through a small mountain of single-author books and articles about depression, I bookmarked three quotes that caught my eye and which described the experience of being depressed in more personal and non-technical terms:

ROLLO MAY, BDIV, PHD: *"Depression is the inability to construct a future."*

J.K. ROWLING, CBE, CH: *"Depression is that absence of being able to envision you will ever be cheerful again…It is the most unpleasant thing I have ever experienced."*

HALLEY CORNELL: *"Depression lies. It tells you you've always felt this way, and you always will…but you haven't, and you won't."*

These quotes really moved me, and I decided to go ahead and text them across town to my friend as evidence that I was beginning to understand the situation. He responded within a few minutes: "She started to cry." Alarmed, I asked: "Why? There's hope. All three of them experienced depression and recovered from it." He responded: "That's why she's crying. There's hope. Please keep going."

Almost by accident we had learned a vital principle: that heartfelt assessments from experienced people can be a very powerful tool in understanding complex emotions, and that insightful comments are often more helpful than dry clinical analyses or definitions found in dictionaries or technical references. Reference works can describe emotions from an *objective* or measurable standpoint, but they don't always provide *subjective* experience, context, or a way forward. *What it looks like* is essential to the scientist, but *what it feels like* is even more essential to the patient or person. The best contributors to understanding emotions are often veteran experts with direct personal experience.

So Many More Unexpected Discoveries to Share

What started out as urgent informal research into the world of complex emotions of depression, trauma, and related emotions proved to be surprisingly helpful, and then it burgeoned into an expanded exploration of over 250 emotions, and ultimately into this book. What we learned is that emotions can be vastly underserved by most standard reference works, which center on technical descriptions, but not on the *subjective* insights of how we feel—and especially what we think, say, or do about the way we feel.

Emotions are, after all, personal interpretations, and so scientific, technical, or academic descriptions can fall short. Where life poses emotional issues, the solutions start best with relating and connecting right where we are. What resonates best is often what emerges from the insights of veteran personal experience.

Remarkably, very few current reference books or authors undertake to define 'emotion' or specific emotions at all. (This is addressed more fully in Appendices B and C.) In addition, few if any readily-available reference works even *begin* to address popular expressions or heart-based phrases and quotes which represent the vast majority of how emotions are communicated in daily conversation. One leading reason for this is because it can be difficult to produce relatable emotional definitions in a few concise words. (Try it yourself, it can be a real challenge.) Another reasonable explanation for this is that science (and lexicography, or the study of meanings and usage) prefer the discipline of stable, measurable, and objective terms—yet emotions are subjective/nuanced states which can vary widely by circumstance and experience. A third reason is that reference works traditionally avoid 'slang' as either potentially offensive or too trendy. *But the bulk of how emotions are used and expressed in everyday language is through these popular and heart-based phrases and quotes.* William Shakespeare and ten thousand authors, songwriters, and poets long ago proved the enduring value of resonant subjective words and phrases. We are now taking the space to elevate these heart-based usages to their long-overdue first-tier status.

Emotions often become, by default, the most-used but least-understood aspects of being human. We overlook them because we are *in* them. So we undertake here a far more useful understanding of emotions by adding vital perspective through using both heart-based *subjective* viewpoints as well as through more standard classical *objective* definitions. This is what is new, different, and fully innovative in this book.

In these pages you will also find that these popular and heart-based phrases and quotes can become *solid gold* in day-to-day communications because they simply resonate better with people. If you truly want to connect well with someone about emotions, a really good way to do it is by using heart-based language. It's how friends talk. The way we speak to ourselves and others matters, and we can start by learning as our own best friend.

Where a happy life is having our head and heart working together in harmony, we are introducing a new framework or paradigm for both defining and understanding emotions, and for living a more balanced and richer life. *Choosing Emotions* is a new *emotionary* format for understanding emotions which has not been developed before, and we may be taking a significant step closer to *emotional super power*. Learn here from among the world's most experienced and thoughtful observers, and move with confidence from your head and heart into the world.

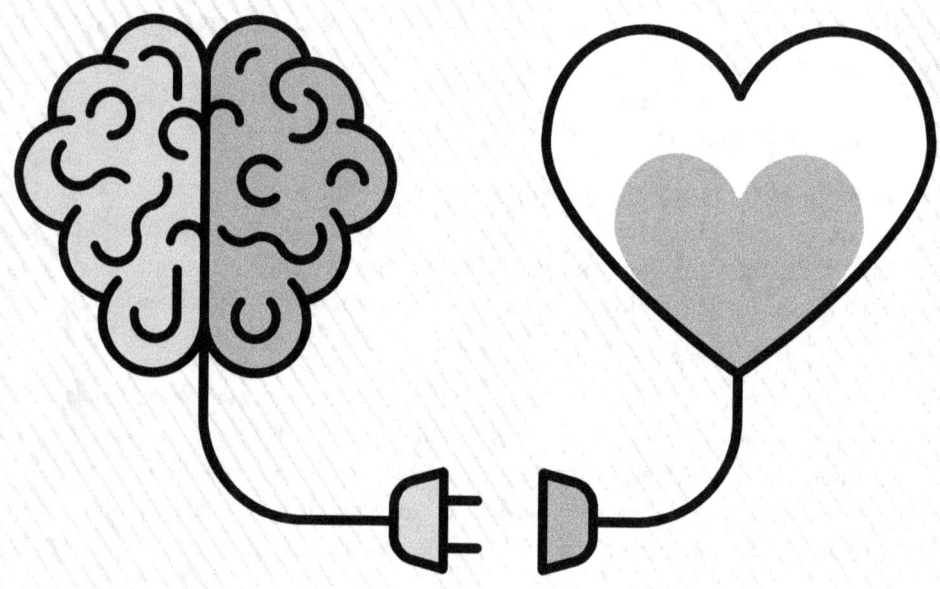

272
EMOTIONS
— AND —
EMOTIONAL
CONDITIONS

Abundance. Experiencing a condition of plenty, including the fulfillment of all primary needs. *Popular or Heart-Based Usage: (1) Doing just fine. (2) Easy Street. (3) The Land of Milk and Honey. (4) Having the wind at your back. (5) Ticking all the boxes. (6) Riding on the gravy train. (7) Living large. (8) 'Harvest time.' (9) Reaping the Horn of Plenty/Cornucopia. (10) Enjoying 'the works.' (11) Having it all. (12) 'It's all good.'*

SUZE ORMAN: *"Abundance is about being rich, with or without money."*

ECKHART TOLLE: *"Acknowledging the good that you already have in your life is the foundation for all abundance."*

MARCUS AURELIUS: *"When you arise in the morning, think of what a precious privilege it is to be alive, to breathe, to think, to enjoy, to love."*

OPRAH WINFREY: *"If you concentrate on what you have, you will always end up having more. If you focus on what you don't have, you will never, ever have enough."*

WAYNE DYER: *"Abundance is not something we acquire. It is something we tune into."*

MARIANNE WILLIAMSON: *"The key to abundance is meeting limited circumstances with unlimited thoughts."*

J. PITTMAN MCGEHEE, DD: *"The three things a human being needs for an abundant life are: meaning in general, purpose in particular, and a place to belong."*

EURIPIDES: *"Enough is abundance to the wise."*

BASHAR: *"Abundance is the ability to do what you need to do when you need to do it."*

LAURA EMILY: *"Abundance is already within you. Let it out."*

SIVANANDA: *"Giving is the secret of abundance."*

PAM GREGORY: *"Your abundance will be linked to the frequency of your heart."*

MARK TWAIN: *"If you want love and abundance in your life, give it away."*

SAYING: *"I am attracting endless abundance by keeping a gratitude mindset."*

LAO TZU: *"When you realize there is nothing lacking, the whole world belongs to you."*

JOHN 10:10: *"I am come that they might have life, and that they might have it more abundantly."*

DEUTERONOMY 11:8–9: *"Therefore shall ye keep all the commandments I you this day, that ye may be strong, and go in and possess the land, ye go to possess it; And that ye may prolong your days in the land, which the Lord sware unto your fathers to give unto them and unto their seed, a land flowing with milk and honey."*

Similar: prosperity, bountifulness, affluence, profusion, splurging, plenty
Opposite: scarcity, hardship, poverty, lack, want

Acceptance. Acknowledging without resistance the factual reality of your situation or circumstances. *Popular or Heart-Based Usage: (1) Keeping it real. (2) Taking off the rose-colored glasses. (3) Checking your ego at the door. (4) Getting the full story, good and bad. (5) Comprehension without bias. (6) Seeing the actual situation. (7) 'I've got it.' (8) 'It is what it is.' (9) Opening your eyes. (10) Getting over yourself.*

ECKHART TOLLE: *"Accept—then act. Whatever the present moment contains, accept it as if you had chosen it. Always work with it, not against it."*

JOEL OSTEEN: *"The first step to overcoming a weakness is to get it out in the open."*

CARL JUNG, MD: *"We cannot change anything unless we accept it."*

JOSEPH GOLDSTEIN: *"You can't stop the waves but you can learn to surf."*

SHANNON ABLES: *"What self-acceptance does is open up more possibilities of succeeding because you aren't fighting yourself along the way."*

DANIELLE LA PORTE: *"It's when we fully accept something that we increase our capacity to transform it."*

CATE BLANCHETT: *"Mind the gap—it's the difference between life as you dream it and life as it is."*

REINHOLD NIEBUHR: *"God grant me the serenity to accept the things I cannot change, the courage to change the things I can, and the wisdom to know the difference."*

RUMI: *"Yesterday I was clever, so I wanted to change the world. Today I am wise, so I am changing myself."*

LEXI JOHNSTON: *"I would tell my younger self that God's grace is sufficient. That your greatest strength is honesty in weakness."*

SIGMUND FREUD, MD: *"Being entirely honest with yourself is a good exercise."*

CARL ROGERS, PHD: *"The curious paradox is that when I accept myself just as I am, then I can change."*

MARSHA LINEHAN, PHD: *"Acceptance is the only way out of hell."*

GAUTAMA BUDDHA: *"Serenity comes when you trade expectations for acceptance."*

ECKHART TOLLE: *"When you live in complete acceptance of what is, that is the end of all drama in your life."*

GEORGE ORWELL: *"Happiness can only exist in acceptance."*

JOHN HEYWOOD: *"Nothing is impossible to a willing heart."*

JACKIE GREER: *"Make friends with change."*

Similar: acquiescence, assent, willingness, embracing
Opposite: resistance, rejection, denial, antagonism

Acting. (1) The art of performance. (2) Portraying characters and telling stories through dialogue, emotions, timing, and body language. (3) The behavioral dimension of emotion. *Popular or Heart-Based Usage: (1) Getting your point across. (2) Credibly suspending disbelief. (3) Committing to your craft. (4) Hitting your marks. (5) Keeping in character. (6) 'Stand and deliver.' (7) 'Break a leg.' (8) Breaking in. (9) Feeling one with the role. (10) 'No false notes.' (11) Going deeper. (12) Channeling. (13) Paying dues. (14) Doing summer stock. (15) Doing off-Broadway. (16) The Great White Way. (17) Making it. (18) The Oscars. (19) The Biz. (20) 'The show must go on.' (21) 'That's Entertainment!'*

STELLA ADLER: *"Acting is in everything but the words."*

SANFORD MEISNER: *"If you want to reach every person in the audience, it's not about being bigger, it's about going deeper."*

MERYL STREEP: *"What makes you different or weird, that's your strength."*

MARLON BRANDO: *"Never surrender to the momentum of mediocrity."*

ROBERT REDFORD: *"Not taking a risk is a risk. That's how I see it."*

BRAD PITT: *"You must lose everything in order to gain anything."*

JACK NICHOLSON: *"The minute that you're not learning I believe you're dead."*

CATE BLANCHETT: *"Mind the gap—it's the difference between life as you dream it and life as it is."*

KATHERINE HEPBURN: *"You are the only person you can actually change."*

TOM CRUISE: *"I don't pretend to be the character. I am the character."*

SANFORD MEISNER: *"Acting is behaving truthfully under imaginary circumstances."*

STELLA ADLER: *"The only excuse for not coming to a class or performance is death."*

CONSTANTIN STANISLAVSKI: *"The language of the body is the key that can unlock the soul."*

LEE STRASBERG: *"A great actor is independent of the poet, because the supreme essence of feeling does not reside in prose or in verse, but in the accent in which it is delivered."*

DAVID DASTMALCHIAN: *"My job as an actor is to use all my tools to manufacture (often many times in a row) an emotional state of being that feels authentic to my scene partners and audience."*

SEAN PENN: *"...(A)udiences don't always know when they are being lied to, but ... they always know when they are being told the truth."*

MARLON BRANDO: *"An actor must interpret life, and in order to do so he must be willing to accept all experiences that life can offer."*

BERTOLT BRECHT: *"If you don't have fun, you don't have a show."*

STELLA ADLER: *"You act with your soul."*

Similar: stagecraft, portrayal, interpretation, depiction, theatrics, drama, expression
Opposite: unemotional, inertial, non-responsive, blank

Addiction. (1) Elevating personal escape over responsibilities to yourself and others. (2) Manifesting a major emotional deficit which leads to a chronic reliance on a substitute reality. (3) Adhering to a path which provides diminishing short-term benefits while also creating longer-term challenges. *Popular or Heart-Based Usage: (1) Hiding from the pain. (2) Craving or 'Jonesing' for an escape. (3) Getting hooked. (4) Having a tiger by the tail. (5) Fooling yourself. (6) Making a deal with the Devil. (7) Slipping into darkness. (8) 'Throwing your life away.' (9) 'Short-term gain, long-term pain.'*

ANNE LAMOTT: *"You can get the monkey off your back, but the circus never leaves town."*

MARK TWAIN: *"Giving up smoking is easy. I've done it hundreds of times."*

JOHN GRISHAM: *"Addicts know no shame. You disgrace yourself so many times you become immune to it."*

JEAN KILBOURNE: *"Addiction begins with the belief that something 'out there' can instantly fill up the emptiness inside."*

ANNA DAVID: *"The problem is that all that brilliance that so many addicts have is focused on the wrong thing."*

STELLA ADLER: *"An addict is someone who uses their body to tell society that something is wrong."*

CARL JUNG, MD: *"Every form of addiction is bad, whether it be alcoholism, morphine, or idealism."*

RINGO STARR: *"That's all drugs and alcohol do. They cut off your emotions in the end."*

NANCY REAGAN: *"Just say no."*

C. DEVILLE: *"Addiction is a symptom of not growing up."*

APHORISM: *"Emotional growth ends where addiction begins."*

GABOR MATE, MD, CM: *"The attempt to escape from pain, is what creates more pain."*

ECKHART TOLLE: *"Every addiction starts with pain and ends with pain. Whatever the substance you are addicted to—alcohol, food, legal or illegal drugs, or a person—you are using something or somebody to cover up your pain."*

DR. JOE DISPENZA: *"We're addicted to our beliefs. We're addicted to the emotions of the past. We see our beliefs as truths, and not as ideas we can change."*

ANTHONY ROBBINS: *"Change happens when the pain of staying the same is greater than the pain of change."*

ANNA DAVID: *"The number one solution to recovery besides having a Miracle Morning is community."*

12 KEYS REHAB: *"To stop craving the escape, you have to learn to face your emotions."*

Similar: dependency, enslavement, evasion, self-destruction
Opposite: sobriety, self-determined, sacrificing, responsible, confronting

Admiration. (1) Acknowledging greatness in another person. (2) Holding a profound or emulative respect for the efforts of others. *Popular or Heart-Based Usage: (1) Looking up to someone. (2) Respecting a class act in others. (3) Seeing in someone else how to sharpen your own game. (4) 'Well played!' (5) 'Bravo Zulu.' (6) 'Take a bow.'*

ALLEGRA HUSTON: *"Be a big person; be generous of spirit; be the person you'd admire."*

GRETCHEN RUBIN: *"Knowing what you admire in others is a wonderful mirror into your deepest, as yet unborn, self."*

THEODORE GAUTIER: *"To love is to admire with the heart; to admire is to love with the mind."*

LUDWIG VAN BEETHOVEN: *"This is the work of a really admirable man: steadfastness in the face of trouble."*

VINCENT VAN GOGH: *"Admire as much as you can. Most people do not admire enough."*

JUSTICE THURGOOD MARSHALL: *"I never worked hard until I got to Howard Law School and met Charlie Houston ... I saw this man's dedication, his vision, his willingness to sacrifice, and I told myself, 'You either shape up, or ship out.' When you are being challenged by a great human being, you know you can't ship out."*

DAVID M. HENDRICKS: *"A good coach is a second father. He's a mentor and a friend who turns boys' hearts. He takes all the blame and knows he can expect very few rewards. He's a man who knows that a boy needs someone he can look up to. A boy remembers his coach all his life."*

SCOUTMASTER BILLY JIM VAUGHN: *"Good leadership is quietly admired and respected."*

PABLO CASALS: *"As long as one can admire and love, one can stay young forever."*

WARREN BUFFETT: *"Enjoy your work and work for whom you admire."*

ANN LANDERS: *"Don't accept your dog's admiration as conclusive evidence that you are wonderful."*

Similar: reverence, emulation, commendation, appreciation, esteem
Opposite: disregard, detestation, disrespect, condemnation

Aggression. (1) Demonstrating the inclination to assert your viewpoint or dominance. (2) Being ready to confront or attack, and often without provocation. *Popular or Heart-Based Usage: (1) Getting seriously pushy. (2) 'Not being shy about it at all.' (3) Ratcheting up the rhetoric. (4) Not taking 'Yes' for an answer. (5) Pushing the envelope. (6) Flipping someone off. (7) Taking off the gloves. (8) Saber-rattling. (9) Carrying a big stick. (10) Squaring off with someone. (11) Demonstrating your Mars influence. (12) Picking a fight. (13) Rolling out the big guns. (14) Taking no prisoners. (15) Getting in someone's face.*

BETTE DAVIS: *"My passions were all gathered together like fingers that made a fist. Drive is considered aggression today; I knew it then as purpose."*

THOMAS JEFFERSON: *"No man has a natural right to commit aggression on the equal rights of another; and this is all from which the laws ought to restrain him."*

BARON DE MONTESQUIEU: *"There are only two cases in which war is just: first, in order to resist the aggression of an enemy, and second, in order to help an ally who has been attacked."*

LYNDON JOHNSON: *"Success only feeds the appetite of aggression."*

JOHN FOSTER DULLES: *"Our capacity to retaliate must be, and is, massive in order to deter all forms of aggression."*

MARGARET WHEATLEY, ED.D: *"Aggression is the most common behavior used by many organizations, an invisible medium that influences all decisions and actions."*

MOMENTOUSINSTITUTE.ORG: *"Boys are more physical, girls are more verbal."*

MARSHALL MCLUHAN, PHD: *"Madison Avenue is a very powerful aggression against private consciousness. A demand that you yield your private consciousness to public manipulation."*

SIGMUND FREUD, MD: *"I take up the standpoint that the tendency to aggression is an innate, independent, instinctual disposition in man, and I come back now to the statement that it constitutes the most powerful obstacle to culture."*

MARGARET MEAD: *"Human nature is potentially aggressive and destructive and potentially orderly and constructive."*

GEORGE CARLIN: *"Comedy is a socially acceptable form of hostility and aggression. That is what comics do, stand the world upside down."*

MAYA ANGELOU: *"I love to see a young girl go out and grab the world by the lapels."*

Similar: assertiveness, drive, combativeness, hostility, domineering, forcefulness
Opposite: passivity, shyness, reluctance, demureness, reticence, deference

Anger. Expressing hostility about an unwelcome situation to stop it or to place blame. *Expanded:* In anger, details are often conflated, altered, or exaggerated to achieve a dramatic effect. *Popular or Heart-Based Usage: (1) Getting triggered. (2) Seeing red. (3) Fuming. (4) Getting your back up. (5) Hot under the collar. (6) Clenching your jaw. (7) Getting bent out of shape. (8) Popping off. (9) Losing your cool. (10) Being pissed off. (11) Breaking eye contact. (12) Lashing out. (13) Going ALL CAPS. (14) 'Let 'em have it.' (15) 'Kick ass and take names.' (16) Pounding the table. (17) Flying off the handle. (18) 'Not happy' about it. (19) 'What were you **thinking**?!?' (20) 'Cut it out!' (21) 'Stop it!'*

PROVERB: *"An angry man rarely speaks the truth."*

BENJAMIN FRANKLIN: *"Whatever is begun in anger ends in shame."*

ECKHART TOLLE: *"Where there is anger, there is always pain underneath."*

PETER A. LEVINE, PHD: *"Anger almost always goes to (issues about) power."*

GAUTAMA BUDDHA: *"Holding on to anger is like drinking poison and expecting the other person to die."*

EPICTETUS: *"Any person capable of angering you becomes your master."*

JUSTICE RUTH BADER GINSBURG: *"Acting in anger or annoyance will not advance one's ability to persuade."*

LINCOLN STOREY: *"Anger is often an attempt to blame someone else for a problem that we know deep down we should have seen coming."*

APHORISM: *"When you have the facts on your side, pound the facts. When you don't have the facts on your side, pound the table."*

D. EARL JOHNSTON: *"In anger, ego grows and reason flees."*

ELEANOR ROOSEVELT: *"Anger is one letter short of danger."*

LAO TZU: *"The best fighter is never angry."*

ABRAHAM LINCOLN: *"Never signed and never delivered."* (Lincoln's practice of 'cooling off' in anger by writing a scathing letter to his adversary, but never sending it.)

ACHARYA NAGARJUNA: *"Although you may spend your life killing, You will not exhaust all your foes. But if you quell your anger, your real enemy will be slain."*

MUHAMMAD: *"The powerful man is not the one who can wrestle, but the powerful man is the one who can control himself at the time of anger."*

PSALM 86:15: *"But you, Lord, are a compassionate and gracious God, slow to anger, abounding in love and faithfulness."*

MATTHEW 5:39: *"Whosoever shall smite thee on thy right cheek, turn to him the other also."*

H. HILL MCALISTER: *"Control your temper, or it will control you."*

PROVERB: *"The greatest remedy for anger is delay."*

PROVERB: *"When angry, count to ten."*

Similar: fury, rage, antagonism, annoyance, acrimony, irritation, intimidation
Opposite: calm, pacifying, serene, relaxed, accepting, defusing, moderating, mediating

Annoyed. (1) Experiencing a condition of irritation or reaction to minor offense(s) from others. (2) Having a minor upset with recent developments. *Popular or Heart-Based Usage: (1) Feeling bugged about something. (2) Having a pet peeve about something. (3) Being tweaked (or triggered). (4) Feeling pestered. (5) Getting rubbed the wrong way. (6) Letting something get under your skin. (7) Rolling your eyes. (8) Dealing with a nuisance. (9) Getting heartburn about something. (10) Having a bug up your ass. (11) Getting hassled. (12) Pushing back. (13) Getting edgy. (14) Getting cranky. (15) Flipping someone off. (16) Getting hacked off. (17) Getting peeved. (18) Getting torqued off. (19) Getting pissed off. (20) Being a sorehead. (21) Getting tasked by a twit. (22) Harassed by a jagoff. (23) Getting irked. (24) Asking: 'What the hell is going on?' (25) 'For crying out loud!' (26) 'Stop it!' (27) 'Knock it off!' (28) 'Get off my back!' (29) 'Buzz off.' (30) 'Get lost!' (31) 'Pound sand!' (32) 'Go away!' (33) 'Get a life!' (34) 'Get off my back!' (35) 'WTF.' [What the Frick.] (36) 'SMH.' [Shaking My Head.] (37) 'NFW!' [No Freaking Way!]*

> MARK TWAIN: *"Few things are harder to put up with than the annoyance of a good example."*
>
> NOEL COWARD: *"I like long walks, especially when they are taken by people who annoy me."*
>
> ISAAC ASIMOV, PHD: *"People who think they know everything are a great annoyance to those of us who do."*
>
> WHOOPI GOLDBERG: *"I don't have pet peeves like some people. I have whole kennels of irritation."*
>
> JEAN DE LA BRUYERE: *"The first day one is a guest, the second day a burden, and the third a pest."*
>
> CAMRYN MANHEIM: *"Parents know how to push your buttons because, hey, they sewed them on."*
>
> ELIZABETH TAYLOR: *"The problem with people who have no vices is that generally you can be pretty sure they're going to have some pretty annoying virtues."*
>
> WOODY ALLEN: *"After I am dead, I suspect very little will get on my nerves, even that annoying noise the neighbors make with their leaf blower."*
>
> JOHNNY MCGREW: *"An unfinished job can just sit there quietly alone but still annoy the hell out of you."*
>
> EDGAR ALLEN POE: *"The past is a pebble in my shoe."*
>
> CARL JUNG, MD: *"Everything that irritates us about others can lead us to an understanding of ourselves."*
>
> JACK BENNY: *"If you don't mind, it doesn't matter."*

Similar: tweaked, triggered, exasperated, vexed, irritated, piqued, edgy, peeved
Opposite: comforted, calm, pleased, satisfied, enjoying

Antagonism. (1) Pursuing a course of opposition or hostility toward a person or issue. (2) Seeking to stop or to challenge an opposing viewpoint, including for the sake of argument or to demean. *Popular or Heart-Based Usage: (1) Getting in someone's grill. (2) Being abrasive. (3) Telling someone where to go. (4) Butting heads with someone. (5) Being a troublemaker. (6) Wanting a piece of someone. (7) Comin' in hot. (8) Having an axe to grind. (9) Throwing someone under the bus. (10) Hassling someone. (11) Having it in for someone. (12) Being ornery. (13) Picking a fight. (14) Lawyering up. (15) Getting a pound of flesh. (16) Squaring off. (17) Getting radicalized. (18) Having a showdown. (19) Letting them have it. (20) Having bad blood. (21) Going after someone. (22) Coming at someone. (23) Nay-saying. (24) Breaking eye contact. (25) Peeing in their Post Toasties. (26) Being a horse's ass. (27) Getting snarky. (28) 'No more Mr. Nice Guy.' (29) 'Ain't gonna happen.' (30) 'Nothing doing.' (31) 'Talk to the hand!' (32) 'Haters gonna hate.' (33) 'Fuhgeddaboutit.' (34) 'Get lost.' (35) 'Go pound sand!' (36) 'Up yours!'*

ALFRED HITCHCOCK: *"Seeing a murder on television can help work off one's antagonisms. And if you haven't any, the commercials will give you some."*

CHAIM POTOK: *"It is impossible to fuse totally with a culture for which you feel a measure of antagonism."*

SALVATORE QUASIMODO: *"The antagonism between the poet and the politician has generally been evident in all cultures."*

PUNEEET ISSAR: *"Every antagonist is a protagonist in his own right."*

ECKHART TOLLE: *"Most humans live in antagonism with the present moment."*

GEN. ERWIN ROMMEL: *"Don't fight a battle if you don't gain anything by winning."*

TOM FEINBERG: *"The protagonist Faust is a hero searching for knowledge, love, and power. His antagonist, Mephistopheles, promises to satisfy Faust's thirst for knowledge and the meaning of life."*

GEORGE HENRY LEWES: *"Originality is independence, not rebellion; it is sincerity, not antagonism."*

EDMUND BURKE: *"He who wrestles with us, strengthens our nerves, and sharpens our skill. Our antagonist is our helper."*

RALPH WALDO EMERSON: *"Nature is upheld by antagonism. Passions, resistance, danger, are educators. We acquire the strength we have overcome."*

FRIEDRICH NIETSZCHE: *"Out of life's school of war—what doesn't kill me, makes me stronger."*

CHRISTINE BERGSMA: *"You are the protagonist of your story, decide if you want to be the hero."*

Similar: argumentation, hostility, opposition, enmity, attack, criticism, confrontation
Opposite: cooperation, togetherness, support, serenity, endorsement, union

Anxiety. [See also **Stress** and **Worry**] (1) Experiencing repetitive worries or fixations over personal irritants. (2) Becoming distressed over apparently unsolvable triggers, issues, or contradictions. (3) Trying to control the future. *Popular or Heart-Based Usage: (1) Getting stressed out. (2) Having the agita. (3) Feeling angst. (4) Touching your ears a lot. (5) Getting heartburn about something. (6) Worrying yourself sick. (7) Grinding on something. (8) Getting fixated on something.*

DAN MILLMAN: *"You don't have to control your thoughts. You just have to stop letting them control you."*

WILLIAM JAMES, MD: *"The greatest weapon against stress is our ability to choose one thought over another."*

SETH GODIN, BS, MBA: *"I define anxiety as experiencing failure in advance."*

JACK NICKLAUS: *"Concentration is a fine antidote to anxiety."*

JOSEPH GOLDSTEIN: *"You can't stop the waves but you can learn to surf."*

PROVERB: *"Whatever you focus upon, expands."*

ECKHART TOLLE: *"Anxiety, tension, stress, worry—all forms of fear—are caused by too much future, and not enough presence ... Be in the now."*

LAO TZU: *"If you are depressed you are living in the past, if you are anxious you are living in the future, if you are at peace you are living in the present."*

RACHEL H.: *"I'm telling you, anxiety is always feeling like something is out of place, and when you can't find what it is—you start to think it's you."*

CINDY DAVIS, BS, MFA: *"Having an anxiety disorder feels like you're in a plane that's about to crash, but the feeling can last for weeks or months."*

PHILIPPIANS 4:6–7: *"Be careful for nothing; but in every thing by prayer and supplication with thanksgiving let your requests be made known unto God. And the peace of God, which passeth all understanding, shall keep your hearts and minds through Christ Jesus."*

AUGUSTINE OF HIPPO: *"Our hearts are restless until they rest in You."*

MATTHEW 6:34: *"Take therefore no thought for the morrow; for the morrow shall take thought for the things of itself. Sufficient unto the day is the evil thereof."*

H. HILL MCALISTER: *"Ninety-five percent of the things you worry about never happen."*

ROLLO MAY, BDIV, PHD: *"One of the few blessings of living in an age of anxiety is that we are forced to become aware of ourselves."*

ALBERT ELLIS, PHD: *"If human emotions largely result from thinking, then one may appreciably control one's feelings by controlling one's thoughts—or by changing the internalized sentences, or self-talk, with which one largely created the feeling in the first place."*

GAUTAMA BUDDHA: *"Don't rush anything. When the time is right it will happen."*

PROVERB: *"The way you speak to yourself matters."*

Anxiety. *(continued)*

AMIT RAY, PHD: *"If you want to conquer the anxiety of life, live in the moment, live in the breath."*

LINCOLN STOREY: *"Hungry? Go eat. Thirsty? Get a drink. And when life brings anxiety, stress, or depression, you can help find normal in conscious breathing."*

JOHANN HARI: *"The scientific evidence is clear that exercise significantly reduces depression and anxiety."*

DANIEL GOLEMAN, PHD: *"If you rely solely on medication to manage depression or anxiety, for example, you have done nothing to train the mind, so that when you come off the medication, you are just as vulnerable to a relapse as though you had never taken the medication."*

JOHNS HOPKINS UNIVERSITY SCHOOL OF MEDICINE: *"In our study, meditation appeared to provide as much relief from some anxiety and depression symptoms as what other studies have found from anti-depressants...They also found no harm came from meditation."*

CLEVELAND CLINIC: *"The mind-body connection means that you can learn to use your thoughts to positively influence some of your body's physical responses, thereby decreasing stress. If you recall a time when you were happy, grateful or calm, your body and your mind tend to relax."*

MAYO FOUNDATION FOR MEDICAL EDUCATION AND RESEARCH: *"Yoga is a mind-body practice that combines physical poses, controlled breathing, and meditation or relaxation. Yoga may help reduce stress, lower blood pressure and lower your heart rate. And almost anyone can do it."*

NATALIE GOLDBERG: *"Stress is basically a disconnection from the earth, a forgetting of the breath."*

AMIT RAY, PHD: *"Conscious breathing is the best antidote to stress, anxiety and depression."*

Similar: worry, conflictedness, foreboding, apprehension, dread, powerlessness
Opposite: peacefulness, calm, resolve, expectancy, confidence

Apathy. (1) Being indifferent to a given situation or to life in general. (2) Abandoning attention, care, or concern. *Popular or Heart-Based Usage: (1) 'Who cares?' (2) Not giving a damn. (3) Taking things for granted. (4) Just drifting along. (5) Going through the motions. (6) Being laissez-faire. (7) Not lifting a finger. (8) Being lackadaisical. (9) Having 'no pulse' about a topic. (10) 'No interest.' (11) 'Not my job.' (12) 'Why bother?' (13) 'So what?'*

GEORGE CARLIN: *"Scientists announced today that they have discovered a cure for apathy. However, they claim no one has shown the slightest interest in it."*

JIMMY BUFFETT: *"Is it ignorance or apathy? Hey, I don't know and I don't care."*

ALDOUS HUXLEY: *"Most human beings have an almost infinite capacity for taking things for granted."*

ARISTOPHANES: *"I'll be a lousy lay, not move a limb."*

LEO BUSCAGLIA, PHD: *"I have a very strong feeling that the opposite of love is not hate—it's apathy. It's not giving a damn."*

H. HILL MCALISTER: *"Apathy becomes evident when the Law of Minimum Effort is applied."*

ELIE WIESEL, NOBEL: *"The opposite of love is not hate, it's indifference. The opposite of art is not ugliness, it's indifference. The opposite of faith is not heresy, it's indifference. And the opposite of life is not death, it's indifference."*

PLATO: *"The price of apathy toward public affairs is to be ruled by evil men."*

WILLIAM BERNBACH: *"In communications, familiarity breeds apathy."*

SIR JAMES GOLDSMITH: *"Tolerance is a tremendous virtue, but the immediate neighbors of tolerance are apathy and weakness."*

EMILIANO SALINAS: *"Fear is better than apathy because fear makes us do something."*

HORACE GREELEY: *"Apathy is a sort of living oblivion."*

ALBERT EINSTEIN, PHD, NOBEL: *"The world will not be destroyed by those who do evil, but by those who watch them and do nothing."*

TODD STOCKER: *"While ignorance might be bliss, apathy can be deadly."*

LINCOLN STOREY: *"Apathy is to emotion what inertia is to science."*

JOHNNY MCGREW: *"Apathy is just pathetic."*

Similar: emotionlessness, numbness, indifference, passivity, unconcern, abstention
Opposite: interest, curiosity, empathy, compassion, sensitivity, concern, focus

Apology. Communicating regret or remorse for an offense arising from an action either taken or not taken. *Popular or Heart-Based Usage: (1) Patching things up. (2) Backing down. (3) Backing off. (4) Throwing it in reverse. (5) Doing a 180. (6) 'My bad.' (7) 'Oops.' (8) 'Sorry.' (9) 'Mea culpa.' (10) 'Our people will get back to you.' (11) 'We're getting some pushback on that.' (12) 'We'll have to circle back on that.' (13) 'We'll need to regroup on that.' (14) 'There's been some miscommunication about this.' (15) 'We're re-thinking this.' (16) Walking it back. (17) Going hat in hand. (18) Bending the knee.*

MUHAMMAD ALI: *"If you even dream of beating me you'd better wake up and apologize."*

JOHANNES BRAHMS: *"If there is anyone here whom I have not insulted, I beg his pardon."*

REAR ADM. GRACE HOPPER, PHD: *"If it's a good idea, go ahead and do it. It's much easier to apologize than it is to get permission."*

GOV. ELIOT SPITZER: *"I have acted in a way that violates my obligations to my family and violates my, or any, sense of right and wrong. I apologize first and most importantly to my family. I apologize to the public, whom I owed better."*

LANCE ARMSTRONG: *"I'll spend the rest of my life trying to earn back trust and apologize to people."*

GREG LEMOND: *"More people should apologize, and more people should accept apologies when sincerely made."*

MARK TWAIN: *"I apologize for such a long letter—I didn't have time to write a short one."*

JOAN RIVERS: *"We don't apologize for a joke. We are comics. We are here to make you laugh. If you don't get it, then don't watch us."*

JOHNNY MCGREW: *"If lying is pre-varication, then the cover-up should be called post-varication."*

LEANN RIMES: *"I'm not gonna apologize for who I am and what I've gone through."*

SONYA DEVILLE: *"Don't be afraid. Don't be ashamed. Don't ever apologize for your sexuality. Just be you."*

AMBROSE BIERCE: *"To apologize is to lay the foundation for future offense."*

SIR BENJAMIN DISRAELI: *"Never apologize for showing feeling. When you do so, you apologize for the truth."*

HARRY S. TRUMAN: *"Carry the battle to them. Don't let them bring it to you. Put them on the defensive and don't ever apologize for anything."*

Similar: sorrow, regret, concession, admission, excuse, acknowledgment, explanation, compromise

Opposite: denial, refusal, repudiation, rejection, attack

Appreciation. Acknowledging the efforts, support, or contributions of others. *Popular or Heart-Based Usage: (1) Giving props to someone. (2) Paying respects. (3) Giving a tip of the hat. (4) 'You da man!' (5) 'Good on ya!' (6) 'Well-played!' (7) 'Giving it up' for someone. (8) Giving a shout-out to someone. (9) Paying it forward. (10) Pointing to the sky. (11) Forming a heart with your fingers.*

ALAN COHEN, MA: *"Appreciation is the highest form of prayer."*

HANSA PROVERB: *"Give thanks for a little and you will find a lot."*

DAVID STENDL-RAST, PHD: *"It is not joy that makes us grateful, it is gratitude that makes us joyful."*

GLADYS KNIGHT: *"Sometimes the best things are right in front of you; it just takes some time to see them."*

VOLTAIRE: *"Appreciation is a wonderful thing. It makes what is excellent in others belong to us as well."*

ALBERT SCHWEITZER, BTH, MD, PHD, NOBEL: *"We should all be thankful for those people who rekindle the inner spirit."*

WILLIAM JAMES, MD: *"The deepest craving of human nature is the need to be appreciated."*

ANTHONY ROBBINS: *"Change your expectation for appreciation and the world changes instantly."*

D. EARL JOHNSTON: *"In times of distress or for things that we lack, thanks move us forward while rage turns us back."*

MAHATMA GANDHI: *"Relationships are based on four principles: respect, understanding, acceptance, and appreciation."*

H. HILL MCALISTER: *"Five Rules for Success in Business:*
1) Thank you and I appreciate your work.
2) Thank you and I appreciate your work.
3) Thank you and I appreciate your work.
4) Thank you and I appreciate your work.
5) Thank you and I appreciate your work."

Similar: gratitude, recognition, regard, esteem, accolades, praise
Opposite: disparagement, criticism, disregard, neglect, rejection

Argument. Having a dispute about facts, issues, or viewpoints, often marked by conflict and acrimony. *Popular or Heart-Based Usage: (1) Picking a fight. (2) Having it out. (3) Squabbling. (4) Having your back up. (5) Not backing down. (6) Not being on the same page. (7) Chewing the fat. (8) Litigating the issue. (9) Giving someone 'the business.' (10) Scrapping about it. (11) Having a brouhaha. (12) Throwing a monkey-wrench into someone's viewpoint. (12) Having an old-fashioned rhubarb. (13) Going in circles. (14) Having a beef. (15) Going toe-to-toe. (16) Clearing the air. (17) 'Well, the thing is ...'*

WHITE HOUSE PRESS SECRETARY: *"Was there a heated argument today in the Oval Office? Why, of course not. The President and the Minority Leader just concluded a very frank and productive exchange of views. And from what we overheard, they each became very efficient in their dialogue, quickly ending their visit with words of just one syllable."*

MARK TWAIN: *"Never argue with a fool. Onlookers may not be able to tell the difference."*

WILL ROGERS: *"There are two theories to arguing with a woman. Neither works."*

LINCOLN STOREY: *"Most disputes are sorted out after the event, and where a clever defense can win out over the temptations of finger-pointing: 'I believe I've been misled' can get you further a lot faster than 'You're just a dirty rotten liar.'"*

MAHATMA GANDHI: *"Honest differences are often a healthy sign of progress."*

YASSER ARAFAT: *"All religious wars are about people arguing over who has the biggest invisible friend."*

WILL ROGERS: *"People's minds are changed through observation and not through argument."*

LOIS FARFEL STARK: *"Don't waste time arguing with someone who cannot change the situation."*

ALLEN CHENG: *"When you get into an argument or conflict with someone, observe your defensiveness when being attacked, as well as the aggression in your counterattack (if you do so). Notice your attachment to your views or opinions, your need to be right and prove the other person wrong. Recognize that your ego is fueling your reaction; acknowledging this will help ..."*

SAYING: *"You don't have to attend every argument you're invited to."*

CARL BECKER: *"Fact-finding is more effective than fault-finding."*

CHE GUEVARA: *"Silence is argument carried out by other means."*

PLUTARCH: *"Adversity is the only balance to weigh friends."*

TONY GASKINS: *"Arguing isn't communication, it's noise."*

JOSEPH JOUBERT: *"Never cut what you can untie."*

LAO TZU: *"The best fighter is never angry."*

RUMI: *"Raise your words, not your voice."*

Similar: quarreling, squabbling, bickering, disputing, challenging, undercutting
Opposite: reasoning, listening, accepting, harmonizing, compromising, concurring

Art (Aesthetics). (1) Undertaking a creative presentation to express an interpretation of life. (2) Organizing light, color, sound, space, shape, texture, design, motion, language, geometry, and/or their inter-relational placements, in order to explore essences and/or to evoke emotion. *Popular or Heart-Based Usage: (1) Interpreting life. (2) Creative self-expression. (3) Transformative energy. (4) Exploring viewpoints and dimensions.*

SAYING: *"Art doesn't read like a book, it makes you think."*
DUANE HANSON: *"Art doesn't have to be pretty. It has to be meaningful."*
JEAN-LUC GODARD: *"Art attracts us by what it reveals of our most secret self."*
FRIEDRICH NIETZSCHE: *"The essence of all beautiful art, all great art, is gratitude."*
OSCAR WILDE: *"Art is the most intense form of individualism the world has ever known."*
ELLIOT EISNER: *"Art is literacy of the heart."*
AUGUSTE RODIN: *"I invent nothing. I rediscover."*
HAROLD ROSENBERG: *"It is not logical for art to be logical."*
AGNES MARTIN: *"Art is the concrete representation of our most subtle feelings."*
CAMILLE PAGLIA: *"Art is something out of the ordinary commenting on the ordinary."*
LEO TOLSTOY: *"Art is not a handicraft, it is the transmission of feeling the artist has experienced."*
YUKITAKA YAMAMOTO: *"To be fully alive is to have an aesthetic perception of life."*
NILE ROGERS: *"Art is something that opens up and enhances your emotions and that's what I like to think I'm doing."*
LEONARDO DA VINCI: *"Where the spirit does not work with the hands there is no art."*
STEVEN PINKER, PHD: *"The art of photography is all about directing the attention of the viewer."*
LINCOLN STOREY: *"Art is a medium for expressing higher dimensions through the tools and crafts of the 4th Dimension."*
SYDNEY POLLACK: *"Almost every single art form is involved in film, in a way."*
CONSTANTIN STANISLAVSKI: *"Love the art in yourself, not yourself in the art."*
EDGAR DEGAS: *"Art is not what you see, but what you make others see."*
BOB DYLAN, PULITZER, NOBEL: *"The purpose of art is to stop time."*
PABLO PICASSO: *"Art is the lie that enables us to realize the truth."*
GUSTAVE FLAUBERT: *"Of all lies, art is the least untrue."*
GIUSEPPE MAZZINI: *"Art does not imitate, but interpret."*
LINCOLN STOREY: *"Art is giving back."*

Similar: creativity, multidimensional, transcendent, inspired, emotional, aspirational
Opposite: crass, bland, insensitive, unaware, plain, two-dimensional, uninspired

Astrology. (1) How angular aspects of planets and stars influence behavioral tendencies on Earth. (2) How matter manifests around energy. *Popular or Heart-Based Usage: (1) Knowing your birth chart. (2) Charting the planets, signs, and houses. (3) Planetary alignments. (4) The clockwork of Creation. (5) The music of the spheres. (6) The cosmic code. (7) The celestial language. (8) The etheric influences. (9) The cosmic weather forecast. (10) Geo-cosmic research. (11) The Age of Aquarius. (12) Co-creating your life.*

ANCIENT ADAGE: *"As above, so below."*

THOMAS AQUINAS: *"The celestial bodies are the cause of all that takes place in the sublunar world."*

SIR WALTER SCOTT: *"Do not Christians and Heathens, and Jews and Gentiles, and poets and philosophers, unite in allowing the starry influences?"*

JOHANNES KEPLER: *"A most unfailing experience … of the excitement of the sublunary (that is, human) natures by the conjunctions and aspects of the planets has instructed and compelled my unwilling belief."*

CONFUCIUS: *"Heaven sends down its good and evil symbols and wise men act accordingly."*

WILLIAM SHAKESPEARE: *"There's some ill planet reigns; I must be patient till the heavens look with an aspect more favorable."*

THEODORE ROOSEVELT, NOBEL: *"I always keep my weather eye on the opposition of my seventh house Moon to my first house Mars."*

J. P. MORGAN: *"Millionaires don't have astrologers, billionaires do."*

SECRETARY OF THE TREASURY DONALD T. REGAN: *"It's common knowledge that a large percentage of Wall Street brokers use astrology."*

BENJAMIN FRANKLIN: *"Oh the wonderful knowledge to be found in the stars. Even the smallest things are written there if you had but skill to read."*

ARISTOTLE: *"This world is inescapably linked to the motions of the worlds above. All power in this world is ruled by these options."*

SIR ISAAC NEWTON, FRS: *"I have studied these things—you have not."* [In defense of astrology, to Edmund Halley, Royal Astronomer]

LOUIS PASTEUR: *"The controls of life are structured as forms and nuclear arrangements, in a relation with the motions of the universe."*

PAULO COELHO: *"Coincidence is the language of the stars. For something to happen, so many forces have to be put into action."*

HIPPOCRATES: *"A physician without a knowledge of Astrology has no right to call himself a physician."*

PAM GREGORY: *"Astrology is a language of mathematical probability. We don't have to obey astrology. It is not deterministic. It is not fated. It is the potentiality made manifest. It is the sheet of music not yet played. It is like a cosmic weather forecast. The weather forecast is helpful and you can say: 'I now have a choice.'"*

Astrology. *(continued)*

ELIZABETH CLARE PROPHET: *"Astrology is like any other branch of knowledge. It can be used for good or ill, properly or improperly, by skilled and unskilled practitioners alike."*

RALPH WALDO EMERSON: *"Men should take their knowledge from the Sun, the Moon and the Stars."*

DANIEL 12:3: *"And they that be wise shall shine as the brightness of the firmament; and they that turn many to righteousness as the stars for ever and ever."*

MATTHEW 2:1–2: *"Now when Jesus was born in Bethlehem of Judea in the days of Herod the king, behold, there came wise men from the east to Jerusalem, saying, 'Where is he that is born King of the Jews? for we have seen his star in the east, and are come to worship him.'"*

MATTHEW 6:10: *"Thy kingdom come, Thy will be done, on earth, as it is in heaven."*

CARL JUNG, MD: *"My evenings are taken up very largely with astrology. I make horoscopic calculations in order to find a clue to the core of psychological truth."*

D. H. LAWRENCE: *"Who knows the power that Saturn has over us, or Venus? But it is a vital power, rippling exquisitely through us all the time."*

CARL JUNG, MD: *"The puzzling thing is that there is really a curious coincidence between astrological and psychological facts, so that one can isolate time from the characteristics of an individual, and also, one can deduce characteristics from a certain time."*

STEVEN PINKER, PHD: *"Astrology had an important role in the ancient world. You can't understand many things unless you know something about astrology—the plays of Shakespeare and so on."*

CARL SAGAN, PHD: *"That we can now think of no mechanism for astrology is relevant but unconvincing. No mechanism was known, for example, for continental drift when it was proposed by Wegener. Nevertheless, we see that Wegener was right, and those who objected...were wrong."*

ALBERT EINSTEIN, PHD, NOBEL (attributed): *"We are slowed down sound and light waves, a walking bundle of frequencies tuned in to the cosmos. We are souls dressed up in sacred biochemical garments and our bodies are the instruments though which our souls play their music."*

G. DAVID LOW, NASA ASTRONAUT, CAPCOM, MS, MBA, PHD: *"Jupiter radiates at least two times as much energy as it absorbs from sunlight."*

FRANCOIS ENGLERT, PHD, NOBEL: *"Gravitational and electromagnetic interactions are long-range interactions, meaning they act on objects no matter how far they are separated from each other."*

DANE RUDHYAR: *"When you don't follow your nature there is a hole in the universe where you were supposed to be."*

Astrology. *(continued)*

Alternative Viewpoints on Astrology:

NANCY REAGAN: *"I have been criticized and ridiculed for turning to astrology, but after a while, I reached the point where I didn't care."*

MARK TWAIN: *"I was born with Halley's Comet and I expect to die upon its return."*

JOHN KENNETH GALBRAITH: *"The only function of economic forecasting is to make astrology look more respectable."*

PAM GREGORY: *"You Don't Really Believe in Astrology, Do You?"* (Book)

LINCOLN STOREY: *"The coincidence of major corporate, political, and religious events (plus product names and brands) with major astrological aspects should probably not be dismissed. The number of prominent leaders who have quietly followed astrology over the centuries and into the present era is surprising."*

REV. COLIN NEWTON: *"Spacetime expresses itself as celestial bodies and individuals, so of course astrology is a means to read that expression through their relationships."*

ASTROLOGY.COM: *"In some ways, the forces between the planets involved in astrology can be simplified into one word: gravity."*

GOOGLE GENERATIVE AI: *"Esoteric astrology views your birth chart as a map of your soul's purpose in this lifetime, highlighting the lessons and challenges you've chosen to work on."*

EDGAR CAYCE: *"The signs of the zodiac are karmic patterns; the planets are the looms; the will is the weaver.... There is no force in the universe more powerful than your will or power."*

ARTHUR C. CLARKE: *"I don't believe in astrology; I'm a Sagittarius and we're skeptical."*

EDWARD ABBEY: *"Who needs astrology? The wise man gets by on fortune cookies."*

MAIMONIDES: *"Astrology is a disease, not a science."*

PETER DE VRIES: *"Do you believe in astrology? I don't even believe in astronomy."*

JOHNNY MCGREW: *"Astrology is one of those things that 'educated' people deny, but somehow pretty much everybody can still tell you their sign."*

THE 5TH DIMENSION/GALT MACDERMOT, JAMES RADO, GEROME RAGNI: *"Aquarius/Let the Sunshine In"* (Song)

Similar: divine, sacred, celestial, geo-cosmic, etheric, synchronistic, harmonic, prophetic, probabilistic, coincidental, co-creative
Opposite: two-dimensional, terrestrial, geomantic, visible, regular, tangible

Attention. [See also **Concentration** and **Intention**] Directing your thoughts, focus, or awareness to something. *Popular or Heart-Based Usage: (1) Being alert. (2) Noticing. (3) Pivoting. (4) Turning your head. (5) Fixing your gaze. (6) Narrowing your focus. (7) Hollering. (8) Getting a head's up. (9) 'Listen up!' (10) 'Pay attention or pay the price.'*

ASTRONAUT JAMES LOVELL: *"Okay, Houston, we've had a problem here."*

HENRY DAVID THOREAU: *"It's not what you look at that matters, it's what you see."*

JOSE ORTEGA Y GASSET: *"Tell me to what you pay attention and I will tell you who you are."*

MAHARISHI MAHESH YOGI: *"Whatever we put our attention on will grow stronger in our life."*

RICHARD MOSS, MD: *"The greatest gift you can give another is the purity of your attention."*

SIMONE WEIL: *"Attention is the rarest and purest form of generosity."*

EDGAR DEGAS: *"Art is not what you see, but what you make others see."*

JAMES REDFIELD: *"Where Attention goes Energy flows; Where Intention goes Energy flows!"*

EDWARD DE BONO, MD, PHD: *"What is urgent will always take precedence over what is important."*

DAVID MOREHOUSE, PHD: *"Most of us spend the vast majority of our lives looking backward into the past, dwelling on the illusion of some event that we choose to keep giving energy."*

ROBERT J. SHILLER, PHD, NOBEL: *"The ability to focus attention on important things is a defining characteristic of intelligence."*

PAULO COELHO: *"All you have to do is pay attention; lessons always arrive when you are ready."*

PAUL LEVY: *"Quantum Physics reveals to us that turning the gaze of our attention towards anything is a powerful creative act that alters, energizes, and potentiates whatever our gaze falls upon. Focus is food. Focusing our attention is an act of creation in and of itself."*

EMMET FOX: *"Attention is the key to life. Whatever you really give your attention to, you become. Whatever you really concentrate on will come into your life. We grow into the thing that fills our thoughts as inevitably as the stream merges into the ocean at last."*

D. EARL JOHNSTON: *"The difference between attention and intention is all about our level of engagement. It is the beginning of emotion."*

MAXIME LEGACE: *"Your attention has value. Don't give it away."*

ANCIENT WISDOM: *"That which we focus upon expands."*

Similar: focus, notice, observation, heed, concentration, narrowing
Opposite: ignorance, diffusion, confusion, distraction, incoherence, splayed

Attitude. Bringing a specific predisposition or a pattern-style response to a topic or situation. *Popular or Heart-Based Usage: (1) How you roll. (2) How you hang your jaw. (3) Going with the flow (or not). (4) The way you portray your day. (5) How you frame your own picture. (6) Checking your ego at the door. (7) Bringing the right stuff. (8) Being young at heart. (9) Playing Oscar da Grouch. (10) Behaving yourself or being (way) out of line. (11) Standing out. (12) Acting out. (13) 'What kinda baggage you totin' today?' (14) 'Is that the best you got?' (15) Being a 'Dude with a Tude.' (16) 'Are you cheerful or tearful? Victor or victim?'*

> VENUS WILLIAMS: *"Some people say I have attitude—maybe I do … but I think you have to. You have to believe in yourself when no one else does—that makes you a winner right there."*
>
> BARBARA CORCORAN: *"You can catch a great attitude from great people."*
>
> EPICTETUS: *"It's not what happens to you, but how you react to it that matters."*
>
> SCOTT HAMILTON: *"The only true disability in life is a bad attitude."*
>
> H. HILL MCALISTER: *"Successful people know that an 'attitude of gratitude' is a winner."*
>
> MARK TWAIN: *"Do the right thing. It will gratify some people and astonish the rest."*
>
> WILLIAM JAMES, MD: *"The greatest discovery of my generation is that a human being can alter his life by altering his attitudes."*
>
> SIR WALTER SCOTT: *"For success, attitude is equally important as ability."*
>
> MEISTER ECKHARDT: *"When you are thwarted, it is your own attitude that is out of order."*
>
> THOMAS JEFFERSON: *"Nothing can stop the man with the right mental attitude from achieving his goal: nothing on earth can help the man with the wrong mental attitude."*
>
> ALBERT EINSTEIN, PHD, NOBEL: *"Weakness of attitude becomes weakness of character."*
>
> JOHN C. MAXWELL: *"People may hear your words, but they feel your attitude."*
>
> JILL BOLTE TAYLOR, PHD: *"Take responsibility for the energy you bring."*
>
> RALPH MARSTON: *"Excellence is not a skill. It is an attitude."*
>
> DIANE VON FURSTENBERG: *"Attitude is everything."*
>
> MAYA ANGELOU: *"If you don't like something, change it. If you can't change it, change your attitude."*
>
> MICHAEL LANDON: *"The tougher the fight, the more important the mental attitude."*

Similar: mindset, predisposition, approach, perspective, stance, proclivity
Opposite: indifference, disinterest, disregard, non-involvement, unconcern

Authenticity. Being yourself, without pretense or guile. *Popular or Heart-Based Usage: (1) Being true to yourself. (2) Keeping it real. (3) Staying 'down-to-earth.' (4) 'Honest-to-goodness.' (5) Being legit. (6) The real deal.*

JANIS JOPLIN: *"Don't compromise yourself. You are all you've got."*

HENRY DAVID THOREAU: *"We are constantly invited to be who we are."*

MARCUS BUCKINGHAM: *"Authenticity is your most precious commodity as a leader."*

MARGARET THATCHER: *"Power is like being a lady ... if you have to tell people you are, you aren't."*

JUDY GARLAND: *"Always be a first-rate version of yourself, and not a second-rate version of someone else."*

MOTHER TERESA, NOBEL: *"Honesty and transparency make you vulnerable. Be honest and transparent anyway."*

BRENE BROWN, MSW, PHD: *"If you trade your authenticity for safety, you may experience the following: anxiety, depression, eating disorders, addiction, rage, blame, resentment, and inexplicable grief."*

COCO CHANEL: *"Hard times arouse an instinctive desire for authenticity."*

ALBERT EINSTEIN, PHD, NOBEL: *"The main task of the spirit is to free man from his ego."*

STEVE JOBS: *"Don't let the noise of others' opinions drown out your own inner voice."*

CRAIG GROESCHEL: *"Be yourself. Authenticity trumps cool every time."*

ERIC CANTONA: *"Children go where they find sincerity and authenticity."*

W. H. AUDEN: *"Some writers confuse authenticity, which they ought always to aim at, with originality, which they should never bother about."*

NEIL BLUMENTHAL: *"Details matter. They create depth, and depth creates authenticity."*

EDGAR CAYCE: *"Your spiritual level is determined by your lowest behavior, not your highest understanding."*

DESHAUN FOSTER: *"Sometimes authenticity resonates more deeply than perfection."*

SØREN KIERKEGAARD: *"The most common form of despair is not being who you are."*

CARL JUNG, MD: *"The privilege of a lifetime is to become who you truly are."*

ECKHART TOLLE: *"Only the truth of who you are, if realized, will set you free."*

MILES DAVIS: *"Man, sometimes it takes you a long time to sound like yourself."*

SOCRATES: *"To find yourself, think for yourself."*

Similar: genuine, legitimate, true blue, undisputed, authoritative, purpose-driven
Opposite: fake, counterfeit, phony, copying, sketchiness, leveraging

Awareness. Perceiving the existence and relevance of developments, experiences, or vital facts. *Popular or Heart-Based Usage: (1) Picking up on something. (2) Getting a clue. (3) Having a light come on. (4) Reading the room. (5) Getting filled in. (6) Getting a head's up. (7) Joining the club. (8) Being 'in the know.' (9) Getting your bearings. (10) Grasping the big picture. (11) Re-booting. (12) Seeing the full field. (13) Responding with a wink and a nod. (14) Getting your head in the game. (15) Knowing the score. (16) Re-setting. (17) Looking with fresh eyes. (18) Wrapping your head around it. (19) Pattern recognition. (20) Connecting the dots. (21) Getting up to speed. (22) Sensing a presence. (23) Opening your mind. (24) Sensing God winks. (25) Embracing the noosphere. (26) Feeling touched by an angel. (27) Seeing life show out. (28) 'Got it!' (29) 'Where was I?' (30) 'I should have known it.' (31) 'Wake up and smell the coffee!' (32) 'Newsflash!'*

L. FRANK BAUM/'THE WONDERFUL WIZARD OF OZ'/DOROTHY GALE: *"Toto, I've a feeling we're not in Kansas anymore."*

ASTRONAUT JAMES LOVELL: *"Okay, Houston, we've had a problem here."*

AMARILLO SLIM: *"Look around the table. If you don't see a sucker, get up, because you're the sucker."*

JAMES HOLLIS: *"That of which we are not aware, owns us."*

DEAN ORNISH: *"Awareness is the first step in healing."*

TIGER WOODS: *"Money and fame made me believe I was entitled. I was wrong and foolish."*

DAVID BOWIE: *"Aging is an extraordinary process whereby you become the person you always should have been."*

ECKHART TOLLE: *"The first glimpse of awareness is recognizing there is a voice in your head."*

CARL JUNG, MD: *"Until you make the subconscious conscious it will direct your life and you will call it fate."*

GRETCHEN RUBIN: *"Self-awareness is a key to self-mastery."*

ABRAHAM MASLOW, PHD: *"What is necessary to change a person is to change his awareness of himself."*

JOHNNY MCGREW: *"Pro tip ... You're not Einstein ... and 7 times out of 10 if you stay aware of the basic issues you'll beat all the smarty pants anyway."*

MADHAV GOYAL, MD, MPH: *"A lot of people have this idea that meditation means sitting down and doing nothing, but that's not true. Meditation is an active training of the mind to increase awareness."*

ROBERT BURNS/POET LAUREATE OF SCOTLAND: *"Oh wad some power the giftie gie us, to see ourselves as others see us."* [sic]

JAMES THURBER: *"Let us not look back in anger, nor forward in fear, but around in awareness."*

Similar: realization, circumspection, cognizance, examination, focus, aha
Opposite: ignorance, obliviousness, disregard, inattention

Belief. Accepting and repeating a particular thought or set of thoughts. *Popular or Heart-Based Usage: (1) Having your own take on something. (2) Making a thought your own. (3) Buying in to something. (4) Taking a stand on a matter. (5) Having your convictions. (6) Following your heart. (7) Holding to something as Gospel. (8) Reaching your own conclusions. (9) Being on board with something. (10) Outlining your path.*

ANTON CHEKHOV: *"Man is what he believes."*

JAMES ALLEN: *"A person is limited only by the thoughts he chooses."*

MARK TWAIN: *"Religion consists in a set of things which the average man thinks he believes, and wishes he was certain."*

D. EARL JOHNSTON: *"We should be really sure about what we believe in. Our beliefs set out our path and goals. What we believe drives all emotions and creates all scenes."*

PAM GREGORY: *"Your belief system will arrange and present your reality to you … The universe is just a mirror."*

LILLIAN HELLMAN: *"Belief is a moral act for which the believer is to be held responsible."*

MAHATMA GANDHI: *"To believe in something, and not to live it, is dishonest."*

SETH GODIN, BS, MBA: *"People don't believe what you tell them. They rarely believe what you show them. They often believe what their friends tell them. They always believe what they tell themselves."*

CARL JUNG, MD: *"The word 'belief' is a difficult thing for me. I don't believe. I must have a reason for a certain hypothesis. Either I know a thing, and then I know it—I don't need to believe it."*

SIGMUND FREUD, MD: *"The more the fruits of knowledge become accessible to men, the more widespread is the decline of religious belief."*

MAYA ANGELOU: *"It is this belief in a power larger than myself and other than myself which allows me to venture into the unknown and even the unknowable."*

EDITH HAMILTON: *"Faith is not belief. Belief is passive. Faith is active."*

LAURELL K. HAMILTON: *"If you only believe when it's easy, you don't really believe."*

THOMAS SZASZ: *"Delusion: belief said to be false by someone who does not share it."*

JOHN F. KENNEDY: *"Tolerance implies no lack of commitment to one's own beliefs. Rather it condemns the oppression or persecution of others."*

RONALD REAGAN: *"All great change in America begins at the dinner table."*

DR. JOE DISPENZA: *"When you change your mind, you change your life."*

THOMAS CARLYLE: *"A man lives by believing something."*

WAYNE DYER: *"You'll see it when you believe it."*

PROVERB: *"Believe in yourself."*

Similar: faith, credo, trust, conviction, stance, opinion, view, internalization
Opposite: doubt, vacillation, disbelief, uncertainty, suspicion, skepticism, mistrust

Betrayal. (1) Refuting or sabotaging an agreement or trust. (2) Bringing harm or ruin to the trusting or unaware. *Popular or Heart-Based Usage: (1) Stabbing someone (getting stabbed) in the back. (2) Turning your back on an ally. (3) Being a Benedict Arnold. (4) Double-crossing someone. (5) Double-dealing. (6) Getting screwed/Screwing someone. (7) Being 'in on it' (in a coordinated betrayal). (8) Being a Judas. (9) Being a turncoat. (10) Selling out.*

MARTIN LUTHER: *"Each betrayal begins with trust."*

GOETHE: *"We are never deceived. We deceive ourselves."*

WILLIAM SHAKESPEARE: *"Et tu, Brute? Then fall, Caesar!"*

PROVERB: *"Fool me once, shame on you; fool me twice, shame on me."*

GEN. GEORGE S. PATTON, JR.: *"I would rather have a German division in front of me than a French division behind me."*

WILLIAM BLAKE: *"It is easier to forgive an enemy than to forgive a friend."*

D. EARL JOHNSTON: *"We can be our most vulnerable when we want to believe."*

SIR EDWARD GEORGE BULWER-LYTTON: *"The easiest person to deceive is yourself."*

FRANK HERBERT: *"When we try to conceal our innermost drives, the entire being screams betrayal."*

LUKE 22:48: *"Judas, betrayest thou the Son of man with a kiss?"*

PROVERB: *"The saddest thing about betrayal is that it never comes from your enemies."*

DEEPAK CHOPRA: *"The person you call an enemy is an exaggerated aspect of your own shadow self."*

TAYLOR CALDWELL: *"I like animals because they are not consciously cruel and don't betray each other."*

MARIANNE WILLIAMSON: *"Always seek less turbulent skies. Hurt. Fly above it. Betrayal. Fly above it. Anger. Fly above it. You are the one who is flying the plane."*

OBSERVATION: *"Forgive yourself for the blindness that let others betray you. Sometimes a good heart doesn't see the bad."*

BENJAMIN FRANKLIN: *"Tricks and treachery are the practice of fools, that don't have the brains enough to be honest."*

RUSSIAN PROVERB: *"Trust, but verify."*

Similar: defection, treachery, disloyalty, breach of faith, reneging, opportunistic
Opposite: trustworthiness, integrity, constancy, fidelity, reliability

Blame. Assigning responsibility or culpability for a problem or mistake to someone else. *Popular or Heart-Based Usage: (1) Pointing the finger. (2) Fault-finding. (3) Pinning it on someone else. (4) Lining up the usual suspects. (5) Ganging up on others. (6) Scapegoating someone. (7) 'But **you** started it!' (8) 'Not my job.' (9) 'Whoever is not in the room gets blamed.' (10) 'The two big guys always blame it on the little guy.'*

ROBERT HALF: *"The search for someone to blame is always successful."*

GEORGE ELIOT: *"Blameless people are always the most exasperating."*

JOHNNY MCGREW: *"The newest employee or the one that just left always gets blamed. Or anyone else not standing there. Blame is like a can of Raid. Watch people scatter like cockroaches when the 'blame' spotlight comes on."*

ROBIN SHARMA: *"Blaming others is nothing more than excusing yourself."*

PROVERB: *"When you point your finger in criticism, remember the other three fingers that are pointing back at you."*

DON SHULA: *"The superior man blames himself. The inferior man blames others."*

CARL BECKER: *"Fact-finding is more effective than fault-finding."*

ELDRIDGE CLEAVER: *"You are either part of the solution or you're part of the problem."*

BILLY SUNDAY: *"If you don't do your part, don't blame God."*

JOHNNY MCGREW: *"After months of patiently listening to me complain about how my ex-wife was to blame for all my problems, my step-mother finally had enough and set me straight. 'So show me the gun,' she demanded quietly, 'where anyone forced you to marry her.'"*

GEN. BRUCE CLARKE: *"When things go wrong in your command, start searching in increasingly large circles around your own desk."*

D. EARL JOHNSTON: *"Sometimes a leader learns the hard way that counseling or blaming a subordinate should be handled in private."*

EPICTETUS: *"An ignorant person is inclined to blame others for his own misfortune. To blame oneself is proof of progress. But the wise man never has to blame another or himself."*

SAYING: *"Comparison leads to blame."*

PROVERB: *"If you don't like your life, build another one."*

Similar: censure, condemn, criticize, denounce, scapegoating
Opposite: praise, applaud, extol, support, cooperate, laud

Blushing. (1) Experiencing a reddening of the face in reaction to unexpected attention or to a matter of personal sensitivity. (2) Demonstrating an outward display of unease or self-consciousness about a matter of the heart. *Popular or Heart-Based Usage: (1) Feeling suddenly and uncomfortably transparent. (2) Turning beet red. (3) Realizing you have a crush on someone. (4) Realizing you've been found out.*

ANTOINE DE SAINT-EXUPERY: *"When someone blushes, doesn't that mean 'yes'?"*

KEITH ABLOW: *"People blush when one of their core truths is revealed."*

JEAN-FRANCOIS DE LA HARPE: *"We never forget those who make us blush."*

CHARLES DARWIN: *"Blushing is the most peculiar and human of all expressions."*

SENECA: *"Certain people have good, ordinary blood and others have an animated, lively sort of blood that comes to the face quickly."*

JOHN KEATS: *"There's a blush for won't, and a blush for shan't, and a blush for having done it: There's a blush for thought and a blush for naught, and a blush for just begun it."*

CHARLES DARWIN: *"It is not the sense of guilt, but the thought that others might think or know us to be guilty which crimsons the face."*

ELIZABETH TAYLOR: *"When a woman stops blushing, she has lost the most powerful weapon of her charm."*

SØREN KIERKEGAARD: *"On the secretly blushing cheek is reflected the glow of the heart."*

SOPHIE KINSELLA: *"I'm blushing at my own stupid, nonsensical, meaningless thought process, which, by the way, nobody knows about except me."*

RAY BRADBURY: *"Her cheeks glowed with pink charcoals."*

BILL VAUGHAN: *"Blushes are the rainbow of modesty."*

PROM QUEEN: *"But it's **normal** for me to turn fuchsia!"*

Similar: embarrassment, hiding, coyness, shame, shyness, flushing, hot flashes
Opposite: boldness, effrontery, confronting, directness, frankness, impertinence

Bold. Pursuing an advantage by taking unexpected initiative or by assuming a calculated risk. *Popular or Heart-Based Usage: (1) Making your move. (2) Having the nerve. (3) Not being bashful about it. (4) Not holding back. (5) Calling your own number. (6) 'Let's do it!' (7) Jumping in with both feet. (8) Leaping without a net. (9) Taking the plunge. (10) Having brass balls. (11) Going for it. (12) Crossing the Rubicon. (13) Taking no prisoners. (14) Going for all the marbles. (15) Being a badass. (16) Reaching for the brass ring. (17) Being bodacious. (18) Having chutzpah. (19) Pre-empting others. (20) 'That's a savage move.' (21) 'How do you like them apples?' (22) Trying to pull something off.*

AMARILLO SLIM: *"If you are going to bluff, make it a big one."*

HELEN KELLER: *"Life is either a daring adventure or nothing."*

FYODOR DOSTOEVSKY: *"Only one thing matters, one thing; to be able to dare."*

GOETHE: *"Whatever you can do or dream you can, begin it. Boldness has genius, power, and magic in it."*

SIR ISAAC NEWTON, FRS: *"No great discovery was ever made without a bold guess."*

SIR BENJAMIN DISRAELI: *"Man is never so manly as when he feels deeply, acts boldly, and expresses himself with frankness and fervor."*

SIR ANDREW LLOYD WEBBER: *"I've always tried with my shows—win, lose, or draw—to take the boundaries of the music as far as I can."*

SIR RICHARD BRANSON: *"Screw it. Let's do it."*

DONALD TRUMP: *"As long as you're going to be thinking anyway, why not think big?"*

HILLARY CLINTON: *"In America, if you can dream it, you should be able to build it."*

GOETHE: *"Daring ideas are like chessmen moved forward; they may be beaten, but they may start a winning game."*

JOHN BURROUGHS: *"Leap and the net will appear."*

RALPH WALDO EMERSON: *"The world makes way for the man who knows where he is going."*

GRAHAM GREENE: *"A single feat of daring can alter the whole conception of what is possible."*

SIR FRANCIS DRAKE: *"Disturb us, Lord, to dare more boldly*
To venture on wider seas,
Where storms will show your mastery;
Where losing sight of land,
We shall find the stars."

JULIUS CAESAR: *"The die is cast."*

VIRGIL: *"Fortune favors the bold."*

Similar: confronting, intrepid, spirited, pre-emptive, fearless, presumptuous
Opposite: timid, vacillating, indecisive, reticent

Boredom. Finding your situation or circumstances uninteresting or worthy of little participation. *Popular or Heart-Based Usage: (1) Dullsville. (2) Humdrum. (3) The same old same old. (4) Having your eyes glaze over. (5) Having no interests or pursuits. (6) Having nothing to tackle. (7) Being stuck like a stick-in-the-mud. (8) Enduring a dud. (9) Having to listen to someone drone on (or bang on) about something. (10) 'It's all so cliché.' (11) 'This is like watching paint dry.' (12) 'Same lame tame shame.' (13) 'Nothing doing.' (14) 'It's just one big yawn.' (15) 'No zip here.'*

PROVERB: *"An idle mind is the devil's playground."*

SØREN KIERKEGAARD: *"Boredom is the root of all evil."*

D. EARL JOHNSTON: *"Boredom is usually the last thing that happens before you find something new. Or it finds you."*

JOHNNY MCGREW: *"Boredom begs for new beginnings."*

RAVI SHANKAR: *"Boredom is a blessing when it leads you to wisdom. And boredom is a curse when it leads you to frustration and depression."*

VICTOR HUGO: *"There is something more terrible than a hell of suffering—a hell of boredom."*

VOLTAIRE: *"Work spares us from three evils: boredom, vice, and need."*

PETER KREEFT: *"The most total opposite of pleasure is not pain but boredom, for we are willing to risk pain to make a boring life interesting."*

WILLIAM F. BUCKLEY: *"Boredom is the deadliest poison."*

KILROY J. OLDSTER: *"Tedium is lethal to the human soul."*

LEO TOLSTOY: *"Boredom: the desire for desires."*

G. K. CHESTERTON: *"There are no uninteresting things, only uninterested people."*

DENNIS PRAGER: *"'I am bored' generally means 'I am boring.'"*

HELEN GURLEY BROWN: *"Never fail to know that if you are doing all the talking you are boring somebody."*

VOLTAIRE: *"The secret of being a bore is to tell everything."*

CATHERYNNE M. VALENTE: *"A clever person is never bored, and a bored person is never clever."*

PETER MCWILLIAMS: *"If you are not playing a big enough game, you'll screw up the game you're playing just to give yourself something to do."*

DOROTHY PARKER: *"The cure for boredom is curiosity. There is no cure for curiosity."*

Similar: monotony, tedium, sameness, indifference, lassitude, purposelessness
Opposite: curiosity, interest, fascination, excitement, liveliness, vigor, concern

Brave. Having the willingness to pursue an action or decision despite the risk of harm or loss. *Popular or Heart-Based Usage: (1) Doing the right thing, no matter what. (2) Hanging in there. (3) Being stout. (4) Having pluck. (5) Manning up. (6) Wearing your big boy (big girl) pants. (7) Facing the music. (8) Growing a spine. (9) Standing tall. (10) Stepping up/Stepping into the breach. (11) Gutting it out. (12) 'To boldly go where no one has gone before.'*

ROBIN SHARMA: *"Speak your truth, even if your voice shakes."*

PAULO COELHO: *"The brave are always stubborn."*

NELSON MANDELA, NOBEL: *"Courage is not the absence of fear but the triumph over it."*

JOHN WAYNE: *"Courage is being scared to death, and saddling up anyway."*

MAHATMA GANDHI: *"Bravery is not a quality of the body. It is of the soul."*

HERODOTUS: *"Great deeds are usually wrought at great risks."*

MARY TYLER MOORE: *"Take chances, make mistakes. That's how you grow. Pain nourishes your courage. You have to fail in order to practice being brave."*

THOMAS PAINE: *"I love the man who can smile in trouble, gather strength from distress, and grow brave by reflection."*

JOAN DIDION, PULITZER: *"There's a point where you go with what you've got. Or you don't go."*

BRUCE BARTON: *"Nothing splendid has ever been achieved except by those who dared believe that something inside them was superior to circumstance."*

DOLLY PARTON: *"You'll never do a whole lot unless you're brave enough to try."*

MARK TWAIN: *"Braveness is resistance to concern—mastery of panic, not absence of anxiety."*

SAYING: *"We're all brave until we realize the cockroach has wings."*

RONALD REAGAN: *"The future doesn't belong to the fainthearted; it belongs to the brave."*

Similar: courage, valor, audacity, gallantry, unflinchingness, dauntlessness
Opposite: cowardice, timidity, weakness, hiding

Bullying. Imposing belittlement, threat, or harm in order to compel obedience or conformity. *Popular or Heart-Based Usage: (1) Throwing your weight around. (2) Being heavy-handed. (3) Getting pushy/Pushing someone around. (4) Carrying a big stick. (5) Saber rattling. (6) Flexing with someone. (7) Creating downside for someone. (8) Selling woof tickets. (9) Ganging up on someone. (10) Leaning hard on someone. (11) Playing the Bad Cop. (12) Being mean/mean-spirited. (13) Pantsing someone. (14) Being a badass to someone. (15) Dropping some nasty hints. (16) Making somebody feel small.*

SHAY MITCHELL: *"It's the bully who's insecure."*

D. EARL JOHNSTON: *"Bullying is often just bluffing."*

JOHNNY MCGREW: *"The bully usually looks around for the easiest targets first."*

GEORGE ELIOT: *"Any coward can fight a battle when he's sure of winning."*

LADY GAGA: *"There really is no difference between the bully and the victim."*

LINCOLN STOREY: *"Bullying and cruelty are twin marks of a crippled heart trying to cover a deep emotional vulnerability by enforcing one-way dominance over normal two-way communication. Somebody inflicted deep hurt in the past, and so the bully is trying to pass that on by recreating what first hurt him."*

TOM HIDDLESTON: *"When people don't like themselves very much, they have to make up for it. The classic bully was actually a victim first."*

DAN PEARCE: *"People who love themselves don't hurt other people. The more we hate ourselves, the more we want others to suffer."*

JEAN-JACQUES ROUSSEAU: *"The greatest braggarts are usually the biggest cowards."*

SIR WINSTON CHURCHILL: *"You have enemies? Good. That means you've stood up to something, sometime in your life."*

LADY GAGA: *"Never bully anyone because Karma has everyone's address and a motherf***ing stamp."*

MOMENTOUSINSTITUTE.ORG: *"Boys are more physical, girls are more verbal."*

PAM GREGORY: *"When we are in victim mode, we will always attract bullies; however, when we are in empowerment mode, it simply does not happen."*

JOEL OSTEEN: *"People may lure you into playing their game. Don't take the bait."*

STEFANIE MARRONE: *"1. Take the high road—don't engage with the harmful things people say about you...2. Kill them with kindness...3. Do not engage or counterattack...4. Problem solve...5. Find your tribe...6. Support and lift up others...7. Don't take it personally...8. Neutralize your naysayers...9. Stand up for others...10. Don't fall into the mean girl trap..."*

JAIME ESCALANTE: *"The greatest thing you have is your self-image, a positive opinion of yourself. You must never let anyone take it from you."*

ELEANOR ROOSEVELT: *"No one can make you feel inferior without your consent."*

Similar: intimidating, domineering, coercive, abusive, blustering, aggressive, imperious
Opposite: encouraging, supportive, reassuring, caring, nurturing

Calm. [See also **Meditation** and **Prayer**] (1) Having quiet command of your thoughts, with minimal distractions. (2) Being untroubled by upset. *Popular or Heart-Based Usage: (1) Keeping cool. (2) Laying low. (3) Emptying your mind. (4) Turning off the sound track in your head. (5) Creating space. (6) Taking it easy. (7) Being chill. (8) Being laid back. (9) Having an easy grip on yourself. (10) Praying the rosary. (11) Delegating your problems to God. (12) Kicking it all upstairs. (13) Having grace under pressure. (14) Trusting the Universe. (15) 'I'm right here.'*

LUKE 1:38: *"Let it be."*
ENGLISH PROVERB: *"Still waters run deep."*
GERMAN PROVERB: *"In your calm is your strength."*
JON STEWART: *"The enemy is noise. The goal is clarity."*
MASON COOLEY: *"Romance is tempestuous. Love is calm."*
JOSIAH GILBERT HOLLAND: *"Calmness is the cradle of power."*
THOMAS JEFFERSON: *"Nothing gives one person so much advantage over another as to remain always cool and unruffled under all circumstances."*
PROVERB: *"Today start your day with a smile, calmness of mind, coolness of emotions, and a heart filled with gratitude."*
ELISABETH KUBLER-ROSS, MD: *"Learn to get in touch with the silence within yourself, and know that everything in life has purpose."*
Copyright: Elisabeth Kubler-Ross Family Limited Partnership
ROBERT LOUIS STEVENSON: *"To be idle requires a strong sense of personal identity."*
TAYLOR SWIFT: *"People haven't always been there for me, but my music always has."*
ECKHART TOLLE: *"You are never more truly yourself than when you are still."*
MA JAYA SATI BHAGAVATI: *"Quiet the mind, and the soul will speak."*
H. HILL MCALISTER: *"If it doesn't really matter, let it go."*
PROVERB: *"You create your own calm."*

Similar: tranquil, quiet, serene, peaceful, spacious
Opposite: chaotic, agitated, unrest, violent, disturbed, crowded, paroxysm

Catharsis. [See also **Release**] Achieving emotional release after resolving a confusion or troubling issue. *Popular or Heart-Based Usage: (1) Having a light come on. (2) Suddenly connecting the dots. (3) Adding 2 + 2. (4) Figuring it all out. (5) Having an 'Aha' moment. (6) Getting emotional clearance. (7) Letting go. (8) 'Yessss!' (9) 'Bingo!' (10) 'That's it!' (11) 'OMG!' [Oh My God!] (12) 'Eureka!' (13) 'Thank God!' (14) 'Finally!'*

TYLER PERRY: *"I didn't have a catharsis for my childhood pain, most of us don't, and until I learned how to forgive those people and let it go, I was unhappy."*

DESMOND TUTU, NOBEL: *"Catharsis is about cleansing and healing at one and the same time—healing memories and attitudes, healing the spirit and the heart."*

DIONNE WARWICK: *"Crying is cleansing. There's a reason for tears, happiness or sadness."*

GLENN CLOSE: *"There is something about a catharsis that is very important."*

DOROTHY PARKER: *"Art is a form of catharsis."*

BESSEL VAN DER KOLK, MD: *"The injured person's reaction to the trauma only exercises a complete 'cathartic' effect if it is an adequate reaction."*

OBSERVATION: *"Sometimes you don't feel the weight of something you've been carrying until you feel its release."*

SYLVIA PLATH: *"God, it was good to let go, let the tight mask fall off, and the bewildered, chaotic fragments pour out. It was the purge, the catharsis."*

GOOGLE GENERATIVE AI: *"Freud believed that making repressed memories conscious could help relieve symptoms and discharge associated emotions. This is known as catharsis."*

ROBIN WILLIAMS: *"Comedy can be a cathartic way to deal with personal trauma."*

MAURICE SENDAK: *"And it is through fantasy that children achieve catharsis. It is the best means they have for taming Wild Things."*

MICHAEL TIERNO: *"Catharsis leaves the audience with a renewed sense of clarity and better able to function in life."*

J. PITTMAN MCGEHEE, DD: *"Aha is the sound of energy coming into consciousness."*

D. EARL JOHNSTON: *"Catharsis is figuring it out, and then soaring."*

Similar: realization, understanding, epiphany, release, euphoria, aha
Opposite: frustration, confliction, confusion, stuck, suspenseful, unresolved

Caution. Taking care to avoid danger or error. *Popular or Heart-Based Usage: (1) Thinking things through. (2) Re-reading the fine print. (3) Making sure you understand. (4) Taking stock of the situation. (5) Heeding the warnings. (6) Putting it on pause. (7) Getting a second opinion. (8) Playing 'Red Light, Green Light.' (9) Fact-checking. (10) Avoiding misinformation. (11) Double-checking. (12) Putting something 'off limits.' (13) Backing away for another look. (14) Using your discretion. (15) Being prudent.*

CHARLOTTE BRONTE: *"Look twice before you leap."*

RUSSELL BAKER, PULITZER: *"Caution: These verses may be hazardous to your solemnity."*

BENJAMIN FRANKLIN: *"Keep your eyes wide open before marriage, half shut afterwards."*

EURIPIDES: *"Among mortals second thoughts are wisest."*

VICTOR HUGO: *"Caution is the eldest child of wisdom."*

PROVERB: *"Measure twice cut once."*

EPICTETUS: *"Confident because of our caution."*

MIGUEL DE CERVANTES: *"Be slow of tongue and quick of eye."*

SUN TZU: *"The enlightened ruler is heedful, and the good general full of caution."*

OTTO VON BISMARCK: *"A little caution outflanks a large cavalry."*

THOMAS S. MONSON: *"Choose your friends with caution. Plan your future with purpose. Frame your life with faith."*

PROVERBS 4:23: *"Keep thy heart with all diligence: for out of it are the issues of life."*

ROBERT HERJAVEC: *"Too much thinking leads to paralysis by analysis. It's important to think things through, but many use thinking as a means of avoiding action."*

BAHYA IBN PAQUDA: *"One of the rules of caution is not to be too cautious."*

WERNHER VON BRAUN: *"I have learned to use the word 'impossible' with the greatest caution."*

FRANK HERBERT: *"Caution is the path to mediocrity. Gliding, passionless mediocrity is all that most people think they can achieve."*

JEROME: *"The scars of others should teach us caution."*

LYMAN ABBOTT: *"Courage is caution overcome."*

JACK LONDON: *"It was my refusal to take cautious advice that made me."*

CARRIE UNDERWOOD: *"Throw caution to the wind and just do it."*

JIM MORRISON: *"The time to hesitate is through."*

SIR RICHARD BRANSON: *"Screw it. Let's do it."*

ROBIN WILLIAMS (TOM SCHULMAN): *"There's a time for daring and there's a time for caution, and a wise man understands which is called for."*

Similar: wariness, prudence, analysis, hesitation, review, double-checking
Opposite: haste, speculation, unpreparedness, imprudence

Certainty. Having reached a firm conviction or conclusion that something is so. *Popular or Heart-Based Usage: (1) Leaving no room for doubt. (2) 'That's sure-fire.' (3) Reaching a unanimous verdict. (4) Using 'on the nose' dialogue. (5) Nailing it. (6) Reaching crystal clarity. (7) 'Just the facts, Ma'am.' (8) 'It's a lead-pipe cinch.' (9) 'I've got this.' (10) 'Done deal.'*

JON STEWART: *"The enemy is noise. The goal is clarity."*

MAY SARTON: *"The minute one utters a certainty, the opposite comes to mind."*

PROVERB: *"A fool starts in certainty and ends in doubt, while a wise man starts in doubt and ends in certainty."*

RUMI: *"Everyone sees the unseen in proportion to the clarity of his heart."*

MATTHEW 5:8: *"Blessed are the pure in heart: for they shall see God."*

ANNE LAMOTT: *"The opposite of faith is not doubt, it's certainty."*

JOHN F. KENNEDY: *"There is nothing more certain and unchanging than uncertainty and change."*

LUDWIG VON MISES, PHD: *"Science does not give us absolute and final certainty. It only gives us assurance within the limits of our mental abilities and the state of scientific thought."*

ERICH FROMM, PHD: *"The quest for certainty blocks the search for meaning. Uncertainty is the very condition to impel man to unfold his powers."*

ECKHART TOLLE: *"When you become comfortable with uncertainty, infinite possibilities open up in your life."*

MARTIN REES, PHD: *"Absence of evidence is not evidence of absence."*

MARGARET HEFFERNAN: *"Certainty is no guarantor of correctness."*

VOLTAIRE: *"Doubt is not a pleasant condition, but certainty is absurd."*

ANATOLE FRANCE, NOBEL: *"It is the certainty that they possess the truth that makes men cruel."*

BERTRAND RUSSELL, FRS, NOBEL: *"What men really want is not knowledge but certainty."*

WILLIAM DERESIEWICZ, PHD: *"We proceed by doubt, by trial and error, by resisting the impulse to lunge after certainty."*

VINCE LOMBARDI: *"Perfection is not attainable, but if we chase perfection we can catch excellence."*

Similar: conviction, clarity, assuredness, confidence, resolve
Opposite: doubt, confusion, hesitation, bewilderment, indecision

Challenge. Facing (or mounting) a major obstacle or threat. *Popular or Heart-Based Usage: (1) Calling a bluff. (2) A stare-down. (3) Taking the bull by the horns. (4) Having your work cut out for you. (5) Speaking truth to power. (6) Seeing what you're made of.*

ALBERT EINSTEIN, PHD, NOBEL: *"In the middle of every difficulty lies opportunity."*

CARL JUNG, MD: *"I am not what happened to me. I am what I choose to become."*

MARTIN LUTHER KING, JR., NOBEL: *"The ultimate measure of a man is not where he stands in moments of comfort and convenience, but where he stands in times of challenge and controversy."*

GAIL SHEEHY: *"To be tested is good. The challenged life may be the best therapist."*

JUSTICE THURGOOD MARSHALL: *"I never worked hard until I got to Howard Law School and met Charlie Houston…I saw this man's dedication, his vision, his willingness to sacrifice, and I told myself, 'You either shape up, or ship out.' When you are being challenged by a great human being, you know you can't ship out."*

JOSEPH CAMPBELL: *"Opportunities to find deeper powers within ourselves come when life seems most challenging."*

D. EARL JOHNSTON: *"Few in severe distress have arrived there without asking: 'Why me?' And nearby, hopeful angels have whispered back: 'Of course you. Of course now. Now is your time to show up and to shine.'"*

WILLIAM BLAKE: *"Great things are done when men and mountains meet."*

HANNIBAL: *"We will either find a way, or make one."*

MARGARET CHASE SMITH: *"When people keep telling you that you can't do a thing, you kind of like to try it."*

CAROL BURNETT: *"I have always grown from my problems and challenges, from the things that don't work out, that's when I've really learned."*

ALBERT ELLIS, PHD: *"The best years of your life are the ones in which you decide your problems are your own. You do not blame them on your mother, the ecology, or the president. You realize that you control your own destiny."*

ARNOLD PALMER: *"The most rewarding things you do in life are often the ones that look like they cannot be done."*

PAULO COELHO: *"Avoiding problems you need to face is avoiding the life you need to live."*

ROBERT H. SCHULLER: *"Never underestimate your problem or your ability to deal with it."*

LINCOLN STOREY: *"Ego's great challenge is separating out the good from the bad."*

MERYL STREEP: *"What makes you different or weird, that's your strength."*

PROVERB: *"When God closes a door, he opens a window."*

Similar: contest, doubt, confrontation, disability, impairment, incapacitation
Opposite: greenlight, streamline, robust, proceeding, underway

Change. Experiencing the process of adjusting, transforming, or moving from one condition to another. *Popular or Heart-Based Usage: (1) Moving from A to B. (2) Having a different conversation. (3) Pivoting. (4) Getting traction. (5) Having a metamorphosis.*

MARK TWAIN: *"I'm all for prosperity, it's change I object to."*

ALBERT EINSTEIN, PHD, NOBEL (attributed): *"If you always do what you always did, you'll always get what you always got."*

RONALD REAGAN: *"All great change in America begins at the dinner table."*

HENRY DAVID THOREAU: *"Things do not change; we change."*

WAYNE DYER: *"If you change the way you look at things, the things you look at change."*

DALAI LAMA: *"A genuine change must first come from within the individual."*

LEO TOLSTOY: *"True life is lived when tiny changes occur."*

ERNEST HEMINGWAY, PULITZER, NOBEL/'THE SUN ALSO RISES': *"How did you go bankrupt? Two ways. Gradually and then suddenly."*

GAIL SHEEHY: *"If we don't change, we don't grow. If we don't grow, we aren't really living."*

R. BUCKMINSTER FULLER: *"There is nothing in a caterpillar that tells you it is going to be a butterfly."*

JOEL OSTEEN: *"You will never change what you tolerate."*

D. EARL JOHNSTON: *"You are never more than one thought or realization away from your breakthrough."*

LINCOLN STOREY: *"We interpret life through windows colored by our emotions. But we can change those windows."*

MAYA ANGELOU: *"If you don't like something, change it. If you can't change it, change your attitude."*

TODD STOCKER: *"When I tell, I inform. When I ask, I transform."*

REAR ADM. GRACE HOPPER, PHD: *"People have an enormous tendency to resist change. They love to say, 'We've always done it this way.' I try to fight that."*

JANE GOODALL: *"Change happens by listening and then starting a dialogue with the people who are doing something you don't believe is right."*

SIR WINSTON CHURCHILL: *"To improve is to change, to be perfect is to change often."*

CHARLES DARWIN: *"The world will not be inherited by the strongest, it will inherited by those most able to change."*

BENJAMIN FRANKLIN: *"When you're finished changing, you're finished."*

MAHATMA GANDHI: *"You must be the change you wish to see in the world."*

CAROL BURNETT: *"Only I can change my life. No one can do it for me."*

LEXI JOHNSTON: *"Change begins with one person."*

Similar: transformation, transition, modification, revision, amendment, mutation
Opposite: stasis, fixed, stability, unyieldingness, firm

Character. Relating to the distinct traits of your core beliefs or guiding values. *Popular or Heart-Based Usage: (1) Who you are down deep. (2) How you roll. (3) Channeling your inner self. (4) Knowing your own heart. (5) Showing your true colors. (6) Standing for something. (7) Heeding your call. (8) Being a one-of-a-kind. (9) Having backbone. (10) Sticking with your convictions. (11) Having your heart in the right place. (12) Showing what you're made of. (13) Keeping it all real. (14) Having a pair. (15) Learning in the school of hard knocks. (16) Having gumption. (17) Having chutzpah. (18) Knowing what really matters. (19) Being a Made Man. (20) Having 'street cred.' (21) Standing tall. (22) Being built to last. (23) Being 'someone of substance.' (24) Being 'well-rounded.' (25) Being 'salt of the earth.' (26) Being known as 'good people.' (27) Being down to earth. (28) Having your head screwed on right. (29) Following your conscience. (30) Being true to yourself. (31) Answering the bell. (32) Living a purpose-driven life. (33) Digging deep within yourself. (34) "What's it gonna be?' (35) Maintaining spiritual sovereignty. (36) Being nobody's fool. (37) Finding your true voice. (38) Being authentic.*

CARL JUNG, MD: *"The privilege of a lifetime is to become who you truly are."*

JUDY GARLAND: *"Always be a first-rate version of yourself, and not a second-rate version of someone else."*

MILES DAVIS: *"Man, sometimes it takes you a long time to sound like yourself."*

ROBERT LOUIS STEVENSON: *"Life is not a matter of holding good cards, but of playing a poor hand well."*

SIGMUND FREUD, MD: *"Before you diagnose yourself with depression or low self-esteem, first make sure you are not, in fact, just surrounded by assholes."*

JOHN WOODEN: *"Be more concerned with your character than your reputation. Reputation is what others think you are. Character is who you really are."*

ABRAHAM LINCOLN: *"Nearly all men can stand adversity, but if you want to test a man's character, give him power."*

NICK SABAN: *"Your character is your accumulation of your thoughts, habits, and priorities on a day-to-day basis."*

ELEANOR ROOSEVELT: *"Great minds discuss ideas, average minds discuss events, and small minds discuss people."*

ANN LANDERS: *"Keep in mind that the true measure of an individual is how he treats a person who can do him absolutely no good."*

EPICTETUS: *"The key is to keep company only with people who uplift you, whose presence calls forth your very best."*

STEVE MARABOLI: *"Life doesn't get easier or more forgiving, we get stronger and more resilient."*

DALE EARNHARDT: *"You win some, lose some and wreck some."*

MALCOLM X: *"A man who stands for nothing will fall for anything."*

CHRISTIAN A. LARSON: *"Believe in yourself and all that you are. Know that there is something inside of you that is greater than any obstacle."*

Character. *(continued)*

ANDREW NIKOU: *"Good thoughts. Good words. Good deeds."*

WALT WHITMAN: *"Nothing endures but personal qualities."*

PROVERB: *"How high you go is a measure of how deep you are."*

JEFF GORDON: *"You've got to be the best person you can be in your life."*

D. EARL JOHNSTON: *"We become known both for what we repeatedly do, as well as for what we repeatedly do not do."*

JOHNNY MCGREW: *"It's important to have a compass in life—your own compass."*

QUENTIN TARANTINO: *"Don't write what you think people want to read. Find your voice and write about what's in your heart."*

TODD STOCKER: *"Principle comes first; action thereafter."*

BROOKE SHIELDS: *"Someone said adversity builds character, but someone else said adversity reveals character."*

ABRAHAM LINCOLN: *"You have to do your own growing no matter how tall your grandfather was."*

THOMAS WOLFE/'A MAN IN FULL': *"The Manager has given every person a spark from His own divinity, and no one can take that away from you, not even the Manager himself, and from that spark comes your character."*

MARK TWAIN: *"A man's character may be learned from the adjectives which he habitually uses in conversation."*

JOHN WOODEN: *"The true test of a man's character is what he does when no one is watching."*

RICK WARREN: *"People are interested by talent. God is impressed by character."*

DR. JOE DISPENZA: *"Whenever you say 'I am' anything, you're commanding your mind and your body towards a destiny."*

GLEN BALLARD, SIEDAH GARRETT, MICHAEL JACKSON: *"Man in the Mirror"* (Song)

WILLIAM SHAKESPEARE: *"To be, or not to be, that is the question."*

HAFEZ: *"The words you speak become the house you live in."*

ARISTOTLE: *"95% of everything you do is the result of habit."*

ALBERT EINSTEIN, PHD, NOBEL: *"Be a voice not an echo."*

FYODOR DOSTOEVSKY: *"Above all, don't lie to yourself."*

WILLIAM SHAKESPEARE: *"To thine own self be true."*

JIM ROHN: *"Let others lead small lives, but not you."*

BENJAMIN FRANKLIN: *"A right heart exceeds all."*

LOIS FARFEL STARK: *"We are what we build."*

TONY HSIEH: *"Character is destiny."*

Similar: decency, ethics, right-mindedness, honor, probity, rectitude, scrupulousness
Opposite: degeneracy, lowness, meanness, depravity, wishy-washiness

Charisma. Projecting a special quality of communication which inspires connection and belief. *Popular or Heart-Based Usage: (1) Building aura points. (2) Being larger than life. (3) 'Charm in a bottle.' (4) Having special magnetism. (5) Having 'star quality.' (6) Having the 'X' factor. (7) Living resonance. (8) Mic drop moments. (9) Having personal gravitas. (10) Winning both hearts and minds. (11) 'Glowing' it right. (12) Having rizz.*

JOHN F. KENNEDY: *"Ask not what your country can do for you, ask what you can do for your country."*

MARTIN LUTHER KING, JR., NOBEL: *"I Have a Dream"* (Speech)

MEAN JOE GREENE: *"Hey Kid, Catch!"* (Television Commercial)

SIR WINSTON CHURCHILL: *"History will be kind to me, for I intend to write it."*

MARIANNE WILLIAMSON: *"Charisma is a sparkle in people that money can't buy. It's an invisible energy with visible effects."*

RALPH ARCHBOLD: *"Charisma is the transference of enthusiasm."*

ROBERT BREAULT: *"Charisma is a fancy name given to the knack of giving people your full attention...Charisma is not just saying hello. It's dropping what you're doing to say hello."*

LINCOLN STOREY: *"Charisma is a special style of communication which melts resistance and builds enthusiasm. It carries more than the message itself. An enigmatic person can intrigue you, but a charismatic presence lifts you up."*

VANESSA VAN EDWARDS: *"Charisma is the perfect blend of warmth and confidence."*

DAVID HENDRICKS: *"Charismatic leaders inspire confidence and win devotion."*

DONALD T. PHILLIPS: *"Charisma refers to a leader's undeniable ability to bring out the best in people by connecting with them—physically, intellectually, and emotionally."*

STEPHANIE SARKIS, PHD: *"Even people that are fundamentally opposed to a charismatic person quickly find themselves changing their position once they meet him or her."*

MAX WEBER: *"Charisma is the gift from above where a leader knows from inside himself what to do."*

D. EARL JOHNSTON: *"On the stage of life, your charisma is a measure of the lines you can deliver better than anyone else."*

JOHN C. MAXWELL: *"It's true that charisma can make a person stand out for a moment, but character sets a person apart for a lifetime."*

QUENTIN CRISP: *"Charisma is the ability to influence people without logic."*

JOHNNY MCGREW: *"Charisma is charming but it's no guarantee of being right."*

PETER HEATHER: *"Charisma often flows from total self-confidence."*

RONALDINHO: *"I am ugly, but what I do have is charm."*

Similar: captivation, resonance, persuasion, dynamism, rapport, charm, attraction
Opposite: repulsive, uninspiring, abrasive, trivial, bland, boring, uninteresting

Charity. Giving your money, possessions, or time to another who is disadvantaged or in need. *Popular or Heart-Based Usage: (1) Giving to the poor. (2) Gifting someone. (3) Chipping in. (4) Passing the hat. (5) Being a do-gooder. (6) Being a Good Samaritan. (7) Giving (or getting) a hand-out. (8) Giving back. (9) Giving from the heart, not the wallet. (10) Doing the right thing.*

SIR WINSTON CHURCHILL: *"We make a living by what we get, but we make a life by what we give."*

JOHN BUNYAN: *"You have not lived today until you have done something for some-one who can never repay you."*

MUHAMMAD ALI: *"Service to others is the rent you pay for your room here on earth."*

MARTIN LUTHER KING, JR., NOBEL: *"Life's most persistent and urgent question is, 'What are you doing for others?'"*

CHARLES DICKENS: *"No one is useless in this world who lightens the burdens of another."*

MATTHEW 6:4: *"That thine alms may be in secret; and thy Father which seeth in secret himself shall reward thee openly."*

PABLO CASALS: *"I feel the capacity to care is the thing that gives life its greatest significance."*

PRAYER OF IGNATIUS OF LOYOLA: *"To give, and not to count the cost."*

MUHAMMAD: *"A man's wealth is the good he does in this world."*

GEORGE ELIOT: *"What do we live for, if not to make life less difficult for each other?"*

ADAM SMITH: *"Beneficence is always free, it cannot be extorted by force."*

AESOP: *"No act of kindness no matter how small is ever wasted."*

PROVERB: *"Your time is the greatest gift you can give someone."*

MOLIÈRE: *"Every good act is charity. A man's true wealth hereafter is the good that he does in this world to his fellows."*

MOTHER TERESA, NOBEL: *"Charity isn't about pity, it is about love."*

ANNE FRANK: *"No one has ever become poor by giving."*

Similar: assistance, gifting, welfare, alms, relief, indulgences
Opposite: greed, miserliness, selfishness

Cheating. (1) Breaking the rules to gain an unfair advantage. (2) Being unfaithful to a partner. *Popular or Heart-Based Usage: (1) Making up new rules. (2) Cutting corners. (3) Stretching the truth. (4) Being a player. (5) Fooling around. (6) Having a wandering eye. (7) Being a two-timer. (8) Being a home wrecker. (9) Being a dirty rotten scoundrel. (10) Being a rat bastard.*

PROVERB: *"What goes around, comes around."*

BRUCE LANSKY: *"On a recent survey, 80 percent of golfers admitted cheating. The other 20 percent lied."*

WILL ROGERS: *"Income tax has made more liars out of the American people than golf has."*

GEORGE CLOONEY: *"One thing you learn selling women's shoes is that all women lie about their shoe size. And I mean **all** women."*

SAYING: *"An envious lover can dig deeper than the FBI."*

FRANK BUNKER GILBRETH, JR.: *"As long as there are final examinations in school, there will be prayers."*

YIDDISH PROVERB: *"A half-truth is a whole lie."*

JEAN-JACQUES ROUSSEAU: *"There are always four sides to a story: your side, their side, the truth, and what really happened."*

JOHN WOODEN: *"Never lie, never cheat, never steal."*

MARK TWAIN: *"If you tell the truth, you don't have to remember anything."*

CORNELIUS VANDERBILT: *"You have undertaken to cheat me. I won't sue you, for the law is too slow. I'll ruin you."*

CLARENCE DARROW: *"Cheating, having 'hoes,' none of that is cute. To be honest, it's really immature. I don't see how people take pride in breaking someone's heart."*

LINCOLN STOREY: *"Most disputes are sorted out after the event, and where a clever defense can win out over the temptations of finger-pointing: 'I believe I've been misled' can get you further a lot faster than 'You're just a dirty rotten liar.'"*

APHORISM: *"Don't let the bastards grind you down." ("Illegitimi non carborundum.")*

TERRENCE MCNALLY: *"Cheating is not the American way. It is small, while we are large. It is cheap, while we are richly endowed. It is destructive, while we are creative. It is doomed to fail, while our gifts and responsibilities call us to achieve. It sabotages trust and weakens the bonds of spirit and humanity, without which we perish."*

DANIEL DEFOE: *"'Tis no sin to cheat the devil."*

Similar: lying, fibbing, deceiving, defrauding, prevaricating
Opposite: frankness, honesty, truthfulness, constancy, fidelity, steadiness

Choice. Selecting a course of action, thought, or emotion from among the alternatives. *Popular or Heart-Based Usage: (1) Navigating issues. (2) Evaluating your options. (3) Sensing binary outcomes. (4) Thinking on it. (5) Weighing pros/cons. (6) Leaning this way or that. (7) Between a rock and a hard place. (8) Between Scylla and Charybdis. (9) Drawing straws. (10) Picking your poison. (11) 'Any gray areas?' (12) Flipping a coin. (13) Splitting the baby. (14) Picking the lesser of evils. (15) Thumbs up or down. (16) 'Yea or Nay.' (17) Reaching the moment of truth. (18) Checking the box. (19) Pulling the lever.*

NELSON MANDELA, NOBEL: *"May your choices reflect your hopes, not your fears."*

CARL JUNG, MD: *"I am not what happened to me. I am what I choose to become."*

ALBERT ELLIS, PHD: *"The best years of your life are the ones in which you decide your problems are your own. You do not blame them on your mother, the ecology, or the president. You realize that you control your own destiny."*

ALBERT EINSTEIN, PHD, NOBEL: *"The most important decision we make is whether we believe in a friendly or hostile universe."*

MARTIN SELIGMAN, PHD: *"Happiness is just one-fifth of what human beings choose to do."*

MARTIN LUTHER KING, JR., NOBEL: *"The choice is not between violence and nonviolence but between nonviolence and nonexistence."*

GAMAL ABDEL NASSER: *"I don't act; I react."*

SAMMY DAVIS, JR.: *"You always have two choices: your commitment versus your fear."*

JEWISH PROVERB: *"A pessimist, confronted with two bad choices, chooses both."*

RUMI: *"And so it is, that both the Devil and the angelic Spirit present us with objects of desire to awaken our power of choice."*

JERRY GARCIA: *"Constantly choosing the lesser of two evils is still choosing evil."*

MATTHEW 7:7–8: *"Ask, and it shall be given to you; seek, and ye shall find;*
       Knock, and it shall be opened unto you:
       For every one that asketh receiveth; and he that seeketh findeth;
       And to him that knocketh it shall be opened."

JILL BOLTE TAYLOR, PHD: *"We have the power to choose, moment by moment, and how we want to be in the world."*

D. EARL JOHNSTON: *"Re-selecting our thoughts and emotions, and not falling prey to first reactions, can re-charge our lives. Wisdom is rooted in choices."*

ROBERT FROST: *"Two roads diverged in a wood, and I—*
       I took the one less traveled by,
       And that has made all the difference."

DEUTERONOMY 30:19–20; PROVERBS 18:21: *"Choose life."*

Similar: selection, pick, discernment, preference, resolution, confirmation, bracketing
Opposite: duty, obligation, force, coercion, compulsion, insistence

Clarity. (1) Reducing an issue to its most fundamental elements. (2) Gaining mastery. *Popular or Heart-Based Usage: (1) Fully unpacking a problem. (2) Getting down to the basics. (3) Cutting though the clutter. (4) Seeking transparency. (5) Eliminating chatter. (6) 'Through the looking glass, then face to face.' (7) 'Reading you 5 by 5.' (8) A to B. (9) 'KISS.' ['Keep It Simple, Stupid.'] (10) Seeing it like it is. (11) Maintaining a laser focus.*

DANIEL J. SIEGEL, MD: *"Name it to tame it."*

WARREN BUFFETT: *"There is nothing like writing to force you to think and get your thoughts straight."*

WILLIAM ZINSSER: *"Four basic premises of writing: clarity, brevity, simplicity, and humanity."*

HIPPOCRATES: *"The chief virtue that language can have is clarity."*

JON STEWART: *"The enemy is noise. The goal is clarity."*

VOLTAIRE: *"If you wish to converse with me, define your terms."*

CHARLES KETTERING: *"A problem well-stated is a problem half-solved."*

JOHN MILTON: *"Light shone, and order from disorder sprung."*

RUMI: *"Everyone sees the unseen in proportion to the clarity of his heart."*

TIBETAN WISDOM: *"Recognition is liberation."*

CORINTHIANS 13:12: *"For now we see through a glass, darkly; but then face to face."*

LES BROWN: *"You need to make a commitment, and once you make it, then life will give you some answers."*

ROBIN SHARMA: *"Clarity precedes mastery. Craft clear and precise plans/goals/ deliverables. And then block out all else."*

STEVE ARTERBURN: *"Great relationships are based on clarity, not mind-reading."*

DIANE VON FURSTENBERG: *"I can compare clarity to pruning in gardening. You know, you need to be clear. If you are not clear, nothing is going to happen..."*

MARY ANNE RADMACHER: *"In service, there is clarity and compassion."*

LINCOLN STOREY: *"Tween bidding Shores of White and Black,*
    Roll ponderous Waves of Gray;
    The Goal, To chart the Proper Course,
    Bright Harbor! Night or Day."

FRIEDRICH NIETZSCHE: *"Profundity of thought belongs to youth, clarity of thought to old age."*

F. SCOTT FITZGERALD: *"Eighteen might look at thirty-four through a rising mist of adolescence, but twenty-two would see thirty-eight with discerning clarity."*

D. EARL JOHNSTON: *"An ounce of clarity is worth ten pounds of narrative."*

VINCE LOMBARDI: *"Success demands singleness of purpose."*

CHRISTIE GOLDEN: *"Clarity is often found in stillness."*

Similar: coherence, lucidity, intelligibility, plainness, explicitness, discernment
Opposite: indecision, murkiness, fogginess, hallucination, waffling, vacillating

Coaching. [See also **Teaching**] Giving or receiving personalized observation and instruction to improve the attitude, technique, or performance of a client, player, or team. *Popular or Heart-Based Usage: (1) Schooling them. (2) 'Show them, don't tell them.' (3) Setting the drills. (4) Calling the plays. (5) Hoarse whispering. (6) Hurting when they hurt. (7) Being a second father. (8) Understanding 'Boyz 2 Men.' (9) Being the fans' and parents' favorite target. (10) Having broad shoulders. (11) Turning hearts and minds.*

MIA HAMM (2X OLYMPIC GOLD MEDALIST, 2X FIFA CHAMPION): *"My coach said I ran like a girl. I said if he could run a little faster he could too."*

LANE KIFFIN: *"I don't know if God is a sports fan or not, but I do know this: He loves a good comeback."*

RICK WARREN: *"People are interested by talent. God is impressed by character."*

VENUS WILLIAMS: *"Set realistic goals, keep re-evaluating, and be consistent."*

PAT SUMMITT: *"Confidence is what happens when you've done the hard work that entitles you to succeed."*

SUE BIRD: *"Don't underestimate yourself. You are more capable than you think."*

JOHN WOODEN: *"Do not let what you cannot do interfere with what you can do."*

MICHAEL JOSEPHSON: *"A good coach improves your game. A great coach improves your life."*

JOHN WOODEN: *"If you're not making mistakes, then you're not doing anything. I'm positive that a doer makes mistakes."*

RICK PITINO: *"Failure is good. It's fertilizer. Everything I've learned about coaching, I've learned from making mistakes."*

LOU HOLTZ: *"Ability is what you are capable of doing. Motivation determines what you are doing. Attitude determines how well you do it."*

DABO SWINNEY: *"The key to coaching is love. It's not knowledge; it's not discipline. If you love'm, you can discipline them. If you love'm, you can yell at them and laugh about it later."*

NICK SABAN: *"Discipline is not punishment. Discipline is changing someone's behavior."*

KIRBY SMART: *"Change is uncomfortable."*

BRIAN KIGHT: *"Discipline is more reliable than talent ... Discipline is the shortcut."*

JOHN MADDEN: *"Coaches have to watch what they don't want to see and listen to what they don't want to hear."*

TOP COACHES AND ATHLETES: *"Success means keeping focus and having a short memory during a game. You will be distracted if you dwell too long on your mistakes. The next play is happening now."*

BUM PHILLIPS: *"There's two kinds of coaches, them that's fired and them that's gonna be fired."*

Coaching. *(continued)*

DAVID M. HENDRICKS: *"A good coach is a second father. He's a mentor and a friend who turns boys' hearts. He takes all the blame and knows he can expect very few rewards. He's a man who knows that a boy needs someone he can look up to. A boy remembers his coach all his life."*

PHIL JACKSON: *"I think the most important thing about coaching is that you have to have a sense of confidence about what you are doing."*

BILL MCCARTNEY: *"All coaching is, is taking a player where he can't take himself."*

JOHN WOODEN: *"In the end, it's about teaching, and what I always loved about coaching was the practices. Not the games, not the tournament, not the alumni stuff. But teaching the players during practice was what coaching was all about to me."*

BILL BELICHICK: *"What we can control is our performance and our execution, and that's what we're going to focus on."*

ECKHART TOLLE: *"There have been many people for whom limitations, failure, loss, or pain in whatever form turned out to be their greatest teacher. It taught them to let go of false self-images and superficial ego-dictated goals and desires. It gave them depth, humility and compassion. It made them more real."*

TODD STOCKER: *"When I tell, I inform. When I ask, I transform."*

COACHING PROVERB: *"Forget the mistake. Remember the lesson."*

NELSON MANDELA, NOBEL: *"You either win or you learn."*

Similar: teaching, mentoring, training, educating, exhorting, inspiring, developing
Opposite: beginner, pupil, student, player, rookie, recruit

Codependence. (1) Supporting a partner's unhealthy behavior—such as addiction, abuse, underperformance, or irresponsibility—in exchange for something favorable in return. (2) Maintaining an unhealthy emotional reliance pattern with a partner. *Popular or Heart-Based Usage: (1) Enabling each other's poor habits. (2) 'You scratch my back and I'll scratch yours.' (3) Putting up with (and even fostering) all the baloney. (4) 'Hear no evil, see no evil, speak no evil.' (5) Willingly continuing as a battered spouse. (6) Needing to be needed. (7) Staying joined at the hip with someone else and their flaws. (8) Looking the other way about a partner's issues. (9) Being someone's 'fixer.' (10) Logrolling. (11) Supporting a partner's false narrative. (12) Accepting a dysfunctional quid pro quo. (13) Being oddly uncurious about a partner's bad behavior. (14) Making a bad 'arrangement.' (15) Keeping bad patterns alive.*

SAYING: *"I'm not addicted to you. I'm addicted to avoiding my own life."*

DR. PHIL MCGRAW: *"When we engage in codependent behavior, we're saying that our value as a human being comes from pleasing others or trying to control them."*

BARBARA DE ANGELIS: *"In all codependent relationships, the rescuer needs the victim as much as the victim needs the rescuer."*

DYNAMIK: *"Some common traits of codependency include low self-esteem, difficulty setting boundaries, a need for approval and validation from others, a tendency to put the needs of others before their own, and an inability to recognize and assert their own needs."*

SHANNON L. ALDER: *"The truth about codependence is that it's an emotional reliance that causes us to act irrationally, makes us responsible for other people's feelings, and leads us ultimately to sacrifice our own happiness."*

MELODY BEATTIE: *"Codependents have no sense of self; they get their identity through others."*

DYNAMIK: *"Don't mistake love for codependency. True love empowers, not enmeshes."*

TRACY A. MALONE: *"Everything happens because there was a lesson you needed to learn. Move on from the messenger, they were not the lesson. Find the lesson and you will never repeat it again."*

CARL WHITAKER, MD: *"The paradox of codependence is that we cannot give ourselves away until we learn how to be ourselves in the first place."*

MELODY BEATTIE: *"Codependents have difficulty knowing what they feel and difficulty expressing it."*

JOHN BRADSHAW: *"Codependents don't realize that they have rights—their own wants and needs—because they were taught not to assert themselves."*

SAYING: *"Codependency is like a black hole that sucks in everything in its orbit."*

Similar: propping each other up, interdependence, a sad situation of tit for tat
Opposite: abandonment, retaliation, reprisal, making someone take responsibility

Coincidence. The simultaneous occurrence of two or more events which do not have a causal connection. *Popular or Heart-Based Usage: (1) Happenstance. (2) Getting two birds with one stone. (3) A 'coinkydink.' (4) Serendipity. (5) Synchronicity. (6) God winks. (7) Déjà vu. (8) 'Jinx!' (9) Being in the right place at the right time. (10) Having fortune smile on you. (11) Getting a lucky break. (12) Having something drop in your lap. (13) 'That's so Twilight Zone!' (14) 'Who'd a thunk?' (15) 'That's really woo-woo.'*

YOGI BERRA: *"That's too coincidental to be a coincidence."*

SIMON VAN BOOY: *"Coincidences mean you're on the right path."*

ALBERT EINSTEIN, PHD, NOBEL: *"Coincidence is God's way of remaining anonymous."*

CARL JUNG, MD: *"Synchronicity: A meaningful coincidence of two or more events where something other than the probability of chance is involved."*

ADAGE: *"Serendipity is the art of finding something that you were not looking for."*

SAYING: *"God winks are those unforgettable situations when God shows up."*

DEFINITION: *"Déjà vu is a feeling of having already experienced something."*

SAYING: *"'Jinx!': what friends shout right after they say the exact same thing."*

ISAAC ASIMOV, PHD: *"People are entirely too disbelieving of coincidence."*

EMMA BULL: *"Coincidence is the word we use when we can't see the levers and pulleys."*

REAR ADM. GRACE HOPPER, PHD: *"If you do something once, people will call it an accident. If you do it twice, they call it coincidence. But do it a third time and you've just proven a natural law!"*

ELISABETH KUBLER-ROSS, MD: *"Everything in this life has a purpose, there are no mistakes, no coincidences."*

Copyright: Elisabeth Kubler-Ross Family Limited Partnership

ELIE WIESEL, NOBEL: *"In Jewish history there are no coincidences."*

PAULO COELHO: *"Coincidence is the language of the stars. For something to happen, so many forces have to be put into action."*

DEEPAK CHOPRA: *"I don't believe in meaningless coincidences. I believe every coincidence is a message, a clue about a particular facet of our lives that requires our attention."*

ERMA BOMBECK: *"Thanksgiving dinners take eighteen hours to prepare. They are consumed in twelve minutes. Half-times take twelve minutes. This is not a coincidence."*

DICK CAVETT: *"Just think of all the billions of coincidences that don't happen."*

G. K. CHESTERTON: *"Coincidences are spiritual puns."*

YOGI BERRA: *"It's like déjà vu all over again."*

Similar: concurrence, happenstance, correlation, parallelism, simultaneous, serendipity, fluke, lucky break

Opposite: disconnection, discord, non-conformity, dissociation, isolation

Commitment. (1) Taking unswerving action toward a goal. (2) Being dedicated to a cause or course. *Popular or Heart-Based Usage: (1) Getting fully on board. (2) Giving something your all. (3) Being fully engaged in a matter. (4) Leaning in to something. (5) Stretching yourself. (6) 'No turning back.' (7) Signing on the dotted line. (8) 'Buying in' to something. (9) Having skin in the game. (10) Sticking to your guns. (11) Taking no prisoners. (12) Pulling out all the stops. (13) 'No such thing as half-pregnant.' (14) 'Are you in or out?' (15) 'Count on me.' (16) 'Through thick and thin.' (17) 'I'm all in.' (18) 'I'm down for that.' (19) Sticking to your convictions. (20) 'Ride or die.' (21) 'No matter what.'*

> BILL MURRAY: *"Whatever you do, always give 100%. Unless you're donating blood."*
>
> PROVERB: *"In a breakfast of bacon and eggs, the chicken is involved but the pig is committed."*
>
> PROVERB: *"You are either pregnant or you are not."*
>
> PAT RILEY: *"There are only two options regarding commitment; you're either in or you're out."*
>
> ANTHONY ROBBINS: *"There's no abiding success without commitment."*
>
> CARL JUNG, MD: *"You are what you do, not what you say you'll do."*
>
> SAMMY DAVIS, JR.: *"You always have two choices: your commitment versus your fear."*
>
> LES BROWN: *"You need to make a commitment, and once you make it, then life will give you some answers."*
>
> MARTIN LUTHER KING, JR., NOBEL: *"No one really knows why they are alive until they know what they'd die for."*
>
> HERNANDO CORTES: *"Burn the ships. We will not leave here without victory."*
>
> THE WOMEN OF SPARTA: *"Come back with your shield—or on it."*
>
> DAVID MCNALLY: *"Commitment is the enemy of resistance."*
>
> JEAN-PAUL SARTRE: *"Commitment is an act not a word."*

Similar: allegiance, constancy, devotedness, steadfastness, vow, promise
Opposite: breach, denial, fickleness, refusal

Compassion. Concern and care for the sufferings and misfortunes of others. *Popular or Heart-Based Usage: (1) Brotherly love. (2) Looking out for others. (3) Helping someone from the heart. (4) Dealing with someone else's distress as if it is your own. (5) Giving someone a helping hand. (6) Holding space for someone. (7) 'Mi casa es su casa.'*

HELEN KELLER: *"Life is an exciting business, and most exciting when it is lived for others."*

BILLY GRAHAM: *"We must never minimize the suffering of another. Scripture's mandate is: Weep with those who weep."*

MEISTER ECKHART: *"You may call God love, you may call God goodness. But the best name for God is compassion."*

DALAI LAMA, NOBEL: *"Love and compassion are necessities. Without them, humanity cannot survive."*

MAHATMA GANDHI: *"Compassion is a muscle that gets stronger with use."*

THICH NHAT HANH: *"Compassion is a verb."*

LAO TZU: *"I have just three things to teach: simplicity, patience, compassion. These three are your greatest treasures."*

SHARON SALZBERG: *"Compassion isn't morose; it's something replenishing and opening; that's why it makes us happy."*

PABLO CASALS: *"I feel the capacity to care is the thing that gives life its greatest significance."*

GEORGE ELIOT: *"What do we live for, if not to make life less difficult for each other?"*

ARTHUR SCHOPENHAUER: *"Compassion is the basis for all morality."*

JACK KORNFIELD: *"If your compassion does not include yourself, it is incomplete."*

LORD BYRON: *"The dew of compassion is a tear."*

SAYING: *"There but for the grace of God go I."*

Similar: empathy, humanity, commiseration, sympathy, charity, kindness, helpfulness
Opposite: cruelty, meanness, mercilessness, selfishness

Complaining. (1) Utilizing monologue, often elevated in pitch or tone, to express opposition to an issue or situation. (2) Expressing helpless disgust. *Popular or Heart-Based Usage: (1) Bitching. (2) Whining. (3) Griping. (4) Moaning. (5) Being a grump. (6) Being a fussbudget. (7) Bellyaching. (8) Getting cranky. (9) Throwing a tantrum. (10) Kicking and screaming. (11) Being fed up. (12) Being a crybaby about something. (13) Being a noodge. (14) Being a sourpuss. (15) Pounding sand. (16) Playing the victim. (17) Taking it out on others. (18) Venting. (19) Letting off steam. (20) Swearing like a sailor. (21) Not having it. (22) Giving full-on push-back. (23) Giving someone a piece of your mind.* Alternately, as opposite behavior: *(24) 'Bitch. Bitch. Bitch.' (25) 'I've had it up to here with your whining.' (26) 'Quit your bellyaching.' (27) 'Talk to the hand.'*

JOHNNY MCGREW: *"If your voice is whining, you are losing."*

CONFUCIUS: *"It is better to light one small candle than to curse the darkness."*

ALBERT ELLIS, PHD: *"Neurosis is just a high-class word for whining."*

ANONYMOUS: *"Being offended doesn't make you right."*

D. EARL JOHNSTON: *"Complaining is the lazy person's answer to a problem."*

BERNARD BARUCH: *"You can overcome anything if you don't bellyache."*

ECKHART TOLLE: *"When you complain, you make yourself into a victim."*

OG MANDINO: *"Do not listen to those who weep and complain, for their disease is contagious."*

DENNIS PRAGER: *"The more we complain, the more unhappy we get."*

IMMANUEL KANT: *"If man makes himself a worm, he must not complain when he is trodden on."*

ECKHART TOLLE: *"Complaining is a key method the ego uses to reinforce itself."*

APHORISM: *"The only thing complaining does is to convince other people you are not in control."*

PSALM 38:9: *"Lord all my desire is before thee; And my groaning is not hid from thee."*

BRACHA GOLDSMITH: *"The opposite of complaining is appreciation."*

SHIRLEY CHISHOLM: *"If they don't give you a seat at the table, bring in a folding chair."*

JOEL OSTEEN: *"When you complain, you remain; but when you praise, you are raised."*

JAMES JOYCE: *"All Moanday, Tearday, Wailsday, Thumpsday, Frightday, Shatterday."*

BAHA'U'LLAH: *"A thankful person is thankful under all circumstances. A complaining soul complains even in paradise."*

SIR BENJAMIN DISRAELI: *"Never complain and never explain."*

SAYING: *"Grin and bear it."*

Similar: protesting, whining, griping, grumbling, bellyaching, finger-pointing
Opposite: solving, developing, supporting, appreciating, praising

Conceit. Demonstrating excessive pride, self-absorption, or self-promotion. *Popular or Heart-Based Usage: (1) Being stuck up. (2) Being full of yourself. (3) Being an empty suit. (4) 'All hat no cattle.' (5) Too cool for school. (6) Flexing. (7) Being a 'wise guy.' (8) Being a know-it-all. (9) Going bougie. (10) Being uppity. (11) Being a snob. (12) Having a big fat say. (13) Playing big shot. (14) Being a blowhard. (15) 'The world according to...' (16) Sucking all the air out of the room. (17) Always having a hand mirror ready. (18) Being hot stuff. (19) Getting caught up in yourself. (20) Being 'too clever by half.' (21) 'Holding court' about something. (22) 'Get a load of me!' (23) Dropping the mic. (24) Quoting yourself. (25) Referring to yourself in the third person. (26) Having false modesty. (27) Engaging in 'humblebrag.' (28) Getting a big head. (29) Being a 'real piece of work.' (30) Expecting to be treated like 'God's gift to the world.' (31) Having a big attitude. (32) Acting saddity. (33) Behaving like you're 'all that.'*

JOHN WOODEN: *"Talent is God-given. Be humble. Fame is man-given. Be grateful. Conceit is self-given. Be careful."*

WILL ROGERS: *"It's great to be great, but it's better to be human."*

WILSON MIZNER: *"Don't talk about yourself. It will be done when you leave."*

AESOP: *"Outside show is a poor substitute for inner worth."*

C. S. LEWIS: *"If a man thinks he is not conceited, he is very conceited indeed."*

LEO TOLSTOY: *"An arrogant person considers himself perfect. This is the chief harm of arrogance. It interferes with a person's main task in life—becoming a better person."*

D. EARL JOHNSTON: *"Conceit is an insecurity which pushes real dialogue aside. It's when your two-way conversation gets hijacked into a monologue."*

ALBERT EINSTEIN, PHD, NOBEL: *"The horizon of many people is a circle with a radius of zero. They call this their point of view."*

GORE VIDAL: *"A narcissist is someone better looking than you."*

DR. PHIL MCGRAW: *"These people have to be the center of attention."*

DIANA VREELAND: *"I loathe narcissism, but I approve of vanity."*

TONY HSIEH: *"Don't be cocky. Don't be flashy. There's always someone better than you."*

PERCY BYSSHE SHELLEY: *"Nothing wilts faster than laurels that have been rested upon."*

ROMANIAN PROVERB: *"Self-praise is no recommendation."*

JOHNNY MCGREW: *"People acting that way? My first response is usually a big fat yawn."*

EMILY DICKINSON: *"I'm nobody! Who are you?"*

TEXAS ADAGE: *"But it ain't braggin' if it's true."*

Similar: narcissism, egotism, arrogance, superciliousness, self-absorption, self-aggrandizement, bloviating, boastfulness, illeism

Opposite: humility, bashfulness, reserve, self-effacement, modesty, selflessness

Concentration. [See also **Attention** and **Intention**] Focusing or narrowing one's primary thoughts or attention to an identified concept or goal. *Popular or Heart-Based Usage: (1) Being into something. (2) Keeping your eye on the ball. (3) Applying yourself. (4) Hitting the books. (5) Being riveted by something. (6) Being absorbed by something. (7) Being glued to something. (8) Keeping something 'top of mind.' (9) Wrapping your head around something. (10) Building an inner monologue. (11) Bringing something into focus. (12) Keeping it all straight in your head. (13) Going for 'intellectual brutality.' (14) Keeping the seat of your pants fixed to the seat of the chair. (15) Being all dialed in. (16) Avoiding distractions.*

VINCE LOMBARDI: *"Success demands singleness of purpose."*

BRUCE LEE: *"The successful warrior is the average man, with laser-like focus."*

GEORGE LUCAS: *"Always remember, your focus determines your reality."*

PROVERB: *"Whatever you focus upon, expands."*

ANTHONY ROBBINS: *"Where focus goes, energy flows."*

JACK NICKLAUS: *"Concentration is a fine antidote to anxiety."*

PUBLILIUS SYRUS: *"To do two things at once is to do neither."*

MAXIME LEGACE: *"Your attention has value. Don't give it away."*

WARREN BUFFETT: *"Knowing what to leave out is just as important as knowing what to focus on."*

RALPH WALDO EMERSON: *"Concentration is the secret of strength in politics, in war, in trade, in short in all management of human affairs."*

D. EARL JOHNSTON: *"When challenged, confidence digs in to refocus and reset. Insecurity throws in the towel to fear."*

DANIEL GOLEMAN, PHD: *"Those who focus best are relatively immune to emotional disturbance."*

ELIZABETH A. STANLEY, PHD: *"In fact, the only thing that's truly under our control is where, when, and how we repeatedly direct our attention, and whether we're directing it consciously."*

JOEL OSTEEN: *"Think this, not that."*

FRANZ KAFKA: *"Evil is whatever distracts."*

GREG MCKEOWN: *"Focus is more important than genius."*

EMMET FOX: *"Supply yourself with a mental equivalent, and the thing must come to you."*

MENACHEM MENDEL SCHNEERSON: *"And how can you achieve such concentration? By recognizing that everything you do is important to God, and is one vital piece of the larger picture of your life."*

Similar: focus, attention, single-mindedness, dedication, intention, purposefulness

Opposite: distractedness, confusion, diffusion, muddlement, chaos, having ADD or ADHD

Condescension. Adopting a posture of superiority and advice-giving to others. *Popular or Heart-Based Usage: (1) Patronizing others. (2) Being snooty. (3) Acting highfalutin. (4) Being a snob. (5) Identifying with the elites. (6) Living among the Brahmins. (7) Lecturing from a high horse. (8) Looking down your nose at others. (9) Associating with 'the great unwashed.' (10) Having Long Island lockjaw. (11) Having disgust for the hoi polloi. (12) Virtue signaling. (13) Stoking your ego. (14) Talking down to people.*

LINCOLN STOREY: *"Condescension is a way of trivializing the other person."*

JOHN STEINBECK: *"There are no ugly questions except those clothed in condescension."*

SCOTT ADAMS: *"If you have any trouble sounding condescending, find a Unix user to show you how it's done."*

MARY BARNETT GIBSON: *"No one who has not experienced the condescension of a buyer towards an ordinary salesgirl can have any conception of its withering effect."*

SPIRO AGNEW: *"[Beware of] an effete corps of impudent snobs."*

HERMAN MELVILLE: *"Of all insults, the temporary condescension of a master to a slave is the most outrageous and galling. That potentate who most condescends, mark him well."*

PAUL GIGOT, PULITZER: *"Obama's style of argumentation is unlike any president I've ever met, and I've met a lot of them. And the condescension that oozes from him when he's talking about his opponents, is really striking."*

SØREN KIERKEGAARD: *"Do you know any more overwhelming and humbling expression for God's condescension and extravagance towards us human beings than that He places himself, so to say, on the same level of choice with the world, just so that we may be able to choose; that God, if language dare speak thus, woos humankind..."*

ISAK DINESEN: *"The true art of the gods is comic. The comic is a condescension of the divine to the world of man; it is the sublime vision, which cannot be studied, but must ever be celestially granted. In the comic the gods see their own being reflected as in a mirror..."*

SIR BERNARD CRICK, PHD: *"The praise of free men is worth having, for it is the only praise which is free from either servility or condescension."*

AMANDA PALMER: *"Asking for help with shame says:*
You have the power over me.
Asking with condescension says:
I have the power over you.
But asking for help with gratitude says:
We have the power to help each other."

Similar: pretentiousness, elitism, pomposity, self-righteousness, arrogance, disgust
Opposite: common, regular, normal, easy-going, tolerant, assimilating

Confidence. Having a predisposition of self-assurance or a firm belief in your prospects for success. *Popular or Heart-Based Usage: (1) 'I've got this!' (2) 'Can do' spirit. (3) 'Hell, yes!' (4) 'Let's roll.' (5) Being cocky. (6) 'Thumbs up!' (7) Having swagger. (8) 'Bring it on!' (9) Being a self-starter. (10) Having your own motor. (11) Knowing that you have what it takes. (12) Having a bounce in your step. (13) Sassiness. (14) Walking the walk. (15) Strutting your stuff. (16) Having your horns on. (17) Being ready to rumble. (18) Betting on yourself. (19) Manspreading your legs. (20) Standing hands on hips. (21) Trusting your gut. (22) Trusting your wits/instincts. (23) Feeling 'it's in the bag.' (24) Giving a reassuring nod. (25) Having positivity bias. (26) 'I'll show you.' (27) 'Of course.' (28) 'Have no fear.' (29) 'Sure thing.' (30) 'No problem.' (31) 'Just watch.' (32) 'Bring it on.' (33) 'I'm in it to win it.' (34) 'Is that all ya got?' (35) 'You ain't seen nothing yet.'*

PAT SUMMITT: *"Confidence is what happens when you've done the hard work that entitles you to succeed."*

VINCE LOMBARDI: *"Confidence is contagious. So is lack of confidence."*

DAVID M. HENDRICKS: *"When you try new things and succeed—even small things—you build confidence. That's damned important to living a happy life."*

PETER MCINTYRE: *"Confidence comes not from always being right but from not fearing to be wrong."*

RICHARD RODGERS: *"I Have Confidence"* (Song)

E. E. CUMMINGS: *"Once we believe in ourselves, we can risk curiosity, wonder, spontaneous delight, or any experience that reveals the human spirit."*

BLAKE LIVELY: *"The most beautiful thing you can wear is confidence."*

CURTIS JACKSON (50 CENT): *"Just be confident. I think confidence is the most attractive part of a person."*

GOLDA MEIR: *"Trust yourself. Create the kind of self that you will be happy to live with all your life. Make the most of yourself by fanning the tiny inner sparks of possibility into flames of achievement."*

JAIME ESCALANTE: *"The greatest thing you have is your self image, a positive opinion of yourself. You must never let anyone take it from you."*

HELEN KELLER: *"Optimism is the faith that leads to achievement. Nothing can be done without hope and confidence."*

HASIDIC SAYING: *"The man who has confidence in himself gains the confidence of others."*

BILL PARCELLS: *"Knowledge is confidence. And confidence lets you play fast."*

TED WILLIAMS: *"Ya gotta be ready for the fastball."*

RON HOWARD: *"Confidence is preparation in action."*

MIGUEL DE CERVANTES: *"Thou hast seen nothing yet."*

SUN TZU: *"You have to believe in yourself."*

Similar: self-assuredness, optimism, boldness, intrepidness, sassy, bodacious
Opposite: fearful, demoralized, shattered, disorganized, disoriented, flustered

Confusion. (1) Experiencing indecision or a lack of clarity from incomplete or conflicting information. (2) Being disorganized. *Popular or Heart-Based Usage: (1) Getting lost. (2) Feeling disoriented. (3) Having a mix-up. (4) Getting your signals crossed. (5) Wrapped around the axle. (6) Things going sideways. (7) Feeling stuck on the fence. (8) Getting all bollixed up. (9) Feeling bumfoozled. (10) Feeling discombobulated. (11) Things going haywire. (12) 'Mayday!' (13) Tossing a cat amongst pigeons. (14) Being flummoxed. (15) Getting misdirected. (16) Feeling misinformed. (17) Eyes glazing over. (18) Scratching your head. (19) Being out of kilter. (20) Getting it all twisted. (21) Being a lost ball in high weeds. (22) 'Out of the loop.' (23) Being 'at sea.' (24) Not getting the memo. (25) Stuck in Malfunction Junction. (26) Being in over your head. (27) Having a brain freeze. (28) 'Not making a lick of sense.' (29) Stuck in a brain fog. (30) Being all turned around. (31) Having something mess with your mind.*

JON STEWART: *"The enemy is noise. The goal is clarity."*

THOMAS FULLER: *"All things are difficult before they are easy."*

YOGI BERRA: *"When you come to a fork in the road, take it."*

DELSON DELMAR: *"Some things are hard to pronounce, others are hard to say."*

ALBERT EINSTEIN, PHD, NOBEL: *"I used to go away for weeks in a state of confusion."*

JOHNNY MCGREW: *"When in confusion or panic, I can stay calm. I remember there's always one thing left that I can still do, and do easily ... Run like hell."*

LES BROWN: *"You need to make a commitment, and once you make it, then life will give you some answers."*

STEVE JOBS: *"Don't let the noise of others' opinions drown out your own inner voice."*

D. EARL JOHNSTON: *"Being confused is not a sin. But staying confused might be."*

SIR ISAAC NEWTON, FRS: *"Truth is ever to be found in simplicity, and not in the multiplicity and confusion of things."*

YOGI BERRA: *"If you don't know where you're going, you might wind up someplace else."*

LARRY KING: *"There is nothing in your destiny, nothing in your future that you cannot accomplish. Getting your house in order and reducing the confusion gives you more control over your life."*

LINCOLN STOREY: *"Which path leads to the best long-term outcome? Choose that one. Anything else is almost always just a distraction."*

SIR WINSTON CHURCHILL: *"Never let a good crisis go to waste."*

PSALM 30:5: *"Weeping may endure for a night, but joy cometh in the morning."*

JOHN MILTON: *"Light shone, and order from disorder sprung."*

MACHIAVELLI: *"Good order makes men bold, and confusion, cowards."*

RUDY RUETTIGER: *"Eliminate the confusion in your life."*

Similar: disorder, chaos, muddlement, uncertainty, crisis, conflict, bafflement
Opposite: clear, certain, resolute, confident, serene, organized

Conscience. Having an inner sense about the inherent rightness or wrongness of your behavior. *Popular or Heart-Based Usage: (1) Knowing right from wrong. (2) Abiding by the Golden Rule. (3) Having scruples. (4) Maintaining your principles. (5) Staying true to your North Star. (6) Living by a code. (7) Being ethical. (8) Acknowledging your higher self. (9) Recognizing your metasystem. (10) Having a Superego. (11) Listening to the still small voice in the back of your head. (12) Taking the long view. (13) 'Let your conscience be your guide.'*

JOHN WOODEN: *"There is no pillow so soft as a clean conscience."*

VICTOR HUGO: *"Conscience is God present in man."*

JEAN-JACQUES ROUSSEAU: *"Reason deceives us; conscience, never."*

ROBERT REDFORD: *"Health food may be good for the conscience but Oreos taste a hell of a lot better."*

MARK TWAIN: *"A clear conscience is the sure sign of a bad memory."*

STANISLAW I. LESZCZYNSKI: *"Conscience warns us as a friend before it punishes us as a judge."*

SOPHOCLES: *"There is no witness so terrible, no accuser so powerful as conscience which dwells within us."*

ALBERT EINSTEIN, PHD, NOBEL: *"Never do anything against conscience even if the state demands it."*

STOKELY CARMICHAEL: *"There is a higher law than the law of government. The law of conscience."*

HARPER LEE: *"The one thing that does not abide by majority rule is a person's conscience."*

OSCAR WILDE: *"Nothing makes one so vain as being told that one is a sinner."*

GEORGE ELIOT: *"The beginning of compunction is the beginning of a new life."*

QUEEN ELIZABETH I: *"A clear and innocent conscience fears nothing."*

BENJAMIN FRANKLIN: *"A good conscience is a continual Christmas."*

WILLIAM SHAKESPEARE: *"I feel within me a peace above all earthly dignities, a still and quiet conscience."*

SUN TZU: *"Having intelligence without conscience is like owning a field that you never cultivate."*

D. EARL JOHNSTON: *"We act out of both science and conscience. Where the brain analyzes the angles, the heart already knows the score."*

WILL ROGERS: *"People are getting smarter nowadays; they are letting lawyers, instead of their conscience, be their guide."*

VINCENT VAN GOGH: *"Conscience is a man's compass."*

PROVERB: *"Follow your heart."*

Similar: principles, guidance, standards, values, morality, ethics, character, superego
Opposite: immorality, sociopathy, disregard, uncaring, ignorance, obliviousness

Conscious Breathing. (1) Undertaking controlled, measured, or rhythmic breathing, or breathing by an assisted or predetermined pattern. (2) Doing oxygen therapy. *Popular or Heart-Based Usage: (1) Breathwork. (2) Centering yourself. (3) Taking a good deep 'blow' for rest. (4) Filling up your lungs all the way. (5) Doing biofeedback. (6) Doing hyperbaric therapy. (7) Supercharging your intentions through your breath. (8) Doing yoga. (9) Ujjayi breathing. (10) Alternate nostril breathing. (11) Doing belly breathing.*

MARY OLIVER, PULITZER: *"Listen—are you breathing just a little, and calling it a life?"*

STEVE MARTIN: *"I've got to keep breathing. It'll be my worst business mistake if I don't."*

DAN BRULE, EMRS, BS, MA: *"If you need to control yourself—your mind, body, emotions, posture or behavior—then start by getting control of your breathing."*

GENESIS 2: *"And the Lord God formed man of the dust of the ground, and breathed into his nostrils the breath of life; and man became a living soul."*

SANSKRIT PROVERB: *"For breath is life, and if you breathe well you will live long on earth."*

DESMOND GREEN: *"Shallow breathing is the root of all evil but conscious deep breathing restores and secures our souls."*

HERMAN HUPFIELD: *"A sigh is just a sigh."*

LINCOLN STOREY: *"Hungry? Go eat. Thirsty? Get a drink. And when life brings anxiety, stress, or depression, you can help find normal in conscious breathing."*

ECKHART TOLLE: *"Being aware of your breath forces you into the present moment— the key to all inner transformation. Whenever you are conscious of the breath, you are absolutely present."*

DR. JOE DISPENZA: *"The breath is a way of pulling the mind out of the body."*

THICH NHAT HANH: *"Breath is the bridge which connects life to consciousness, which unites your body to your thoughts."*

D. EARL JOHNSTON: *"It is so very normal to breathe simple shallow breaths merely to survive, and to react emotionally to whatever life presents us. But when we choose instead to breathe consciously and deeply, and when we deliberately choose our emotions, our world transforms."*

CANDACE BEEBE PERT, PHD: *"Simply bringing awareness to the process of breathing initiates the release of peptide molecules from the hindbrain to regulate breathing while unifying all systems."*

MAYO FOUNDATION FOR MEDICAL EDUCATION AND RESEARCH: *"Yoga is a mind-body practice that combines physical poses, controlled breathing, and meditation or relaxation. Yoga may help reduce stress, lower blood pressure and lower your heart rate. And almost anyone can do it."*

B. K. S. IYENGAR: *"Pranayama teaches the aspirant to regulate his breathing and thereby control the mind."*

Conscious Breathing. *(continued)*

AMIT RAY, PHD: *"Conscious breathing is the best antidote to stress, anxiety and depression."*

CLEVELAND CLINIC: *"Supplemental oxygen therapy helps people with COPD, COVID–19, emphysema, sleep apnea and other breathing problems get enough oxygen to function and stay well. Low blood oxygen levels (hypoxemia) can damage organs and be life threatening ... Healthy blood oxygen levels help you feel and sleep better."*

BESSEL VAN DER KOLK, MD: *"The more you stay focused on your breathing, the more you will benefit, particularly if you pay attention until the very end of the out breath and then wait a moment before you inhale again."*

BYRON NELSON: *"One way to break up any kind of tension is good deep breathing."*

BARBARA CARRELLAS, ACS, AASECT: *"Breathing a bit more deeply and fully than you currently do is not just good advice for sex and orgasm. It applies to every aspect of life."*

L. FRANK BAUM/'THE WONDERFUL WIZARD OF OZ': *"Whenever I feel blue, I start breathing again."*

PROVERB: *"When you own your breath, nobody can steal your peace."*

NATIONAL LIBRARY OF MEDICINE: *"Slow deep breathing (SDB) is commonly employed in the management of pain ..."*

GIOVANNI PAPINI: *"Breathing is the greatest pleasure in life."*

SAYING: *"Don't resist your pain, just breathe through it."*

ADAGE: *"Oxygen drives out confusion and fear."*

JOHNNY MCGREW: *"Breath brought you here. Without breath there's nothing."*

DAN BRULE, EMRS, BS, MA: *"Opening and relaxing the breath is like opening the doors to your soul. Use your breath to allow every fiber of your being to be bathed in the life force that flows from the source."*

MARTHA GRAHAM: *"In the end, it all comes down to the art of breathing."*

Similar: respiration, centering, rhythmic inhalation-exhalation
Opposite: gasping, coughing, wheezing, choking, expiration

Consciousness. Experiencing an awareness of being aware and/or recognizing your own cognitive processes. *Popular or Heart-Based Usage: (1) Recognizing that you are thinking. (2) Understanding the voice in your head. (3) Figuring stuff out. (4) The Zero Point. (5) The Divine Matrix. (5) Thanking God. (6) 'Look around.' (7) Being aware of time. (8) Left-brained/right-brained. (9) Remote viewing. (10) Out-of-body experience.*

PLATO: *"Thinking is the soul talking with itself."*

LEONARDO DA VINCI: *"All thoughts start with emotion."*

RENÉ DESCARTES: *"I think, therefore I am."* (*"Cogito ergo sum."*)

ECKHART TOLLE: *"You are awareness, disguised as a person."*

PROVERB: *"The way you speak to yourself matters."*

DAVID CHALMERS, PHD: *"How does the water of the brain turn into the wine of consciousness?"*

DR. JOE DISPENZA: *"How you think, how you act, and how you feel is called your personality, and your personality creates your personal reality."*

HEALTHLINE.COM: *"If you're mostly analytical and methodical in your thinking, the theory says that you're left-brained. If you tend to be more creative or artistic, you're right-brained."*

JILL BOLTE TAYLOR, PHD: *"Hemispheres of the brain are very different places and they don't share any cell bodies. They are completely separate entities."*

ROGER WOLCOTT SPERRY, PHD, NOBEL: *"There appear to be two modes of thinking, verbal and nonverbal, represented rather separately in left and right spheres respectively and that our educational system, as well as science in general, tends to neglect the nonverbal form of intellect."*

ECKHART TOLLE: *"The brain does not create consciousness, but consciousness created the brain, the most complex physical form on earth, for its expression."*

ALBERT EINSTEIN, PHD, NOBEL: *"Our separation from each other is an optical illusion of consciousness."*

BERNARD HAISCH, PHD: *"Consciousness creates reality."*

AMIT GOSWAMI, PHD: *"Consciousness, not matter, is fundamental."*

PAM GREGORY: *"The whole universe is one consciousness. We are fractals of that."*

MAX PLANCK, PHD, NOBEL: *"I regard consciousness as fundamental. I regard matter as derivative from consciousness."*

GREGG BRADEN: *"A new school of thought suggests that consciousness informs itself through its creations—through its art, music, books, and movies."*

JOSEPH NGUYEN: *"Our mind's duty is to keep us alive. Our consciousness's duty is help us feel fulfilled."*

SAYING: *"Believe in the you who believes in yourself."*

LYNNE MCTAGGART: *"Thoughts become things."*

Similar: awareness, self-discovery, wakefulness, cognitive penetrability, mindfulness
Opposite: blank, void, unconsciousness

Conservative. (1) Having an inclination to adhere to what is traditional, known, or the status quo. (2) Resisting the unknown or unproven. *Popular or Heart-Based Usage: (1) Being 'old school.' (2) 'Making do' with something. (3) The 'right' as often contrasted with the 'left' or 'liberal' in politics.* Alternately, as opposites: *(4) Conservative vs. liberal. (5) Red-pilled vs. blue-pilled. (6) Right vs. left. (7) Right-wing (or conservative/reactionary) vs. left-wing (or progressive/socialist).*

WILL ROGERS: *"You've got to admit that each party is worse than the other. The one that's out always looks the best."*

CHARLES BARKLEY: *"I do not use words like 'liberal' or 'conservative.' You can ask me a question and I will give you an answer. Those are words rich people on television use to divide and conquer."*

SIR ELTON JOHN: *"I grew up conservative because my mum was conservative, and when I finally realized what conservatives were, I changed my mind immediately."*

ROBERT FROST: *"I never dared to be radical when young for fear it would make me conservative when old."*

AMBROSE BIERCE: *"Conservative, n.: A statesman who is enamored of existing evils, as distinguished from the Liberal who wishes to replace them with others."*

THOMAS WOLFE: *"If a conservative is a liberal who's been mugged, a liberal is a conservative who's been arrested."*

DANIEL PATRICK MOYNIHAN: *"The central conservative truth is that it is culture, not politics, that determines the success of a society. The central liberal truth is that politics can change a culture and save it from itself."*

JOHN KENNETH GALBRAITH: *"The modern conservative is engaged in one of man's oldest exercises in moral philosophy; that is, the search for a superior moral justification for selfishness."*

WOODROW WILSON, PHD, NOBEL, PRESIDENT: *"A conservative is a man who sits and thinks, mostly sits."*

CANDACE OWENS: *"I like to say now that the reason I am conservative is because I used to be liberal, and I learned a lot."*

WILL ROGERS: *"Democrats are the only reason to vote Republican."*

Similar: traditional, classical, orthodox, reactionary, old-fashioned, retro
Opposite: liberal, progressive, nonconformist, contemporary

Contentment. Recognizing a general satisfaction with your circumstances. *Popular or Heart-Based Usage: (1) 'It's all good.' (2) Being happy with your lot in life. (3) Putting your feet up. (4) Popping a cold one. (5) Having things in good measure. (6) Nothing in excess. (7) Smiling on the inside. (8) Having your life under control. (9) 'Everything is copacetic.' (10) Having good health and cash flow. (11) 'No complaints.' (12) 'So far, so good.' (13) 'Living the dream.' (14) Being in a good place.*

SOCRATES: *"He is rich who is content with the least; for contentment is the wealth of nature."*

OSCAR WILDE: *"The best way to enjoy your job is to imagine yourself without one."*

DALE CARNEGIE: *"It isn't what you have or who you are or where you are or what you are doing that makes you happy or unhappy. It is what you think about it."*

MAYA ANGELOU: *"Moderation in all things. And even moderation in moderation. Don't get too much moderation, you know?"*

JACOB BRONOWSKI, PHD: *"It is vain to say human beings ought to be satisfied with tranquility: they must have action; and they will make it if they cannot find it."*

EPICTETUS: *"Fortify yourself with contentment, for this is an impregnable fortress."*

OSCAR WILDE: *"True contentment is not having everything, but in being satisfied with everything you have."*

JOE ROGAN: *"The key to happiness doesn't lay in numbers in a bank account but in the way we make others feel."*

ACHARYA NAGARJUNA: *"Contentment is the greatest form of wealth."*

JOB 36:11: *"If they obey and serve him, they will spend their days in prosperity, and their years in pleasures."*

OPRAH WINFREY: *"There is no paycheck that can equal the feeling of contentment that comes from being the person you were meant to be."*

PROVERB: *"Count your blessings."*

Similar: accepting, fulfilled, happy, well-being, blessed
Opposite: misery, wretchedness, woe, anxiety, emptiness

Control. Having the power to manage or determine your own behavior and situational outcomes. *Popular or Heart-Based Usage: (1) Having a good handle on things. (2) Having something under your thumb. (3) Being in the saddle. (4) Pulling the levers (or strings) about a situation. (5) Having someone by the short hairs. (6) Dealing with your plight. (7) 'I've got this.' (8) Taking care of business. (9) 'Everything's under control.'*

JACK WELCH: *"Control your own destiny or someone else will."*

ALI KRIEGER: *"I can control only myself, my actions, my work ethic, and my attitude."*

ALBERT ELLIS, PHD: *"The best years of your life are the ones in which you decide your problems are your own. You do not blame them on your mother, the ecology, or the president. You realize that you control your own destiny."*

BILL BELICHICK: *"What we can control is our performance and our execution, and that's what we're going to focus on."*

AMELIA EARHART: *"You can do anything you decide to do. You can act to change and control your life; and the procedure, the process is its own reward."*

MICHAEL PHELPS: *"I can only control my own performance. If I do my best, then I can feel good at the end of the day."*

ELIZABETH A. STANLEY, PHD: *"In fact, the only thing that's truly under our control is where, when, and how we repeatedly direct our attention, and whether we're directing it consciously."*

NAPOLEON BONAPARTE: *"Men are more easily governed through their vices than through their virtues."*

HENRI NOUWEN, DRS: *"It is easier to control people than to love people, easier to own life than to love life."*

GEORGE BERNARD SHAW: *"To be in hell is to drift; to be in heaven is to steer."*

JASON DAY: *"Anything can happen, so you have to control your attitude and stay strong."*

BRIAN KIGHT: *"Discipline is the shortcut."*

Similar: rule, subjection, influence, purview, domination, supervision, regulation
Opposite: chaotic, unchecked, neglected, unregulated, mismanaged, free-wheeling

Courage. Confronting a known challenge or adversary despite the risk of harm, loss, or failure. *Popular or Heart-Based Usage: (1) Standing your ground. (2) Digging deep. (3) Crossing the line in the sand. (4) Having (or growing) a spine. (5) Being stout. (6) To 'man up' about something. (7) Having pluck. (8) Growing a pair. (9) Speaking truth to power. (10) Facing something head-on. (11) Squaring your shoulders. (12) Biting the bullet. (13) Being the tip of the spear. (14) Wearing a big red 'S' on your chest. (15) Doing the right thing.*

DOROTHY BERNARD: *"Courage is fear that has said its prayers."*

MAHATMA GANDHI: *"It is easy to stand in the crowd, but it takes courage to stand alone."*

ROBIN SHARMA: *"Speak your truth, even if your voice shakes."*

BRENE BROWN, MSW, PHD: *"Show up. Be seen. Answer the call."*

SIR WINSTON CHURCHILL: *"Fear is a reaction. Courage is a decision."*

NORA EPHRON: *"Above all, be the heroine of your life, not the victim."*

MUHAMMAD ALI: *"He who is not courageous enough to take risks will accomplish nothing in life."*

ABRAHAM LINCOLN: *"Be sure you put your feet in the right place, then stand firm."*

THE WOMEN OF SPARTA: *"Come back with your shield—or on it."*

UMBERTO ECO: *"Nothing gives a fearful man more courage than another's fear."*

SIR WINSTON CHURCHILL: *"Courage is what it takes to stand up and speak. Courage is also what it takes to sit down and listen."*

BILLY GRAHAM: *"Courage is contagious. When a brave man takes a stand, the spines of others are often stiffened."*

ROLLO MAY, BDIV, PHD: *"The opposite of courage in our society is not cowardice, but conformity."*

MARY ANNE RADMACHER: *"Courage doesn't always roar. Sometimes courage is the quiet voice at the end of the day saying, 'I will try again tomorrow.'"*

GLORIA ESTEFAN: *"Don't Wanna Lose You"* (Song)

BRENE BROWN, MSW, PHD: *"We can have courage or we can have comfort, but we cannot have both."*

MACHIAVELLI: *"Never was anything great achieved without danger."*

EURIPIDES: *"I would rather die on my feet than live on my knees."*

JOAN OF ARC: *"I fear nothing for God is with me."*

PLATO: *"Courage is knowing what not to fear."*

Similar: boldness, bravery, resolve, assurance, calmness, confidence, forthrightness
Opposite: retreat, withdrawal, fright, alarm, panic, dread, terror

Crazy. (1) Behaving in an irrational, imprudent, or destructive manner. (2) Being mentally unfit or unsound. *Popular or Heart-Based Usage: (1) Being out of your mind. (2) Having a screw loose. (3) Going nuts. (4) Becoming unhinged. (5) Losing your marbles. (6) Losing it. (7) Spinning out of control. (8) Being moonstruck. (9) Going around the bend. (10) Going off the reservation. (11) Becoming unglued. (12) Going looney tunes. (13) Not playing with a full deck. (14) Going (nutsy) cuckoo. (15) Having taken leave of your senses. (16) Flipping out. (17) 'They gone cray-cray.' (18) 'Gonzo.'*

GROUCHO MARX: *"I'm not crazy about reality, but it's still the only place to get a decent meal."*

RODNEY DANGERFIELD: *"My psychiatrist told me I was crazy and I said I want a second opinion. He said OK, you're ugly too."*

NORA EPHRON: *"Insane people are always sure they're fine. It's only the sane people who are willing to admit they're crazy."*

DOUGLAS HORTON: *"No one can drive us crazy unless we give them the keys."*

C. S. LEWIS: *"When the whole world is running towards a cliff, he who is running in the opposite direction appears to have lost his mind."*

FRIEDRICH NIETZSCHE: *"Insanity in individuals is something rare—but in groups, parties, nations, and epochs, it is the rule."*

GEORGE CARLIN: *"Those who dance are considered insane by those who cannot hear the music."*

NIELS BOHR, PHD, NOBEL: *"Your theory is crazy, but it's not crazy enough to be true."*

GOETHE: *"We do not have to visit a madhouse to find disordered minds; our planet is the mental institution of the universe."*

DWIGHT D. EISENHOWER: *"Any man who wants to be president is either an egomaniac or crazy."*

RITA MAE BROWN: *"If the world were a logical place, men would ride side saddle."*

LUDWIG WITTGENSTEIN, PHD: *"If people did not sometimes do silly things, nothing intelligent would ever get done."*

NOLAN RYAN: *"It helps if the hitter thinks you're a little crazy."*

SIGMUND FREUD, MD: *"Dreams are often most profound when they seem the most crazy."*

CARL JUNG, MD: *"Show me a sane man and I will cure him for you."*

ARISTOTLE: *"No excellent soul is exempt from a mixture of madness."*

JACKIE CHAN: *"I'm crazy, but I'm not stupid."*

Similar: mad, insane, incoherent, unbalanced, daft, nutty, whacked
Opposite: rational, coherent, sane, balanced, composed, measured

Criticism. Expressing analytical viewpoints, especially including disapproval, regarding someone's efforts. *Popular or Heart-Based Usage: (1) Calling someone out. (2) Cutting (or putting) someone down. (3) Being picky. (4) Chewing them out. (5) Name-calling. (6) Dishing on someone. (7) Mocking someone. (8) Sneering at someone. (9) Getting snarky. (10) Making someone feel small. (11) Pooh-poohing. (12) Giving a piece of your mind. (13) Taking pot shots at someone. (14) Dissing someone. (15) Trashing something. (16) Chirping about something. (17) Being sarcastic with someone. (18) Straining gnats. (19) Fault-finding. (20) Giving someone a hard time. (21) Torching someone. (22) Talking smack. (23) Being a hater. (24) 'Call me a cynic, but...' (25) 'Othering' someone. (26) Giving someone lots of static. (27) Cutting someone to the quick. (28) Busting their chops. (29) Giving somebody tough love. (30) Dunking on someone. (31) Lowering the boom. (32) Dressing someone down. (33) 'Grow the hell up!'* Alternately, where you are the target of criticism: *(34) Getting ratioed. (35) Catching Hell. (36) Getting slimed. (37) Getting beat up over something. (38) Getting roasted or grilled. (39) Taking your lumps. (40) Getting the silent treatment. (41) Being left out. (42) Not getting cut any slack. (43) Having to walk something back. (44) Getting bashed. (45) Getting savaged. (46) Getting ripped. (47) Catching static. (48) Being scolded. (49) Enduring a beatdown.*

LIBERACE: *"Your review hurt me! I cried all the way to the bank!"*

OSCAR WILDE: *"If you cannot prove a man wrong, don't panic. You can still call him names."*

BELIZE PROVERB: *"Don't call the alligator 'Big Mouth' until you have crossed the river."*

GROUCHO MARX: *"I didn't like the play. But I saw it under unfavorable circumstances—the curtains were up."*

SAM RAYBURN: *"Any jackass can kick a barn down, but it takes a carpenter to build it."*

CHRISTOPHER HAMPTON: *"Asking a working writer what he thinks about critics is like asking a lamppost what it thinks about dogs."*

MEL BROOKS: *"Did you say crickets? I just hate crickets. Always making such a racket, those damned crickets."*

APHORISM: *"Don't let the bastards grind you down."* ("Illegitimi non carborundum.")

AFRICAN PROVERB: *"The axe forgets, but the tree remembers."*

SIR BENJAMIN DISRAELI: *"How much easier it is to be critical than to be correct."*

DANIEL KAHNEMAN, MD, NOBEL: *"The brains of humans contain a mechanism that is designed to give priority to bad news."*

JOHANNES KEPLER: *"I much prefer the sharpest criticism of a single intelligent man to the thoughtless approval of the masses."*

D. H. LAWRENCE: *"Instead of chopping yourself down to fit the world, chop the world down to fit yourself."*

Criticism. *(continued)*

LEBRON JAMES: *"I like criticism. It makes you strong."*

WALT WHITMAN: *"Dismiss whatever insults your soul."*

HENRIK IBSEN: *"To live is to war with trolls."*

JOSEPH JOUBERT: *"When you go in search of honey you must expect to be stung by bees."*

ARISTOTLE: *"To avoid criticism say nothing, be nothing, do nothing."*

RUSKIN C. NORMAN, MD: *"Remember when people criticize you they are attacking from below you. You are already above them."*

ELEANOR ROOSEVELT: *"Do what you feel in your heart to be right—for you'll be criticized anyway. You'll be dammed if you do, and damned if you don't."*

APHORISM: *"When you point your finger in criticism, remember the other three fingers that are pointing back at you."*

BENJAMIN FRANKLIN: *"Any fool can criticize, condemn, and complain—and most fools do."*

CARL BECKER: *"Fact-finding is more effective than fault-finding."*

ELEANOR ROOSEVELT: *"Great minds discuss ideas; average minds discuss events; small minds discuss people."*

ALBERT ELLIS, PHD: *"Most people would have given up when faced with the criticism I've received over the years."*

MATTHEW 7:3–5: *"And why beholdest thou the mote that is in thy brother's eye, but considerest not the beam that is in thy own eye?"*

MARCUS AURELIUS: *"Whenever you are about to find fault with someone, ask yourself the following question: What fault of mine most nearly resembles the one I am about to criticize?"*

GERMAN PROVERB: *"Sweep in front of your own door."*

ABRAHAM LINCOLN: *"He has a right to criticize, who has a heart to help."*

CHINESE PROVERB: *"Deal with the faults of others as gently as your own."*

CAMILLE PAGLIA: *"Criticism at its best is re-creative, not spirit-killing."*

JOSEPH JOUBERT: *"Children need models rather than critics."*

DAVID HUME: *"It is harder to avoid censure than to gain applause."*

ELBERT HUBBARD: *"The final proof of greatness lies in being able to endure criticism without resentment."*

MAHATMA GANDHI: *"First they ignore you, then they ridicule you, then they fight you, and then you win."*

Similar: chastising, undercutting, castigating, fault-finding, disparaging, carping

Opposite: approving, commending, complimenting, praising, supporting

Crying. (1) Responding tearfully to being injured, saddened, or overwhelmed. (2) Surrendering to a deeply emotional event. *Popular or Heart-Based Usage: (1) Sniffling. (2) Boo-hooing. (3) Bawling your eyes out. (4) Sobbing. (5) Weeping. (6) 'Bwaah!' (7) Turning on the water works. (8) 'Like Niagara Falls.' (9) 'Tears for fears.' (10) Shedding full-on tears.*

JOHN 11:35: *"Jesus wept."*

ADAGE: *"Sometimes you just need a good cry."*

LEONARDO DA VINCI: *"Tears come from the heart and not from the brain."*

MUHAMMAD: *"Verily, tears are a mercy that God has placed in the essence of His Servants."*

PEARL OF GREAT PRICE, MOSES 7:28–29: *"And it came to pass that the God of heaven looked upon the residue of the people, and he wept."*

ANTOINE DE SAINT-EXUPERY: *"It is such a secret place, the land of tears."*

ADAGE: *"Crying does not mean the person is weak. It means the person has a heart."*

ROGER HUTCHISON: *"Weeping is energy, longing to be released. Weeping became a superpower and a place I visited but did not stay."*

SAYING: *"Only a strong man can cry. The other kind doesn't know how."*

DIONNE WARWICK: *"Crying is cleansing. There's a reason for tears, happiness or sadness."*

GOLDA MEIR: *"Those who don't know how to weep with their whole heart, don't know how to laugh either."*

CHARLES DICKENS: *"I like to cry for joy. It's so delicious to cry for joy."*

PSALM 30:5: *"Weeping may endure for a night, but joy cometh in the morning."*

LOWELL GANZ, BABALOO MANDEL: *"There's no crying in baseball!"*

HENRY DAVID THOREAU: *"'Tis healthy to be sick sometimes."*

BEBE LORD GOW: *"The best part of being sick is feeling well again."*

PROVERB: *"The prettiest eyes have cried the most tears."*

VICTOR HUGO: *"Those who do not weep, do not see."*

Similar: tearfulness, weeping, releasing, bawling, overwhelmed, moved
Opposite: stoic, repressed, unemotional, uncaring, flat

Curious. (1) Expressing a spirit of inquiry or investigation. (2) Wanting to know more about the background, workings, or reasons for things. *Popular or Heart-Based Usage: (1) To be lit up (by an interest). (2) Poking around. (3) Sniffing around. (4) Being nosy. (5) Sneaking a peek. (6) Perking up your ears. (7) Keeping your ear to the ground. (8) Checking something (or someone) out. (9) Dialing (or getting the) 411 on something. (10) Googling something. (11) Digging into something. (12) Asking around. (13) Pinging the universe. (14) Wanting to know the skinny. (15) Getting the low-down. (16) Playing the cub reporter. (17) 'Casing the joint.' (18) Peeling back the layers of the onion. (19) Trying out a new idea for size. (20) Wanting to do a deeper dive. (21) 'Listening in' about something. (22) Asking 'Wassup?' or 'Supwidat?' (23) 'Inquiring minds want to know.'*

DOROTHY PARKER: *"The cure for boredom is curiosity. There is no cure for curiosity."*

B. F. SKINNER, PHD: *"When you run into something interesting, drop everything else and study it."*

WILLIAM HAZLITT: *"I'm not smart, but I like to observe. Millions saw the apple fall, but Newton was the one to ask why."*

ALBERT EINSTEIN, PHD, NOBEL: *"The mind that opens to a new idea never returns to its original size."*

WILLIAM ARTHUR WARD, MA: *"Curiosity is the wick in the candle of learning."*

LINUS PAULING, MD (2X NOBEL): *"Satisfaction of one's curiosity is one of the greatest sources of happiness in life."*

JAMES THURBER: *"It is better to know some of the questions than all of the answers."*

WILL ROGERS: *"There are three kinds of men. The one that learns by reading. The few who learn by observation. The rest of them have to pee on the electric fence for themselves."*

BILL MAHER: *"Curious people are interesting people. I wonder why that is."*

WALT WHITMAN: *"Be curious, not judgmental."*

TODD STOCKER: *"When I tell, I inform. When I ask, I transform."*

CHARLIE MUNGER, JD: *"In my whole life I have known no wise people (over a broad subject matter area) who didn't read all the time—none. Zero."*

DOUGLAS JOHNSTON: *"The greatest gift of all is an inquiring mind."*

LEONARDO DA VINCI: *"To become an artist you have to be curious."*

PLUTARCH: *"The mind is not a vessel to be filled, but a fire to be kindled."*

Similar: inquisitive, nosy, marveling, interested, piqued
Opposite: indifferent, heedless, disregarding, oblivious, uncaring

Dance. (1) Moving expressively to beat, rhythm, sound, and space. (2) Acting out your personal language of self-expression and joy. *Popular or Heart-Based Usage: (1) Bustin' a move. (2) Hitting the floor. (3) Cutting a rug. (4) Shaking a leg. (5) Being a hoofer. (6) Breaking / toeing / flipping / tapping / swinging / tangoing / foxtrotting / salsaing / waltzing. (7) Boogieing down. (8) Grooving to the beat. (9) Steppin' out.*

AUGUSTINE: *"Learn to dance, so when you get to heaven the angels know what to do with you."*

JAMES BROWN: *"The one thing that can solve most of our problems is dancing."*

ALBERT EINSTEIN, PHD, NOBEL (attributed): *"We dance for laughter, we dance for tears, we dance for madness, we dance for fears, we dance for hopes, we dance for screams, we are the dancers, we create the dreams."*

GABRIELLE ROTH: *"We dance to fall in love with the spirit in all things, to wipe out memory or transform it into moves that nobody else can make because they didn't live it."*

BESSEL VAN DER KOLK, MD: *"The capacity of art, music, and dance to circumvent the speechlessness that comes with terror may be the one reason they are used as trauma treatments in cultures around the world."*

RUDOLPH NUREYEV: *"The main thing is dancing, and before it withers away from my body, I will keep dancing until the last moment, the last drop."*

MARTHA GRAHAM: *"Dance is communication, and so the challenge is to speak clearly, beautifully, and with inevitability."*

FRED ASTAIRE: *"Do it big, do it right, and do it with style."*

GINGER ROGERS: *"My mother told me I was dancing before I was born. She could feel my toes tapping wildly inside her for months."*

BOB THAVES (attributed): *"Ginger Rogers did everything Fred Astaire did, but backwards and in high heels."*

MARY SCHMICH: *"Dance, even if you have nowhere to do it but your living room."*

GEORGE CARLIN: *"Those who dance are considered insane by those who cannot hear the music."*

MARTHA GRAHAM: *"Dance is the hidden language of the soul, the body."*

FRIEDRICH NIETZSCHE: *"Every day I count wasted in which there has been no dancing."*

TED SHAWN: *"Dance is the only art of which we ourselves are the stuff of which it is made."*

VICKI BAUM: *"There are shortcuts to happiness, and dancing is one of them."*

CONSTANZE MOZART: *"Dancing is like dreaming with your feet."*

ALVIN AILEY: *"The most unique thing in the world is you."*

GEORGE BALANCHINE: *"Dance is music made visible."*

Similar: twisting, twirling, spinning, gyrating, whirling, skipping, cavorting, stomping
Opposite: sitting, reclining, lying, dead

Death. (1) The ending of life. (2) Having no pulse or breath. (3) Cessation of growth, regeneration, or function. *Popular or Heart-Based Usage: (1) Being that time/the end time. (2) Hearing St. Peter calling. (3) The long goodbye. (4) Facing the Grim Reaper. (5) Doing a life review. (6) 'Die before you die.' (7) Leaving nothing unsaid. (8) Ushering yourself out. (9) Feeling no pain. (10) Breaking even. (11) Checking out. (12) Kicking the bucket. (13) Cashing in your chips. (14) Keeling over. (15) Croaking. (16) Buying the farm. (17) Not making it. (18) Giving up the ghost. (19) Passing away. (20) Doing the big sleep. (21) Six feet under. (22) Pushing up daisies. (23) Davy Jones's Locker. (24) Sleeping with the fishes. (25) Transitioning. (26) Going home. (27) Going to Heaven. (28) Arriving at the Pearly Gates. (29) Being in a better place. (30) Meeting your Maker. (31) Getting your reward. (32) Listening to harp music. (33) Hanging out with the angels. (34) Being among your friends. (35) Resting In Peace. (36) Leaving your legacy.*

MARK TWAIN: *"The report of my death is an exaggeration."*

WILLIAM SAROYAN, PULITZER: *"Everybody has got to die, but I've always believed an exception would be made in my case."*

DOUGLAS JOHNSTON: *"At the moment, I am a little more concerned with life after birth than life after death."*

WILLIAM WALLACE: *"Every man dies. Not every man really lives."*

STEVE JOBS: *"Remembering that you are going to die is the best way I know to avoid the trap of thinking you have something to lose."*

JOHN DONNE: *"Any man's death diminishes me, because I am involved in Mankind; Therefore never send to know for whom the bell tolls; it tolls for thee."*

ELISABETH KUBLER-ROSS, MD: *"I know beyond a shadow of a doubt that there is no death the way we understood it. The body dies, but not the soul. The highest spiritual values can originate from the thought and study of death."*

Copyright: Elisabeth Kubler-Ross Family Limited Partnership

HELEN KELLER: *"Death is no more than passing from one room into another. But there is a difference for me, you know. Because in that other room I shall be able to see."*

CHARLES BUKOWSKI: *"We are here to laugh at the odds and to live our lives so well that Death will tremble to take us."*

AMERICAN INDIAN SAYING: *"The tragedy of life is not death but what we let die inside us while we live."*

GOETHE: *"Life is the childhood of our immortality."*

PERCY BYSSHE SHELLEY: *"Death is the veil which those who live call life. They sleep, and it is lifted."*

ECKHART TOLLE: *"Life has no opposite. The opposite of death is birth. Life is eternal."*

FEDERICO GARCIA LORCA: *"As I have not worried to be born, I do not worry to die."*

Death. *(continued)*

PLATO: *"Death is not the worst that can happen to men."*

CHIEF SEATTLE: *"There is no death. Only a change of worlds."*

JOHN DONNE: *"Death be not proud."*

GURU NANAK: *"Death would not be called bad, O people, if one knew how to truly die."*

CARL JUNG, MD: *"Shrinking away from death is something unhealthy and abnormal which robs the second half of life of its purpose."*

2 TIMOTHY 4:7: *"I have fought a good fight, I have finished my course, I have kept the faith."*

SOGYAL RINPOCHE: *"Two people have been living in you all your life. One is the ego—garrulous, demanding, hysterical, calculating—the other is the hidden spiritual being, whose still voice of wisdom you have only rarely heard or attended to—you have uncovered in yourself your own wise guide."*

HANNA JACOB DOUMETTE: *"Through death we put away the perishable and renew our activities through new forms suited to duties to higher spheres, vibrations, and laws of functioning. Thus the spirit uses various forms in fulfilling its divine mission."*

ECKHART TOLLE: *"Death is a stripping away of all that is not you. The secret of life is to 'die before you die'—and find there is no death."*

WALT WHITMAN: *"I know I am deathless. No doubt I have died myself ten thousand times before. I laugh at what you call dissolution, and I know the amplitude of time."*

JAMES JOYCE: *"We are all born the same way but we all die in different ways."*

WILD BILL HICKOK: *"Can you let me go to hell the way I want to?"*

LEONARDO DA VINCI: *"A well spent day brings happy sleep, so life well used brings happy death."*

RITA LEVI-MONTALCINI, MD, NOBEL: *"If I die tomorrow or in a year, it is the same—it is the message you leave behind you that counts."*

DOUGLAS JOHNSTON: *"It's important to know that you've mattered to people."*

JOEL OSTEEN: *"It's not over until God says it is."*

WILL ROGERS: *"Lord let me live until I die."*

TOMBSTONE: *"Here lies a good person."*

Similar: end, demise, expiration, annihilation, destruction, cessation, eight bells, Taps

Opposite: birth, beginning, creation, commencement, renaissance, revival

Deception. Using misinformation, false appearances, or subterfuge in order to lie, to mislead someone, or to gain an undisclosed advantage. *Popular or Heart-Based Usage: (1) Putting someone on. (2) Being downright sneaky. (3) Baiting someone. (4) Being cagey. (5) Shining someone on. (6) Speaking with forked tongue. (7) Telling it with a straight face. (8) Pulling the wool over someone's eyes. (9) Laying on a head fake. (10) Pulling someone's leg. (11) Being a crook. (12) Pushing fake news. (13) Being a four-flusher. (14) Double-dealing. (15) Being a spy/double agent. (16) Creating a false flag operation. (17) Jobbing someone. (18) Pulling some trickeration. (19) Fleecing someone. (20) Being a Wiley Coyote. (21) Acting dumb like a fox. (22) Playing possum. (23) Doing a flop. (24) Being sketchy. (25) Being shady. (26) Being slippery. (27) Conning someone. (28) Doing a snow job on someone. (29) Being in cahoots with someone. (30) Pulling a fast one. (31) Spoofing. (32) Whitewashing. (33) Fronting something. (34) Pulling a switcheroo. (35) Sliding something past someone. (36) Getting 'cute' with someone. (37) Crossing someone up. (38) Faking someone out. (39) Fooling someone. (40) Leading someone on. (41) Stretching the truth. (42) Duping someone. (43) Ginning something up. (44) 'Playing' someone. (45) Blinking excessively. (46) Outsmarting someone. (47) 'The fix is in.' (48) Cheating. (49) Capping. (50) Scamming. (51) Trolling someone.*

ROBIN MARANTZ HENIG: *"The English language has 112 words for deception, according to one account, each with a different shade of meaning: collusion, fakery, malingering, self-deception, confabulation, prevarication, exaggeration, denial."*

PROVERB: *"Not everyone who smiles at you is your friend."*

THOMAS BECKET: *"Those who tread among serpents, and along a tortuous path, must use the cunning of the serpent."*

MACHIAVELLI: *"You will always find people willing to be deceived."*

DEVIL: *"Such a sweet surprise. They never see me coming."*

ANTHONY WELDON: *"Fool me once, shame on you; Fool me twice, shame on me."*

D. EARL JOHNSTON: *"Trouble shows up, often disguised as something attractive."*

JOHNNY MCGREW: *"Remember this. Ten percent of everybody you meet will smile at you and then steal your lunch money if you let them. Your best friend in life is a foolproof BS detector."*

ADAGE: *"All warfare is based on deception."*

MARTIN L. GROSS: *"Politicians are masters of the art of deception."*

MACHIAVELLI: *"It is double pleasure to deceive the deceiver."*

D. EARL JOHNSTON: *"The first seducers of Integrity have usually been either Cool, Cash, or Convenient."*

FYODOR DOSTOEVSKY: *"When reason fails, the devil helps!"*

WILLIAM GOLDMAN: *"Follow the money."*

Similar: ruse, artifice, lying, fakery, guile, slyness, embellishment, plotting, scheming
Opposite: honesty, straightforwardness, transparency, frankness, forthrightness, candor

Decision. Selecting a path or course of action among available alternatives. *Popular or Heart-Based Usage: (1) Hashing it out. (2) Weighing the pros and cons. (3) Reading the tea leaves. (4) Picking your poison. (5) Casting lots. (6) Drawing straws. (7) Choosing 'Rock, Paper, Scissors.' (8) Flipping a coin. (9) Cutting the deck. (10) Going back to the well for guidance. (11) Getting down to the short strokes. (12) Making up your mind. (13) Calling the ball. (14) Giving the nod. (15) Crossing the line in the sand. (16) Crossing the Rubicon. (17) Going over to the Dark Side. (18) Calling balls and strikes. (19) Biting the bullet. (20) Pulling the trigger. (21) Giving thumbs up or down. (22) Going for it. (23) 'Choose it or lose it.' (24) 'Lead, follow, or get out of the way.' (25) Following a confirming coincidence. (26) Reaching a resolution. (27) Weighing in on a matter. (28) Making the call.*

ROY E. DISNEY: *"When your values are clear to you, making decisions comes easier."*

RALPH WALDO EMERSON: *"Once you make a decision, the universe conspires to make it happen."*

LIN-MANUEL MIRANDA: *"I try to let my decisions be guided not by what I think will succeed or fail, but what I'm going to learn from the process."*

ADVICE: *"My father told me this: You either get paid for the decisions you made long ago, or you get to pay for the decisions you made long ago."*

AMELIA EARHART: *"The most difficult thing is to act. The rest is merely tenacity."*

CAROLINE KENNEDY: *"When you make the right decision, it really doesn't matter what anyone else thinks."*

DALTON MCGUINTY: *"There's no wrong time to make the right decision."*

JILL BOLTE TAYLOR, PHD: *"We have the power to choose, moment by moment, who and how we want to be in the world."*

SAQUON BARKLEY: *"Sometimes in life, you have to make a selfish decision and do what's best for you."*

MAHATMA GANDHI: *"Honest disagreement is often a sign of good progress."*

GARY HALBERT: *"HALT stands for hungry, angry, lonely, and tired, and you should never make a decision when you are any of those things."*

BRIAN TRACY: *"Almost any decision is better than no decision at all."*

GOVINDA: *"All of us start from zero. We take the right decision and become a hero."*

RICHARD PETTY: *"Never put a question mark where God puts a period."*

SIR WINSTON CHURCHILL: *"Fear is a reaction. Courage is a decision."*

ANTHONY ROBBINS: *"If there's no action, you haven't truly decided."*

ADAGE: *"Measure twice and cut once."*

SAM GORES: *"Never let yourself be misunderstood."*

PROVERB: *"Forget the mistake. Remember the lesson."*

Similar: selection, choice, determination, resolution, ruling, judgment
Opposite: deferral, wavering, postponement, vacillation, wobbling, muddlement

Defiant. (1) Rejecting the control, demands, or requirements set by another person. (2) Remaining steadfast despite the demands of others. *Popular or Heart-Based Usage: (1) Leading with your chin. (2) Holding out. (3) Snorting your disapproval. (4) Crossing the line in the sand. (5) Giving them the middle finger/flipping them off. (6) Resisting to the max. (7) 'No way.' (8) 'Talk to the hand!' (9) 'Go to Hell!' (10) 'Up yours.' (11) 'Is that all you got?' (12) 'Oh yeah?' (13) 'Try me.' (14) 'I dare you.' (15) 'Not gonna happen.' (16) Sticking to your principles/sticking to your guns. (17) 'That's baloney!' (18) 'Don't tread on me.' (19) 'Back off!' (20) 'Come and take it.' (21) 'Spit in your eye!' (22) 'Not the boss of me!' (23) 'Make me!'*

TWYLA THARP: *"Creativity is an act of defiance."*

AYN RAND: *"Defiance, not obedience, is the American's answer to overbearing authority."*

WALT WHITMAN: *"There is no week nor day nor hour when tyranny may not enter upon this country, if the people lose their roughness and spirit of defiance."*

SIR WINSTON CHURCHILL: *"In War: Resolution; In Defeat: Defiance; In Victory: Magnanimity; In Peace: Good Will."*

WILLIAM ERNEST HENLEY: *"It matters not how strait the gate, How charged with punishments the scroll; I am the master of my fate: I am the captain of my soul."*

MAX LUCADO: *"Sin is not an unfortunate slip or a regrettable act; it is a posture of defiance against a holy God."*

JOHN MILTON/'PARADISE LOST' (SATAN): *"Better to reign in Hell than serve in Heaven."*

J. K. ROWLING, OBE, CH: *"When people are very damaged, they can often meet the world with a kind of defiance."*

NORMAN MAILER: *"With the pride of the artist, you must blow against the walls of every power that exists the small trumpet of your defiance."*

HANNAH ARENDT, PHD: *"The defiance of established authority, religious and secular, social and political, as a world-wide phenomenon may well one day be accounted the outstanding event of the last decade."*

BOB WOODWARD: *"Good work is always done in defiance of management."*

Similar: resistant, steadfast, contemptuous, self-reliant, bold, headstrong, uncooperative
Opposite: obedient, passive, submissive, accepting, cooperative

Definition(s). (1) Describing the unique essence, qualities, or properties of a thing. (2) Identifying how a thing is different from other things. *Popular or Heart-Based Usage: (1) Knowing what you are talking about. (2) 'What it's all about is ...' (3) Making it simple. (4) Linguistic referencing. (5) Getting down to the short strokes about something. (6) Wordsmithing. (7) Making a long story short. (8) Taking it down to CliffsNotes. (9) Getting to the bottom line. (10) Getting down to the nitty gritty. (11) Making it short and snappy. (12) 'KISS.' ['Keep It Simple, Stupid.'] (13) Saying it in your own words. (14) 'Here's what it really means.' (15) Knowing all you really need to know about something.*

LEONARDO DA VINCI: *"The noblest pleasure is the joy of understanding."*

PLATO: *"He who can properly define and divide is to be considered a god."*

CHARLES KETTERING: *"A problem well-stated is a problem half-solved."*

TIBETAN WISDOM: *"Recognition is liberation."*

DANIEL J. SIEGEL, MD: *"Name it to tame it."*

SIR ISAAC NEWTON, FRS: *"Truth is ever to be found in the simplicity, and not in the multiplicity and confusion of things."*

BUMPER STICKER: *"Hire a teenager while they still know everything."*

LUDWIG WITTGENSTEIN, PHD: *"All I know is what I have words for."*

NOAM CHOMSKY, PHD: *"Language etches the grooves through which your thoughts must flow."*

DAME AGATHA CHRISTIE: *"Words, Mademoiselle, are only the outer clothing of ideas."*

JAMES WHITCOMB RILEY: *"When I see a bird that walks like a duck and swims like a duck and quacks like a duck, I call that bird a duck."*

MIGUEL DE CERVANTES: *"A proverb is a short sentence based on long experience."*

D. EARL JOHNSTON: *"An ounce of definition is worth ten pounds of narrative."*

IMMANUEL KANT: *"Science is organized knowledge. Wisdom is organized life."*

OSHO: *"Wisdom is experience, not information."*

ARISTOTLE: *"It is the mark of an educated man to look for precision in each class of thing in so far as its nature admits."*

LINCOLN STOREY: *"A good definition describes what something is, and so it also helps rule out what it isn't."*

DR. JOE DISPENZA: *"When your thoughts and words are aligned, you create a powerful state of coherence."*

THE REV. LAURENS A. HALL, DD: *"Biblically, the adjective 'good' is a more comprehensive understanding of the nature and essence of God and the things of God than the more traditional application of the word 'great.'"*

NIELS BOHR, PHD, NOBEL: *"What is it that we human beings ultimately depend on? We depend on our words. We are suspended in language. Our task is to communicate experience and ideas to others."*

Definition(s). *(continued)*

VOLTAIRE: *"If you wish to converse with me, define your terms."*

WALT WHITMAN: *"Either define the moment or the moment will define you."*

LINCOLN STOREY: *"Definitions are the foundation of confidence. Confidence is the foundation of a better life."*

GEORGES BRAQUES: *"To define a thing is to substitute the definition for the thing itself."*

D. EARL JOHNSTON: *"Mastery is knowing when to set aside unproven definitions, and to replace them with new knowledge."*

BRENE BROWN, MSW, PHD: *"Language is our portal to meaning-making. Having access to the right words can open up entire universes."*

LINCOLN STOREY: *"Emotions represent the Rosetta Stone of human behavior."*

OCCAM'S RAZOR: *"The simplest explanation is usually the best."*

Similar: understanding, clarity, conciseness, precision, identity, exactness
Opposite: confusion, muddlement, uncertainty, doubt, indecision, malaise

Delusional. Persisting in belief despite the existence of ample contrary facts. *Popular or Heart-Based Usage: (1) Kidding yourself. (2) Hiding from the truth. (3) Wearing rose-colored glasses. (4) Wearing blinders. (5) Doing a head trip/Tripping. (6) Wanting to believe. (7) Wishful thinking. (8) Wanting it so bad. (9) Having cognitive bias. (10) Not using common sense. (11) Becoming untethered to reality. (12) Taking leave of your senses. (13) Chasing rainbows (or fighting windmills).*

CONAN O'BRIEN: *"When all else fails there's always delusion."*

MARK TWAIN: *"It's easier to fool people than to convince them that they have been fooled."*

D. EARL JOHNSTON: *"We can be our most vulnerable when we want to believe."*

LINCOLN STOREY: *"The realist observes, the optimist plans, the pessimist avoids, and the delusionist distorts."*

EDWARD ABBEY: *"Better a cruel truth than a comfortable delusion."*

ROGER COHEN: *"Never underestimate the human capacity for delusion."*

DANIEL DAY-LEWIS: *"I suppose I have a highly developed capacity for self-delusion, so it's no problem for me to believe that I'm somebody else."*

LADY GAGA: *"It was my delusion and naivety that brought me here."*

HORACE: *"One wanders to the left, another to the right. Both are equally in error, but are seduced by different delusions."*

CARL SAGAN, PHD: *"It is far better to grasp the universe as it really is than to persist in delusion, however satisfying and reassuring."*

ROBERT TODD CARROLL, PHD: *"A delusion held by one person is a mental illness, held by a few is a cult, held by many is a religion."*

EDMUND BURKE: *"The people never give up their liberties but under some delusion."*

ARTHUR D. HLAVATY: *"Paranoia is the delusion that your enemies are organized."*

THOMAS SZASZ: *"Delusion: belief said to be false by someone who does not share it."*

RONALD REAGAN: *"If history teaches anything, it teaches that self-delusion in the face of unpleasant facts is folly."*

ALBERT GORE, JR., NOBEL: *"An Inconvenient Truth"* (Film)

SGT. JOE FRIDAY: *"Just the facts, ma'am."*

Similar: unrealistic, self-deceiving, hallucinatory, quixotic, going mad, misinformed
Opposite: realistic, fact-centered, observant, clearheaded, sober, well-grounded

Denial. (1) Choosing to disavow, dismiss, or reject undesired information. (2) Declaring that something is not true or not applicable. *Popular or Heart-Based Usage: (1) 'No way!' (2) 'Not having it.' (3) 'Ain't so.' (4) 'Never happened.' (5) 'Don't even think it.' (6) Looking the other way. (7) Playing ostrich. (8) 'Hear no evil. See no evil. Speak no evil.' (9) 'Where's the beef?' (10) Hiding from inconvenient truths. (11) Washing your hands of a matter. (12) Climate denying. (13) Postponing a day of reckoning. (14) 'There's no "there" there.' (15) 'Negatory on that.' (16) 'That's a complete non-starter.' (17) 'Talk to the hand.' (18) 'No. Never. And that means never in a million years.'*

TEENAGER: *"I am not spoiled. I'm not. I'm not. I'm not!"*

FLORIANO MARTINS: *"I protect myself by refusing to know myself."*

COLLEGE STUDENT: *"Yes I have my morals. I just choose to ignore them from time to time."*

JIM BUTCHER: *"Everything was perfectly healthy and normal here in Denial Land."*

GROUCHO MARX: *"Who are you going to believe, me or your lying eyes?"*

JENNIFER SALAIZ: *"How 'bout a shot of truth in that denial cocktail."*

TAYLOR JENKINS REID: *"Denial is like an old blanket. I loved to get on under that thing and curl up and sleep."*

SHANNON L. ALDER: *"Evil originates not in the absence of guilt; but in our effort to escape it."*

BOB DYLAN, PULITZER, NOBEL: *"How many times can a man turn his head, and pretend that he just doesn't see?"*

GABOR MATE, MD, CM: *"The attempt to escape from pain, is what creates more pain."*

WILLIAM SHAKESPEARE: *"Methinks thou dost protest too much."*

OSCAR WILDE: *"To deny one's own experiences is to put a lie into the lips of one's own life. It is no less than a denial of the soul."*

D. EARL JOHNSTON: *"How often vehement denial comes just before real answers."*

ROBERT LOUIS STEVENSON: *"Sooner or later, everyone sits down to a banquet of consequences."*

ADAGE: *"The chickens do come home to roost."*

ALBERT GORE, JR., NOBEL: *"An Inconvenient Truth"* (Film)

CAROLE RADZIWILL: *"Delusion and denial does not equal an apology."*

THE FIVE STAGES OF GRIEF: *"Denial. Anger. Bargaining. Depression. Acceptance."*

SHANNON L. ALDER: *"Lies don't end relationships; the truth does."*

WILLIAM E. GLADSTONE: *"Justice delayed is justice denied."*

Similar: rejection, dismissal, refutation, rebuttal, repudiation, rebuff

Opposite: acceptance, endorsement, confirmation, cooperation

Depression. (1) Experiencing an extended outlook of sadness, emptiness, or deep disappointment. (2) Feeling no sense of purpose. *Popular or Heart-Based Usage: (1) Being way down in the dumps. (2) Just going through the motions. (3) Losing your mojo. (4) Feeling like you are up a creek without a paddle. (5) Having an identity crisis. (6) Feeling gripless. (7) Feeling totally lost. (8) Waking up in fear. (9) Experiencing soul-crushing times. (10) Believing there is no hope. (11) Seeing no way out.*

J. K. ROWLING, OBE, CH: *"Depression is that absence of being able to envisage that you will ever be cheerful again…It is the most unpleasant thing I have ever experienced."*

ROLLO MAY, BDIV, PHD: *"Depression is the inability to construct a future."*

SUSAN POLIS SCHUTZ: *"It's often difficult for those who are lucky enough to have never experienced what true depression is to imagine a life of complete hopelessness, emptiness, and fear."*

SIGMUND FREUD, MD (attributed): *"Before you diagnose yourself with depression or low self-esteem, first make sure you are not, in fact, just surrounded by assholes."*

JULIETTE LEWIS: *"The bravest thing I have ever done was continuing to live when I wanted to die."*

HALLEY CORNELL: *"Depression lies. It tells you you've always felt this way, and you always will. But you haven't, and you won't."*

DOROTHY ROWE: *"Depression is a prison where you are both the suffering prisoner and the cruel jailer."*

GEORGE SANTAYANA: *"Depression is rage spread thin."*

ALBERT ELLIS, PHD: *"You largely constructed your depression. It wasn't given to you. Therefore you can deconstruct it."*

DOUGLAS JOHNSTON: *"Times can get really tough, and it helps to keep a sense of humor. My friend told me after his dog died and his wife left him that he got so depressed he could have flown a kite under a rug."*

ATTICUS: *"Depression is being colorblind and constantly being told how colorful the world is."*

SOPHOCLES: *"The greatest griefs are those we cause ourselves."*

LAO TZU: *"If you are depressed you are living in the past, if you are anxious you are living in the future, if you are at peace you are living in the present."*

CINDY DAVIS, BS, MFA: *"The difference between garden-variety depression and clinical depression is the difference between a sore muscle and a muscle that has been ripped in half and partially eaten by wild hogs."*

MAXIME LEGACE: *"Being depressed, all I needed was someone who could listen to me, believe in me, encourage me, but most of all, understand me."*

ALEXANDER PUSHKIN: *"Don't be sad, don't be angry, if life deceives you! Submit to your grief—your time for joy will come, believe me."*

Depression. *(continued)*

TREVOR NOAH: *"One of the best things that helps depression is work, and socializing with other people and connecting. Because when you work you find purpose."*

SOGYAL RINPOCHE: *"Light must come from inside. You cannot ask the darkness to leave; you must turn on the light."*

DANIEL GOLEMAN, PHD: *"If you rely solely on medication to manage depression or anxiety, for example, you have done nothing to train the mind, so that when you come off the medication, you are just as vulnerable to a relapse as though you had never taken the medication."*

JOHANN HARI: *"The scientific evidence is clear that exercise significantly reduces depression and anxiety."*

AUNG SAN SUU KYI, NOBEL: *"When you feel helpless, help someone."*

AMIT RAY, PHD: *"Conscious breathing is the best antidote to stress, anxiety and depression."*

HARVARD T.H. CHAN SCHOOL OF PUBLIC HEALTH: *"Drinking enough water each day is crucial for many reasons: to regulate body temperature, keep joints lubricated, prevent infections, deliver nutrients to cells, and keep organs functioning properly. Being well-hydrated also improves sleep quality, cognition, and mood."*

JOHNS HOPKINS UNIVERSITY SCHOOL OF MEDICINE: *"In our study, meditation appeared to provide as much relief from some anxiety and depression symptoms as what other studies have found from anti-depressants...They also found no harm came from meditation."*

VICTOR HUGO: *"Even the darkest night will end and the sun will rise."*

MAXIME LEGACE: *"Winter always comes to an end, always."*

DR. JOE DISPENZA: *"Love your future more than your past."*

RODGERS & HAMMERSTEIN: *"My Favorite Things"* (Song)

Similar: purposelessness, dejection, withdrawal, sadness, despondency, dysphoria
Opposite: hope, optimism, confidence, enthusiasm, expansion, volunteering

Despair. Arriving at a point of deep disappointment or absence of purpose, verging on hopelessness. *Popular or Heart-Based Usage: (1) Abandoning hope. (2) Giving up on your dreams. (3) Feeling like you are up a creek without a paddle. (4) Crying your eyes out. (5) Feeling that all is lost. (6) Experiencing the dark night of the soul. (7) Feeling you have no place to turn. (8) Seeing no future. (9) Wanting to unzip your skin and change lives. (10) Hitting rock bottom. (11) 'I'm totally screwed.'*

JOHN DONNE: *"Despair is the damp of hell, as joy is the serenity of heaven."*

F. SCOTT FITZGERALD: *"In a real dark night of the soul, it is always three o'clock in the morning, day after day."*

AESCHYLUS: *"He who learns must suffer. And even in our sleep pain that cannot forget falls drop by drop upon the heart. And in our own despair, against our will, comes wisdom to us by the awful grace of God."*

PERCY BYSSHE SHELLEY: *"Then black despair, the shadow of a starless night, was thrown over the world in which I moved alone."*

ELIE WIESEL, NOBEL: *"Because I remember, I despair. Because I remember, I have the duty to reject despair."*

GEORGE ELIOT: *"There is no despair so absolute as that which comes with the first moments of our first great sorrow, when we have not yet known what it is to have suffered and be healed, to have despaired and have recovered hope."*

ROLLO MAY, BDIV, PHD: *"Courage is not the absence of despair; it is, rather, the capacity to move ahead in spite of despair."*

CHARLIE CHAPLIN: *"Despair is a narcotic. It lulls the mind into indifference."*

ALFRED, LORD TENNYSON: *"I must lose myself in action, lest I wither from despair."*

WILLIAM MAKEPEACE THACKERAY: *"Despair is perfectly compatible with a good dinner, I promise you."*

JOEL OSTEEN: *"God loves you too much to let you miss your purpose."*

JEAN-PAUL SARTRE: *"Life begins on the other side of despair."*

APHORISM: *"Hope is a greater warrior than despair."*

LORD BYRON: *"The busy have no time for tears."*

JOAN BAEZ: *"Action is the antidote to despair."*

PSALM 30:5: *"Weeping may endure for a night, but joy cometh in the morning."*

Similar: despondency, hopelessness, rejection, joylessness, uselessness
Opposite: elation, confidence, bullishness, sanguinity

Desperation. Having an inclination toward radical or erratic behavior when the odds of success or survival are fading. *Popular or Heart-Based Usage: (1) Having your back against the wall. (2) Being in dire straits. (3) Doubling (or tripling) down. (4) Throwing caution to the wind. (5) Acting like there's no tomorrow. (6) Seeing your life flash before your eyes. (7) Throwing a 'Hail Mary.' (8) Going flat out. (9) Trying to dial up a miracle. (10) Making a last-ditch effort. (11) 'Any port in a storm.' (12) Betting it all on red. (13) Holding a fire sale. (14) Laying everything on the line. (15) 'Going for broke.'*

HORATIO NELSON: *"Desperate affairs require desperate measures."*

CANELO ALVAREZ: *"The more desperate you are, the more mistakes you make."*

MARK TWAIN: *"Under certain circumstances, urgent circumstances, desperate circumstances, profanity provides a relief denied even to prayer."*

HENRY DAVID THOREAU: *"Most men lead lives of quiet desperation and will go to the grave with the song still in them."*

SIR BENJAMIN DISRAELI: *"Desperation is sometimes as powerful an inspirer as genius."*

DAISAKU IKEDA: *"A person who, no matter how desperate the situation, gives others hope, is a true leader."*

ROBERTO BOLAÑO: *"We interpret life at moments of the deepest desperation."*

SARAH JESSICA PARKER: *"When men attempt bold gestures, generally it's considered romantic. When women do it, it's often considered desperate or psycho."*

LIVY: *"In difficult and desperate cases, the boldest counsels are the safest."*

HENRY DAVID THOREAU: *"It is a characteristic of wisdom not to do desperate things."*

MAC DAVIS: *"In the Ghetto"* (Song)

ANTHONY ROBBINS: *"In life you need either inspiration or desperation."*

SUN RA: *"The possible has been tried and failed. Now it's time to try the impossible."*

D. EARL JOHNSTON: *"In truly desperate times, there is only one person left. The real you."*

MOOJI: *"If you are curious, you will learn. If you are desperate, you will discover."*

HANNIBAL: *"We will either find a way, or make one."*

AMARILLO SLIM: *"If you are going to bluff, make it a big one."*

Similar: daring, frantic, frenzied, impetuous, over-reaching
Opposite: calm, confident, contented, unworried, stable

Determination. [See also **Grit** and **Perseverance**] (1) Maintaining firmness of purpose toward a desired outcome. (2) Deciding to continue on your path despite resistance or obstacles. *Popular or Heart-Based Usage: (1) Doubling down. (2) Bearing down. (3) Hunkering down. (4) Buckling down. (5) Having grit. (6) Having moxie. (7) Showing up. (8) Sucking it up. (9) Taking it up a notch. (10) Making it happen. (11) Digging in your heels. (12) Shaking something off. (13) Hanging tough. (14) Getting over it. (15) Grinding it out. (16) Sticking it out. (17) Knocking yourself out. (18) Going for it. (19) Making no excuses. (20) 'Put up or shut up.' (21) Taking no prisoners. (22) Showing what you're made of. (23) Holding your own. (24) Giving a project the full-court press. (25) Taking it to the hoop. (26) Being in it to win it. (27) Doing the heavy lifting. (28) Committing yourself to go the distance. (29) Continuing 'no matter what.' (30) 'So what. Now what.' (31) Being built to last. (32) Deciding to be unstoppable. (33) Going 'all in.'*

REBA MCENTIRE: *"Be different, stand out, and work your butt off."*

MARY KAY ASH: *"The only difference between successful people and unsuccessful people is extraordinary determination."*

GEN. GEORGE S. PATTON, JR.: *"The object of war is not to die for your country but to make the other bastard die for his."*

WOODY HAYES: *"They may outsmart me, or be luckier, but they can't outwork me."*

ELON MUSK: *"We're going to make it happen. As God is my bloody witness, I'm hell-bent on making it work."*

MICHAEL JORDAN: *"Some people want it to happen, some wish it would happen, others make it happen."*

SIR WINSTON CHURCHILL: *"Never give in, never give in, never, never, never—in nothing, great or small, large or petty—never give in except to convictions of honor and good sense. Never yield to force; never yield to the apparently overwhelming might of the enemy."*

MARIE CURIE, PHD, NOBEL (2X): *"First principle: never to let one's self be beaten down by persons or events."*

EVA PERON: *"I know that like every woman of the people, I have more strength than I appear to have."*

ALBERT ELLIS, PHD: *"Most people would have given up when faced with the criticism I've received over the years."*

SHIRLEY CHISHOLM: *"If they don't give you a seat at the table, bring in a folding chair."*

LISA FERNANDEZ: *"I make my weaknesses my strengths, and my strengths stronger."*

ROLANDA BELL: *"You can't stop a woman that will not quit."*

LEONARDO DA VINCI: *"It had long since come to my attention that people of accomplishment rarely sat back and let things happen to them. They went out and happened to things."*

Determination. *(continued)*

HANNIBAL: *"We will either find a way, or make one."*

BEBE LORD GOW: *"Once a job is first begun, never leave it 'til it's done. Be the labor great or small, do it well or not at all."*

DOUGLAS JOHNSTON: *"A woman may put on a bathing suit and never go near the water; another woman may put on a tennis dress and never set foot on a court; but friend, when a woman puts on a wedding dress, she means business."*

DALAI LAMA, NOBEL: *"If you think you are too small to make a difference, try sleeping with a mosquito."*

MATTHEW REILLY: *"We didn't come this far just to come this far."*

JOHN WAYNE: *"True grit is making a decision and standing by it, doing what must be done."*

ABRAHAM LINCOLN: *"Determine that the thing can and shall be done and then find the way."*

ALFRED, LORD TENNYSON: *"To strive, to seek, to find, and not to yield."*

PETER MAGOWAN: *"If somebody says you can't do something, roll up your sleeves."*

WILLIAM ERNEST HENLEY: *"I am the master of my fate. I am the captain of my soul."*

GEN. FERDINAND FOCH: *"The most powerful weapon on earth is the human soul on fire."*

MARY LOU RETTON: *"I'm very determined and stubborn. There's a desire in me that makes me want to do more and more, and to do it right. Each one of us has a fire in our heart for something. It's our goal in life to find it and to keep it lit."*

AYN RAND: *"The question isn't who is going to let me; it's who is going to stop me."*

ANGELA LEE DUCKWORTH, PHD: *"Enthusiasm is common. Endurance is rare."*

HERNANDO CORTES: *"Burn the ships. We will not leave here without victory."*

NAPOLEON BONAPARTE: *"The truest wisdom is resolute determination."*

TIM NOTKE: *"Hard work beats talent when talent doesn't work hard."*

THOMAS H. PALMER: *"If at first you don't succeed, try, try again."*

LEONARDO DA VINCI: *"Every obstacle yields to stern resolve."*

DESIDERIUS ERASMUS: *"Fortune favors the audacious."*

APHORISM: *"Knocked down seven times, stand up eight."*

JOHNNY CASH: *"Life is rough so you gotta be tough."*

JOHN PAUL JONES: *"I have not yet begun to fight."*

STEVE MARTIN: *"Be so good they can't ignore you."*

DR. JOE DISPENZA: *"Feel it. Believe it. Become it."*

ADAGE: *"Where there is a will, there is a way."*

FRAN CHILDRESS: *"Keep coming back."*

EURIPIDES: *"Leave no stone unturned."*

Similar: tenacity, resolve, doggedness, steadfastness, relentlessness, single-mindedness
Opposite: fickle, ambivalent, compromising, wishy-washy, spineless, wobbly

Devotion. Having dedication, loyalty, or commitment to a person or cause, or to God. *Popular or Heart-Based Usage: (1) Being all in. (2) Standing by your man. (3) Being in someone's corner. (4) Supporting something no matter what. (5) 'Through thick and thin.' (6) 'Until the cows come home.' (7) 'Come Hell or high water.' (8) 'You can count on me.' (9) 'Semper Fi.' (10) 'I'm all yours.'*

ELIZABETH GILBERT: *"Devotion is diligence without assurance."*

G. K. CHESTERTON: *"To be simple is the best thing in the world."*

JOHN RUSKIN: *"When love and skill work together, expect a masterpiece."*

IGNATIUS OF LOYOLA: *"Work as if everything depends on you. Pray as if everything depends on God."*

OSCAR WILDE: *"There is nothing in the world like the devotion of a married woman. It is a thing no married man knows anything about."*

IMMANUEL VELIKOVSKY: *"It is difficult to describe in short the enthusiasm and devotion provoked by and given to my research. We lived almost in poverty. I used pencils, two for a nickel, and could not buy a fountain pen, when I lost mine."*

FRANK LLOYD WRIGHT: *"I know the price of success: dedication, hard work, and an unremitting devotion to the things you want to see happen."*

FRANK GAINES: *"Only he who can see the invisible can do the impossible."*

DAVID M. HENDRICKS: *"A charismatic leader inspires confidence and wins devotion."*

MUHAMMAD ALI JINNAH: *"With faith, discipline, and selfless devotion to duty, there is nothing worthwhile that you cannot achieve."*

GURU NANAK: *"I bow at His Feet constantly, and pray to Him, the Guru, the True Guru, has shown me the Way."*

INSPIRATION.ORG: *"As you pray, remember that God does not have limits, and that with Him, nothing is impossible. He has asked us to be bold, to boldly ask Him in faith, to believe Him for miracles, and to expect answers."*

JOHN 15:13: *"Greater love hath no man than this, that a man lay down his life for his friends."*

PLEDGE OF ALLEGIANCE: *"I pledge allegiance to the Flag of the United States of America, and to the Republic for which it stands, one Nation under God, indivisible, with liberty and justice for all."*

ABRAHAM LINCOLN/GETTYSBURG ADDRESS: *"It is rather for us to be here dedicated to the great task remaining before us, that from these honored dead we take increased devotion to that cause for which they here gave the last full measure of devotion."*

Similar: adherence, allegiance, dedication, steadfastness
Opposite: animosity, coolness, fickleness, indifference

Disappointment. Acknowledging the unhappy reality of an unfulfilled hope or expectation. *Popular or Heart-Based Usage: (1) Coming up short. (2) Having dashed hopes. (3) Getting a rejection response or a 'Dear John.' (4) Taking the L. (5) Living with a downer. (6) Having something fizzle out. (7) Coming up empty-handed. (8) Moping around. (9) Getting short-changed. (10) 'It's just total crap.' (11) Feeling bummed out. (12) Dealing with a setback. (13) Feeling sorry for yourself. (14) Pushing a lost cause. (15) Dealing with a broken heart. (16) Feeling torn up about something. (17) Wearing the brown helmet. (18) Getting the rug pulled out from under you. (19) Getting shafted. (20) 'There's no joy in Mudville.' (21) Dealing with a soul-crushing loss. (22) 'Epic fail.' (23) Eating a dirt sandwich. (24) Trying to keep your chin up. (25) Trying to deal with it. (26) 'Aye Yai Yai!' (27) 'Now what.'*

ERNEST LAWRENCE THAYER: *"Mighty Casey has struck out."*

ECKHART TOLLE: *"When something gets in your way, it is still the way."*

HENRY DAVID THOREAU: *"If we will be quiet and ready enough, we shall find compensation in every disappointment."*

MARTIN LUTHER KING, JR., NOBEL: *"We must accept finite disappointment, but never lose infinite hope."*

ROBERT KIYOSAKI: *"The size of your success is measured by the strength of your desire; the size of your dream; and how you handle disappointment along the way."*

JIM WEATHERLY: *"Midnight Train to Georgia"* (Song)

JUSTICE RUTH BADER GINSBURG: *"My mother was a powerful influence. She made me toe the line. If I didn't have a perfect report card, she showed her disappointment."*

GEORGE FOREMAN: *"Evil lurks where disappointment lodges."*

NAFESSA WILLIAMS: *"Disappointment builds character and strength."*

DAN BONGINO: *"The Gift of Failure"* (Book)

GEORGE ELIOT: *"The only failure one should fear, is not hugging to the purpose as they see fit."*

JOEL OSTEEN: *"What you can't see is that trouble is transportation, moving you into your purpose, perhaps into a position to make a difference in someone else's life."*

ARIANNA HUFFINGTON: *"I failed many times in my life. One failure that I always remember was when my second book was rejected by 36 publishers. Many years later, I watched HuffPost come alive."*

RUMI: *"You have to keep breaking your heart until it opens."*

APHORISM: *"Dust yourself off, get back on your horse, and ride."*

Similar: setback, deflated, crestfallen, blow, blunder, obstacle, impasse, downdraft, anticlimactic, downer

Opposite: achievement, accomplishment, attainment, success, winning

Discernment. (1) Having the ability to judge well, especially in complex circumstances or affairs of the heart. (2) Embracing spiritual guidance in the absence of objective clarity. *Popular or Heart-Based Usage: (1) Weighing the pros and cons. (2) Navigating tricky situations. (3) Figuring out what is best. (4) Trusting your gut. (5) Doing the calculus. (6) Separating the wheat from the chaff. (7) Reading between the lines. (8) Spotting a phony. (9) Choosing the lesser of two evils. (10) Having your heart in the right place. (11) Staying grounded. (12) Having the humility to ask for help. (13) Having a good head on your shoulders. (14) Sticking with your principles. (15) Making tough choices. (16) Getting on your knees. (17) Exercising personal wisdom. (18) Having good acumen.*

JON STEWART: *"The enemy is noise. The goal is clarity."*

ERWIN ROMMEL: *"Don't fight a battle if you don't gain anything by winning."*

ELDRIDGE CLEAVER: *"You're either part of the solution or you're part of the problem."*

MOLLY IVINS: *"My first rule of holes: When you're in one stop digging."*

MARGARET MILLAR: *"Some people become so expert at reading between the lines they don't read the lines."*

CRISS JAMI: *"God gives His deepest discernment and sharpest marksmanship to men who aim to expose His truth before an enemy's lies."*

1 CORINTHIANS 12:10: *"To another the working of miracles; to another prophecy; to another discerning of spirits; to another divers kinds of tongues; to another the interpretation of tongues."*

LAO TZU: *"He who knows others is clever; He who knows himself has discernment."*

BENJAMIN FRANKLIN: *"When in doubt, don't."*

TIM COOK: *"We believe in saying no to thousands of projects so that we can really focus on the few that are truly important and meaningful to us."*

HENRY R. JOHNSTON: *"Before you move forward with a big decision, make sure of three things; that the issue is important, that it is a matter of principle, and that you're right."*

ALDOUS HUXLEY: *"The victim of mind-manipulation does not know he is a victim; to him, the walls of his prison are invisible, and he believes himself to be free."*

SAMUEL JOHNSON: *"The supreme end of education is expert discernment in all things—the power to tell the good from the bad, the genuine from the counterfeit, and to prefer the good and genuine to the bad and counterfeit."*

ANNA LAETITIA BARBAULD: *"Children have an almost intuitive discernment between the maxims you bring forward for their use, and those by which you direct your own conduct."*

JACK KEROUAC: *"One day I will find the right words, and they will be simple."*

Similar: perceptiveness, insight, intuition, acumen, enlightenment, judgment
Opposite: ignorance, uncomprehending, indifference, apathy, unaware, clueless

Discrimination. (1) Demonstrating unjust treatment of others based on their race, culture, religion, age, gender identity, or sexual orientation. (2) Violating someone's dignity. *Popular or Heart-Based: (1) Giving preferences only to your pals. (2) Hating on those that differ from you. (3) Picking on people. (4) Holding certain people back. (5) Denying a person's basic human rights.*

NELSON MANDELA, NOBEL: *"No one is born hating another person because of the color of his skin, or his background, or his religion. People must learn to hate, and if they can learn to hate, they can be taught to love, for love comes more naturally to the human heart than the opposite."*

MARTIN LUTHER KING, JR., NOBEL: *"I have a dream that my four little children will one day live in a nation where they will not be judged by the color of their skin, but by the content of their character."*

ELEANOR ROOSEVELT: *"Where, after all, do universal human rights begin? In small places, close to home—so close and so small that they cannot be seen on any maps of the world... Such are the places where every man, woman and child seeks equal justice, equal opportunity, equal dignity without discrimination. Unless these rights have meaning there, they have little meaning everywhere."*

EDITH STEIN: *"The world doesn't need what women have, it needs what women are... A woman's soul is fashioned as a shelter in which other souls may unfold."*

ELIZABETH TAYLOR: *"I call upon you to draw from the depths of your being—to prove that we are a human race, to prove that our love outweighs the need to hate, that our compassion is more compelling than our need to blame."*

ROGER STAUBACH: *"Discrimination is a disease."*

WILLIAM J. CLINTON: *"It turns out that advancing equal opportunity and economic empowerment is both morally right and good economics. Why? Because discrimination, poverty, and ignorance restrict growth."*

DONALD TRUMP: *"I like the idea of amending the 1964 Civil Rights Act to include a ban of discrimination based on sexual orientation. It would be simple. It would be straightforward."*

ARETHA FRANKLIN: *"We all require and want respect, man or woman, black or white. It's our basic human right."*

RITA LEVI-MONTALCINI, MD, NOBEL: *"If I had not been discriminated against or had not suffered persecution, I would bever have received the Nobel Prize."*

MARTINA NAVRATILOVA: *"Labels are for filing. Labels are for clothing. Labels are not for people."*

ROSA PARKS: *"I would like to be known as a person who is concerned about freedom and justice and equality and prosperity for all people."*

Similar: prejudice, favoritism, intolerance, exclusion, unfairness, hatred, bigotry
Opposite: fairness, acceptance, tolerance, welcome, inclusion, impartiality, objectivity

Disgust. Having a strong aversion to something noted as offensive or well below acceptable standards. *Popular or Heart-Based Usage: (1) Rolling your eyes. (2) Feeling something is deeply inappropriate. (3) Looking around for a can of industrial-strength repellent. (4) Turning away from something shunned or stigmatized. (5) Pivoting about something taboo. (6) Getting a sickening feeling about something. (7) Feeling like you want to puke. (8) Being ready to retch. (9) Shuddering about something unspeakable. (10) Getting the full creeps about something. (11) Spotting a turd in the punchbowl. (12) 'Throwing up' on an idea. (13) 'Yuck.' (14) 'Ew.' (15) 'Gross.' (16) 'That's revolting!' (17) 'Done with this.' (18) 'So out of here.' (19) 'This is an outrage!'*

MARK TWAIN: *"But it is a blessed provision of times like these, as soon as a man's has gotten down to a certain point, there comes a revulsion and he rallies."*

JIM ROHN: *"Disgust and resolve are two of the great emotions that lead to change."*

STEVE ALLEN: *"If there is a God, the phrase that must disgust him is—holy war."*

SOPHOCLES: *"All is disgust when a man leaves his nature and does what is unfit."*

CAMILLA NORD, PHD: *"We've known for some time that when you see something disgusting, your stomach muscles' electrical signals become dysregulated."*

DANIEL KAHNEMAN, MD, NOBEL: *"The psychologist, Paul Rozin, an expert on disgust, observed that a single cockroach will completely wreck the appeal of a bowl of cherries, but a cherry will do nothing for a bowl of cockroaches."*

CHARLES BAUDELAIRE: *"I am unable to understand how a man of honor could take a newspaper in his hands without a shudder of disgust."*

MOTHER TERESA, NOBEL: *"Facing the press is more difficult than bathing a leper."*

DIOGENES: *"The vine bears three kinds of grapes: the first of pleasure, the second of intoxication, and the third of disgust."*

LINCOLN STOREY: *"Incest is widely known as a universal taboo."*

CICERO: *"The greatest pleasures are only narrowly separated from disgust."*

ROSE KENNEDY: *"The time will come when it will disgust you to look in the mirror."*

Similar: disdain, revulsion, loathing, abhorrence, indignation, repugnance, detestation
Opposite: approval, admiration, esteem, respect, pursuit

Doubt. Questioning the validity or likelihood of a fact, situation, or course of action. *Popular or Heart-Based Usage: (1) Having a few misgivings. (2) Having issues. (3) Taking a pause or a time out to reassess. (4) Having second thoughts. (5) Mulling something over. (6) Rubbing your eyes. (7) Double-checking something. (8) Feeling something is far-fetched. (9) Having some scruples. (10) Finding something hard to swallow. (11) Regrouping about something. (12) Tapping the brakes on an idea. (13) Throwing/casting shade on something. (14) Calling BS on something. (15) Pushing back on your heels. (16) Giving it an eye-roll. (17) Coughing on purpose. (18) Casting aspersions. (19) 'Hunh?' (20) 'You sure about that?' (21) 'Back it up!' (22) 'Show me.' (23) 'Dunno about that.' (24) 'Prove it.' (25) 'Baloney!' (26) 'Get out of town!' (27) 'No way!'*

BENJAMIN FRANKLIN: *"When in doubt, don't."*

MARK TWAIN: *"It is better to keep your mouth closed and let people think you are a fool than to open it and remove all doubt."*

JENNIFER LOPEZ: *"Doubt is a killer. You just have to know who you are and what you stand for."*

MOLIÈRE: *"Doubts are more cruel than the worst of truths."*

RICHARD PETTY: *"Never put a question mark where God puts a period."*

DEREK JETER: *"I love it when people doubt me, it makes me work harder to prove them wrong."*

RENÉ DESCARTES: *"If you would be a real seeker after truth, it is necessary that at least once in your life you doubt, as far as possible, all things."*

YOGI BERRA: *"When you come to a fork in the road, take it."*

BARBRA STREISAND: *"Confidence and doubt are at both ends of the scale, and you need both."*

SUZY KASSEM: *"Doubt kills more dreams than failure ever will."*

MIGUEL DE UNAMUNO: *"Faith which does not doubt is dead faith."*

SETH GODIN: *"If not enough people doubt you, you're not making a difference."*

ALFRED, LORD TENNYSON: *"There lives more faith in honest doubt, believe me, than in half the creeds."*

ISAAC BESHEVIS SINGER: *"Doubt is part of all religion. All the religious thinkers were doubters."*

HENRY DAVID THOREAU: *"Faith keeps many doubts in her pay. If I could not doubt, I should not believe."*

WILLIAM SHAKESPEARE: *"Modest doubt is called the beacon of the wise."*

ECKHART TOLLE: *"Observe your thoughts, don't believe them."*

GAUTAMA BUDDHA: *"Doubt everything. Find your own light."*

DIOGENES: *"I know nothing, except the fact of my ignorance."*

AUGUSTINE OF HIPPO: *"Doubt is the origin of wisdom."*

Similar: uncertainty, indecision, hesitancy, misgiving, reluctance, apprehension
Opposite: reliance, assurance, confidence, faith, belief

Dreaming. (1) Focusing on your goals and highest aspirations. (2) Content during sleep. *Popular or Heart-Based Usage: (1) Picturing something in your mind. (2) Exploring your heart of hearts. (3) Watching your path unfold. (4) Seeing your thoughts manifest. (5) Wishing on a star. (6) Understanding REM sleep. (7) 'In dreams, time is not linear.'*

WALT DISNEY: *"If you can dream it, you can do it."*

JUDY GARLAND (HAROLD ARLEN / YIP HARBURG): *"Somewhere over the rainbow, skies are blue, and the dreams that you dare to dream really do come true."*

ALBERT EINSTEIN, PHD, NOBEL: *"Logic will take you from A to B. Imagination will take you everywhere."*

RICHARD BACH: *"To bring anything into your life, imagine it is already there."*

KAHLIL GIBRAN: *"Trust in dreams, for in them is hidden the gate to eternity."*

JEREMY IRONS: *"We all have our time machines. Some take us back, they're called memories. Some take us forward, they're called dreams."*

MIGUEL DE CERVANTES: *"In order to attain the impossible, one must attempt the absurd."*

DR. JOE DISPENZA: *"To be happy with yourself in the present moment while maintaining a dream of your future is a grand recipe for manifestation."*

MARTIN LUTHER KING, JR., NOBEL: *"I have a dream! To be free at last! Free at last! Free at last. And if a man has nothing to die for, then his life is worth nothing."*

MARK TWAIN: *"Focus more on your desire than on your doubt, and the dream will take care of itself."*

JIM ROHN: *"If you really want to do something, you'll find a way."*

LINCOLN STOREY: *"Your dream is your intention, more precious than time."*

EARL NIGHTINGALE: *"Whatever we plant in our subconscious mind and nourish with repetition and emotion will one day become a reality."*

CARL JUNG, MD: *"Man's task is to become conscious of the contents that press upward from the unconscious."*

GOETHE: *"Whatever you can do or dream you can, begin it. Boldness has genius, power and magic in it."*

VINCENT VAN GOGH: *"I dream of painting and then I paint my dream."*

MARGE PIERCY: *"Every artist creates with open eyes what she sees in her dreams."*

EDGAR CAYCE: *"Dreams are today's answers to tomorrow's questions."*

WILLIAM BLAKE: *"What is now proved was once only imagined."*

GLORIA STEINEM: *"Dreaming, after all, is a form of planning."*

PAUL VALERY: *"Breath, dreams, silence, invincible calm, you triumph."*

LYNNE MCTAGGART: *"Thoughts become things."*

Similar: visualizing, imagining, creating, focusing, conceiving, picturing
Opposite: unfocused, scattered, apathetic, disinterested

Ego. Maintaining a cultivated or projected personality different from your true self. *Popular or Heart-Based Usage: (1) Putting on a social mask. (2) Talking around people. (3) Letting your bad self take over. (4) Trolling others. (4) Putting people down. (5) Virtue-signaling. (6) Having it your way. (7) Making others wrong. (8) Puffing up like a cobra. (9) Holding court. (10) Flexing. (11) 'Silence! Oz has spoken!' (12) 'Get a load of me!' (13) Being a drama queen. (14) 'My world, not yours.' (15) Being holier-than-thou.*

JOHNNY MCGREW: *"No way. Not me. I don't have an ego. HE has an ego."*

CARL JUNG, MD: *"The first half of life is devoted to forming a healthy ego, the second half is going inward and letting go of it."*

ECKHART TOLLE: *"The moment you become aware of the ego in you, it is strictly speaking no longer the ego, but just an old, conditioned mind-pattern. Ego implies unawareness. Awareness and ego cannot coexist."*

DEEPAK CHOPRA: *"The ego is your self-image; it is your social mask; it is the role you are playing. Your social mask thrives on approval."*

GELEK RINPOCHE: *"That's the ego talking. But it's not the real you. You are a good and wonderful person. You are kind. You have a compassionate nature."*

MARIANNE WILLIAMSON: *"Ego says, 'Once everything falls into place, I'll find peace.' Spirit says, 'Find your peace, and then everything will fall into place.'"*

ALBERT EINSTEIN, PHD, NOBEL: *"The main task of the spirit is to free man from his ego."*

LINCOLN STOREY: *"Your ego is a superficial personality which you put out there to deal with daily issues. You use it to make yourself right and others wrong."*

ALLEN CHENG: *"Notice your attachment to your views or opinions, your need to be right and prove the other person wrong. Recognize that your ego is fueling your reaction; acknowledging this will help to dissolve it."*

D. EARL JOHNSTON: *"If you fashion your life as a hammer, you will go around steadily looking for nails."*

CULLEN HIGHTOWER: *"Our ego is our silent partner … too often with a controlling interest."*

RYAN HOLIDAY: *"Ego is the Enemy"* (Book)

MAHATMA GANDHI: *"Many could forgo heavy meals, a full wardrobe, a fine house, et cetera. It is the ego they cannot forgo."*

ECKHART TOLLE: *"Complaining is a key method the ego uses to reinforce itself."*

KAMAND KOJOURI, PHD: *"You have no choice. You must leave your ego on the doorstep before you enter love."*

D. H. LAWRENCE: *"When we get out of the glass bottle of our ego … things will happen to us that we don't know ourselves. Cool, unlying life will rush in."*

NIKKI SIXX: *"Your ego is not your amigo."*

Similar: self-righteous, sanctimonious, judgmental, assertive, moralistic
Opposite: humility, shame, disgrace, dishonor, ignominy

Electromagnetism. [See also **Frequency**, **Gravity**, **Light**, and **Quantum Physics**] (1) Relating to one of the four core primary forces of physics, measured in wavelengths and frequencies, and including the visible and invisible universes of energy, matter, space, and time in which life operates. (2) Involving the interactions between particles having electric charge within a magnetic field. (3) Humans may be considered as electromagnetic beings. *Popular or Heart-Based Usage: (1) Living beneath the starry firmament. (2) Living in the silent buzz. (3) Knowing you produce both an EKG and EEG. (4) 'Being in the ozone.' (5) Living in electro-smog. (6) Living in the Akashic universe. (7) Sailing in the solar wind. (8) 'Space is not empty.' (9) Operating in the ether. (10) Being shielded by Earth's magnetic field. (11) Living in the cosmic hologram. (12) 'What is the Matrix?'*

SETH GODIN, BS, MBA: *"Invisible doesn't mean unimportant."*

GOOGLE GENERATIVE AI: *"The heart and the brain generate electromagnetic fields that are affected by emotions. Positive emotions strengthen the field, while negative emotions weaken it."*

KIP THORNE, PHD, NOBEL: *"When Galileo first trained his optic telescope on the heavens and opened up modern optical astronomy, that was the first of the electromagnetic windows out of the universe: light."*

D. EARL JOHNSTON: *"Space is not empty. We have our limited view of the stars based on the very narrow band of wavelengths we know as visible light. But the full electromagnetic spectrum of the universe is far broader."*

MICHAEL FARADAY: *"I happen to have discovered a direct relation between magnetism and light, and also electricity and light, and the field it opens is so large and I think rich."*

JAMES CLERK MAXWELL, FRS: *In his 1865 paper "A Dynamic Theory of the Electromagnetic Field," he demonstrated that electrical and magnetic fields travel through space as waves moving at the speed of light.*

ALBERT EINSTEIN, PHD, NOBEL: *"The special theory of relativity owes its origins to Maxwell's equations of the electromagnetic field."*

GREGORY BENFORD, PHD: *"Electromagnetic theory and experiment gave us the telephone, radio, TV, computers, and made the internal combustion engine practical—thus, the car and airplane, leading inevitably to the rocket and outer space exploration."*

JASON SILVA: *"We have all kinds of limitations as human beings. I mean we can't see the whole electromagnetic spectrum; we can't see the very small; we can't see the very far. So we compensate for these things with technological scaffoldings."*

JOHN TRUDELL: *"What I view life like is about energy. Everything is about energy—everything. We physically are little units of electrical energy, and we vibrate and project electromagnetic thought."*

PAM GREGORY: *"We are essentially electromagnetic beings."*

Electromagnetism. *(continued)*

LINCOLN STOREY: *"The X-ray, EKG, EEG, CT, and MRI are electromagnetic tools."*

BARRY BARISH, PHD, NOBEL: *"Everything we know about the universe is studied by using telescopes or other instruments that look at visible light, infrared, ultraviolet or X-ray—different wavelengths of electromagnetic interactions. Only 4 percent of what's in the universe gives off electromagnetic radiation, so we don't have any handle on the rest."*

FRANCOIS ENGLERT, PHD, NOBEL: *"Gravitational and electromagnetic interactions are long-range interactions, meaning they act on objects no matter how far they are separated from each other."*

NIKOLA TESLA: *"I am trying to awake the energy contained in the air. These are the main sources of energy. What is considered as empty space is just a manifestation of matter that is not awakened."*

ALBERT EINSTEIN, PHD, NOBEL (attributed): *"We are slowed down sound and light waves, a walking bundle of frequencies tuned in to the cosmos."*

LINCOLN STOREY: *"Energy changes permeate life and our being. When our voice drops an octave or two, people are suddenly drawn to our confidence and calm; and when it rises and we start to whine, people quickly sense there's a problem."*

M. BRUCE MACIVER, BSC, MSC, PHD: *"Electromagnetic field (EMF) theories of mind/brain integration have been proposed to explain brain function for over seventy years. Interest in this theory continues to this day because it explains mind-brain integration and it offers a simple solution to the 'binding problem' of our unified conscious experience."*

DIANE HENNACY POWELL, MD: *"In fact, that's how the electroencephalograph was actually created by Hans Berger, who was in the military. His sister sent him a telegraph asking if he was okay right after he had a near-miss accident....So he thought, 'Wow! This must be electromagnetic, this thinking.'"*

HANS BERGER, MD: *"We see in the electroencephalogram a concomitant phenomenon of the continuous nerve processes which take place in the brain, exactly as the electrocardiogram represents a concomitant phenomenon of contractions of the individual segments of the heart."*

THE DAILY CHRONICLE: *"1937...the patent for the electric guitar to George D. Beauchamp...The use of electromagnetic pickups to capture and amplify the acoustic guitar's sound paved the way for the evolution of rock and roll."*

DR. JOE DISPENZA: *"Every thought has a frequency."*

PAM GREGORY: *"We need to become masters of frequency and energy."*

ALAN COHEN, MA: *"God is a frequency. Stay tuned."*

Similar: radiation, ultraviolet, infrared, radio, microwave, gamma rays, cosmic rays
Opposite: void, null, dead, lacking charge

Embarrassment. Being inclined toward shame or withdrawal after becoming aware of your own errors or awkwardness. *Popular or Heart-Based Usage: (1) 'Cringe' or feeling that something is cringe-worthy. (2) Wincing. (3) Making a gaffe. (4) Self-owning. (5) Being chagrined. (6) Wanting to have something back. (7) Feeling sheepish. (8) Having spinach in your teeth. (9) Blowing the punchline. (10) Stepping on a rake. (11) Having your plan backfire. (12) 'Now I've really stepped in it.' (13) Feeling mortified. (14) Screwing the pooch. (15) Getting 'pantsed' (or caught with your pants down). (16) Not getting the memo. (17) Being red-faced. (18) Having your ears turn red. (19) Walking something back. (20) Beating a fast retreat. (21) Having your tail between your legs. (22) Seeking a quick exit. (23) Going low-profile. (24) Facing up to your own foibles. (25) Going into hiding. (26) 'Wanting to die (or just disappear).' (27) 'Ulp!' (28) 'Oh, no!' (29) 'Oh God, I did WHAT?' (30) Self-editing. (31) Going hiding. (32) 'Oops outta here!'*

JULIA NICKSON-SOUL: *"If you are never scared, embarrassed, or hurt, it means you never take chances."*

JOYCE BROTHERS, PHD: *"Accept that all of us can be hurt, that all of us can and will surely at times fail. Other vulnerabilities like being embarrassed or risking love, can be terrifying, too. I think we should follow a simple rule: if we can take the worst, take the risk."*

SUE JOHANSON: *"It's sad that the most glorious of sexual experiences can make us feel guilty, ashamed, embarrassed, and abnormal."*

JANET MORRIS: *"Nothing powers hate better than embarrassment."*

SARAH JESSICA PARKER: *"I cringe inside when anybody gives me something, I don't know why. I just get embarrassed."*

DAVE BARRY: *"To an adolescent, there is nothing in the world more embarrassing than a parent."*

STEVE JOBS: *"Remembering that I'll be dead soon is the most important tool I've ever encountered to help me make the big choices in life. Because almost everything—all external expectations, all pride, all fear of embarrassment or failure—these things just fall away in the face of death, leaving only what is truly important."*

MIKA BRZEZINSKI: *"A fundamental lesson on being fired: Never lie about it. People will know what you're saying is a cover-up for how you really feel—embarrassed, discouraged, and afraid."*

SIR RICHARD BRANSON: *"Do not be embarrassed by your failures. Learn from them and start again."*

ADAGE: *"A thing is embarrassing only if you care what people think."*

WILL ROGERS: *"Eventually you stop lying about your age and start bragging about it."*

Similar: self-consciousness, cringing, blushing, self-deprecation, discomfiture, shyness
Opposite: confidence, boldness, shamelessness, self-assertion

Emotional. (1) Having to do with the bridge between thought and behavior. (2) Relating to your reactions, decisions, and engagement about behavior, whether involuntary or voluntary. *Popular or Heart-Based Usage: (1) Interpreting life. (2) Expressing yourself. (3) Reacting and choosing. (4) Having feelings. (5) Following your heart. (6) Getting all riled up. (7) Getting irrational. (8) 'Fear and loathing.' (9) 'Fight, flight, or freeze.' (10) Recognizing an 'amygdala hijack.' (11) Crying buckets. (12) Being choked up. (13) 'Home is where the heart is.' (14) Knowing what really matters. (15) Making friends. (16) Like kinds attract. (17) Falling in love. (18) Starting a family. (19) Being tempted. (20) Taking risks. (21) Being transparent. (22) Trusting your gut. (23) Baring your heart. (24) Doing your best. (25) 'Cherish, respect, honor.' (26) 'Keeping it close to the vest.' (27) Knowing heartache, betrayal, and suffering. (28) Forgiving and loving. (29) Keeping your beliefs.*

LEONARDO DA VINCI: *"All thoughts start with emotion."*

CARL JUNG, MD: *"Emotion is the chief source of consciousness."*

GENESIS 1:27: *"So God created man in his own image."*

PLATO: *"Human behavior flows from three main sources: desire, emotion, and knowledge."*

BESSEL VAN DER KOLK, MD: *"The emotional brain is at the heart of the central nervous system, and its key task is to look after your welfare."*

JONATHAN HAIDT, PHD: *"It is only because our emotional brain works so well that our reasoning can work at all."*

ANTONIO DAMASIO, MD, PHD: *"Emotion operates, very often when you think about how you react to the world ... but you are constantly reacting to the world."*

TONY ROBBINS: *"Take control of your consistent emotions and begin to consciously and deliberately reshape your daily experience of life."*

HEATHER ENSWORTH, PHD: *"Earth is a planet that is about emotions."*

JODY WILLIAMS, NOBEL: *"Emotion without action is irrelevant."*

STEVEN PINKER, PHD: *"You can't hear a word and just hear it as raw sound; it always evokes an associated meaning and emotion in the brain."*

ANTONIO DAMASIO, MD, PHD: *"Emotions represent a very well orchestrated set of alterations in the body that has, as a general purpose, making life more survivable by taking care of a danger, of taking care of an opportunity, either/or, or something in between."*

BESSEL VAN DER KOLK, MD: *"I want to emphasize that emotions are not opposed to reason; our emotions assign value to experiences and thus are the foundation of reason."*

JILL BOLTE TAYLOR, PHD: *"Emotion only lasts in our bodies for about 90 seconds. After that, the physical reaction dissipates, UNLESS our cognitive brain kicks in and starts connecting our anger with past events."*

HUMORIST: *"Mixed emotions are what a guy can feel when his mother-in-law drives over a cliff in his new car."*

Emotional. *(continued)*

JOHNNY MCGREW: *"Talk about emotional ranges? Get on a call with a computer 'help desk person' and you'll start out with a few moments of normal cheerful conversation. But from there it'll shift pretty quickly to concerns about money, then tech panic sets in, and finally you land at just plain old begging for mercy."*

DICTATOR: *"I use emotion for the many and reason for the few."*

DANIEL GOLEMAN, PHD: *"Emotions are contagious."*

PHIL HELLMUTH: *"Poker is about understanding human behavior and managing emotions—yours and the other guy's. That's huge in poker, and it's huge in business."*

CHRISTOPHER VOSS: *"Emotions aren't the obstacles to a successful negotiation; they are the means."*

COACH CHIP KELLY: *"We talk about this all the time. In a game three things can happen—momentum swings, adversity, and random acts. If you're a competitor, you respond to it. If you're not a competitor, you react."*

ROBERT REDFORD: *"Get emotionally connected to your story so you can deliver it, you know, if you can't deliver the emotions to your script there's no point to your story."*

GOOGLE GENERATIVE AI: *"The heart and the brain generate electromagnetic fields that are affected by emotions. Positive emotions strengthen the field, while negative emotions weaken it."*

SUSAN DAVID, PHD: *"Emotions are data, they are not directives."*

SHANNON L. ALDER: *"Feelings are something you have, not something you are."*

RINGO STARR: *"That's all drugs and alcohol do. They cut off your emotions in the end."*

BETTY GRECO SHER: *"When you bury an emotion, you bury it alive."*

BRENE BROWN, MSW, PHD: *"We cannot selectively numb emotions. When we numb the painful emotions, we also numb the positive emotions."*

ADAGE: *"The problems of this world are almost always emotional problems."*

BO CALVERT: *"Play with emotion, but don't let your emotions play with you."*

JOHNNY MCGREW: *"There is nothing more personal than your emotions."*

LINCOLN STOREY: *"Emotions are the shared language of humanity, and very possibly the shared language of the intelligent universe."*

ABDU'L BAHA: *"Be not the slave of your moods but their master."*

COACH JIM VALVANO: *"I just got one last thing. I urge all of you, all of you, to enjoy your life, the precious moments that you have. To spend each day with some laughter and some thought, to get your emotions going."*

D. EARL JOHNSTON: *"Think with your head, and act with your heart."*

Similar: behavioral, expressive, feeling, sensitive, responsive, reactive, demonstrative
Opposite: indifferent, non-responsive, cold, dispassionate, tone-deaf, unengaged

Empathy. Duplicating the emotions and mindset of another, especially where the other person is experiencing difficulty. *Popular or Heart-Based Usage: (1) Picking up on someone else's vibes. (2) Getting on the same wavelength with someone. (3) Reading the room. (4) Reading people's faces. (5) Reaching out to someone. (6) Connecting at a deep level. (7) Walking a mile in their shoes. (8) Reacting as if it happened to you. (9) Feeling someone else's pain. (10) Doing the Vulcan mind-meld. (11) Being relatable. (12) Coming alongside someone. (13) Tilting your head to listen. (14) Holding space for someone. (15) 'I feel your pain.' (16) Love-flooding. (17) Responding in the highest octave of love.*

MAHATMA GANDHI: *"I saw that a man of truth must also be a man of care."*

MOHSIN HAMID: *"Empathy is about finding echoes of another person in yourself."*

JOHN STEINBECK: *"You can only understand other people if you feel them in yourself."*

LAWRENCE J: *"Empathy is like giving someone a psychological hug."*

ELISABETH KUBLER-ROSS, MD: *"Those who have known defeat, known suffering, known struggle, known loss, and have found their way out of the depths. These persons have an appreciation, a sensitivity, and an understanding of life that fills them with compassion, gentleness, and a deep loving concern."*
Copyright: Elisabeth Kubler-Ross Family Limited Partnership

D. EARL JOHNSTON: *"Empathy is walking a mile in someone else's shoes, encouragement is helping someone grow into their shoes, happiness is being really comfortable in your own shoes, and fun is running barefoot together."*

EURIPIDES: *"When a good man is hurt all who would be called good must suffer with him."*

CARL ROGERS, PHD: *"We think we listen, but very rarely do we listen with full understanding, true empathy. Yet listening, of this very special kind, is one of the most potent forces for change that I know."*

WALT WHITMAN: *"I do not ask the wounded person how he feels, I myself become the wounded person."*

ALEXANDER POPE: *"Teach me to feel another's woe, To hide the fault I see, That mercy I to others show, That mercy show to me."*

THEODORE ROOSEVELT, NOBEL: *"No one cares how much you know, until they know how much you care."*

HOMER: *"Yet, taught by time, my heart has learned to glow for others' good, and melt for others' woe."*

Similar: sympathy, nurturing, mothering, co-creating, intuiting, mentoring, like-mindedness, duplication, compassion, rapport
Opposite: disdain, indifference, anger, rejection, selfishness, coldness, righteousness

Empowerment. Providing support and the means to help someone realize their goals and aspirations. *Popular or Heart-Based Usage: (1) Taking someone under your wing. (2) Lifting someone up. (3) Planting a seed of greatness in someone. (4) Teaching to DIY. (5) Backing someone. (6) Helping someone see a vision of their future. (7) Providing someone a runway long enough to take off. (8) Being 'big' toward others. (9) Helping someone to develop coping skills. (10) Helping someone to 'blow up.' (11) Being a role model. (12) Being someone for others to look up to. (13) Touching someone's heart. (14) Bringing out the best in someone.*

MACHIAVELLI: *"Make no small plans for they have no power to stir the soul."*

JEFFERSON FISHER: *"Every word you say has the power to shape your world."*

CRAIG GROESCHEL: *"When you delegate tasks, you create followers. When you delegate authority, you create leaders."*

STEPHEN KING: *"You can, and should, and if you're brave enough to start, you will."*

NINA SHAW: *"If you want to be a woman in power, then empower other women."*

TYRA BANKS: *"I am learning how to delegate and how to empower people."*

GLORIA STEINEM: *"Dreaming, after all, is a form of planning."*

BRACHA GOLDSMITH: *"Love is empowerment. Fear is disempowerment."*

J. K. ROWLING, OBE, CH: *"We carry all of the power we need inside ourselves already."*

STEVEN PINKER, PHD: *"Societies that empower women are less violent in every way."*

ABRAHAM MASLOW, PHD: *"The fact is that people are good. Give people affection and security, and they will give affection and be secure in their feelings and in their behavior."*

GUILLAUME APOLLINAIRE: *"Come to the edge.*
We might fall.
Come to the edge.
It's too high.
Come to the edge.
And they came,
And he pushed,
And they flew."

KEVIN BACON: *"A good director creates an environment which gives the actor the encouragement to fly."*

JEFF SILBAR & LARRY HENLEY: *"Wind Beneath My Wings"* (Song)

JOHN BURROUGHS: *"Leap and the net will appear."*

DAVID M. HENDRICKS: *"I believe in you."*

Similar: nurturing, validation, grant, facilitating, enabling, endorsing, warranting
Opposite: deny, disavow, veto, reject, disapprove

Emptiness. Lacking meaning, goals, or a purpose. *Popular or Heart-Based Usage: (1) Having nothing to live for. (2) Feeling tapped out. (3) Being toast. (4) Feeling like you've had the rug pulled out from under you. (5) Feeling like you're a circle without the rim. (6) Void of course. (7) Feeling dead inside. (8) Feeling washed up. (9) Losing the plot in life. (10) Just going through the motions.*

HARUKI MURAKAMI: *"There is nothing so cruel in this world as the desolation of having nothing to hope for."*

ANTONIO PORCHIA: *"In a full heart there is room for everything, and in an empty heart there is room for nothing."*

JAMES DE LA VEGA: *"Why does the feeling of emptiness occupy so much space?"*

HELEN KELLER: *"Once I knew only darkness and stillness…my life was without past or future…but a little word from the fingers of another fell into my hand that clutched at emptiness, and my heart leaped to the rapture of living."*

ECKHART TOLLE: *"A person dies, or something you identified with completely is gone…There is extreme pain at first. But whenever a form dissolves, which is called 'death,' what remains is an opening into emptiness."*

VINCENT VAN GOGH: *"I am unable to describe exactly what is the matter with me; now and then there are horrible fits of anxiety, apparently without cause, or otherwise a feeling of emptiness and fatigue in the head."*

DOUGLAS JOHNSTON: *"Times can get really tough, and it helps to keep a sense of humor. My friend told me after his dog died and his wife left him that he got so depressed he could have flown a kite under a rug."*

NORA ROBERTS: *"Feeling too much is a hell of a lot better than feeling nothing."*

OSHO: *"Meditation is nothing but coming to terms with your inner emptiness: recognizing it, not escaping; living through it, not escaping; being through it, not escaping. Then suddenly the emptiness becomes the fullness of life."*

LAO TZU: *"Become totally empty. Quiet the restlessness of the mind. Only then will you realize everything unfolding from restlessness."*

BRUCE LEE: *"The usefulness of the cup is its emptiness."*

OSHO: *"The inner emptiness is the door to God."*

ABRAHAM JOSHUA HESCHEL: *"Prayer begins at the edge of emptiness."*

MEISTER ECKHART: *"To be full of things is to be empty of God; to be empty of things is to be full of God."*

PHILIPPIANS 2:7: *"…but emptied himself, taking the form of a servant, being born in the likeness of men."*

MAX LUCADO: *"When you're full of yourself, God can't fill you. But when you empty yourself, God has a vessel."*

Similar: purposelessness, unmotivated, deflated, lost, forlorn, hopeless, adrift, void
Opposite: inspired, passionate, driven, focused, obsessed, motivated

Encouragement. (1) Expressing support or uplift for the efforts or activities of another. (2) Cheering someone on. *Popular or Heart-Based Usage: (1) Giving someone a shout-out. (2) Talking something up. (3) Helping someone over the hump. (4) Pulling for someone. (5) Giving someone a boost. (6) Rooting for someone. (7) Pumping someone up. (8) Bringing out the best in others. (9) 'Thumbs up!' (10) 'You can do it!' (11) 'Totally legit!' (12) 'You've got this!' (13) 'I'm here for you.' (14) 'Go for it!' (15) 'Now's your time!' (16) 'Bring it!' (17) 'Booyah!' (18) 'You da man!' (19) 'You go girl!' (20) 'Got your back!' (21) 'That's what I'm talkin' about!' (22) 'You do you!' (23) 'Arriba!' (24) 'Bravo!' (25) 'Way to go!' (26) 'Now you're talking!'*

IGNATIUS OF LOYOLA: *"Go forth, and set the world on fire."*

ANATOLE FRANCE, NOBEL: *"Nine tenths of education is encouragement."*

GOETHE: *"Correction does much, but encouragement does more."*

PABLO PICASSO: *"The meaning of life is to find your gift. The purpose of life is to give it away."*

CHARLES M. SCHWAB: *"I consider my ability to arouse enthusiasm among the greatest assets I possess. The way to develop the best that is in a man is by appreciation and encouragement."*

HAROLD S. GENEEN: *"The best way to inspire people to superior performance is to convince them by everything you do and your everyday attitude that you are wholeheartedly supporting them."*

JOEL OSTEEN: *"Encouragement to others is something everyone can give. Somebody needs what you have to give. It may not be your money; it may be your time. It may be your listening ear. It may be your arms to encourage. It may be your smile to uplift. Who knows?"*

EUGENE KENNEDY: *"There would be no need for love if perfection were possible. Love arises from our imperfection, from being different and always in need of the forgiveness, encouragement and that missing half of ourselves that we are searching for, as the Greek myth tells us, to complete ourselves."*

KEVIN BACON: *"A good director creates an environment, which gives the actor the encouragement to fly."*

SCOUTMASTER BILLY JIM VAUGHN: *"We are in the encouragement business."*

WALT WHITMAN: *"Now, Voyager, sail thou forth, to seek and find."*

DR. SEUSS: *"Oh, the Places You'll Go!"*

TOM GORES: *"Take it up a notch."*

Similar: exhortation, uplift, cheering, backing, reassurance, extroversion, support
Opposite: discouragement, jeering, derision, criticism, denunciation, trashing

Enthusiasm. Being convinced about the merits of something, to the point of joining in or enlisting the participation of others. *Popular or Heart-Based Usage: (1) Being a go-getter. (2) Chomping at the bit. (3) Getting pumped up. (4) Being amped up. (5) Being gung ho. (6) Having a gleam in your eye. (7) Getting on board. (8) Drinking the Kool Aid. (9) Poised on the balls of your feet. (10) Getting all lit up. (11) Being rarin' to go. (12) Pressing the pedal to the metal. (13) Jumping in with both feet. (14) Hitting the ground running. (15) Being totally dialed in. (16) Being all over it. (17) Pulling out all the stops. (18) Going to town. (19) Being high-spirited. (20) 'Blowing up.' (21) Going Rambo. (22) Being stoked. (23) 'Ain't no stoppin' us now!' (24) 'Now you're talking!' (25) 'Booyah!' (26) 'Bombs away!' (27) 'Bottoms up!' (28) 'Cheers!' (29) 'I'm so up for that!' (30) 'Let 'er rip!' (31) 'Let's roll!' (32) 'High five!' (33) 'You ain't seen nothin' yet!' (34) 'Game On!' (35) 'I'm all in!' (36) 'Ooh! Yes!' (37) '!!!' (38) 'LFG!' ['Let's Freaking Go!'] (39) 'Let's GOOOOO!'*

PELE: *"Enthusiasm is everything."*
FRED ASTAIRE: *"Do it big, do it right, and do it with style."*
TONY HSIEH: *"Whatever you are thinking, think bigger."*
SAMUEL TAYLOR COLERIDGE: *"Nothing is so contagious as enthusiasm."*
HELEN KELLER: *"Life is either a daring adventure or nothing."*
ADAGE: *"Enthusiasm is the Spirit of God working within you."*
BO BENNETT: *"Enthusiasm is excitement with inspiration, motivation, and a pinch of creativity."*
SIR EDWARD APPLETON: *"I rate enthusiasm even above professional skill."*
SIR EDWARD GEORGE BULWER-LYTTON: *"Enthusiasm is the genius of sincerity, and truth accomplishes no victories without it."*
HENRY DAVID THOREAU: *"None are so old as those who have outlived enthusiasm."*
RALPH WALDO EMERSON: *"Enthusiasm is the mother of effort, and without it nothing great was ever achieved."*
DANNY KAYE: *"Life is a blank canvas and you need to throw all the paint on it you can."*
ANGELA LEE DUCKWORTH, PHD: *"As much as talent counts, effort counts twice."*
DADA VASWANI: *"Enthusiasm is the greatest asset you can possess, for it can take you further than money, power, or influence."*
SIR ISAAC NEWTON, FRS: *"Live your life as an exclamation rather than an explanation."*
JEFF BEZOS: *"Work hard, have fun, and make history."*
ARTHUR BALFOUR: *"Enthusiasm moves the world."*
SIR RICHARD BRANSON: *"Screw it. Let's do it."*

Similar: eagerness, exuberance, fervor, keenness, zest, zealousness, extroversion
Opposite: passive, disinterested, bored, reluctant, introverted, withdrawn, isolated

Envy. [See also **Insecurity, Jealousy,** and **Selfish**] (1) Feeling inferior based on your relative deficiencies in comparison to someone else. (2) Seeking redress or remedy when observing someone else's success. *Popular or Heart-Based Usage: (1) Feeling uncomfortably deficient. (2) Wanting deeply to be in another person's shoes. (3) Being a wannabe. (4) Wanting to keep up with the Joneses. (5) Acting 'all bougie' about something. (6) Wanting to hold someone else back. (7) Wanting to take someone down a peg. (8) Wanting to 'fix somebody's little red wagon.' (9) Wanting to level the playing field. (10) 'Eat your heart out!'*

KERRY SHOOK: *"Envy is not only wanting your grass to be greener than your neighbor's, but also wanting your neighbor's grass to turn brown."*

ECCLESIASTES 4:4: *"Envy … is like chasing the wind."*

PROVERBS 14:30: *"A heart at peace gives life to the body, but envy rots the bones."*

F. DE LA ROCHEFOUCAULD: *"Envy is more irreconcilable than hatred."*

DANISH PROVERB: *"Rust consumes iron and envy consumes itself."*

THOMAS FULLER: *"Nothing sharpens sight like envy."*

SAYING: *"An envious lover can dig deeper than the FBI."*

AESCHYLUS: *"It is in the character of very few men to honor without envy a friend who has prospered."*

SAYING: *"Some people want to see you do good, but never better than them. Remember that."*

WILLIAM HAZLITT: *"Envy is a littleness of soul, which cannot see beyond a certain point, and if it does not occupy the whole space feels itself excluded."*

MARGARET THATCHER: *"The spirit of envy can destroy; it can never build."*

JEAN VANIER: *"Envy comes from people's ignorance of, or lack of belief in, their own gifts."*

JOAN DIDION, PULITZER: *"To cure jealousy is to see it for what it is, a dissatisfaction with self."*

HAROLD COFFIN: *"Envy is the art of counting the other fellow's blessings instead of your own."*

JOHNNY MCGREW: *"Envy is about pushing your belief in God to the back burner."*

APHORISM: *"Don't worry about the people who aren't happy for you. They probably aren't happy for themselves either."*

CHARLEY REESE: *"It is never wise to seek or wish for another's misfortune. If malice or envy were tangible and had a shape, it would be the shape of a boomerang."*

JOE ROGAN: *"Someone else's success does not equal a failure for you."*

PROVERB: *"Run your own race."*

Similar: covetousness, resentment, begrudging, disparagement, self-loathing, separation, alienation

Opposite: friendliness, kindness, liking, support, positivity, inclusion

ESP or Extra Sensory Perception. [See also **Intuition**] Manifesting information, knowledge, and/or communication beyond the traditional physical pathways. *Popular or Heart-Based Usage: (1) Having ESP. (2) Going with your hunches. (3) Discerning patterns/advance pattern recognition. (4) Activating your spider sense. (5) Having your antennae up. (6) Feeling the vibes. (7) Having a strong gut feeling. (8) Using muscle testing. (9) Reading the room. (10) Having second sight. (11) Using your 'third eye.' (12) Remote viewing. (13) Being clairvoyant. (14) Activating your chakras. (15) Kundalini awakening. (16) Being telepathic. (17) Having Siddhi powers. (18) Doing Sufi magic. (19) Performing Jedi mind control. (20) Being a shaman. (21) Pulling an answer out of thin air. (22) Channeling spirits. (23) Talking to dead people. (24) Scrying. (25) Operating on the astral plane. (26) Demonstrating telekinesis. (27) Having a spirit guide. (28) Being a seer or prophet. (29) Being in woo-woo territory. (30) Seeing around corners. (31) Being way out there. (32) In the Twilight Zone. (33) Having a 'sixth sense.'*

AMIT RAY, PHD: *"The reality of you lies much beyond your sensory perceptions and boundaries."*

ALEXIS CARREL, MD, NOBEL: *"Intuition comes very close to clairvoyance; it appears to be the extrasensory perception of reality."*

NIKOLA TESLA: *"If you want to find the secrets of the universe, think in terms of energy, frequency, and vibration."*

DIANE HENNACY POWELL, MD: *"One consistent observation is that psychic phenomena (telepathy, precognition, and clairvoyance) are at their strongest when the earth's magnetic field is at its lowest intensity."*

ALAN TURING, PHD, OBE, FRS: *"These disturbing phenomena [Extra Sensory Perception] seem to deny all our scientific ideas. How we should like to discredit them! ... The statistical evidence, at least for telepathy, is overwhelming."*

J. ROBERT OPPENHEIMER, PHD: *"There are children playing in the streets who could solve some of my top problems in physics, because they have modes of sensory perception that I lost long ago."*

ELIZABETH GOULD DAVIS: *"In ... the twenty-first century, not physical force but spiritual force will lead the way. Mental and spiritual gifts will be more in demand than gifts of a physical nature. Extrasensory perception will take precedence over sensory perception. In this ... women will again dominate."*

D. EARL JOHNSTON: *"What transcends the day-to-day limits of our tedious cause-and-effect world is a universe of unlimited intention, which we know of as God."*

1 CORINTHIANS 12:10: *"To another the working of miracles; to another prophecy; to another discerning of spirits; to another divers kinds of tongues; to another the interpretation of tongues."*

Similar: clairvoyance, divination, prophecy, vision, telepathy, telekinesis, sixth sense
Opposite: sensory, mundane, terrestrial, straightforward, evidence-based

Euphoria. Experiencing peak joys after a success, realization, or transformation. *Popular or Heart-Based Usage: (1) Having a mountaintop experience. (2) Having an out-of-body experience. (3) Feeling the 'runner's high.' (4) Experiencing the thrill of a lifetime. (5) Being over the Moon. (6) Being on Cloud Nine. (7) Sitting on top of the world. (8) Dancing on the ceiling. (9) Dancing in the streets. (10) Being unspeakably happy. (11) 'The greatest feeling you'll ever know.' (12) Visiting the land of endorphins. (13) 'I did it!' (14) 'Hallelujah!' (15) 'Words fail me.' (16) 'It's a miracle come true!' (17) 'Nirvana!' (18) 'Seventh Heaven!'*

LINCOLN STOREY: *"Euphoria is earned joy. Nobody can take it away from you."*

LAILAH GIFTY AKITA: *"The excitement of dreams coming true is beyond the description of words."*

NIKOLA TESLA: *"I do not think there is any thrill that can go through the human heart like that felt by the inventor as he sees some creation of the brain unfolding to success ... such emotions make a man forget food, sleep, friends, love, everything."*

ANTHONY KIEDIS: *"You can't buy it, you can't get it on a street corner, you can't steal it or inject it or shove it up your (rear), you have to earn it."*

ERNEST HEMINGWAY, PULITZER, NOBEL: *"Live the full life of the mind, exhilarated by new ideas, intoxicated by the romance of the unusual."*

GEORGE SOROS: *"The same thing applies to me as to everybody else, so I'm given to euphoria and despair. And I would say that I basically have survived by recognizing my mistakes."*

JAMES REDFIELD: *"The true, or higher part of the self is aways seeking the state that mystics talk about, the state in which we are filled with a universal love and a peaceful euphoria."*

VENUS WILLIAMS: *"But at the end, when it's done, I feel euphoric. I'm like, 'Yes, the work is done.' You just feel like a glowing feeling inside.'"*

JARED PADALECKI: *"There are no words to describe the euphoria you feel when your baby recognizes you for the first time and smiles."*

JOHNNY MCGREW: *"Muffled euphoria can be a very suitable emotional response when your mother-in-law announces she has postponed her visit by a year."*

WARREN BUFFETT: *"When investing, pessimism is your friend, euphoria the enemy."*

TORI AMOS: *"Being in your forties—any woman who isn't there yet, I just have to say to you: Euphoria is coming to you."*

D. EARL JOHNSTON: *"You are never more than one thought or realization away from your breakthrough."*

BILL WATTERSON: *"Happiness isn't good enough for me! I demand euphoria!"*

Similar: exhilaration, bliss, elation, jubilation, ecstasy, joy
Opposite: discouragement, sadness, sorrow, dejection, self-pity, failure, withdrawal

Evil. Promoting the least amount of good and/or the most amount of harm or fear within a situation. *Popular or Heart-Based Usage: (1) Falling for temptation. (2) Taking the bait. (3) Getting it twisted. (4) Knowing it's wrong. (5) Looking the other way. (6) Sympathy for the Devil. (7) Moving to the Dark Side. (8) Abandoning your true purpose. (9) Playing the short game. (10) Selling your soul. (11) Opening your portal to Hell. (12) Hanging with vampires. (13) Wearing a black hat. (14) 'Just this once. Who cares. Do it.' (15) 'Take the cash.' (16) The Devil's bid. (17) Living in fear. (18) 'Here comes trouble.'*

JOSEPH CONRAD: *"The belief in a supernatural source of evil is not necessary. Men are quite capable of every wickedness."*

ALBERT EINSTEIN, PHD, NOBEL: *"God did not create evil. Just as darkness is the absence of light, evil is the absence of God."*

W. H. AUDEN: *"Evil is unspectacular and always human, and shares our bed and eats at our own table."*

WOODY ALLEN: *"There are two types of people in this world: good and bad. The good sleep better, but the bad seem to enjoy the waking hours much more."*

ALEKSANDR SOLZHENITSYN: *"The battleline between good and evil runs through the heart of every man."*

M. SCOTT PECK: *"Evil people hate the light because it reveals themselves to themselves. They will destroy the light, the goodness, the love, in order to avoid the pain of self-awareness."*

MOSES: *"See, I have set before you this day life and good, death and evil…I have set before you life and death, blessing and curse; therefore choose life."*

PYTHAGORAS: *"The most momentous thing in human life is winning the soul to good or evil."*

DAN PEARCE: *"People who love themselves don't hurt other people. The more we hate ourselves, the more we want others to suffer."*

LINCOLN STOREY: *"True evil intends to draw you in, twist you up in doubt and confusion, and then have you voluntarily give up your best hopes and dreams."*

HEINRICH ZSCHOKKE: *"Evil is in antagonism with the entire creation."*

MACHIAVELLI: *"You will always find people willing to be deceived."*

DEVIL: *"Such a sweet surprise. They never see me coming."*

D. EARL JOHNSTON: *"Trouble shows up, often disguised as something attractive."*

JOHNNY MCGREW: *"If Satan really exists, his game is to plant seeds of doubt and to fertilize them with piles of cash."*

PLATO: *"Ignorance, the root and stem of all evil."*

PERCY BYSSHE SHELLEY: *"Sometimes the Devil is a gentleman."*

JERRY GARCIA: *"Constantly choosing the lesser of two evils is still choosing evil."*

MIGUEL DE CERVANTES: *"God bears with the wicked, but not forever."*

Similar: malevolence, immorality, bad, demonic, degenerate, anti-social, harmful
Opposite: decent, upright, helpful, benevolent, auspicious, wonderful

Excitement. (1) Having intense interest in or focus on developing events. (2) Stirring up. *Popular or Heart-Based Usage: (1) Looking forward. (2) 'What's the fuss?' (3) Life in the front row. (4) Being on the edge of your seat. (5) Rubbing your hands together. (6) Holding your breath. (7) Having your pupils dilate. (8) Your eyes lighting up. (9) Getting goosebumps. (10) Feeling the buzz. (11) Being on pins and needles. (12) Having your heart in your throat. (13) Being riveted. (14) Getting hyper about something. (15) Spine-tingling. (16) Heart-stopping. (17) 'What's all the commotion?' (18) Getting lit up by something. (19) Watching a 'barnburner.' (20) Getting amped up. (21) Going bonkers. (22) Chomping at the bit. (23) Going gangbusters. (24) Having an electric atmosphere. (25) Ginning it up. (26) 'It's the Bomb!' (27) 'Whoa, doggies!' (28) 'Just look at this!' (29) 'Holy Toledo!' (30) 'Are you kidding me?' (31) 'Can't sleep!' (32) 'Get out of town!' (33) 'It's the real deal!' (34) "It's going down!' (35) 'Epic!' (36) 'That's what I'm talkin' about!' (37) 'I'm so hype!' (38) 'Yabba dabba doo!' (39) 'Mo bettah!' (40) 'Dope!' (41) 'I'm all in!' (42) 'I'm up for that!' (43) 'I'm down for that!' (44) 'And now. The envelope, please!'*

> ADAGE: *"Excitement is where the action is."*
>
> JOHNNY MCGREW: *"Excitement is the vapor trail my wife leaves when she hears about a half-off sale an hour before the store closes."*
>
> ABRAHAM HICKS: *"If you're not excited about it, it's not the right path."*
>
> ANDY WARHOL: *"The idea of waiting for something makes it more exciting."*
>
> CATE BLANCHETT: *"If I had my way, if I was lucky enough, if I could be on the brink my entire life—that great sense of expectation and excitement without the disappointment—that would be the perfect state."*
>
> LINCOLN STOREY: *"Real excitement is seeing yourself in the game, where the thrill of winning can quickly shift to an edgy fear of losing. Excitement is uncertainty, putting yourself in the arena, relying on your wits, and seeing what comes."*
>
> ERNEST HEMINGWAY, PULITZER, NOBEL: *"Live the full life of the mind, exhilarated by new ideas, intoxicated by the romance of the unusual."*
>
> TAYLOR CALDWELL: *"Learning should be a joy and full of excitement. It is life's greatest adventure; it is an illustrated excursion into the minds of the noble and the learned."*
>
> D. H. LAWRENCE: *"If it doesn't absorb you, if it isn't any fun, don't do it."*
>
> SIR BRIAN MAY: *"The guitar has a kind of grit and excitement possessed by nothing else."*
>
> LYNNE MCTAGGART: *"The excitement that science possesses is its ability to answer the big questions."*
>
> CRISS JAMI: *"Excitement is a crossroad which runs in all directions."*
>
> JOHNNY MCGREW: *"Excitement is what's new and different. It's what brings back the eager kid in us."*

Similar: interest, eagerness, anticipation, captivation, animation
Opposite: disinterest, passivity, stillness, calm, inactivity, boredom, self-absorption

Expectation. Anticipating or believing that something will happen. *Popular or Heart-Based Usage: (1) Looking forward to something. (2) Setting the bar. (3) Being on the balls of your feet. (4) Being primed and ready. (5) Waiting with bated breath. (6) Having high hopes. (7) 'That's what I'm talking about!' (8) 'Wait for it!'*

COACH GARY FRANKE: *"Need a little more from you."*

SAM WALTON: *"High expectations are the key to everything."*

ABRAHAM HICKS: *"Expectation is where desire intersects belief."*

JOHNNY MCGREW: *"Expect little from others and appreciate every surprise."*

ANTHONY ROBBINS: *"Change your expectation for appreciation and the world changes instantly."*

ANNE BANCROFT: *"The best way to get most husbands to do something is to suggest that perhaps they're too old to do it."*

APHORISM: *"Where there are no expectations, there are no disappointments."*

ANDRES GODIN: *"The quality of our expectations determines the quality of our actions."*

RITA LEVI-MONTALCINI, MD, NOBEL: *"My experience in childhood and adolescence of the subordinate role played by the female in a society run entirely by men had convinced me that I was not cut out to be a wife."*

JOHN KENNETH GALBRAITH: *"In the United States, though power corrupts, the expectation of power paralyzes."*

BARRY SCHWARTZ, PHD: *"The secret of happiness is low expectations."*

WILLIAM SHAKESPEARE: *"Expectation is the root of all heartache."*

ALCOHOLICS ANONYMOUS: *"Expectations are premeditated resentments."*

BENJAMIN FRANKLIN: *"Keep your eyes wide open before marriage, half shut afterwards."*

PROVERB: *"Hope for the best and prepare for the worst."*

Similar: anticipation, presumption, presupposition, assumption, hope
Opposite: dismissal, denial, dread, disinterest, disregard

Failure. (1) Experiencing a lack of success. (2) Missing a goal. *Popular or Heart-Based Usage: (1) Falling short. (2) Missing the mark. (3) Going off the rails. (4) Screwing up. (5) Goofing up. (6) Going nowhere fast. (7) Getting a beat-down. (8) 'Things went south.' (9) Drilling a dry hole. (10) Going back to the drawing board. (11) Going over like a lead balloon. (12) Being a huge waste of time. (13) Being a dud. (14) 'Uh-oh.' (15) Stuck behind the 8-ball. (16) Circling the drain. (17) Being a flop. (18) Going belly up. (19) Being a duster. (20) Being a clunker. (21) Being a non-starter. (22) Doing a face plant. (23) Not cutting the mustard. (24) Taking it smack on the chin. (25) 'DNF.' (Did Not Finish.) (26) 'DSQ.' (Disqualified.) (27) Taking an incomplete. (28) Flunking. (29) Taking the L.*

JOHN WOODEN: *"Failure isn't fatal, but failure to change might be."*

THOMAS J. WATSON: *"If you want to increase your success rate, double your failure rate."*

HENRY FORD: *"Failure is the opportunity to begin again, more intelligently."*

W. C. FIELDS: *"If at first you don't succeed, try, try again. Then quit. There's no point being a damn fool about it."*

OPRAH WINFREY: *"There is no such thing as failure. Failure is just life trying to move us in another direction."*

SUMNER REDSTONE: *"Success is not built on success. It is built on failure. It is built on frustration. Sometimes it is built on catastrophe."*

RICK PITINO: *"Failure is good. It's fertilizer. Everything I've learned about coaching, I've learned from making mistakes."*

MICHAEL JORDAN: *"I have missed more than 9,000 shots in my career. I've lost almost 300 games. 26 times I've been trusted to take the game winning shot and missed. I've failed over and over and over again in my life. And that is why I succeed."*

HENRY DAVID THOREAU: *"Men are born to succeed, not to fail."*

NELSON MANDELA, NOBEL: *"You either win or you learn."*

SIR WINSTON CHURCHILL: *"Success is not final; failure is not fatal: it is the courage to continue that counts."*

TOP COACHES AND ATHLETES: *"Success means keeping focus and having a short memory. You cannot dwell on your mistakes. The next play is happening now."*

ELON MUSK: *"When I started SpaceX I thought that the most likely outcome was failure. And I think to have any other expectation would have been irrational."*

ALBERT EINSTEIN, PHD, NOBEL: *"Failure is success in progress."*

GEN. GEORGE S. PATTON, JR.: *"Success is how high you bounce when you hit bottom."*

AUNG SAN SUU KYI NOBEL: *"Saints, it has been said, are the sinners who go on trying."*

APHORISM: *"Dust yourself off, get back on your horse, and ride."*

Similar: loss, defeat, falling short, nonperformance, collapse
Opposite: success, accomplishment, triumph, achievement

Faith. (1) Maintaining guiding principles, and often despite the absence of significant supporting evidence. (2) Consciously believing in something. *Popular or Heart-Based Usage: (1) Having core values. (2) Following a creed. (3) Believing in your heart. (4) Hearing a call. (5) Bringing the Kingdom. (6) 'The substance of things unseen.' (7) 'Semper Fi.' (8) 'In God We Trust.'*

WILLIAM WORDSWORTH: *"Faith is a passionate intuition."*

KAHLIL GIBRAN: *"Faith is a knowledge within the heart, beyond reach of proof."*

CLAIRE LONDON: *"Just because you can't see it doesn't mean it isn't there."*

RALPH WALDO EMERSON: *"All I have seen teaches me to trust the Creator for all I have not seen."*

D. EARL JOHNSTON: *"A short list of invisible things which are part of our daily lives: Gravity, radio waves, X-rays, the past, the future, our emotions, our values, our next breath, and God."*

SIR ISAAC NEWTON, FRS: *"Gravity explains the motions of the planets, but it cannot explain who sets the planets in motion."*

JEREMIAH 31:33: *"After those days, saith the LORD, I will put my law in their inward parts, and write it in their hearts; and will be their God, and they shall be my people."*

MATTHEW 17:20: *"If ye have faith as a grain of mustard seed, ye shall say unto this mountain, Remove hence to yonder place; and it shall remove; and nothing shall be impossible to you."*

HEBREWS 11:1: *"Now faith is the substance of things hoped for, the evidence of things not seen."*

SMITH WIGGLESWORTH: *"I am moved only by what I believe."*

DENIS WAITLEY: *"Belief is the ignition switch that gets you off the launching pad."*

GERMANY KENT: *"Faith in God will elevate you to next level blessings."*

MAHATMA GANDHI: *"Faith is not something to be grasped, it is a state to grow into."*

THE REV. LAURENS A. HALL, DD: *"By faith in God in Christ, when faced with doubt, reason thoroughly and go forth boldly."*

JOEL OSTEEN: *"Faith is not of the mind; faith is of the heart."*

MIGUEL DE UNAMUNO: *"Faith which does not doubt is dead faith."*

VOLTAIRE: *"Faith consists in believing when it is beyond the power of reason to believe."*

FRANK GAINES: *"Only he who can see the invisible can do the impossible."*

ANTOINE DE SAINT-EXUPERY: *"What is essential is invisible to the eye."*

ALBERT EINSTEIN: *"The more I study science, the more I believe in God."*

JOSIAH IDOWU-FEARON: *"Doubt is the prelude to great faith."*

Similar: confidence, trust, conviction, allegiance, reliance, constancy
Opposite: disbelief, disregard, denial, agnosticism, rejection, treachery

Fear. (1) Having heightened concerns about pending danger, pain, or loss. (2) Reacting to a threat, including anxiety, introversion, and withdrawal. *Popular or Heart-Based Usage: (1) Getting queasy. (2) Having a sinking feeling. (3) Having deep misgivings. (4) Getting cold feet. (5) Getting tense. (6) Wimping out. (7) Hiding out. (8) Feeling imprisoned by emotion. (9) Having a pit in your stomach. (10) Having a phobia. (11) Dreading it. (12) Being grip-less. (13) Having a panic attack. (14) Having sweaty palms. (15) Getting cold sweats. (16) Being white-knuckled. (17) Being in 'fight or flight' mode.*

GERMAN PROVERB: *"Fear makes the wolf bigger than he is."*

WALL STREET ADAGE: *"Fear sells."*

D. EARL JOHNSTON: *"Fear shrinks our horizons."*

GAMBLING ADAGE: *"Scared money always loses."*

ARISTOTLE: *"Fear is pain rising from the anticipation of evil."*

MAHATMA GANDHI: *"The enemy is fear. We think it is hate; but it is really fear."*

FLORENCE NIGHTINGALE: *"How little can be done under the spirit of fear."*

EMMET FOX: *"Whenever you are afraid of something you are worshipping it. Whatever you fear, you bow down to and give it power."*

JILL BOLTE TAYLOR, PHD: *"My favorite definition of fear is: False Expectations Appearing Real."*

UNIVERSITY OF ROCHESTER MEDICAL CENTER: *"Fear hormones are secreted by the adrenal gland, an endocrine gland located on top of your kidneys."*

OSHO: *"The greatest fear in the world is of the opinions of others. And the moment you are unafraid of the crowd, you are no longer a sheep, you become a lion."*

MARIE CURIE, PHD, NOBEL (2X): *"Nothing in life is to be feared. It is only to be understood."*

ROBERT LOUIS STEVENSON: *"Keep your fears to yourself, but share your courage with others."*

AUNG SAN SUU KYI, NOBEL: *"The only real prison is fear, and the only real freedom is freedom from fear."*

JOHNNY MCGREW: *"Worship God = live in love; Follow the Devil = live in fear."*

HILLARY CLINTON: *"Fear is always with us, but we just don't have time for it."*

PROVERBS 9:10: *"Fear of the Lord is the beginning of wisdom."*

SIR WINSTON CHURCHILL: *"Fear is a reaction. Courage is a decision."*

JAMES RUSSELL LOWELL: *"Fate loves the fearless."*

JOAN OF ARC: *"I fear nothing for God is with me."*

SETH GODIN, BS, MBA: *"The enemy of fear is creativity."*

JON ACUFF: *"Fear gets a voice, but not a vote."*

DANIEL J. SIEGEL, MD: *"Name it to tame it."*

OSHO: *"Life begins where fear ends."*

Similar: terror, fright, tense, alarm, panic, dread
Opposite: assurance, calmness, confidence, serenity

Flirtation. Making (or pretending) overtures of romantic interest toward another person. *Popular or Heart-Based Usage: (1) Playing coy. (2) Initiating eye contact. (3) Batting your eyelashes. (4) Fixing your hair. (5) Dropping a hint (or a handkerchief). (6) Bumping into someone 'accidentally on purpose.' (7) Catching someone's eye. (8) Deliberately ignoring someone for effect. (9) Making sure to mispronounce their name. (10) Pretending interest in someone else. (11) Playing the field. (12) Chasing skirts. (13) 'Are you from around here?' (14) 'Haven't we met somewhere before?' (15) 'Don't I know you?'*

SOPHIA LOREN: *"A woman's dress should be like a barbed-wire fence; serving its purpose without obstructing the view."*

CHARLOTTE BRONTE: *"Flirting is a woman's trade. One must keep in practice."*

ANNA HELD: *"I think the eyes flirt most. There are so many ways to use them."*

JOYCE JILLSON: *"There are times not to flirt. When you're sick. When you're with children. When you're on the witness stand."*

HONORE DE BALZAC: *"I can no longer think of anything but you. In spite of myself, my imagination carries me to you. I grasp you, I kiss you, I caress you, a thousand of the most amorous caresses take possession of me."*

CHARLES MAURICE DE TALLEYRAND-PERIGORD: *"In order to avoid being called a flirt, she always yielded easily."*

HELEN ROWLAND: *"Flirting is the gentle art of making a man feel pleased with himself."*

HELEN ROWLAND: *"A wise woman puts a grain of sugar into everything she says to a man, and takes a grain of salt with everything he says to her."*

APHORISM: *"Flirt: When you fall for someone's words. Lust: When you fall for someone's body. Love: When you fall for someone's soul."*

TEENAGER: *"Oops I just lost my cell number. Could I have yours?"*

COLLEGE STUDENT: *"You remind me of my next girlfriend."*

DOLLY PARTON: *"Yeah I flirt. I'm not blind and I'm not dead!"*

JOHN RAY: *"Beauty is power; a smile is its sword."*

Similar: courting, teasing, coyness, toying, playfulness, dallying
Opposite: commitment, constancy, faithfulness, steadfastness

Focus. [See **Attention, Concentration,** and **Intention**]

Foolish. (1) Failing to use common sense or good judgment. (2) Pursuing an act or idea without having sufficient facts, experience, or knowledge. *Popular or Heart-Based Usage: (1) Being a blockhead / ding-a-ling / dope / dolt / idiot / nerd / nitwit / jackass. (2) Not using your head. (3) Being scatter-brained. (4) Running around on a wild goose chase. (5) Being a few bricks shy of a load. (6) Being a lost ball in high weeds. (7) Being a bumpkin. (8) Having an elevator that does not go all the way to the top. (9) Not being the sharpest knife in the drawer. (10) Leading with your chin. (11) Kidding yourself. (12) 'Yo. So just hold my beer and watch this.' (13) Leaping before you look. (14) Being an airhead. (15) Getting sucked in. (16) Falling for ruses. (17) Being highly suggestible.*

GEORGE BERNARD SHAW: *"I learned long ago, never to wrestle with a pig. You get dirty, and besides, the pig likes it."*
CZECH ADAGE: *"The fool never undertakes little."*
JAPANESE PROVERB: *"Fools and scissors require good handling."*
MAORI PROVERB: *"Only the fool visits the land of the cannibals."*
SAYING: *"For some people the elevator doesn't go all the way to the top."*
ALEXANDER POPE: *"Fools rush in where angels fear to tread."*
DOGEN ZENJI: *"A fool sees himself as another, but a wise man sees others as himself."*
ROBERTSON DAVIES: *"Only a fool expects to be happy all the time."*
MARK TWAIN: *"Never argue with a fool. Onlookers may not be able to tell the difference."*
SØREN KIERKEGAARD: *"There are two ways to be fooled; One is to believe what isn't true, the other is to refuse to believe what is true."*
PROVERB: *"A fool starts in certainty and ends in doubt, while a wise man starts in doubt and ends in certainty."*
ADAGE: *"Fool me once, shame on you. Fool me twice, shame on me."*
ANATOLE FRANCE, NOBEL: *"If fifty million people say a foolish thing, it is still a foolish thing."*
GEORGE DAVID WEISS, HUGO PERETTI, LUIGI CREATORE: *"Can't Help Falling in Love"* (Song)
JOHNNY MERCER, RUBE BLOOM: *"Fools Rush In"* (Song)
PYTHAGORAS: *"A fool is known by his speech, and a wise man by silence."*
DIOGENES: *"I know nothing, except the fact of my ignorance."*
JOHNNY MCGREW: *"God does not suffer fools either. He wants us to be wise. Follow your heart but by all means first put your brain in gear."*
P. T. BARNUM: *"This Way to the Egress."* (Circus Sign)

Similar: gullible, thoughtless, suggestible, ignorant, stupid, untethered, ungrounded
Opposite: confident, focused, thoughtful, measured, analytical, aware

Forgiveness. Abandoning upset or resentment over a past issue. *Popular or Heart-Based Usage: (1) Putting something behind you. (2) Letting bygones be bygones. (3) Letting it go. (4) Wishing someone well. (5) Getting over it. (6) Smoking the peace pipe. (7) Settling your differences. (8) Dropping it. (9) Calling off the dogs. (10) 'Kiss and make up.' (11) Releasing it. (12) Blotting it out. (13) 'No need to keep score.' (14) 'Go easy on me.' (15) 'All that doesn't matter any more.' (16) 'I'm moving on.' (17) Turning the page.*

JOHN F. KENNEDY: *"Forgive your enemies, but never forget their names."*

LEWIS B. SMEDES: *"To forgive is to set a prisoner free and discover that the prisoner was you."*

GERALD JAMPOLSKY: *"I can have peace of mind only when I can forgive rather than judge."*

SUZANNE SOMERS: *"Forgiveness is a gift you give yourself."*

FRANCIS OF ASSISI: *"It is in pardoning that we are pardoned."*

MARTIN LUTHER KING, JR., NOBEL: *"He who is devoid of the power to forgive is devoid of the capacity to love."*

RUTH GRAHAM: *"A happy marriage is the union of two good forgivers."*

SAYING: *"Forgiveness doesn't mean you excuse the crime. It just means you're no longer willing to be the victim."*

ALBERT ELLIS, PHD: *"To err is human; to forgive people and yourself for poor behavior is to be sensible and realistic."*

MAHATMA GANDHI: *"The weak can never forgive. Forgiveness is the attribute of the strong."*

D. EARL JOHNSTON: *"Withholding forgiveness can be your attempt to imprison someone else behind bars of mistake, guilt, or hatred. But those prison bars you build in silence, and your ego tightly grips the key."*

LOUIS ZAMPERINI: *"Forgiveness has to be complete. If you hate somebody, it's like a boomerang that misses its target and comes back and hits you in the head."*

F. DE LA ROCHEFOUCAULD: *"We pardon to the extent that we love."*

WILLIAM BLAKE: *"It is easier to forgive an enemy than to forgive a friend."*

CHAIM HERZOG: *"I do not bring forgiveness with me, nor forgetfulness. The only ones who can forgive are dead; the living have no right to forget."*

THOMAS SZASZ: *"The stupid neither forgive nor forget; the naïve forgive and forget; the wise forgive but never forget."*

REV. COLIN NEWTON: *"Forgiveness is a consciousness expanding practice."*

ALEXANDER POPE: *"To err is human; to forgive, divine."*

JOHNNY CASH: *"When God forgave me, I figured I'd better do it too."*

HO'OPONOPONO PRAYER: *"I'm sorry, please forgive me; thank you, I love you."*

LES BROWN: *"Forgive yourself first."*

Similar: pardoning, condoning, exculpation, exoneration, absolution, resetting
Opposite: condemn, accuse, blame, censure, harboring, judging

Frequency. [See also **Electromagnetism** and **Gravity**] (1) A measurement of energy in the physical universe. (2) How often things happen. (3) Measuring the number of waves passing a point in a unit of time, such as wave cycles per second (also known as *hertz*). *Popular or Heart-Based Usage: (1) How energy manifests in waves. (2) Recognizing the cycles of the universe. (3) Tuning in. (4) Feeling the vibes. (5) Hearing the musical scales. (6) Distinguishing the 88 piano keys. (7) Adjusting the pitch. (8) Feeling the thrum of bass notes. (9) Seeing the colors of the rainbow (e.g., violet is the highest frequency). (10) Monitoring the radio. (11) Broadcasting, transmission, reception. (12) Understanding planetary orbits. (13) 'Music of the spheres.' (14) Feeling gravity. (15) Cycling energy.*

NIKOLA TESLA: *"If you want to find the secrets of the universe, think in terms of energy, frequency and vibration."*

ALBERT EINSTEIN, PHD, NOBEL (attributed): *"Everything is energy and that's all there is to it. Match the frequency of the reality you want and you cannot help but get that reality. It can be no other way. This is not philosophy. This is physics."*

DR. JOE DISPENZA: *"Every thought has a frequency."*

FREDERICK LENZ, PHD: *"Every living being is psychic. Whether or not we are consciously aware of it, we feel vibrations and energies coming to us from other people all the time. The vast majority of the thoughts you think and the emotions you feel aren't your own."*

CLINT EASTWOOD: *"I've had moments when I've thought about somebody, picked up the phone to call them and they are on the line already, and I think that maybe there's some vibration, some connection."*

JOHN COLTRANE: *"One positive thought produces millions of positive vibrations."*

ALBERT EINSTEIN, PHD, NOBEL: *"Concerning matter, we have been all wrong. What we have called matter is energy, whose vibration has been so lowered as to be perceptible to the senses. There is no matter."*

JACK CANFIELD, PHD: *"Remember that your thoughts are the primary cause of everything. So when you think a sustained thought it is immediately sent out into the Universe. That thought magnetically attaches itself to the like frequency, and then within seconds sends the reading of that frequency back to you through your feelings."*

NIKOLA TESLA: *"Our entire biological system, the brain, and the Earth itself, work on the same frequencies."*

RHONDA BYRNE: *"The feeling of love is the highest frequency you can emit. The greater the love you feel and emit, the greater the power you are harnessing."*

PAM GREGORY: *"We need to become masters of frequency and energy."*

ALAN COHEN, MA: *"God is a frequency. Stay tuned."*

Similar: pulsation, beat, oscillation, wavelength, timing, periodicity, harmonics
Opposite: random, chaotic, disjointed, separate, infrequent, haphazard, staccato

Friendship. Enjoying each other's presence and spirit in mutual trust and support. *Popular or Heart-Based Usage: (1) Being close. (2) Being buddies/pals. (3) Hitting it off with someone. (4) Being a wingman. (5) Being a sidekick. (6) Having an alter ego. (7) Looking out for each other. (8) Getting along. (9) Being tight. (10) Being on the same wavelength. (11) Having good chemistry. (12) Couchsurfing together. (13) Coming alongside. (14) Standing shoulder to shoulder. (15) Hanging out. (16) Having a bromance. (17) Being a 'bro.' (18) 'BFFs.' ('Best Friends Forever.') (19) 'Bottoms up!' (20) 'Rolling in the deep.' (21) 'I've got your back.' (22) 'I'm here for you.' (23) Showing up.*

WALT WHITMAN: *"I no doubt deserved my enemies, but I don't believe I deserved my friends."*

DONNA ROBERTS: *"A friend is someone who knows the song in your heart, and can sing it back to you when you have forgotten the words."*

ALBERT CAMUS: *"Don't walk behind me; I may not lead. Don't walk in front of me; I may not follow. Just walk beside me and be my friend."*

BENJAMIN FRANKLIN: *"Be slow in choosing a friend, slower in changing."*

THOMAS AQUINAS: *"There is nothing on this earth more to be prized than true friendship."*

ARISTOTLE: *"A friend is a second self."*

BETTY GRECO SHER: *"You know you are best friends when you can be totally happy doing nothing together."*

DANISH PROVERB: *"The road to a friend's house is never long."*

MURRAY BURNETT, JOAN ALISON: *"Louis, I think this is the start of a beautiful friendship."*

PROVERB: *"Friends listen to what you say. Best friends listen to what you don't say."*

EPICTETUS: *"The key is to keep company only with people who uplift you, whose presence calls forth your very best."*

PEGGY NOONAN: *"Candor is a compliment; it implies equality. It's how true friends talk."*

D. EARL JOHNSTON: *"Your closest friends will always remember your heart."*

HEBREW PROVERB: *"Who is mighty? He who makes an enemy into a friend."*

WALTER WINCHELL: *"A real friend is one who walks in when the rest of the world walks out."*

STEFANIE MARRONE: *"A frenemy is someone masquerading as your friend."*

ADAGE: *"Keep your friends close and your enemies even closer."*

PROVERB: *"Not everyone who smiles at you is your friend."*

RALPH WALDO EMERSON: *"To have a friend, be a friend."*

ARISTOTLE: *"The antidote for fifty enemies is one friend."*

Similar: affinity, rapport, buddies, attachment, companionship
Opposite: enmity, antagonism, incompatibility

Frustration. Experiencing delay, blockage, or a repeated lack of success in the pursuit of a goal. *Popular or Heart-Based Usage: (1) Beating your head into a wall. (2) Spinning your wheels. (3) Feeling bottled up. (4) Having things go sideways. (5) Gnashing your teeth. (6) Venting your spleen. (7) Being caught in the rat race/stuck on the hamster wheel. (8) Living through another 'Groundhog Day.' (9) Pounding sand. (10) Being stuck in neutral. (11) 'Life in the slow lane'/encountering another detour/pounding the steering wheel. (12) 'Nothing to see here. Move along.' (13) 'Hurry up and wait.' (14) 'What a crock!' (15) 'Give me a break.' (16) 'WTF.' ['What the f***.'] (17) 'Same old same old.' (18) Grinding away at life. (19) Getting nowhere.*

ECKHART TOLLE: *"When something gets in your way, it is still the way."*

TOM BODETT: *"The difference between school and life? In school, you're taught a lesson and then given a test. In life, you're given a test that teaches you a lesson."*

ALBERT EINSTEIN, PHD, NOBEL: *"Insanity is doing the same thing over and over again and expecting different results."*

ANTONIO BANDERAS: *"Expectation is the mother of all frustration."*

MEISTER ECKHART: *"When you are thwarted, it is your own attitude that is out of order."*

LEE IACOCCA: *"In times of great stress or adversity, it's always best to keep busy, to plow your anger and your energy into something positive."*

GILLIAN MICHAELS: *"Whenever I've had a rough day, I like to pour my frustration into my workouts."*

BEYONCE KNOWLES: *"My way of dealing with frustration is to sit down and to think and speak logically."*

H. HILL MCALISTER: *"On most days, rough or not, I pour some frustration reliever into a small glass, with ice."*

RICK WARREN: *"A sense of humor is God's antidote for anger and frustration."*

RYAN HOLIDAY: *"The Obstacle is the Way"* (Book)

PROVERB: *"When God closes a door, he opens a window."*

HELEN KELLER: *"When one door closes, another opens. But often we look so long, so regretfully, upon the closed door, that we fail to see the one that is opened for us."*

Similar: delay, exasperation, annoyance, vexation, hindrance, obstacle, detour
Opposite: success, satisfaction, breakthrough, streamline, fast tracking

Generosity. Sharing or providing support to others in voluntary and meaningful ways. *Popular or Heart-Based Usage: (1) Having a big heart. (2) Giving someone a helping hand. (3) Noblesse oblige. (4) Being a giver and not a taker. (5) Being a good sport. (6) Being a volunteer. (7) Stepping up for others. (8) Pulling strings to help someone. (9) Making something possible for others. (10) Giving back.*

SIVANANDA: *"Giving is the secret of abundance."*

LEONARD NIMOY: *"The miracle is this: the more we share the more we have."*

FRANK A. CLARK: *"Real generosity is doing something nice for someone who will never find out."*

C. S. LEWIS: *"The only things we can keep are the things we freely give to God."*

MARTHA ALTER HINES: *"Please release the idea that giving means giving from lack."*

ADAGE: *"Your time is the greatest gift you can give someone."*

AESOP: *"No act of kindness no matter how small is ever wasted."*

MATTHEW 6:4: *"That thine alms may be in secret; and thy Father which seeth in secret himself shall reward thee openly."*

MAYA ANGELOU: *"I have found that among its other benefits, giving liberates the soul of the giver."*

ARIANNA HUFFINGTON: *"Be a go-giver, not a go-getter."*

ALLAN LOKOS: *"It is a powerful practice to be generous when you are the one feeling in need."*

JOEL OSTEEN: *"We need to be willing to be interrupted and inconvenienced if it means we can help meet someone's needs."*

SIR WINSTON CHURCHILL: *"We make a living by what we get, but we make a life by what we give."*

CONFUCIUS: *"Benevolence is the characteristic element of humanity."*

WALT WHITMAN: *"The gift is to the giver, and comes back most to him—it cannot fail."*

H. HILL MCALISTER: *"Giving and abundance walk the same road holding hands."*

SETH GODIN, BS, MBA: *"Your generosity is more important than your perfection."*

ADAGE: *"When we do things to help mankind, we help ourselves."*

IGNATIUS OF LOYOLA: *"To give and not to count the cost."*

ANNE FRANK: *"No one has ever become poor by giving."*

GAELIC PROVERB: *"A thing is bigger for being shared."*

JIM MCINGVALE: *"The essence of living is giving."*

Similar: magnanimity, consideration, benevolence, hospitality, charity, largesse
Opposite: greedy, inconsiderate, stingy, miserly, self-absorbed

Genius. (1) Creating, achieving, or doing something innovative or extraordinary, and often with limited instruction. (2) Having rare vision or insight. *Popular or Heart-Based Usage: (1) Being an Einstein. (2) Making hard stuff look easy. (3) Having the chops to get something difficult done. (4) Solving what nobody else has solved. (5) Creating a new paradigm. (6) Being in a class of one.*

SIR BERNARD WILLIAMS: *"Talent is a flame. Genius is a fire."*

NIKOLA TESLA: *"Imagination is the life force of the genius code."*

ARISTOTLE: *"There is no great genius without some touch of madness."*

ADAGE: *"Genius is comprehension without instruction."*

DAVID R. HAWKINS, MD, PHD: *"Genius is confused with a high IQ. This is a gross misunderstanding … Genius is an extraordinarily high degree of savvy in a given area of human activity."*

THOMAS EDISON: *"Genius is 99% perspiration and 1% inspiration."*

GEN. GEORGE S. PATTON, JR.: *"Never tell people how to do things. Tell them what to do and they will surprise you with their ingenuity."*

CHARLES KETTERING: *"A problem well stated is a problem half solved."*

MICHELANGELO: *"Every block of stone has a sculpture inside it, and it is the job of the sculptor to discover it."*

OSHO: *"Creativity is the greatest rebellion in existence."*

MARGARET FULLER: *"The especial genius of women I take to be electrical in movement, intuitive in function, spiritual in tendency."*

MINNA ANTRIM: *"To know one's self is wisdom, but to know one's neighbor is genius."*

R. BUCKMINSTER FULLER: *"Everyone is born a genius, but the process of living de-geniuses them."*

ALBERT EINSTEIN, PHD, NOBEL: *"Everybody is a genius. But if you judge a fish by its ability to climb a tree, it will live its whole life believing it is stupid."*

WILLIAM JAMES, MD: *"Genius … means little more than the faculty of perceiving in an unhabitual way."*

JAMES JOYCE: *"A man of genius makes no mistakes. His errors are volitional and are the portals of discovery."*

MICHAEL DELL: *"You don't have to be a genius or a visionary or even a college graduate to be successful. You just need a framework and a dream."*

EDWIN LAND, FRS: *"If you dream of something worth doing and then simply go to work on it … it is amazing how quickly you get through those 5,000 steps."*

D. EARL JOHNSTON: *"What a genius conceives, a lawyer usually helps nudge across the finish line."*

JOHNNY MCGREW: *"Nobody truly understands my special genius like my dog."*

Similar: adept, savant, gifted, prodigy, visionary, inspired, brilliant, luminous
Opposite: ignorant, incapable, inept, incompetent, pedestrian

Glory. Achieving recognition and renown from many for a very uncommon or grand achievement. *Popular or Heart-Based Usage: (1) Turning the tide. (2) Making the big score. (3) Landing the big one. (4) Bringing down the house. (5) Beating all the odds. (6) Wresting victory from the jaws of defeat. (7) Spiking the ball. (8) Basking in hard-earned success. (9) Taking a deep bow. (10) Earning all the accolades. (11) Hoisting the trophy. (12) Taking a victory lap. (13) Wearing the olive wreath. (14) Hearing the crowd roar. (15) Posing for your bust. (16) Getting mobbed by your supporters.*

JOHN MILTON: *"For what is glory but the blaze of fame?"*

ALFRED, LORD TENNYSON: *"There's no glory like those who save their country."*

GEN. GEORGE S. PATTON, JR.: *"A slave stood behind the conqueror holding a golden crown and whispering in his ear a warning: that all glory is fleeting."*

EPICTETUS: *"The greater the difficulty, the more glory in surmounting it. Skillful pilots gain their reputation from storms and tempests."*

CONFUCIUS: *"Our greatest glory is not in never failing, but in rising every time we fall."*

EDWIN MARKHAM: *"Defeat may serve as well as victory to shake the soul and let the glory out."*

APHORISM: *"The pain you experience may last an hour, but the glory of your finish will last a lifetime."*

JOEL OSTEEN: *"Glory means honor, favor, and influence… When you do the right thing when the wrong thing is happening, you're getting ready to carry the weight of glory."*

VINCE LOMBARDI: *"The real glory is being knocked to your knees and then coming back. That's real glory. That's the essence of it."*

HARRIET BEECHER STOWE: *"The pain of discipline is short, but the glory of the fruition is eternal."*

AUGUSTUS CAESAR: *"If you want a rainbow, you have to deal with the rain."*

THOMAS PAINE: *"The harder the conflict, the more glorious the triumph."*

NAPOLEON BONAPARTE: *"Glory is fleeting, but obscurity is forever."*

WALT WHITMAN: *"Simplicity is the glory of expression."*

GOETHE: *"The deed is everything. Glory is naught."*

JULIUS CAESAR: *"I came; I saw; I conquered."*

CICERO: *"Life is short but glory is eternal."*

Similar: triumph, renown, fame, magnificence, grandeur, splendor
Opposite: insignificance, irrelevance, unimportance, ignominy, ill-repute

Goosebumps. (1) Having a short-term skin-level reaction to a profound coincidence, an affair of the heart, or to an unexpected stimulus. (2) Experiencing something that is deeply thrilling. *Popular or Heart-Based Usage: (1) Getting chill bumps. (2) Having a shiver run up your spine. (3) Experiencing a hair-raising event. (4) Having a skin orgasm. (5) 'Words don't do it justice.'*

TARA STILES: *"Go after what gives you goosebumps."*

CASEMIRO: *"When you hear the Champions League anthem, it gives you goosebumps."*

CHRISTOPHER JACKSON: *"I get goosebumps going out on stage every night."*

RUSSELL CROWE: *"I want to make movies that pierce people's hearts and touch them in some way, even if it's just for the night while they're in the cinema; in that moment, I want to bring actual tears to their eyes and goosebumps to their skin."*

SAMMY HAGAR: *"In Van Halen there were moments, like in some of the ballads, I put my heart and soul into those records. Those lyrics when I sang 'em, I gave myself goosebumps."*

EDDY MERCKX: *"I wore the yellow jersey 96 times. It is the best memory of my career. It still gives me goosebumps."*

JEREMY SPENCER: *"Give me anything that moves my heart, that gives me goosebumps."*

LINCOLN STOREY: *"We get goosebumps when we experience an event of joy that brings out our deepest life forces."*

PAT WILLIAMS: *"Don't hide your goosebumps."*

D. EARL JOHNSTON: *"Goosebumps are a reminder of how good it is to be alive."*

JOHNNY MCGREW: *"Do stuff that gives your Guardian Angel goosebumps."*

Similar: chill bumps, goose pimples, piloerections, butterflies
Opposite: creeps, willies, heebie-jeebies, cold shudders

Gossip. The spreading of idle talk or rumors which are usually demeaning to others. *Popular or Heart-Based Phrases: (1) Sharing juicy tidbits. (2) 'Just passing idle time with old friends.' (3) Filling in the blanks. (4) Helping an interesting story along. (5) Adding fuel to the fire. (6) 'I can tell you a thing or two about a thing or two.' (7) Loving someone 'to pieces.' (8) Helping to separate the wheat from the weevils. (9) Passing notes. (10) Whispering campaigns.*

JOSEPH CONRAD: *"Gossip is what no one claims to like, but everybody enjoys."*

BERTRAND RUSSELL: *"No one gossips about other people's secret virtues."*

ELEANOR ROOSEVELT: *"Great minds discuss ideas; average minds discuss events; small minds discuss people."*

ERICA JONG: *"Men have often detested women's gossip because they suspect the truth: their measurements are being taken and compared."*

MARGARET WALKER, PHD: *"Talk had feet and could walk and gossip had wings and could fly."*

CHARLES H. SPURGEON: *"A lie can travel halfway around the world and back while the truth is putting on its boots."*

SIR BERNARD INGHAM: *"Blood sport is brought to its ultimate refinement in the gossip columns."*

SIR PHILIP SIDNEY: *"Whoever gossips to you will gossip about you."*

WILSON MIZNER: *"Don't talk about yourself. It will be done when you leave."*

HERB SHRINER: *"Conversation is three women stand on the corner talking. Gossip is when one of them leaves."*

HERMANN HESSE: *"When you hate a person, you hate something in him that is part of yourself. What isn't part of ourselves doesn't disturb us."*

ERNEST HEMINGWAY, PULITZER, NOBEL: *"The best ammunition against lies is the truth, there is no ammunition against gossip. It is like a fog and the clear wind blows it away and the sun burns it off."*

STEFANIE MARRONE: *"1. Take the high road—don't engage with the harmful things people say about you...2. Kill them with kindness...3. Do not engage or counterattack...4. Problem solve...5. Find your tribe...6. Support and lift up others...7. Don't take it personally...8. Neutralize your naysayers...9. Stand up for others...10. Don't fall into the mean girl trap..."*

WILL ROGERS: *"Live in such a way that you would not be ashamed to sell your parrot to the town gossip."*

NAPOLEON BONAPARTE: *"The best way to keep one's word is not to give it."*

Similar: embellishing, exaggerating, fabricating, slandering, chattering, babbling, hearsay
Opposite: circumspection, probity, fact-checking, truth, silence

Gratitude. (1) Acknowledging the contribution or support of another person. (2) Expressing respect or deference toward a benefactor. *Expanded Aspects*: Gratitude reflects awareness and respect for the assistance of others. In certain respects, it may also represent subservience, as toward a superior, or to God. *Popular or Heart-Based Usage: (1) Giving it up for someone. (2) Giving a shout-out to someone. (3) Giving props to someone. (4) Letting someone know how much they mean to you. (5) Giving someone a hug. (6) Giving the nod to God. (7) Pointing to the sky.*

PROVERB: *"A grateful heart is a magnet for miracles."*
CICERO: *"Gratitude is not only the greatest of all virtues, it is the parent of all others."*
ADAGE: *"Gratitude is a holy emotion which transforms both the giver and receiver."*
DENNIS PRAGER: *"Of all the characteristics needed for both a happy and morally decent life, none surpasses gratitude. Grateful people are happier, and grateful people are more morally decent."*
ANTHONY ROBBINS: *"When we have an attitude of gratitude we see life as it is; an unbelievable gift."*
MELODY BEATTIE: *"Gratitude unlocks the fullness of life. It turns what we have into enough, and more. It turns denial into acceptance, chaos to order, confusion to clarity. It can turn a meal into a feast, a house into a home, a stranger into a friend."*
ECKHART TOLLE: *"Acknowledging the good that you already have in your life is the foundation for all abundance."*
AESOP: *"Gratitude is the sign of noble souls. He that is hard to please may get nothing in the end."*
DAVID STENDL-RAST, PHD: *"It is not joy that makes us grateful, it is gratitude that makes us joyful."*
LINCOLN STOREY: *"Saying thanks seals good outcomes. It shows respect for the giver, and it allows everyone to share the moment."*
D. EARL JOHNSTON: *"Gratitude is the universal solvent. Stepping back, and looking again in gratitude, shrinks the issues down to a size we can handle."*
GERMANY KENT: *"It's a funny thing about life, once you begin to take note of the things you are grateful for, you begin to lose sight of the things that you lack."*
PLATO: *"A grateful mind eventually attracts to itself great things."*
SIR BENJAMIN DISRAELI: *"Never take anything for granted."*
GLADYS B. STERN: *"Silent gratitude isn't much use to anyone."*
PROVERB: *"You get more bees with honey."*
SAYING: *"Count your blessings."*

Similar: appreciation, acknowledgment, recognition, thankfulness, respect
Opposite: disdainful, dismissive, condemning, criticizing, disrespect

Gravity. [See also **Electromagnetism** and **Quantum Physics**] Relating to one of the four primary forces of physics, whereby every particle attracts every other particle with a force which varies inversely as the square of their distance from each other. *Popular or Heart-Based Usage: (1) Experiencing the universal constant. (2) 'What goes up.' (3) Being drawn in to something. (4) 'Like kinds attract.' (5) 'Money goes to money.' (6) Experiencing mutual attraction. (7) Keeping your feet on the ground. (8) 'Astrology 101.' (9) Having personal gravitas. (10) 'Black holes suck.' (11) Wrapping your head around curved space-time.*

R. BUCKMINSTER FULLER: *"Love is metaphysical gravity."*

SIR ISAAC NEWTON, FRS: *"Gravity explains the motions of the planets, but it cannot explain who sets the planets in motion."*

FRANCOIS ENGLERT, PHD, NOBEL: *"Gravitational and electromagnetic interactions are long-range interactions, meaning they act on objects no matter how far they are separated from each other."*

LIGO.CALTECH.EDU: *"Gravitational waves…are fundamentally unrelated to EM radiation. They are as distinct from light as hearing is from vision."*

ALBERT EINSTEIN, PHD, NOBEL: *"When forced to summarize the general theory of relativity in one sentence: Time and space and gravitation have no separate existence from matter."*

LIGO.CALTECH.EDU: *"Technically speaking, every physical object that accelerates produces gravitational waves."*

SCIENCE.NASA.GOV: *"To move in a curved path, a planet must have an acceleration toward the center of the circle."*

LINCOLN STOREY: *"Electricity, magnetism, and gravity each operate a little bit differently. Together they make the universe go around."*

HOME.CERN: *"There are four fundamental forces at work in the universe: the strong force, the weak force, the electromagnetic force, and the gravitational force. They work over different ranges and have different strengths. Gravity is the weakest but it has infinite range."*

BRIAN GREENE, DPHIL: *"Einstein comes along and says, space and time can warp and curve, that's what gravity is. Now string theory comes along and says, yes, gravity, quantum mechanics, electromagnetism—all together in one package, but only if the universe has more dimensions than the ones we see."*

ALBERT EINSTEIN, PHD, NOBEL: *"Gravitation cannot be held responsible for people falling in love."*

ADAM SAVAGE: *"Gravity. It's not just a good idea; it's the law!"*

Similar: attraction, weight, pull, magnetism, drawing-in
Opposite: repulsion, levitation, lightness, expansion, zero gravity

Greed. Seeking to accumulate money, power, or influence in an obsessive manner which is beyond common standards of self-interest or fairness. *Popular or Heart-Based Usage: (1) Falling for the mean green. (2) Being all about the Benjamins. (3) 'Things trump people.' (4) Acting like a pig. (5) Being a Scrooge. (6) Getting bedazzled. (7) Going all out for bling mania. (8) 'Cha-ching!' (9) Being a glory hog. (10) 'Mine ... all mine!'*

BOB DYLAN, PULITZER, NOBEL: *"All the money you make will never buy back your soul."*

ANDY STANLEY: *"Greed is not a financial issue. It is a heart issue."*

VANNA BONTA: *"Greed is a lack of confidence in one's own ability to create."*

MAYA ANGELOU: *"There is a very fine line between loving life and being greedy for it."*

WILLIAM GOLDMAN: *"Follow the money."*

ADAM SMITH: *"Individual ambition serves the common good."*

HENRY DAVID THOREAU: *"It is preoccupation with possessions, more than anything else, that prevents us from living freely and nobly."*

ALEKSANDR SOLZHENITSYN: *"Just as King Midas turned everything to gold, Stalin turned everything to mediocrity."*

BLAISE PASCAL: *"It is not good to be too free. It is not good to have everything one wants."*

ACTS 20:35: *"It is more blessed to give than to receive."*

JEAN-JACQUES ROUSSEAU: *"The money you have gives you freedom; the money you pursue enslaves you."*

THOMAS HARRIS: *"Nothing makes us more vulnerable than loneliness except greed."*

SIR FRANCIS BACON: *"If money be not thy servant, it will be thy master."*

WILLIAM SHAKESPEARE: *"All that glitters is not gold."*

JOHNNY MCGREW: *"Build your mansion in your heart."*

DEMOCRITUS: *"It is greed to do all the talking but not to want to listen at all."*

PUBLILIUS SYRUS: *"Poverty wants much; but avarice, everything."*

PROVERBS 11:28: *"He that trusteth in riches shall fall; but the righteous shall flourish as a branch."*

HEBREWS 13:5: *"Let your conversation be without covetousness; and be content with such things as ye have: for he hath said, I will never leave thee, nor forsake thee."*

Similar: stinginess, miserliness, self-absorption, obsessive, manic, unipolar
Opposite: benevolence, magnanimity, charity, generosity, caring

Grief. Experiencing anguish or profound sorrow over a death or loss. *Popular or Heart-Based Usage: (1) Being beside yourself. (2) Knowing heartbreak. (3) Living with a deep soul-wrenching loss. (4) Losing your other half. (5) Sadness beyond words. (6) Being stuck in the past. (6) Having difficulty creating a future. (7) 'Ain't no sunshine.'*

QUEEN ELIZABETH II: *"Grief is the price we pay for love."*

ANN VOSKAMP: *"When grief is deepest, words are fewest."*

C. S. LEWIS: *"No one ever told me that grief felt so like fear."*

HENRY ROLLINS: *"It's sad when someone you know becomes someone you knew."*

KEANU REEVES: *"Grief changes shape, but it never ends."*

DAVID KESSLER: *"Your grief is as unique as your fingerprint. The six stages of grief are: Denial, Anger, Bargaining, Depression, Acceptance, and Finding Meaning."*

JOAN DIDION: *"Grief turns out to be a place none of us know until we reach it."*

HENRY CLOUD, PHD: *"Grief is accepting the reality of what is. That is grief's job and purpose—to allow us to come to terms with the way things really are, so that we can move on. Grief is a gift of God. Without it, we would all be condemned to a life of continually denying reality, arguing or protesting against reality, and never growing from the realities we experience."*

ANN ROIPHE: *"Grief is in two parts. The first is loss. The second is the remaking of life."*

ELISABETH KUBLER-ROSS, MD: *"In our grief process, we are moving into life from death, without denying the devastation that came before."*

Copyright: Elisabeth Kubler-Ross Family Limited Partnership

GEORGE ELIOT: *"She was no longer wrestling with the grief, but could sit down with it as a lasting companion and make it a sharer in her thoughts."*

CICERO: *"Friendship improves happiness and abates misery, by the doubling of our joy and the dividing of our grief."*

PATTI SMITH: *"But if you transform it (grief) into remembrance, then you're magnifying the person you lost, and also giving something of that person to other people, so they can experience something of that person."*

GEORGE ELIOT: *"To have suffered much is like knowing many languages. Thou hast learned to understand all."*

ECKHART TOLLE: *"Life has no opposite. The opposite of death is birth. Life is eternal."*

KERRY SHOOK: *"If you don't grieve your losses then you can't experience great joy."*

MARCEL PROUST: *"It is grief that develops the powers of the mind."*

GEORGE HENRY LEWES: *"The only cure for grief is action."*

Similar: anguish, mourning, bereavement, agony, sorrow, misery, melancholy, ordeal
Opposite: advantage, blessing, contentedness, joyfulness, centeredness, comfort

Grit. [See **Determination** and **Perseverance**]

Guilt. (1) Experiencing remorse about having done something you know was wrong. (2) Knowingly breaking a firm promise or understanding. (3) Having transgressed against a known legal or moral code. *Popular or Heart-Based Usage: (1) Breaking the rules or the law. (2) Getting busted. (3) Getting caught with your hand in the cookie jar. (4) Getting caught red-handed. (5) Getting caught dead to rights. (6) Violating the code. (7) Getting hoisted by your own petard. (8) Feeling schadenfreude. (9) Guilt-tripped. (10) Getting pinched. (11) Doing a perp walk. (12) Trying the orange jumpsuit. (13) Trying on stripes. (14) Going up the river. (15) Heading to the slammer. (16) Ending up behind bars. (17) Doing (hard) time. (18) Being in the pokey. (19) Breaking rocks. (20) Hammering license plates. (21) Being someone's bitch. (22) Being 'back on the chain gang.' (23) Wearing a hair shirt. (24) Wearing sackcloth and ashes. (25) Wearing a scarlet letter. (26) Getting your just deserts. (27) Beating yourself up. (28) Wanting to make it right/make amends.*

ERMA BOMBECK: *"Guilt: the gift that keeps on giving."*

CATHY GUISEWITE: *"Food, love, career, and mothers, the four major guilt groups."*

KEVIN KLINE: *"I've got the Jewish guilt and the Irish shame and it's a hell of a job distinguishing which is which."*

KELSEY GRAMMER: *"How convenient. Your new boyfriend being a geologist, and you having all those faults."*

JOHNNY MCGREW: *"They say misery loves company. But it's more like guilt needs company. And like we see with so many politicians, lotta times guilt pretty much* **insists** *on having company."*

SHANNON L. ALDER: *"Evil originates not in the absence of guilt; but in our effort to escape it."*

WILLIAM SHAKESPEARE: *"The lady doth protest too much, methinks."*

APHORISM: *"Do the crime, serve the time."*

WILLIAM SHAKESPEARE: *"Suspicion always haunts the guilty mind."*

CARL JUNG, MD: *"In each of us there is a pitiless judge who makes us feel guilty … He who is most guilty is most innocent; the most holy man is the one most conscious of his sin."*

DAVID R. HAWKINS, MD, PHD: *"Guilt, so commonly used in our society to manipulate and punish, manifests itself in a variety of expressions, such as remorse, self-recrimination, masochism, and whole gamut of symptoms of victimhood."*

VINCENT F. BERGER, PHD, ABPP, ABFP: *"Almost everyone experiences guilt, off and on, throughout their life. Guilt is not completely negative, unproductive and disruptive. Guilt can be seen in a positive light, although most people do not see it as such."*

BRENE BROWN, MSW, PHD: *"Shame is a focus on self, guilt is a focus on behavior. Shame is: 'I am bad.' Guilt is 'I did something bad.'"*

Guilt. *(continued)*

ERNEST HEMINGWAY, PULITZER, NOBEL: *"I know only that what is moral is what you feel good after, and what is immoral is what you feel bad after."*

DEBBIE FORD: *"An exciting and inspiring future awaits you beyond the noise in your mind, beyond the guilt, doubt, fear, shame, insecurity and heaviness of the past you carry around."*

ZIG ZIGLAR: *"With integrity, you will do the right thing, so you will have no guilt."*

ALBERT ELLIS, PHD: *"Stop shoulding on yourself."*

ALAN COHEN, MA: *"Guilt: punishing yourself before God doesn't."*

JOEL OSTEEN: *"Quit remembering what God has forgotten."*

Similar: culpability, liability, remorse, regret, shame, responsibility, self-condemnation
Opposite: absolution, indemnification, satisfaction, remission, pardon

Happiness. Living with general fulfillment and without undue difficulty. *Popular or Heart-Based Usage: (1) 'Good times.' (2) Having solid friends. (3) Comfortable in your own skin. (4) Having all your stuff. (5) Humming a tune. (6) Living the dream. (7) Liking your lot. (8) Kicking back. (9) Taking it easy. (10) Being fulfilled. (11) 'No big worries.'*

CHINESE PROVERB: *"If you want happiness for an hour, take a nap. If you want happiness for a day, go fishing. If you want happiness for a year, inherit a fortune. If you want happiness for a lifetime, help someone else."*

DANIEL KAHNEMAN, MD, NOBEL: *"It is only a slight exaggeration to say that happiness is the experience of spending time with people you love and who love you."*

MARTIN SELIGMAN, PHD: *"What humans want is not just happiness. They want justice; they want meaning."*

OPRAH WINFREY: *"If you want to feel good, you have to go out and do some good."*

RALPH MARSTON: *"You will not be happy until you choose to be happy."*

DALE CARNEGIE: *"Success is getting what you want. Happiness is wanting what you get."*

ECKHART TOLLE: *"Happiness is alignment with the present moment."*

WILLIAM ARTHUR WARD: *"Happiness is an inside job."*

ELEANOR ROOSEVELT: *"Happiness is not a goal, it is a by-product of a life well-lived."*

VICTOR HUGO: *"The greatest happiness of life is the conviction that we are loved."*

AUDREY HEPBURN: *"I heard a definition once: Happiness is health and a short memory! I wish I'd invented it because it is very true."*

WILLIAM BUTLER YEATS: *"We are happy when we are growing."*

ARTHUR C. BROOKS, MPHIL, PHD: *"The key to happiness is not being rich; it's doing something arduous and creating something of value and then being able to reflect on the fruits of your labor."*

SYDNEY J. HARRIS: *"Happiness is a direction, not a place."*

JOEL OSTEEN: *"Happiness is not dependent on what's going on around you, it's dependent on what's going on in you."*

D. EARL JOHNSTON: *"Happiness is when both your head and heart are fulfilled."*

WILLIAM MAKEPEACE THACKERAY: *"A good laugh is sunshine in the house."*

GEORGE SAND: *"There is only one happiness in life, to love and be loved."*

ABRAHAM LINCOLN: *"Folks are usually about as happy as they make up their minds to be."*

ANONYMOUS: *"Happiness is two things: good health and positive cash flow."*

PROVERB: *"Happiness is enjoying the little things in life."*

Similar: contentment, fulfillment, satisfaction, expansiveness
Opposite: depression, discouragement, melancholy, introversion, fear

Hate. (1) Harboring intense animosity or rejection toward a person or thing. (2) Maintaining an extreme and enduring form of personal opposition. *Popular or Heart-Based Usage: (1) Wishing someone ill. (2) Having major issues with someone. (3) Utterly despising someone or something. (4) Detesting the ground he/she walks on. (5) Having a hard heart. (6) Seeing red. (7) 'That makes my blood boil.' (8) Giving someone a full-on rejection. (9) 'Oil and water don't mix.' (10) 'I can't stand him/her.' (11) 'My mind is a steel trap.' (12) 'No quarter.' (13) 'When Hell freezes over!'*

CLARENCE DARROW: *"I have never killed a man, but I have read some obituaries with great pleasure."*

W. C. FIELDS: *"I am free of all prejudice. I hate everyone equally."*

TERRI GUILLEMETS: *"Hate cages all the good things about you."*

LAURELL K. HAMILTON: *"Hatred makes us all ugly."*

WILLIAM F. DEVAULT: *"Hatred unlocks no doors in Heaven."*

BILLY GRAHAM: *"You cannot pray for someone and hate them at the same time."*

D. EARL JOHNSTON: *"Better to avoid than to hate. Better to resolve than to avoid."*

MARTIN LUTHER KING, JR., NOBEL: *"Darkness cannot drive out darkness, only light can do that. Hate cannot drive out hate, only love can do that."*

DALAI LAMA, NOBEL: *"Hatred first will disturb your mind, the mental peace. Secondly, it will create mental suffering."*

PAUL EKMAN, PHD: *"Hatred…blocks your access to your own memories."*

HERMANN HESSE: *"When you hate a person, you hate something in him that is part of yourself. What isn't part of ourselves doesn't disturb us."*

GOETHE: *"Hatred is something peculiar. You will find it strongest and most violent where there is the lowest degree of culture."*

TACITUS: *"It is human nature to hate the one whom you have hurt."*

HENRY EMERSON FOSDICK: *"Hating people is like burning down your house to get rid of a rat."*

JOHNNY MCGREW: *"Hatred is a nasty place we go when we want to feel superior."*

JOE ROGAN: *"The time you spend hating on someone robs you of your own time. You are literally hating on yourself and you don't even realize it."*

H. HILL MCALISTER: *"True forgiveness negates hate."*

ELON MUSK: *"Life is too short for long-term grudges."*

JOHNNY MCGREW: *"Hatred can stunt your growth."*

MARY BAKER EDDY: *"Reject hatred without hating."*

GRAHAM GREENE: *"Hate is a lack of imagination."*

HOSEA BALLOU: *"Hatred is self-punishment."*

RENE MARAN: *"Hatred is one long wait."*

APHORISM: *"Hate hardens the heart."*

Similar: loathing, detestation, abhorrence, resentment, animosity
Opposite: friendship, goodwill, approval, cooperation, love

Heart. (1) Adhering to your treasured motives, dreams, and aspirations. (2) Emotional coherence. *Popular or Heart-Based Usage: (1) Doing the right thing. (2) Optimizing your energies. (3) Being right-brained. (4) Pursuing your metaphysical/intuitive side.*

PROVERB: *"Home is where the heart is."*

TODD STOCKER: *"A change of heart changes everything."*

JOE ROGAN: *"You can't measure what's inside a man's heart."*

L. FRANK BAUM/'THE WONDERFUL WIZARD OF OZ': *"Remember that a heart is not measured by how much you love, but how much you are loved by others."*

MATTHEW 5:8: *"Blessed are the pure in heart: for they shall see God."*

ALBERT EINSTEIN, PHD, NOBEL: *"Don't let your brain interfere with your heart."*

PROVERBS 4:23: *"Keep thy heart with all diligence: for out of it are the issues of life."*

STEVE JOBS: *"Have the courage to follow your heart and intuition. They somehow already know what you truly want to become."*

HELEN KELLER: *"The best and most beautiful things in the world cannot be seen or even touched—they must be felt with the heart."*

GOETHE: *"What is uttered from the heart alone, will win the hearts of others to your own."*

KIRA AUSTIN-YOUNG: *"God does not see or value the things that humans value but looks on the heart."*

EVANDER HOLYFIELD: *"It's not the size of the man but the size of his heart that matters."*

ELEANOR ROOSEVELT: *"To handle yourself, use your head; to handle others, use your heart."*

GABRIEL GARCIA MARQUEZ: *"The heart's memory eliminates the bad and maximizes the good."*

JEREMY SPENCER: *"Give me anything that moves my heart, that gives me goosebumps."*

RUMI: *"Everyone sees the unseen in proportion to the clarity of his heart."*

JOEL OSTEEN: *"Hold tightly to what God has put in your heart. Hold loosely to how it happens."*

ARISTOTLE: *"Educating the mind without educating the heart is no education at all."*

D. EARL JOHNSTON: *"Think with your head, and act with your heart."*

JEWISH PROVERB: *"As he thinks in his heart, so he is."*

PROVERB: *"Follow your heart."*

Similar: conscience, character, core, foundation, essence
Opposite: superficiality, image, appearance, façade, ego

Heartache. (1) Experiencing deep anguish or grief from a loss. (2) Feeling chest pain without physical explanation and stemming from apparent emotional origins. *Popular or Heart-Based Usage: (1) Suffering a wrenching loss. (2) Feeling totally deflated. (3) Experiencing unrequited love. (4) Feeling deprived or robbed of someone or something deeply cherished. (5) Knowing rejection. (6) Beating yourself up with 'what ifs' and 'what might have beens.' (7) Feeling rejected and naive. (8) Not seeing it coming.*

WILLIAM SHAKESPEARE: *"Expectation is the root of heartache."*

ELIZABETH GILBERT: *"Someday you're gonna look back on this moment of your life as such as sweet time of grieving. You'll see that you were in mourning and your heart was broken, but your life was changing."*

KAHLIL GIBRAN: *"Out of suffering have emerged the strongest souls; the most massive characters are seared with scars."*

HENRY ROLLINS: *"It's sad when someone you know becomes someone you knew."*

MARK TWAIN: *"Never allow someone to be your priority while allowing yourself to be their option."*

LAUREN CONRAD: *"Don't cry over someone who wouldn't cry over you."*

MEDICALNEWSTODAY.COM: *"The research shows that rejection appears to be in a class by itself in terms of its similarity to physical pain."*

MARILYN MONROE: *"Sometimes good things fall apart so better things can fall together."*

HENNY YOUNGMAN: *"You can't buy love, but you can pay heavily for it."*

RED SKELTON: *"No matter what your heartache may be, laughing helps you forget it for a few seconds."*

MARGARET GEORGE: *"The cure for a broken heart is simple, my lady. A hot bath and a good night's sleep."*

ANDRE GIDE: *"Sadness is almost never anything but a form of fatigue."*

ABRAHAM LINCOLN: *"To ease another's heartache is to forget one's own."*

RABBI NACHMAN OF BRESLOV: *"Charity cures heartaches."*

SAYING: *"When you can tell your story and it doesn't make you cry, you know you have healed."*

ROBERT FROST: *"In three words I can sum up everything I've learned about life. It goes on."*

FREDDIE PERREN, DINO FEKARIS (& GLORIA GAYNOR): *"I Will Survive"* (Song)

RUMI: *"You have to keep breaking your heart until it opens."*

PROVERB: *"This too shall pass."*

Similar: grief, bereavement, sorrow, depression, sadness, misery, loss
Opposite: cheer, delight, joy, bullishness, enthusiasm

Heroism. Demonstrating service above self in the pursuit or defense of a core belief. *Popular or Heart-Based Usage: (1) Taking one for the team. (2) Having guts. (3) Standing tall. (4) Setting a good example. (5) Volunteering your life. (6) Fighting for what is right. (7) Doing what must be done. (8) Making the ultimate sacrifice. (9) 'Do the right thing.'*

MAYA ANGELOU: *"I think a hero is a person really intent on making this a better place for all people."*

WILL ROGERS: *"We can't all be heroes because someone has to sit on the curb and clap as they go by."*

GEORGE F. KENNAN: *"Heroism is endurance for one moment more."*

SØREN KIERKEGAARD: *"Only the noble of heart are called to difficulty."*

WADE DAVIS: *"Heroes are never perfect, but they're brave, they're authentic, they're courageous, determined, discreet, and they've got grit."*

CHRISTOPHER REEVE: *"A hero is an ordinary individual who finds the strength to persevere and endure in spite of overwhelming obstacles."*

ERNEST HEMINGWAY, PULITZER, NOBEL: *"As you get older, it is harder to have heroes but it is sort of necessary."*

JOHN 15:13: *"Greater love hath no man than this, that a man lay down his life for his friends."*

CHRISTINE BERGSMA: *"You are the protagonist of your story, decide if you want to be the hero."*

JIMMY STEWART: *"I think one day you'll find that you're the hero you've been looking for."*

RALPH WALDO EMERSON: *"Self-trust is the essence of heroism."*

WALT WHITMAN: *"A man can be a hero in any profession."*

PHILIP ZIMBARDO, PHD: *"Heroism is the antidote to evil."*

JOSH BILLINGS: *"Everyone who does the best he can is a hero."*

JOE ROGAN: *"Be the hero of your own story."*

Similar: courageousness, bravery, stoutheartedness, valor, dauntlessness
Opposite: afraid, disconcerted, skittish, timid, indecisive, cowardice

Honesty. (1) Telling the truth. (2) Communicating with an absence of guile, deception, or falsehood. *Popular or Heart-Based Usage: (1) Being true blue. (2) Being a 'stand up' person. (3) Holding your hands open/palms up. (4) Telling it like it is. (5) Talking turkey. (6) Being transparent. (7) Keeping things on the up and up. (8) Being a reliable source. (9) Keeping it real. (10) 'Cross my heart.' (11) 'It is what it is.'*

SPENCER JOHNSON: *"Integrity is telling myself the truth. And honesty is telling the truth to other people."*

YIDDISH PROVERB: *"A half-truth is a whole lie."*

WILLIAM SHAKESPEARE: *"The eyes are the window to the soul."*

LEMUEL WASHBURN: *"Honesty is never seen sitting astride the fence."*

JOHN RUSKIN: *"To make your children capable of honesty is the beginning of education."*

THOMAS JEFFERSON: *"Honesty is the first chapter in the book of wisdom."*

BENJAMIN FRANKLIN: *"Write to please yourself. When you write to please others you end up pleasing no one."*

JAMES ALTUCHER: *"Honesty is the fastest way to prevent a mistake from becoming a failure."*

JADA PINKETT SMITH: *"Love and honesty are the things that make a good wife and mother."*

WILLIAM SHAKESPEARE: *"Honesty is the best policy. And if I lose mine honor, I lose myself."*

ALBERT BEL FAY: *"When somebody starts a sentence with 'Well, to be honest with you...' does it mean they haven't been telling the truth the rest of the time?"*

WAYLON JENNINGS: *"Honesty is something you can't wear out."*

Similar: truthfulness, integrity, veracity, probity, uprightness
Opposite: deceptive, crooked, lying, dissembling, double-dealing

Hope. Having a wish, goal, or expectation about events to come. *Popular or Heart-Based Usage: (1) Having a wish list. (2) Wishing on a star. (3) Having your heart leap. (4) Believing in your dreams. (5) 'Aim high.' (6) 'Tomorrow will be a better day.'*

HELEN KELLER: *"Hope sees the invisible, feels the intangible, and achieves the impossible."*

PROVERB: *"When God closes a door, He opens a window."*

OSCAR WILDE: *"Second marriage is the triumph of hope over experience."*

FRANK DARABONT: *"Remember hope is a good thing, maybe the best of things. And no good thing ever dies."*

DESMOND TUTU, NOBEL: *"Hope is being able to see there is light despite all the darkness."*

J. R. R. TOLKIEN: *"There is some good in this world, and it's worth fighting for."*

ALBERT EINSTEIN, PHD, NOBEL: *"Learn from yesterday, live for today, hope for tomorrow."*

AGA KHAN IV: *"The right to hope is the most powerful human motivation I know."*

NELSON MANDELA, NOBEL: *"May your choices reflect your hopes, not your fears."*

SIR BENJAMIN DISRAELI: *"I am prepared for the worst, but hope for the best."*

MICHAEL J. FOX: *"To me, hope is informed optimism."*

NAPOLEON BONAPARTE: *"Courage is like love: it must have hope for nourishment."*

THICH NHAT HANH: *"If we believe that tomorrow will be better, we can bear a hardship today."*

FYODOR DOSTOEVSKY: *"To live without hope is to cease to live."*

ENGLISH PROVERB: *"The darkest hours are just before the dawn."*

SØREN KIERKEGAARD: *"Hope is passion for what is possible."*

HEBREWS 11:1: *"Now faith is the substance of things hoped for, the evidence of things not seen."*

THALES OF MILETUS: *"Hope is the only good thing that is common to all men; those who have nothing else possess hope still."*

THOMAS FULLER: *"Hopes make great men."*

PROVERB: *"If you have hope you have everything."*

L. FRANK BAUM / 'THE WONDERFUL WIZARD OF OZ' / DOROTHY GALE: *"Somewhere, over the rainbow."*

RALPH WALDO EMERSON: *"Hitch your wagon to a star."*

Similar: aspiration, optimism, faith, dream, wish, aim
Opposite: doubt, despair, discouragement, pessimism, disbelief

Humility. (1) Placing a lesser focus on your own importance. (2) Being aware of your own limitations, and deferential to others. *Popular or Heart-Based Usage: (1) Knowing your proper place. (2) Swallowing your pride. (3) Taking a back seat. (4) Serving as the undercard. (5) Staying out of the limelight. (6) Learning the hard way. (7) Getting your comeuppance. (8) Getting bitch-slapped. (9) Sucking up. (10) Getting schooled. (11) Eating humble pie. (12) Eating crow. (13) Eating a dirt sandwich. (14) Wearing sackcloth and ashes. (15) Bowing and scraping. (16) Kissing ass. (17) 'Here's my two cents.' (18) Poking fun at yourself.*

ROBERT BROWNING: *"Less is more."*

EMILY DICKINSON: *"I'm nobody! Who are you?"*

NELSON MANDELA, NOBEL: *"You either win or you learn."*

JACK NICKLAUS: *"Don't be too proud to take lessons. I'm not."*

THE BEATITUDES: *"Blessed are the meek, for they shall inherit the earth."*

JAMES 4:10: *"Humble yourselves in the sight of the Lord, and he shall lift you up."*

DESMOND TUTU, NOBEL: *"We may be surprised at the people we find in heaven. God has a soft spot for sinners. His standards are quite low."*

RAY DALIO: *"Humility is not weakness. It is strength."*

TIGER WOODS: *"Money and fame made me believe I was entitled. I was wrong and foolish."*

CHRISTOPHER HITCHENS: *"Everyone has a book in them, which is exactly where, it should, I think, in most cases, remain."*

AUGUSTINE OF HIPPO: *"It was pride that changed angels into devils: It is humility that makes men into angels."*

MATTHEW 18:4: *"Whosoever therefore shall humble himself as this little child, the same is the greatest in the kingdom of heaven."*

MAIMONIDES: *"Teach thy tongue to say 'I do not know' and thou shalt progress."*

RICK WARREN: *"Humility is not thinking less of yourself, it is thinking of yourself less."*

JOHN RUSKIN: *"Really great men have a curious feeling that the greatness is not of them, but through them."*

TRYON EDWARDS: *"True humility is not an abject, groveling, self-despising spirit; it is but a right estimate of ourselves as God sees us."*

QURAN: *"The servants of the Most Merciful are those who walk upon the earth in humility, and when the ignorant address them, they say words of peace."*

THE TALMUD: *"He who sacrifices a whole offering shall be rewarded for a whole offering; He who offers a burnt-offering shall receive the reward of a burnt-offering; But he who offers humility to God and man shall be rewarded with a reward as if he had offered all the sacrifices in the world."*

Similar: modesty, self-deprecation, demureness, deference, meekness, lowliness
Opposite: pride, arrogance, hubris, selfishness, boasting, conceit, greed

Humor. Combining surprise with a comparison of unrelated things in order to facilitate emotional release and an elevation of mood. *Popular or Heart-Based Usage: (1) 'Ha!' (2) Being playful. (3) Being lighthearted. (4) Having a few laughs. (5) Pulling someone's leg. (6) Tickling someone's funny bone. (7) Telling Dad Jokes. (8) Sharing good times. (9) Poking fun at yourself. (10) Having a great sense of timing.*

PHYLLIS DILLER: *"Housework can't kill you. But why take a chance?"*

COMEDY CLUB DRESSING ROOM: *"Attention: The beatings will continue until morale improves."*

BUMPER STICKER: *"Hire a teenager while they still know everything."*

WILL ROGERS: *"I am not a member of any organized political party. I'm a Democrat."*

ERMA BOMBECK: *"Seize the moment. Remember all those women on the Titanic who waved off the dessert cart."*

CASEY STENGEL: *"The key to being a good manager is keeping the people who hate me away from those who are still undecided."*

WILL ROGERS: *"Everything is funny, as long as it's happening to somebody else."*

ERMA BOMBECK: *"The only reason I would take up jogging is so that I could hear heavy breathing again."*

DAVE BARRY: *"You can only be young once. But you can always be immature."*

MARK TWAIN: *"Get your facts first, then you can distort them as you please."*

STEVE MARTIN: *"A day without sunshine is like, you know, night."*

HUMORIST: *"You, sir, totally disgust me…Please continue."*

LUCILLE BALL: *"I'm not funny. What I am is brave."*

STU KONIGSBERG: *"Your own shortcomings are the best ground to grow your sense of humor."*

COMEDY CLUB DRESSING ROOM: *"Sarcasm can dig and satire can bite, but self-deprecation makes it go right."*

BOB HOPE: *"I have seen what a laugh can do. It can transform almost unbearable tears into something bearable, even hopeful."*

FRANK A. CLARK: *"I think the next best thing to solving a problem is finding some humor in it."*

RODNEY DANGERFIELD: *"He who laughs last didn't get it in the first place."*

D. EARL JOHNSTON: *"If you can laugh at an emotion, it does not control you."*

ANONYMOUS: *"Emotions are like children. You don't want them driving the car, but you can't stuff them in the trunk, either."*

MAX EASTMAN: *"Humor is the instinct for taking pain playfully."*

ROBIN WILLIAMS: *"Comedy can be a cathartic way to deal with personal trauma."*

ARISTOTLE: *"The secret to humor is surprise."*

Similar: comedy, lightheartedness, wit, playfulness, wisecracking
Opposite: seriousness, tragedy, sadness, melancholy

Hunger. Feeling the urge toward physical or emotional sustenance. *Popular or Heart-Based Usage: (1) Running on empty. (2) Hearing your stomach growling. (3) Having a craving. (4) Having a deep hankering for something. (5) Needing a sugar fix. (6) Raiding the fridge. (7) 'Jonesing' for something. (8) Having the munchies. (9) 'Want it gotta have it!' (10) 'Feed me!' (11) 'I'm starving!' (12) 'Just skin and bones!' (13) 'Snack time!' (14) 'More please!' (15) 'Seconds!' (16) Having a big void to fill. (17) Having a soul-level yearning for something. (18) Wanting to be held. (19) Needing to be needed.*

MOTHER TERESA, NOBEL: *"We think sometimes that poverty is only being hungry, naked, and homeless. The poverty of being unwanted, unloved and uncared for is the greatest poverty."*

PLATO: *"The god of love lives in a state of need. It is a need. It is an urge. It is a homeostatic imbalance. Like hunger and thirst, it's almost impossible to stamp out."*

JOHNNY MCGREW: *"Hunger trumps just about everything."*

ARISTOPHANES: *"Hunger knows no friend but its feeder."*

ALLYN FONTAINE: *"Hunger reflects life at the margins. When a hungry person covers food or any basic challenge, they move up to the next higher level of wanting, because solving the very next need is our basic lot on Earth."*

JOHN STEINBECK: *"Where does the discontent start? You are warm enough, but you shiver. You are fed, yet hunger gnaws you. You have been loved, but your yearning wanders in new fields. And to prod all these there's time, the Bastard Time."*

MARTIN LUTHER KING, JR., NOBEL: *"I have the audacity to believe that peoples everywhere can have three meals a day for their bodies, education and culture for their minds, and dignity, equality, and freedom for their spirits."*

MOTHER TERESA, NOBEL: *"The hunger for love is much more difficult to remove than the hunger for bread."*

GEORGE ELIOT: *"No man can be wise on an empty stomach."*

PEARL S. BUCK, NOBEL: *"A hungry man can't see right or wrong, he just sees food."*

PRANAB MUKHERJEE: *"There is no humiliation more abusive than hunger."*

Similar: yearning, wanting, emptiness, craving, starvation, famine, malnourishment
Opposite: fullness, satisfaction, fill, content, bloat, gluttony

Hurrying. Proceeding with urgency or in haste. *Popular or Heart-Based Usage: (1) Stepping on it. (2) Going for it. (3) Skedaddling. (4) Pushing the envelope. (5) Getting out over your skis. (6) Taking no prisoners. (7) Going high-rev. (8) Going breakneck. (9) Being a Type-A personality.*

WILLA CATHER, PULITZER: *"Life is hurrying past us and running away, too strong to stop, too sweet to lose."*

JOSEPH ADDISON: *"He who hesitates is lost."*

MARCO RUBIO: *"For most of my life I've been in a hurry."*

ALAN WATTS: *"Hurrying and delaying are alike ways of trying to resist the present."*

MAHATMA GANDHI: *"There is more to life than increasing its speed."*

HENRY DAVID THOREAU: *"The hero then will know how to wait, as well as to make haste."*

ABRAHAM LINCOLN: *"Things may come to those who wait, but only the things left by those who hustle."*

G. K. CHESTERTON: *"One of the great disadvantages of hurry is that it takes such a long time."*

NORA ROBERTS: *"'Do you know what happens when you always look before you leap?' She reached out and touched his hand before hurrying toward the door. 'You hardly ever make the jump.'"*

WILL ROGERS: *"We are all here for a spell. Get all the good laughs you can."*

ST. FRANCIS DE SALES: *"Never be in a hurry; do everything quietly and in a calm spirit. Do not lose your inner peace for anything whatsoever, even if your whole world seems upset."*

EMILY DICKINSON: *"A mother is one to whom you hurry when you are troubled."*

A. A. MILNE: *"Rivers know this: there is no hurry. We shall get there some day."*

WILLIAM SHAKESPEARE: *"Go wisely and slowly. Those who rush stumble and fall."*

MARIO LEMIEUX: *"When someone screams at me to hurry up, I slow down."*

ROBERT LOUIS STEVENSON: *"He who sows hurry reaps indigestion."*

DALLAS WILLARD, PHD: *"Ruthlessly eliminate hurry from your life."*

MATTHEW ARNOLD: *"Journalism is literature in a hurry."*

JOHN WOODEN: *"Be quick without hurrying."*

Similar: rushing, hustling, scrambling, scurrying, darting, dashing
Opposite: delaying, dawdling, procrastinating, slow-walking

Hydration. Drinking water to optimize your health. *Popular or Heart-Based Usage: (1) Fluid intelligence. (2) Thirst-busting. (3) Being pee savvy. (4) Topping off your tank.*

LAO TZU: *"Water benefits all things and does not compete."*

LEONARDO DA VINCI: *"Water is the driving force in nature."*

LOREN EISELEY, PHD: *"If there is Magic on this planet, it is contained in water."*

ALBERT SZENT-GYORGYI, PHD, NOBEL: *"Water is life's matter and matrix, mother and medium. There is no life without water."*

SLOVAKIAN ADAGE: *"Pure water is the world's first and foremost medicine."*

W. H. AUDEN: *"Thousands have lived without love, not one without water."*

VEDA AUSTIN: *"Water is not a resource, it is Source."*

MASARU EMOTU: *"Understanding that water exists as a solid, a liquid, a vapor, as a molecule, and at some point as light is to also understand our own nature and possibilities because we are mostly made of water."*

JOHNS HOPKINS UNIVERSITY MAGAZINE: *"Even slight levels of dehydration (as little as 2% water loss) impair your performance in tasks that require attention, cognitive functions, physical movement, and immediate memory skills."*

NATIONAL INSTITUTES OF HEALTH: *"Dehydration may lead to some adverse results such as decreased muscle endurance and strength, or increased chances of kidney stones and urinary tract infections. Furthermore, dehydration may affect cognitive performance, as water accounts for 75% of brain mass."*

HARVARD T.H. CHAN SCHOOL OF PUBLIC HEALTH: *"Drinking enough water each day is crucial for many reasons: to regulate body temperature, keep joints lubricated, prevent infections, deliver nutrients to cells, and keep organs functioning properly."*

HUMAN BRAIN MAPPING: *"The functionality of several organs, our cognitive ability, and our mood are hindered to an alarming degree if our body's water content drops by as little as 1%."*

NATIONAL LIBRARY OF MEDICINE: *"Rehydration after water supplementation alleviated fatigue and improved TMD, short-term memory, attention, and reaction."*

KATHERINE ZERATSKY, RD, LD: *"Alkaline water has a higher PH level than that of plain tap water…Some say that alkaline water can help prevent disease, such as cancer and heart disease."*

NATIONAL LIBRARY OF MEDICINE: *"(Dehydration) has been reported to occur in 17–28% of older adults in the U.S. (It) is a frequent cause of hospital admission."*

LINCOLN STOREY: *"Frequent yawning can be simple dehydration, not tiredness."*

KELLY BARTON: *"Water is the most neglected item in your diet."*

Similar: refreshment, quenching, drinking, slaking, topping off, bloat
Opposite: dehydration, thirstiness, parchedness, desiccation, hallucinating, death

Ignorance. Having a lack of knowledge or awareness. *Popular or Heart-Based: (1) Being a dumb-ass. (2) Not knowing that you don't know. (3) Being lost like an ostrich/ burying your head in the sand. (4) Being both uninformed and uninterested.*

PROVERB: *"Hear no evil, see no evil, speak no evil."*

ALBERT EINSTEIN, PHD, NOBEL: *"The only thing more dangerous than ignorance is arrogance."*

MARTIN LUTHER KING, JR., NOBEL: *"Nothing in the world is more dangerous than sincere ignorance and conscious stupidity."*

BARACK OBAMA, NOBEL: *"When ignorant folks want to advertise their ignorance, you don't really have to do anything, you just let them talk."*

ALDOUS HUXLEY: *"Most ignorance is vincible ignorance. We don't know because we don't want to know."*

GOETHE: *"Nothing is worse than active ignorance."*

WILL ROGERS: *"When ignorance gets started, it knows no bounds."*

MAYA ANGELOU: *"My mother said I must always be intolerant of ignorance but understanding of illiteracy."*

MAHATMA GANDHI: *"Truth is by nature self-evident. As soon as you remove the cobwebs of ignorance that surround it, it shines clear."*

OSHO: *"The less people know, the more stubbornly they know it."*

FREDERICK DOUGLASS: *"Where justice is denied, where poverty is enforced, where ignorance prevails, and where any one class is made to feel that society is an organized conspiracy to suppress, rob and degrade them, neither persons nor property will be safe."*

ANDREW CARNEGIE: *"Mutual ignorance breeds mutual distrust."*

SIR BENJAMIN DISRAELI: *"Ignorance never settles a question."*

TIMOTHY LONG: *"Fear and ignorance are the key roots to racism."*

LYNDON JOHNSON: *"Poverty has many roots, but the tap root is ignorance."*

KATE LANGLEY BOSHER: *"People are generally opposed to things they know nothing about."*

ELIZABETH STUART PHELPS WARD: *"A great idea is usually original to more than one discoverer. Great ideas come when the world needs them. Great ideas surround the world's ignorance and press for admission."*

THOMAS JEFFERSON: *"If ignorance is bliss, why aren't more people happy?"*

DAME EDITH SITWELL: *"I am patient with stupidity, but not those who are proud of it."*

JON STEWART: *"Evil is relatively rare. Ignorance is epidemic."*

Similar: unaware, oblivious, uninformed, uncurious, uninterested, dismissive, stupid
Opposite: informed, aware, educated, briefed, up to speed, read in

Imagination. (1) Having a new idea, flash of creativity, or special insight about a topic. (2) Focusing on the creation of new ideas, concepts, or possibilities. *Popular or Heart-Based Usage: (1) Having a light come on. (2) Flashing on an idea. (3) Thinking outside the box. (4) Looking skyward. (5) Making stuff up. (6) Trail-blazing. (7) Envisioning it in your mind. (8) Floating an idea. (9) Starting with a blank canvas. (10) 'What if...?'*

JOSEPH JOUBERT: *"Imagination is the eye of the soul."*

WALT DISNEY: *"Laughter is timeless. Imagination has no age. And dreams are forever."*

WILLIAM BLAKE: *"What is now proved was once only imagined."*

HENRY DAVID THOREAU: *"The world is but a canvas to our imagination."*

PERCY BYSSHE SHELLEY: *"The great instrument of moral good is the imagination."*

RICHARD WAGNER: *"Imagination creates reality."*

LYNNE MCTAGGART: *"Thoughts become things."*

ALBERT EINSTEIN, PHD, NOBEL: *"Imagination is more important than knowledge. Knowledge is limited. Imagination circles the world."*

RICHARD FEYNMAN, PHD, NOBEL: *"Science is imagination in a straitjacket."*

RICHARD BACH: *"To bring anything into your life, imagine it is already there."*

EDWIN LAND, FRS: *"An essential aspect of creativity is not being afraid to fail."*

ALBERT EINSTEIN, PHD, NOBEL: *"Imagination is everything. It is the preview of life's coming attractions."*

IMMANUEL KANT: *"Happiness is not an ideal of reason, but of imagination."*

GEORGE BERNARD SHAW: *"Imagination is the beginning of creation. You imagine what you desire, you will what you imagine, and at last you create what you will."*

ERNEST HOLMES: *"The universe must exist for the self-expression of God and the delight of God."*

PABLO PICASSO: *"Everything you can imagine is real."*

LINCOLN STOREY: *"Imagination can include dreaming up the new you, and then memorizing and repeating that vision 100X until it becomes real."*

NIKOLA TESLA: *"Facts and ideas are dead in themselves and it is the imagination that brings life to them."*

ELON MUSK, FRS: *"You can study all these things that you have in a book, but if you don't have imagination and then take it to another level, it doesn't mean a thing."*

JOHNNY MCGREW: *"My old girlfriend started a big company. She claimed she got her degree at night school from MSU. You know—'Made Stuff Up.'"*

HENRY JAMES: *"It is time to start living the life you imagined."*

Similar: creativity, insight, vision, innovation, cutting edge, resourcefulness
Opposite: inability, dullness, void, death

Indignant. Reacting sharply and with hostility to a perceived wrong. *Popular or Heart-Based Usage: (1) Getting severely bent out of shape. (2) Hotly rejecting something. (3) 'Hey, no fair!' (4) Feeling something is way out of whack. (5) Being a hothead. (6) Really fuming. (7) 'That's an outrage!' (8) 'Totally ridiculous!' (9) 'Ain't gonna show you no stinkin' badges!' (10) 'In a pig's eye!' (11) 'That's enough!' (12) 'I've had it up to here!' (13) 'I am so outta here!' (14) 'Just look at what they've done!' (15) 'Have they lost their minds?' (16) 'Oh yeah? Well let's just see what happens now!' (17) 'Totally unacceptable!' (18) 'Your turn now. It's about time you did something!' (19) 'Never in a million years!' (20) 'What were you even **thinking**?' (21) 'How dare you!' (22) 'How could you?"*

IRVING STONE: *"What did you use to keep warm? 'Indignation.' Said Michelangelo, 'Best fuel I know. Never burns out.'"*

RALPH WALDO EMERSON: *"A good indignation brings out all of one's powers."*

CHE GUEVARA: *"If you tremble with indignation at every injustice, you are a comrade of mine."*

STEPHANE HESSEL: *"If you want to be a real human being—a real man, a real woman—you cannot tolerate things which put you to indignation, to outrage. You must stand up."*

L. FRANK BAUM/'THE WONDERFUL WIZARD OF OZ'/DOROTHY GALE: *"Don't you dare bite Toto! You ought to be ashamed of yourself, a big beast like you, to bite a poor little dog!"*

THUCYDIDES: *"Man's indignation, it seems, is more excited by legal wrong than violent wrong."*

ABRAHAM LINCOLN: *"You can tell the greatness of a man by what makes him angry."*

JOSHUA OPPENHEIMER: *"I think that indignation is pleasurable, and it's pleasurable because it's self-righteous."*

H.G. WELLS: *"Moral indignation is jealousy with a halo."*

ELBERT HUBBARD: *"Righteous indignation: your own wrath as opposed to the shocking bad temper of others."*

FRIEDRICH NIETZSCHE: *"No one lies so boldly as the man who is indignant."*

ALCOHOLICS ANONYMOUS: *"Rejection before investigation is contempt."*

SIMON BOLIVAR: *"Slavery is the worst human indignity."*

Similar: resentful, annoyed, incensed, contemptuous, derisive
Opposite: peaceful, calm, cheerful, praising, grateful

Insecurity. [See also **Envy**, **Jealousy**, and **Selfish**] Lacking confidence in your own abilities, beliefs, or prospects. *Popular or Heart-Based Usage: (1) Having a few hang-ups. (2) Having low self-esteem. (3) Getting stuck in introversion. (4) Constantly looking over your shoulder. (5) Being a wallflower. (6) Feeling wishy-washy. (7) Always taking the easy way. (8) Being an easy mark/Getting easily talked into things. (9) Being clingy. (10) Feeling antsy. (11) Glomming onto other people. (12) Looking around for support. (13) Fishing for compliments. (14) Being the class clown. (15) Boasting or bragging to impress. (16) Trying hard to act cool. (17) Putting others down/putting yourself down. (18) Taking the lead at Gossip Central. (19) Living in 'FOMO.' ['Fear of Missing Out.'] (20) Acting all saddity. (21) Being a fashion slave. (22) Being a wannabe.*

MARIAH CAREY: *"I'm not vain, I'm insecure."*

ADAGE: *"Confidence is quiet. Insecurities are loud."*

BETH MOORE: *"Jealousy takes root in the soil of insecurity."*

BRANDON SANDERSON: *"The hallmark of insecurity is bravado."*

BLAKE LIVELY: *"People gossip. People are insecure, so they talk about other people so that they won't be talked about. They talk about flaws in other people to make them feel good about themselves."*

JOHN LITHGOW: *"To my mum, I owe security in a very insecure young life. We lived in about 10 different places because of my father's chequered career, and she always made me feel a sense of consistency and security."*

ADELE: *"I have insecurities, of course, but I don't hang out with anyone who points them out to me."*

MARIANNE WILLIAMSON: *"You are a child of God. Your playing small does not serve the world. There is nothing enlightened about shrinking so that other people won't feel insecure about you. You were born to manifest the glory of God that is within us."*

HENRI NOUWEN, DRS: *"The greatest trap in life is not success, popularity, or power, but self-rejection."*

DAG HAMMARSKJOLD: *"It is when we all play safe that we create a world of utmost insecurity."*

JOHN C. MAXWELL: *"Leaders who are kind of insecure or egocentric, they basically sabotage themselves."*

JOAN DIDION, PULITZER: *"To cure jealousy is to see it for what it is, a dissatisfaction with self."*

Similar: inadequacy, anxiety, uncertainty, threatened, apprehensive, vulnerable
Opposite: composed, confident, unafraid, calm, secure

Inspiration. (1) Getting the thought or motivation to begin a new course of action. (2) Giving or receiving insight to help pursue a cherished goal. *Popular or Heart-Based Usage: (1) Getting lit up. (2) Flashing on an idea. (3) Picturing it in your mind. (4) Finding jet fuel for your soul. (5) Discovering your passion. (6) Getting a preview of your future. (7) Getting an inkling of fresh horizons. (8) Reaching a personal inflection point. (9) Ignoring your critics/inner critic. (10) Feeling something new emerge in your heart. (11) Finding someone who brings out the best in you. (12) Moving in a whole new direction. (13) Feeling you're on a mission from God. (14) Connecting with your muse. (15) Getting goosebumps about something. (16) 'You can do it.' (17) 'Go for it!'*

ADAGE: *"When you aspire to inspire, the universe takes note."*

HELEN KELLER: *"The best and most beautiful things in the world cannot be seen or even touched. They must be felt with the heart."*

MAYA ANGELOU: *"I've learned that people will forget what you said, people will forget what you did, but people will never forget how you made them feel."*

TONY HSIEH: *"There's a big difference between motivation and inspiration. Inspire through values and motivation takes care of itself."*

NELSON MANDELA, NOBEL: *"There is no passion to be found playing small—in settling for a life that is less than the one you are capable of living."*

PSALM 121:1–2 *"I will lift up mine eyes unto the hills, from whence cometh my help. My help cometh from the Lord, which made heaven and earth."*

JAMES ALLEN: *"You will become as small as your controlling desire; as great as your dominant aspiration."*

ELEANOR ROOSEVELT: *"Great minds discuss ideas, average minds discuss events, and small minds discuss people."*

MARTHA GRAHAM: *"Some men have thousands of reasons why they cannot do what they want to, when all they need is one reason why they can."*

CONFUCIUS: *"Our greatest glory is not in never failing, but in rising every time we fall."*

KEN VENTURI: *"I don't believe you have to be better than everyone else. You have to be better than you ever thought you could be."*

RUMI: *"Set your life on fire. Seek those who fan the flames."*

RAM DASS: *"Inspiration is God making contact with itself."*

T. S. ELIOT: *"Every moment is a fresh beginning."*

Similar: emboldening, stirring, instilling, imagining, inventing, visualizing
Opposite: depression, discouragement, despair

Integrity. (1) Being truthful to yourself and to others. (2) Adhering to what you know is truthful, moral, and ethical. *Popular or Heart-Based Usage: (1) Being true blue. (2) Being authentic. (3) Keeping it real. (4) Having street cred. (5) Being a stand-up person. (6) Being a role model. (7) Having a strong moral compass. (8) Knowing true north. (9) Walking the walk. (10) Playing it straight. (11) Knowing what you're doing. (12) Avoiding misunderstandings. (13) 'Let's level with each other.' (14) Holding sacred space. (15) Living fully in the Ethisphere. (16) Being a true witness. (17) Having gravitas.*

ABRAHAM LINCOLN: *"If I were two-faced, would I be wearing this one?"*

MARK TWAIN: *"A clear conscience is the sure sign of a bad memory."*

CARLY FIORINA: *"The way you behave when you think you can get away with it is who you really are."*

JOHN WOODEN: *"Be more concerned with your character than your reputation. Reputation is what others think you are. Character is who you really are."*

WARREN BUFFETT: *"In looking for people to hire, look for three qualities: integrity, intelligence, and energy. And if they don't have the first, the other two will kill you."*

PAULETTE KLEIN: *"Being a beautiful woman is not about physical appearance. True beauty comes from character, integrity, intelligence, strength, and compassion."*

GLORIA STEINEM: *"The art of acting morally is behaving as if everything we do matters."*

D. EARL JOHNSTON: *"The first seducers of Integrity have usually been either Cool, Cash, or Convenient."*

GEORGE WASHINGTON: *"Few men have virtue to withstand the highest bidder."*

CLINT EASTWOOD: *"Integrity isn't about the big things, it's about the small ones. The times when no one's looking, and you do the right thing."*

LUKE BRYAN: *"I am just what I am, I'm just what you see. So I'll make it easy, I'll stay me."*

RUMI: *"It's your road, and yours alone, others may walk it with you, but no one can walk it for you."*

D. EARL JOHNSTON: *"Integrity is your duty to yourself. Deep down in your heart you know you will remember."*

D. H. LAWRENCE: *"You've got to know yourself so you can at last be yourself."*

SAM GORES: *"Never let yourself be misunderstood."*

OSCAR WILDE: *"Be yourself, everyone else is already taken."*

WILLIAM SHAKESPEARE: *"To thine own self be true."*

Similar: honor, rectitude, principle, virtue, righteousness, saturnian, high-minded
Opposite: deceit, disgrace, dishonor, phoniness, pettiness, fickleness

Intention. [See also **Attention** and **Concentration**] (1) The carrier wave of decision. (2) Focusing on where and how to pursue your efforts. (3) Bringing the spiritual into the physical. *Popular or Heart-Based Usage: (1) 'Mind over matter.' (2) Setting your goals. (3) Being purpose-driven. (4) Sweeping away confusion. (5) Prioritizing clarity. (6) Developing a laser focus. (7) Building the resolve. (8) Visualizing your plans. (9) Seeing beyond cause, effect, and time. (10) Making up your mind. (11) 'Locking in' to your decision. (12) Proceeding in the language of your heart and mind. (13) Following your mantra. (14) Structuring your life. (15) Keeping clear thoughts from a clean heart. (16) Deciding to get from A to B. (17) Having willpower. (18) 'Going for it.' (19) 'Just do it.'*

PAUL LEVY: *"Focusing our attention is an act of creation in and of itself."*

HSING YUN: *"Intention is the core of all conscious life. Conscious intention colors and moves everything."*

JAMES REDFIELD: *"Where Attention goes Energy flows; Where Intention goes Energy flows!"*

SHARON SALZBERG: *"Each decision we make, each action we take, is born out of an intention."*

JAMES JOYCE: *"Men are governed by lines of intellect; women by curves of emotion."*

MARLO MORGAN: *"When you have a thought that is not in alignment with your highest vision, change to a new thought!"*

ALBERT EINSTEIN, PHD, NOBEL: *"Live with purpose. Don't let people or things around you get you down."*

SAMUEL JOHNSON: *"The road to hell is paved with good intentions."*

STEPHEN COVEY: *"We judge ourselves by our intentions. And others by their actions."*

WAYNE DYER: *"I intend to take time for myself to live the life that I came here to live."*

TRIS THORP: *"The word mantra can be broken down into two parts: 'man,' which means mind, and 'tra' which means transport or vehicle."*

WAYNE DYER: *"Once you put your attention, your thoughts, your energy, your consciousness on a new intention, that's what you begin manifesting into your life. The word 'intention,' I believe, is really important, because it doesn't leave any room for doubt or maneuvering."*

D. EARL JOHNSTON: *"The step from attention to intention is about engagement— first noticing something and then deciding to act. It's where emotions enter."*

JUSTICE THURGOOD MARSHALL: *"What is the quality of your intent?"*

PSALM 119:36/THE DECALOGUE: *"Incline my heart unto thy testimonies."*

MATTHEW 6:10: *"Thy kingdom come, Thy will be done in earth, as it is in heaven."*

Similar: attention, concentration, focus, resolve, decision, initiative, motivation
Opposite: confusion, indecision, muddlement, chaos, waffling

Intimidation. Intending to change someone else's behavior through the threat of embarrassment, pain, or loss. *Popular or Heart-Based Usage: (1) Dropping a few nasty hints. (2) Being plain mean. (3) Planting big seeds of doubt. (4) Making ugly overtures. (5) Staring someone down. (6) Creating major downside for someone. (7) Selling woof tickets. (8) Saber-rattling. (9) Dropping a conversational bomb. (10) Talking smack. (11) Trash talking. (12) Dropping a few 'F Bombs.' (13) Getting in someone's face. (14)* [From baseball] *Throwing a brushback pitch. (15)* [From baseball] *Throwing a little chin music. (16) Making someone feel small. (17) Being overbearing. (18)* [From foot-ball] *Getting in somebody's grill. (19) 'Call yo Momma!' (20) 'Who's your daddy?' (21) Bitch-slapping someone. (22) Slam-dunking someone. (23) 'That all you got?'*

PAULO COELHO: *"If you want to intimidate someone, all you have to do is make them feel afraid."*

JUSTICE SANDRA DAY O'CONNOR: *"The freedom to criticize judges and other public officials is necessary to a vibrant democracy. The problem comes when healthy criticism is replaced with more destructive intimidation and sanctions."*

HILLARY CLINTON: *"Extremism thrives amid ignorance and anger, intimidation and cowardice."*

MO IBRAHIM: *"Intimidation, harassment, and violence have no place in a democracy."*

JANE AUSTEN: *"My courage always rises at every effort to intimidate me."*

REBECCA AGUILAR: *"Lead by inspiration, not intimidation."*

LENNY WILKINS: *"Intimidation doesn't last very long."*

ROGER CLEMENS: *"But Jack (Nicklaus) leaned over to me, and he said, 'Being intimidating, Rocket, is because you win. You can throw very, very hard and not win, not be intimidating.'"*

AUNG SAN SUU KYI, NOBEL: *"If you give in to intimidation, you'll go on being intimidated."*

KOBE BRYANT: *"I realized that intimidation didn't really exist if you're in the right frame of mind."*

KAILIN GOW: *"Courage is taking calculated risks and facing intimidation in the eye."*

NATE SILVER: *"Success makes you less intimidated by things."*

PROVERB: *"Do right and fear no man."*

Similar: bullying, glowering, threatening, harassing, shaming, introverting
Opposite: encouragement, appreciation, extroversion, snapping back

Intuition. [See also **ESP** or **Extra Sensory Perception**] Having understanding or clarity or about something through special insight and/or without physical contact. *Popular or Heart-Based Usage: (1) Trusting your gut. (2) Having your antennae up. (3) Thinking outside the box. (4) Trusting your spider sense. (5) Believing in your powers. (6) Having ESP. (7) Listening to the still small voice inside. (8) Having a strong hunch. (9) Having a visceral reaction to something. (10) Picking up on something. (11) Knowing what's coming next. (12) Connecting the dots. (13) Reading between the lines. (14) Pattern recognition. (15) Seeing where it is going. (16) Feeling it deep in your bones.*

RUMI: *"There is a voice that doesn't use words. Listen."*

OPRAH WINFREY: *"Follow your instincts. That's where true wisdom manifests itself."*

PROVERB: *"A woman's intuition can be her favorite superpower."*

MARGARET FULLER: *"The especial genius of women I take to be electrical in movement, intuitive in function, spiritual in tendency."*

STEVE JOBS: *"Intuition is a very powerful thing, more powerful than intellect."*

D. EARL JOHNSTON: *"The heart and gut are the seats of intuition."*

DR. JOYCE BROTHERS: *"Trust your hunches. They're usually based on facts filed away just below the conscious level."*

JONAS SALK, MD: *"Intuition will tell the thinking mind where to look next."*

DANIEL KAHNEMAN, MD, NOBEL: *"Intuition is nothing more and nothing less than recognition."*

JONATHAN HAIDT, PHD: *"Intuitions come first, strategic reasoning second."*

KRISHNAMURTI: *"Intuition is the whisper of the soul."*

SHAKTI GAWAIN: *"There is a universal, intelligent, life force that exists within everyone and everything. It resides within each of us as a deep wisdom, an inner knowing."*

THE BEATITUDES: *"Blessed are the pure in heart: for they shall see God."*

ALBERT EINSTEIN, PHD, NOBEL: *"The intuitive mind is a sacred gift. The rational mind is a faithful servant. We have created a society that honors the servant and has forgotten the gift."*

BENJAMIN SPOCK, MD: *"Trust yourself, you know more than you think you do."*

ROLLO MAY, BDIV, PHD: *"It is amazing how may hints and guides and intuitions for living come to the sensitive person who has ears to hear what his body is saying."*

STEVE JOBS: *"Have the courage to follow your heart and your intuition. They somehow already know what you truly want to become."*

ADAGE: *"Intuition is knowing without knowing."*

RUMI: *"Close both eyes to see with the other eye."*

Similar: second sight, divination, clairvoyance, hunch, gut feeling, discernment
Opposite: misapprehension, unfamiliarity, ignorance, cluelessness

Jealousy. [See also **Envy**, **Insecurity**, and **Selfish**] Fearing a loss of attention or affection because of the presence or success of a third party. *Popular or Heart-Based Usage: (1) Getting eaten up by someone (or something). (2) Giving someone the evil eye. (3) Sending 'thought daggers' toward someone. (4) Talking 'sour grapes' about someone. (5) Having doubts about yourself. (6) Feeling inadequate and threatened.*

MARC PAUL: *"Nothing sharpened my eyesight more than seeing another man dancing with my wife."*

MARY SCHMICH, PULITZER: *"Do not waste time on jealousy. Sometimes you're ahead, sometimes you're behind."*

WILLIAM PENN: *"The jealous are troublesome to others but a torment to themselves."*

JOSH BILLINGS: *"Love looks through a telescope; envy, through a microscope."*

JOSEPH ADDISON: *"Jealousy is that pain which a man feels from the apprehension that he is not equally loved by the person whom he entirely loves."*

WILLIAM SHAKESPEARE: *"Oh beware, my lord, of jealousy; it is the green-eyed monster which doth mock the meat it feeds on."*

HAVELOCK ELLIS: *"Jealousy, that dragon which slays love under the pretense of keeping it alive."*

MAYA ANGELOU: *"Jealousy is like salt in food. A little can enhance the savor, but too much can spoil the pleasure, and under certain circumstances can be life threatening."*

WASHINGTON IRVING: *"Jealous people poison their own banquet and then eat it."*

SHANNON L. ALDER: *"Love may be blind but jealousy has 20–20 vision."*

HELEN ROWLAND: *"Jealousy is the tie that binds, and binds, and binds."*

JOAN DIDION, PULITZER: *"To cure jealousy is to see it for what it is, a dissatisfaction with self."*

FRANCOISE SAGAN: *"To jealousy, nothing is more frightful than laughter."*

YOKO ONO: *"Transform envy to admiration, and what you admire will become part of your life."*

D. EARL JOHNSTON: *"God gives a special purpose to everyone. Our mission is to find it—sometimes where we least expect it—to be grateful for it, and to expand it."*

PROVERB: *"Run your own race."*

JOE ROGAN: *"I realized a long time ago that instead of being jealous you can be inspired and appreciative. It carries more energy to you."*

Similar: resentment, envy, possessiveness, inadequacy, wariness
Opposite: trust, understanding, unconcern, confidence, self-assurance

Joy. Experiencing extreme happiness, delight, or exultation of the spirit. *Popular or Heart-Based Usage: (1) Being unspeakably happy. (2) Footloose. (3) Having your heart leap. (4) Feeling on top of the world. (5) Having an out-of-body experience. (6) Holding your child for the first time. (7) Dancing in the streets. (8) Happy pandemonium. (9) Envisioning the Rapture. (10) 'Glory to God in the highest.' (11) 'Hosanna in the highest!' (12) 'Hallelujah!' (13) 'Eureka!' (14) Having a song in your heart. (15) 'I'm home!'*

JOEL OSTEEN: *"Joy is deep down within you, a calm delight."*

MOTHER TERESA, NOBEL: *"Joy is the token of a generous personality."*

JEAN PAUL RICHTER: *"Joy descends gently upon us like the evening dew."*

MAYA ANGELOU: *"We need Joy as we need air. We need love as we need water. We need each other as we need the earth we share."*

W. H. AUDEN: *"In times of joy, all of us wished we possessed a tail we could wag."*

MARIANNE WILLIAMSON: *"When we are centered in joy, we attain our wisdom."*

WILLIAM SCHUTZ, PHD: *"Joy is the feeling that comes from the fulfillment of one's potential."*

FREDERICK FABER: *"There are souls in this world who have the gift of finding joy everywhere and of leaving it behind them when they go."*

CARROLL E. IZARD, PHD: *"Joy seems to be more a by-product of events and conditions than a result of a direct effort to obtain it. Joy is characterized by a sense of confidence and significance, a feeling of being loved or being loveable."*

LORD BYRON: *"All who joy would win must share it. Happiness was born a Twin."*

ANN VOSKAMP: *"Joy is always given, never grasped."*

CHARLES DICKENS: *"I like to cry for joy. It's so delicious to cry for joy."*

ECKHART TOLLE: *"Pleasure is always derived from something outside of you, whereas joy arises from within."*

THEODORE ROOSEVELT, NOBEL: *"Comparison is the thief of joy."*

JOHN NEWTON: *"Amazing Grace"* (Song)

LUDWIG VAN BEETHOVEN: *"Ode to Joy"* (Song)

WILLIAM BLAKE: *"He who binds to himself a joy,*
   Does the winged life destroy;
   But he who kisses the joy as it flies,
   Lives in eternity's sunrise."

Similar: delight, rapture, bliss, jubilation, exultation, exhilaration, ecstasy, elation
Opposite: misery, agony, horror, fear, terror, suppression, insecurity

Justice. Applying the mandates of fairness and the law equally to all citizens or affected people. *Popular or Heart-Based Usage: (1) Doing the fair thing. (2) Getting what you got coming to you. (3) Talking to the lady with the blindfold. (4) 'The Man gonna getcha.'*

WILLIAM E. GLADSTONE, FRS: *"Justice delayed is justice denied."*

MARTIN LUTHER KING, JR., NOBEL: *"Injustice anywhere is a threat to justice everywhere."*

DESMOND TUTU, NOBEL: *"If you are neutral in situations of injustice, you have chosen the side of the oppressor. If an elephant has its foot on the tail of a mouse and you say that you are neutral, the mouse will not appreciate your neutrality."*

ROSA PARKS: *"I would like to be known as a person who is concerned about freedom and justice and equality and prosperity for all people."*

MAHATMA GANDHI: *"There is a higher court than courts of justice and that is the court of conscience. It supersedes all other courts."*

ADAM SMITH: *"Mercy to the guilty is cruelty to the innocent."*

REINHOLD NIEBUHR: *"Man's capacity for justice makes democracy possible, but man's inclination to injustice makes democracy necessary."*

BENJAMIN FRANKLIN: *"Justice will not be served until those who are unaffected are as outraged as those who are."*

THOMAS JEFFERSON: *"The system of justice will either protect citizens from tyranny or be one means by which tyranny is exercised over them."*

DECLARATION OF INDEPENDENCE: *"We hold these truths to be self evident, that all men are created equal."*

PREAMBLE TO THE U.S. CONSTITUTION: *"We the People of the United States, in order to form a more perfect union, establish Justice, insure domestic Tranquility, provide for the common defense, promote the general welfare, and secure the blessings of Liberty to ourselves and our Posterity, do ordain and establish this Constitution..."*

PLEDGE OF ALLEGIANCE: *"I pledge allegiance to the Flag of the United States of America, and to the Republic for which it stands, one Nation under God, indivisible, with liberty and justice for all."*

ABRAHAM LINCOLN: *"I've always found that mercy bears richer fruits than strict justice."*

GLORIA STEINEM: *"Law and justice are not always the same."*

ARISTOTLE: *"Justice is the bond of men in states, and the administration of justice, which is the determination of what is just, is the principle of order in political society."*

PLATO: *"Do not expect justice where might is right."*

Similar: righteousness, rectitude, impartiality, fairness, probity
Opposite: arbitrariness, tyranny, dictatorship, suppression

Karma. (1) The principle of cause and effect where nature seeks a balance in human affairs. (2) The tendency of life to reward those who demonstrate net benevolent behavior toward others, and to withhold success from those who demonstrate net negative behavior toward others. (3) The dynamic principle that vice is punished and virtue is rewarded. (4) How a person's positive or negative behavior carries forward in their life and subsequent lives. *Popular or Heart-Based Usage: (1) Reaping what you sow. (2) The invisible principle of cause and effect. (3) 'What goes around, comes around.' (4) 'Actions have consequences.' (5) Living out the Golden Rule. (6) Feeling some Saturnian lessons. (7) The consequences of being a 'giver' or a 'taker.' (8) 'It all comes back to you in the end.' (9) Getting what's coming to you. (10) Notations from the Book of Life. (11) Experiencing poetic justice. (12) Getting your just deserts.*

ADAGE: *"What goes around, comes around."*
ALLAN WILLIAMS: *"Karma is God's girlfriend."*
BARBARA DE ANGELIS: *"Love and kindness are never wasted."*
GALATIANS 6:7: *"Be not deceived; God is not mocked: for whatsoever a man soweth, that shall he also reap."*
LEONARDO DA VINCI: *"Realize that everything connects to everything else."*
WAYNE DYER: *"When you judge another, you do not define them, you define yourself."*
ECKHART TOLLE: *"Life will give you whatever experience is most helpful for the evolution of your consciousness."*
SAKYONG MIPHAM: *"Like gravity, karma is so basic we often don't even notice it."*
ALBERT EINSTEIN, PHD, NOBEL: *"It is every man's obligation to put back into the world at least the equivalent of what he takes out of it."*
ELTON JOHN, HANS ZIMMER, TIM RICE: *"Circle of Life"* (Song)
APHORISM: *"A strong person does not seek revenge. They move on and let karma do the dirty work."*
FREDERICK DOUGLASS: *"When men sow the wind it is rational to expect they will reap the whirlwind."*
LADY GAGA: *"Never bully anyone because Karma has everyone's address and a motherf***ing stamp."*
MATT ALAN: *"We learn what karma is when we have a teenage daughter."*
DUSTIN POIRIER: *"Karma is not a bitch, it's a mirror."*
HUMORIST: *"My dogma got run over by my karma."*

Similar: destiny, fate, kismet, action and reaction, just deserts
Opposite: misfortune, randomness, unpredictability, chaos

Kindness. Expressing gentleness, benevolence, and support to others, especially when it is not expected or required. *Popular or Heart-Based Usage: (1) Being good-hearted. (2) Looking out for others. (3) 'That's so sweet.' (4) Giving someone some TLC. (5) Doing someone a solid. (6) Earning your wings. (7) Doing gently unto others. (8) Going the extra mile for someone.*

DALAI LAMA, NOBEL: *"Be kind whenever possible. It is always possible."*

WILLIAM PENN: *"If there is any kindness I can show, or any good thing I can do to any fellow human being, let me do it now, and not deter or neglect it, as I shall not pass this way again."*

PLATO: *"Be kind, for everyone you meet is fighting a harder battle."*

MARK TWAIN: *"Kindness is the language which the deaf can hear and the blind can see."*

MAX LUCADO: *"I choose kindness. I will be kind to the poor, for they are alone. Kind to the rich, for they are afraid. And kind to the unkind, for such is how God has treated me."*

JACKIE CHAN: *"Sometimes it takes only one act of kindness and caring to change a person's life."*

LAO TZU: *"Kindness in words creates confidence. Kindness in thinking creates profoundness. Kindness in giving creates love."*

DALAI LAMA, NOBEL: *"My religion is kindness."*

THE TALMUD: *"The highest wisdom is loving kindness."*

MOTHER TERESA, NOBEL: *"If you are kind, people may accuse you of selfish ulterior motives; Be kind anyway."*

HENRY JAMES: *"Three things in human life are important. The first is to be kind. The second is to be kind. And the third is to be kind."*

ALBERT EINSTEIN, PHD, NOBEL: *"Be kind to people who are different from you."*

AESOP: *"No act of kindness, however small, is ever wasted."*

Similar: caring, considerate, soft-heartedness, compassion, benevolence, tenderness
Opposite: cruelty, neglect, disdainful, caustic, abrasive, mean

Laughter. Smiling and exhaling in lighthearted emotional release. *Popular or Heart-Based Usage: (1) 'Haha!' (2) Having fun. (3) Cracking up. (4) Living it up. (5) Letting the good times roll. (6) Getting your jollies. (7) Busting loose. (8) 'Hee haw!' (9) 'LOL.' [Laughing Out Loud.] (10) 'ROFLMAO.' [Rolling on the Floor Laughing My Ass Off.]*

WILL ROGERS: *"We are all here for a spell. Get all the good laughs you can."*

MARK TWAIN: *"The human race has only one really effective weapon, and that is laughter."*

GEORGE ELIOT: *"Wear a smile and have friends; wear a scowl and have wrinkles."*

VICTOR BORGE: *"Laughter is the shortest distance between two people."*

THOMAS MANN: *"Laughter is a sunbeam of the soul."*

LORD BYRON: *"Always laugh when you can. It's cheap medicine."*

GOETHE: *"Nothing shows a man's character more than what he laughs at."*

CARL REINER: *"There isn't anything more important than being able to laugh. When you laugh, life is worth living."*

BOB HOPE: *"I have seen what a laugh can do. It can transform almost unbearable tears into something bearable, even hopeful."*

MARK TWAIN: *"The best way to cheer yourself up is to try to cheer someone else up."*

ELSA MAXWELL: *"Laugh at yourself first, before anyone else can."*

WILLIAM MAKEPEACE THACKERAY: *"A good laugh is sunshine in the house."*

D. EARL JOHNSTON: *"If you can laugh at an emotion, it does not control you."*

DAU VOIRE: *"Laughter is, and always will be, the best form of therapy."*

JOHNNY MCGREW: *"Laughter is taking a happy break from your problems."*

PROVERBS 15:15: *"He that is of a merry heart hath a continual feast."*

JOSH BILLINGS: *"Laughter is the fireworks of the soul."*

READER'S DIGEST: *"Laughter is the best medicine."*

JOHN HEYWOOD: *"He who laughs last, laughs best."*

MILTON BERLE: *"Laughter is an instant vacation."*

PLATO: *"Even the gods love jokes."*

Similar: chuckle, chortle, grin, guffaw, ha!, knee-slapping
Opposite: sadness, crying, weeping, frowning, withdrawing, introverting

Leadership. Deciding to act, command, inspire, or to set an example for the benefit of others. *Popular or Heart-Based Usage: (1) Setting the tone/example. (2) Being the boss. (3) Getting hard stuff accomplished. (4) Being the adult in the room. (5) Making it all happen. (6) Taking it up a notch. (7) Taking responsibility. (8) Getting kicked upstairs. (9) Taking the helm. (10) Running with the big dogs. (11) Winning people over. (12) Filling the void. (13) Stepping into the breach. (14) Making the tough calls. (15) Being the tip of the spear. (16) Kicking ass and taking names. (17) Doing what needs to be done. (18) Taking the point on an issue. (19) Winning hearts and minds. (20) Inspiring others.*

ADAGE: *"If you're not the lead dog, the scenery won't be changing."*

SENECA: *"Throw me to the wolves and I will return leading the pack."*

TONY HSIEH: *"Whatever you are thinking, think bigger."*

JUDY GARLAND: *"Always be a first-rate version of yourself and not a second-rate version of someone else."*

ALEXANDER THE GREAT: *"I am not afraid of an army of lions led by a sheep; I am afraid of an army of sheep led by a lion."*

HARRY S. TRUMAN: *"I learned that a great leader is a man who has the ability to get other people to do what they don't want to do and like it."*

GEN. GEORGE S. PATTON, JR.: *"Honor your people. When a true leader's work is done and his aims fulfilled, they should say and believe 'We did this ourselves.'"*

GEN. DOUGLAS MACARTHUR: *"A true leader has the confidence to stand alone, the courage to make tough decisions, and the compassion to listen to the needs of others. He does not set out to be a leader, but becomes one by the equality of his actions and the integrity of his intent."*

D. EARL JOHNSTON: *"Sometimes a leader learns the hard way that counseling or blaming a subordinate should be discussed in private."*

GEN. WILLIAM H. MCRAVEN: *"To be a good leader, you have to be a good communicator."*

THOMAS AQUINAS: *"If the highest aim of a captain were to preserve his ship, he would keep it in port forever."*

GAMAL ABDEL NASSER: *"He who cannot support himself, can not take his own decision."*

CAPT. DAVID MARQUET: *"If you want your people to think, don't give instructions, give intent."*

JOHN D. ROCKEFELLER: *"Good leadership consists of showing average people how to do the work of superior people."*

LAO TZU: *"Leadership is your ability to hide your panic from others."*

DAVID M. HENDRICKS: *"A charismatic leader inspires confidence and wins devotion."*

SAYING: *"Lead, follow, or get out of the way."*

THOMAS EDISON: *"Vision without execution is hallucination."*

Leadership. *(continued)*

FAYE WATTLETON: *"The only safe ship in a storm is leadership."*

CARLY FIORINA: *"The highest calling of leadership is to challenge the status quo and unlock the potential of others."*

JOSEPH JOUBERT: *"Mediocrity is excellence in the eyes of the mediocre."*

CHRISTINE LAGARDE: *"To me, leadership is about encouraging people. It's about stimulating them. It's about enabling them to achieve what they can achieve—and doing that with a purpose."*

JESSE JACKSON: *"Leaders must be tough enough to fight, tender enough to cry, human enough to make mistakes, humble enough to admit them, strong enough to absorb the pain, and resilient enough to bounce back and keep on moving."*

DAISAKU IKEDA: *"A person who, no matter how desperate the situation, gives others hope, is a true leader."*

PAM GREGORY: *"We are meant to turn our wounds into leadership."*

GEN. GEORGE S. PATTON, JR.: *"Never tell people how to do things. Tell them what to do and they will surprise you with their ingenuity."*

PETER F. DRUCKER: *"Management is doing things right; leadership is doing the right things."*

JOHN G. MEDLIN, JR.: *"A leader: 1. Learns the rules. 2. Follows the rules. 3. Knows how to make exceptions."*

ARISTOTLE: *"He who has never learned to obey cannot be a good commander."*

ROY E. DISNEY: *"When your values are clear to you, making decisions comes easier."*

LEO TOLSTOY: *"There is no greatness where there is no simplicity, goodness, and truth."*

HENRY FORD: *"Don't find fault, find a remedy."*

ADAGE: *"Leadership is action not position."*

SCOUTMASTER BILLY JIM VAUGHN: *"Good leadership is quietly admired and respected."*

JAMES A. BAKER III: *"A leader sees what needs to be done, and then does it."*

Similar: authority, command, control, direction, initiative, decisiveness
Opposite: impotence, waffling, indecision, subservience, powerlessness

Liberal. (1) Maintaining support for the integration of new ideas and a wide range of views. (2) Promoting progressiveness and diversity in political and social policies. (3) In the current political environment, *liberal* is a term often contrasted with *conservative*. *Popular or Heart-Based Usage: Being a progressive.* Alternately, as opposites: *(4) Liberal vs. conservative, (5) Blue-pilled vs. red-pilled. (6) Left vs. right. (7) Left-wing (or progressive/socialist) vs. right-wing (or conservative/reactionary).*

WILL ROGERS: *"I remember when being liberal meant being generous with your own money."*

HERBERT HOOVER: *"The spirit of liberalism is to create free men; it is not the regimentation of men."*

AMBROSE BIERCE: *"Conservative, n.: A statesman who is enamored of existing evils, as distinguished from the Liberal who wishes to replace them with others."*

LINCOLN STOREY: *"A liberal often believes in giving away lots of money, as long as most of it is not theirs. A conservative is just fine with new ideas, as long as everything stays the way it used to be."*

THOMAS WOLFE: *"If a conservative is a liberal who's been mugged, a liberal is a conservative who's been arrested."*

CHARLES BARKLEY: *"I do not use words like 'liberal' or 'conservative.' You can ask me a question and I will give you an answer. Those are words rich people on television use to divide and conquer."*

JOHNNY MCGREW: *"In the current environment, there's hardly anything more compelling in Hollywood than what a friend says is trendy or cool."*

BARUCH SPINOZA: *"Freedom is absolutely necessary for progress in science and the liberal arts."*

ARISTOTLE: *"Of all the varieties of virtues, liberalism is the most beloved."*

ELLEN KEY: *"Education can give you a skill, but a liberal education can give you dignity."*

JOHNNY MCGREW: *"If you find me conservative, please quote me liberally."*

DANIEL PATRICK MOYNIHAN: *"The central conservative truth is that it is culture, not politics, that determines the success of a society. The central liberal truth is that politics can change a culture and save it from itself."*

IGNATIUS OF LOYOLA: *"Be generous to the poor and orphans and those in need. The man to whom Our Lord has been liberal ought not to be stingy. We shall one day find in Heaven as much rest and joy as we ourselves have dispensed in this life."*

Similar: progressive, socialist, open-minded, lenient, tolerant, generous, welfare-oriented
Opposite: conservative, narrow-minded, reactionary, right-wing

Life. (1) Pursuing your survival and success as a physical or spiritual being. (2) Solving problems. *Popular or Heart-Based Usage: (1) Going cradle to grave. (2) 'It's just one darned thing after another.' (3) Keeping your head screwed on right. (4) Keeping your perspective. (5) Handling stuff 24/7. (6) 'Some days it rains.' (7) Staying focused. (8) Finding your place. (9) 'What goes around, comes around.' (10) Keeping a sense of humor. (11) Having your time in the sun. (12) Being full of beans. (13) Playing for the whole enchilada. (14) Pursuing the wheel of fortune. (15) Having your fifteen minutes of fame. (16) Livin' the dream. (17) 'Waiting for them Pearly Gates.' (18) 'The show must go on.' (19) What you are doing with your body. (20) Leaving your legacy.*

REBA MCENTIRE: *"To succeed in life, you need three things: a wishbone, a backbone, and a funny bone."*

ELBERT HUBBARD: *"Don't take life too seriously, no one makes it out alive."*

GEORGE BERNARD SHAW: *"Life isn't about finding yourself. Life is about creating yourself."*

SAI BABA: *"Life is a song—sing it. Life is a game—play it. Life is a challenge—meet it. Life is a dream—realize it. Life is a sacrifice—offer it. Life is love—enjoy it."*

JACKIE ROBINSON: *"A life is not important except in the impact it has on other lives."*

ARTHUR RUBINSTEIN: *"I have found that if you love life, life will love you back."*

HELEN KELLER: *"Life is an exciting business, and most exciting when it is lived for others."*

GEORGE ELIOT: *"What do we live for, if not to make life less difficult for each other?"*

DALAI LAMA, NOBEL: *"Our prime purpose in this life is to help others. And if you can't help them, at least don't hurt them."*

HIPPOCRATES: *"First, do no harm."*

MAHATMA GANDHI: *"Live simply, that others may simply live."*

WALT WHITMAN: *"That you are here—and that life exists and identity. That the powerful play goes on and you may contribute a verse."*

ALBERT EINSTEIN PHD, NOBEL: *"Life is like riding a bicycle. To keep your balance, you must keep moving."*

JOSE ORTEGA Y GASSET: *"Human life, by its very nature, has to be dedicated to something."*

ROBERT LOUIS STEVENSON: *"Life is not a matter of holding good cards, but of playing a poor hand well."*

HENRY WADSWORTH LONGFELLOW: *"Into every life some rain must fall."*

AXL ROSE/GUNS N' ROSES: *"Welcome to the Jungle"* (Song)

EVA PERON: *"Time is my greatest enemy."*

APHORISM: *"Life's a bitch and then you die."*

JOHNNY MCGREW: *"Remember this. Ten percent of everybody you meet will smile at you and then steal your lunch money if you let them. Your best friend in life is a foolproof BS detector."*

Life. *(continued)*

ROBERT FROST: *"I can sum up everything I've learned about life. It goes on."*

PAULA D'ARCY: *"God comes to you disguised as your life."*

JORGE LUIS BORGES: *"Any life is made up of a single moment, the moment in which a man finds out, once and for all, who he is."*

ECKHART TOLLE: *"When something gets in your way, it is still the way."*

LOUIS GERSTNER: *"Computers are magnificent tools for the realization of our dreams, but no machine can replace the human spark of spirit, compassion, love, and understanding."*

D. EARL JOHNSTON: *"Through the ages, Earth has been noted as a place where we rediscover ourselves as timeless hyper-dimensional souls lodged for a time in temporary four-dimensional bodies."*

EDGAR CAYCE: *"You have inherited (the) most from yourself, not from your family. The family is only a river through which Soul flows."*

PIERRE TEILHARD DE CHARDIN: *"We are not human beings having a spiritual experience. We are spiritual beings having a human experience."*

OSHO: *"We never ask the meaning of life when we are in love."*

WALT WHITMAN: *"The whole purpose of the universe is unerringly aimed at one thing—you."*

PAM GREGORY: *"Life is NOT happening to us. It is happening FOR us."*

CHARLES ERNEST CARSON: *"The business of life is the acquisition of memories. In the end that's all there is."*

SOPHIA LOREN: *"Mistakes are part of the dues one pays for a full life."*

ECKHART TOLLE: *"Life has no opposite. The opposite of death is birth. Life is eternal."*

ROSE KENNEDY: *"Life isn't a matter of milestones, but of moments."*

GOETHE: *"Life is the childhood of our immortality."*

PABLO PICASSO: *"The meaning of life is to find your gift. The purpose of life is to give it away."*

WILLIAM WALLACE: *"Every man dies. Not every man really lives."*

JOHNNY MCGREW: *"If living good was easy, everybody would do it."*

ECKHART TOLLE: *"Get the inside right, and the outside will take care of itself."*

PAM GREGORY: *"My sense of humor is my #1 survival skill."*

JOHN HENRY NEWMAN: *"Growth is the only evidence of life."*

HENRY DAVID THOREAU: *"Live the life you've dreamed."*

ECKHART TOLLE: *"You don't have a life. You are life."*

OBSERVATION: *"Life is a school. The Earth is a classroom."*

OSHO: *"Love is the goal, life is the journey."*

Similar: survival, being, creation, existence, family, legacy
Opposite: death, cessation, termination, expiration, nonexistence, void

Light. (1) A manifestation of energy making it possible to see things. (2) The segment of the electromagnetic spectrum visible to the human eye in wavelengths from about 380 nanometers (violet) to about 720 nanometers (red). *Popular or Heart-Based Usage: (1) Out of the void. (2) Out of the Big Bang. (3) Flipping on the switch. (4) Being illuminated. (5) Glowing in the dark. (6) 'A thousand points of light.' (7) Chariots of fire. (8) Apollo's kingdom. (9) Heavenly splendor. (10) The Seven Rays. (11) Seeing is believing. (12) A glorious sunrise. (13) The golden dawn. (14) The silvery moon. (15) Our sky canopy. (16) The Starlight Express. (17) Sunlight (moonlight) dancing on the water. (18) Seeing fireflies and moonbeams. (19) Shimmering phosphorescence. (20) Experiencing a luminous presence. (21) Understanding photonic emissions. (22) Seeing prismatic refraction. (23) Getting all lit up. (24) Seeing the colors of the rainbow. (25) Seeing the light. (26) Having your life flash before your eyes. (27) Beholding the divine essence.*

GENESIS 1:3: *"And God said, Let there be light: and there was light."*

ALBERT EINSTEIN, PHD, NOBEL: *"Matter is Energy…Energy is Light…We are all Light Beings."*

HEATHER ENSWORTH, PHD: *"All the cells of our body communicate with light."*

NATIONAL LIBRARY OF MEDICINE: *"Although first proposed about a century ago, another form of communication…has been attracting attention in recent times. This form of communication involves light…indeed all living cells, can generate light and may use this to send messages to each other."*

SIR ISAAC NEWTON, FRS: *"Colours which appear through the Prism are to be derived from the Light of the white one."*

ALBERT EINSTEIN, PHD, NOBEL: *"Light behaves as both a particle and a wave."*

STUDYSMARTER.CO.UK: *"The properties of light are refraction, reflection, diffraction, interference, dispersion, polarization, and scattering."*

OG MANDINO: *"I will love the light for it shows me the way, yet I will endure the darkness because it shows me the stars."*

STEVEN WEINBERG, NOBEL: *"The invisible and non-existent look very much alike."*

FRANCIS OF ASSISI: *"All the darkness in the world cannot extinguish the light of a single candle."*

ALBERT SCHWEITZER, BTH, MD, PHD, OM, NOBEL: *"Just as white light consists of colored rays, so reverence for life contains all the components of ethics: love, kindliness, sympathy, empathy, peacefulness, and power to forgive."*

DIANE ACKERMAN, PHD: *"Love is the white light of emotion."*

ALBERT EINSTEIN, PHD, NOBEL: *"Darkness is in reality the absence of light. Light we can study, but not darkness."*

PLATO: *"The real tragedy of life is when men are afraid of the light."*

Similar: bright, radiant, luminous, photonic, glowing, shining, reflecting, shimmering
Opposite: darkness, void, emptiness, nothingness, blackness

Listening. Giving due attention to receiving, understanding, and acknowledging the verbal communications of others. *Popular or Heart-Based Usage: (1) Tuning in. (2) Picking up on something. (3) Lending an ear. (4) Paying attention. (5) Harkening to others. (6) 'Who's in your ear?' (7) Setting down everything else. (8) Being there for someone else. (9) Being a sounding board. (10) Being a go-to person. (11) 'From your lips to God's ears.' (12) '10–4.' (13) 'I copy.' (14) 'Roger that.' (15) 'Asked and answered.' (16) 'P911!' or 'POS!' ['Parent Over Shoulder!'] (17) 'Back atcha.' (18) 'Got it.'*

PAUL TILLICH: *"The first duty of love is to listen."*

RUTH BADER GINSBURG: *"I'm a very strong believer in listening and learning from others."*

GEN. COLIN POWELL: *"Diplomacy is listening to what the other guy needs. Preserving your own position, but listening to the other guy. You have to develop relationships with other people so when the tough times come, you can work together."*

SIMON SINEK: *"There is a difference between listening and waiting for your turn to speak."*

PROVERB: *"Friends listen to what you say. Best friends listen to what you don't say."*

PAT METHENY: *"The best musicians are not the best players, they're the best listeners."*

DEAN RUSK: *"The best way to persuade people is with your ears—by listening to them."*

DR. JOYCE BROTHERS: *"Listening, not imitation, may be the sincerest form of flattery."*

AMERICAN INDIAN PROVERB: *"Listen or thy tongue will keep thee deaf."*

STEVE JOBS: *"Don't let the noise of others' opinions drown out your own inner voice."*

CONSTANCE WU: *"Listening to an underserved population is how you learn to understand them and serve them better."*

DAVID HOCKNEY: *"Listening is a positive act: you have to put yourself out to do it."*

KARL A. MENNINGER: *"Listening is a magnetic and strange thing, a creative force. The friends we listen to are the ones we move toward. When we are listened to, it creates us, makes us unfold and expand."*

M. SCOTT PECK: *"By far the most important form of attention we can give our loved ones is listening ... True listening is love in action."*

JAN GOSS: *"The quality of our communications determines the quality of our lives."*

ADAGE: *"A good listener is an instantly more likeable person."*

Similar: tuning in, taking notice, hearing, copying, noting, duplicating, heeding
Opposite: ignore, refuse, reject, tune out, disobey, disregard

Logical. (1) Solving problems through the use of reason or scientific principles. (2) Proceeding by evaluating verifiable facts rather than through speculation, imagination, or opinion. *Popular or Heart-Based Usage: (1) Using common sense. (2) Using your head. (3) Being left-brained. (4) Putting on your thinking cap. (5) Keeping your head screwed on right. (6) Engaging your brain before opening your mouth. (7) Assembling the facts. (8) Using your digital brain. (9) Thinking something through.*

WILL ROGERS: *"If pro is the opposite of con, what is the opposite of Congress?"*

RITA MAE BROWN: *"If the world were a logical place, men would ride side saddle."*

LEONARD NIMOY: *"Logic is the beginning of wisdom, not the end."*

NIELS BOHR, PHD, NOBEL: *"No, no, you're not thinking; you're just being logical."*

ALBERT EINSTEIN, PHD, NOBEL: *"Logic will get you from A to B. Imagination will take you everywhere."*

HENRY DAVID THOREAU: *"If a man does not keep pace with his companions, perhaps it is because he hears a different drummer."*

BARBARA DE ANGELIS: *"If you let your mind talk you out of things that aren't logical, you're going to have a very boring life. Because grace isn't logical. Love isn't logical. Miracles aren't logical."*

JACQUES COUSTEAU: *"If we were logical, the future would be bleak, indeed. But we are more than logical. We are human beings, and we have faith, and we have hope, and we can work."*

RUDOLF STEINER: *"Because of their very nature, science and logical thinking can never decide what is possible or impossible. Their only function is to explain what has been ascertained by experience and observation."*

MR. SPOCK: *"May I say that I have not thoroughly enjoyed working with humans? I find their illogic and foolish emotions a constant irritant."*

DALE CARNEGIE: *"When dealing with people, remember you are not dealing with creatures of logic, but creatures of emotion."*

ARISTOTLE: *"The more you know, the more you know you don't know."*

Similar: reason, deduction, level-headedness, common sense, cause-and-effect, analytical, probabilistic

Opposite: irrational, ethereal, unrealistic, illogical, chaotic, random

Loneliness. Experiencing sadness or isolation as a result of loss, disappointment, or limited social interactions. *Popular or Heart-Based Usage: (1) Feeling left out. (2) Going it alone. (3) Feeling like you're on the outside looking in. (4) Finding yourself on an island. (5) Feeling cut off from the world. (6) Being a lonely heart. (7) Batching it. (8) Going it solo. (9) Playing solitaire. (10) Being a hermit. (11) Being a party of one. (12) 'It's just me, myself, and I.' (13) Calling a roll of one. (14) 'I'm single.' (15) Losing your other half. (16) Living in an empty nest. (17) 'Nobody here but the man in the mirror.'*

MOTHER TERESA, NOBEL: *"Loneliness and the feeling of being unwanted is the most terrible poverty."*

SUKARNO: *"The worst cruelty that can be inflicted on a person is isolation."*

ANTOINE DE SAINT-EXUPERY: *"It is such a secret place, the land of tears."*

GEORGE WASHINGTON: *"It is far better to be alone, than to be in bad company."*

GEORGE ELIOT: *"What loneliness is more lonely than distrust?"*

MARTHA BECK: *"Loneliness is proof that your innate search for connection is intact."*

HENRY DAVID THOREAU: *"Not until we are lost do we begin to understand ourselves."*

MAY SARTON: *"Loneliness is the poverty of self; solitude is the richness of self."*

NEIL DIAMOND: *"Solitary Man"* (Song)

SUPERMAN: *The Fortress of Solitude*

ALBERT EINSTEIN, PHD, NOBEL: *"Be a loner. That gives you time to wonder."*

WILLIAM STYRON: *"Reading—the best state yet to keep absolute loneliness at bay."*

ALAN LADD: *"Being a good host offsets the deprivation and loneliness of my youth."*

ADAGE: *"Having a dream in your heart means you're never alone."*

NIKOLA TESLA: *"Originality thrives in seclusion free of outside influences."*

INDRA DEVI: *"Yoga is a way to freedom. By its constant practice, we can free ourselves from fear, anguish, and loneliness."*

PROVERB: *"To have a friend, be a friend."*

JOHNNY MCGREW: *"Ready to say goodbye to loneliness? Every time you enter a room, try smiling at people, and really mean it. Then watch the magic begin."*

ADAGE: *"Find your tribe and love them hard."*

Similar: isolation, estrangement, solitude, dislocation, alienation, withdrawal
Opposite: sociable, affability, popularity, friendship, partnership, mentoring

Love. (1) Experiencing deep affinity and affection for another, and a willingness to put the needs of others first. (2) Experiencing romantic and sexual attraction. *Popular or Heart-Based Usage: (1) Life at its best. (2) Feeling butterflies. (3) 'Splendor in the grass.' (4) Hearts afire. (5) Soul harmony. (6) Philia. (7) Agape. (8) Having great chemistry. (9) Finding your soulmate. (10) Connecting with your tribe or 'family of frequency.' (11) Giving your heart away. (12) Being there. (13) Promise-keeping. (14) Sharing life. (15) Looking out for each other. (16) Bringing out someone's best. (17) Heartwarming stuff.*

BABS SMITH: *"Love helps things grow."*

WILLIAM SHAKESPEARE: *"Love looks not with the eyes but with the mind."*

GOETHE: *"Love does not dominate, it cultivates."*

ARISTOTLE: *"Love is composed of a single soul inhabiting two bodies."*

LAO TZU: *"Being deeply loved by someone gives you strength, while loving someone deeply gives you courage."*

JOHN DONNE: *"More than kisses, letters mingle souls."*

PLATO: *"At the touch of love everyone becomes a poet."*

MOTHER TERESA, NOBEL: *"Let us always meet each other with a smile, for the smile is the beginning of love."*

THOMAS AQUINAS: *"The things that we love tell us what we are."*

FRANCIS OF ASSISI: *"Lord, grant that I might not so much seek to be loved as to love."*

BERNARD OF CLAIRVAUX: *"What we love we shall grow to resemble."*

MAYA ANGELOU: *"I know for sure that love saves me. And that it is here to save us all."*

EVA GABOR: *"Love is a game that two can play and both win."*

DAVID FROST: *"Love is when each person is more concerned with the other than for oneself."*

B. F. SKINNER, PHD: *"What is love but another name for the use of positive reinforcement?"*

ANTOINE DE SAINT-EXUPERY: *"Love does not consist in gazing at each other, but in looking outward together in the same direction."*

SHARON TATE: *"My definition of love is being full. Complete. It makes everything lighter. Beauty is something you see. Love is something you feel."*

GOETHE: *"To be loved for what one is, is the greatest exception."*

CAROL GURNEY: *"Through their unconditional love, animals offer a direct reflection of those areas within ourselves that need nurturing."*

THICH NHAT HANH: *"If you love someone, the greatest gift you can give them is your presence."*

GAUTAMA BUDDHA: *"Love is a gift of one's inner most soul so that both can be whole."*

PAUL TILLICH: *"The first duty of love is to listen."*

BRIDGETT DEVOUE: *"We're starving for connection not attention."*

DALAI LAMA, NOBEL: *"Love and compassion are necessities, not luxuries. Without them humanity cannot survive."*

Love. *(continued)*

BRACHA GOLDSMITH: *"Love is empowering. Fear is disempowering."*

JOSH BILLINGS: *"A dog is the only thing on earth that loves you more than he loves himself."*

DANIEL KAHNEMAN, MD, NOBEL: *"A stable relationship requires that good interactions outnumber bad interactions by 5 to 1."*

BESSEL VAN DER KOLK, MD: *"As long as we feel safely held in the hearts and minds of the people who love us, we will climb mountains and cross deserts and stay up all night to finish projects."*

WALT WHITMAN: *"We were together. I forget the rest."*

ECKHART TOLLE: *"Love is when you recognize yourself in the other person."*

R. BUCKMINSTER FULLER: *"Love is metaphysical gravity."*

THOMAS MERTON: *"Our job is to love others without stopping to inquire whether or not they are worthy."*

EMILY DICKINSON: *"Unable are the loved to die, for love is immortality."*

PAUL: *"Love is patient; love is kind; love is not envious or boastful or arrogant or rude. It does not insist on its own way; it is not irritable or resentful; it does not rejoice in wrongdoing, but rejoices in the truth. It bears all things, believes all things, hopes all things, endures all things. Love never ends. Now faith, hope, and love abide, these three; and the greatest of these is love."*

FRANCIS CHAN: *"God's definition of what matters is pretty straightforward. He measures our lives by how we love."*

GERALD MITTMAN, D.MIN: *"If all the words in the Bible could be reduced to only one word, the word would be 'Love.'"*

EMMET FOX: *"The great difference between the two feelings is that love is always creative, and fear is always destructive."*

JEWISH PROVERB: *"Only love gives us the taste of eternity."*

LEVITICUS 19:18: *"Thou shalt love thy neighbor as thyself."*

MATTHEW 22:37–40: *"Jesus said unto him. Thou shalt love the Lord God with all thy heart, and with all thy soul, and with all thy mind. This is the first and great commandment. And the second is like unto it, thou shalt love thy neighbor as thyself. On these two commandments hang all the law and the prophets."*

MUHAMMAD: *"You will never enter paradise until you have faith, and you will not complete your faith until you love one another."*

Similar: harmony, endearment, fondness, attraction, eros, support, fulfillment, philia
Opposite: fear, hatred, opposition, antagonism, contraction, destruction, withdrawal

Loyalty. Maintaining allegiance to a person, principle, or belief. *Popular or Heart-Based Usage: (1) Being true blue. (2) Honoring your pledge to someone (or something). (3) 'Standing by your man.' (4) Having/being a reliable ally. (5) 'Semper Fi!'*

WOODROW WILSON, PHD, NOBEL, PRESIDENT: *"Loyalty means nothing unless it has at its heart the absolute principle of self-sacrifice."*

GALE SAYERS, 3X NFL MVP: *"The Lord is first, others are second, and I am third."*

MARK TWAIN: *"Loyalty to the country always. Loyalty to the government when it deserves it."*

TOMMY LASORDA: *"You give loyalty, you'll get it back. You give love, you'll get it back."*

ARIANNA HUFFINGTON: *"You can do not just twice as much but 200 times as much when you have a good partner."*

SOLDIER: *"Loyalty isn't grey. It's black and white. You're either loyal completely, or not at all."*

EURIPIDES: *"One loyal friend is worth ten thousand relatives."*

STEPHEN COVEY: *"Be loyal to those who are not present. In so doing, you build the trust of those who are present."*

CLARENCE FRANCIS: *"You cannot buy loyalty; you cannot buy the devotion of hearts, minds, and souls. You have to earn these things."*

ERIC FELTON: *"Without loyalty there can be no love. Without loyalty there can be no family. Without loyalty there can be no friendship."*

DR. PHIL MCGRAW: *"When you get married, your loyalty, first and foremost, is to your spouse, and to the family that you create together."*

THREE PROMISES OF THE SCOUT OATH: *"Duty to God and country, Duty to other people, and Duty to self."*

MOTTO OF THE U.S. MARINE CORPS: *"Semper Fidelis"* (Always Faithful)

DAVID MAMET: *"What I value most in my friends is loyalty."*

Similar: steadfastness, allegiance, devotion, faithfulness, constancy, fidelity, fealty
Opposite: treachery, sabotage, disgrace, dishonor, renegade

Luck. Having the experience or expectation that chance and random outcomes can be influenced by belief, action, charm, or grace. *Popular or Heart-Based Usage: (1) Having mojo. (2) Beating the odds. (3) Catching the breaks. (4) Getting the bounces. (5) Living a charmed life. (6) Going through your special rituals. (7) Knocking on wood. (8) Having a lucky number. (9) Finding a four-leaf clover. (10) 'Jupiter expands everything it touches.' (11) 'By Jove!' (12) Having your planets align. (13) Being on a roll. (14) Having a good hair day. (15) Having your rabbit's foot. (16) Running the table. (17) Capturing lightning in a bottle. (18) Being blessed by grace. (19) Being right for the wrong reasons. (20) Being in the right place at the right time. (21) The universe having your back.*

GAMBLER: *"A lot of luck is just believing you're lucky."*

BRUCE SPRINGSTEEN: *"When it comes to luck, you make your own."*

SENECA: *"Luck is what happens when preparation meets opportunity."*

NAPOLEON BONAPARTE: *"Ability is of little account without opportunity."*

JOEL OSTEEN: *"It's not luck, it's favor. It's God shining down on you, making things happen that you couldn't make happen."*

H. HILL MCALISTER: *"Lucky in love is God's grace in action."*

DORIE CLARK: *"Lucky people have an openness, an authenticity, and a generosity toward embracing people—without overthinking 'what's the value exchange'? It's just that's an interesting person."*

BARBARA SHER: *"The amount of good luck coming your way depends on your willingness to act."*

ROBERT LOUIS STEVENSON: *"Life is not a matter of holding good cards, but of playing a poor hand well."*

D. EARL JOHNSTON: *"A streak of luck is like having a beautiful dove alight near you. You know it's there and it's special, but you don't dare reach for it."*

EARL PICKETT: *"Lotta ball players like a set routine, like maybe it brings them luck or something. I never set foot on the field without repeating my exact same preparation."*

EARL WILSON: *"Success is merely a matter of luck. Ask any failure."*

WILLIAM HAZLITT: *"Keep your misfortunes to yourself."*

GAMBLING ADAGE: *"Scared money always loses."*

THOMAS JEFFERSON: *"I'm a great believer in luck, and I find the harder I work the more I have of it."*

DALAI LAMA, NOBEL: *"Remember that sometimes not getting what you want can be a wonderful stroke of luck."*

Similar: chance, fluke, break, advantage, serendipity, kismet, propitiousness
Opposite: misfortune, disadvantage, predictability, certainty

Lust. (1) Experiencing strong physical or sexual desire, and often without love or commitment. (2) Yearning for the pleasures of the flesh. *Popular or Heart-Based Usage: (1) Feeling horny. (2) Feeling hot to trot. (3) Finding the fleshpots. (4) Going for the eye candy. (5) Getting hot and bothered. (6) Having crotch goblins. (7) Getting the in-and-out urge. (8) Gettin' jiggy. (9) Feeling randy. (10) Feeling hot-hot-hot. (11) 'Thinkin' with yer John Henry.' (12) Bustin' a move. (13) Getting horizontal in a hurry. (14) Gettin' down 'n' dirty. (15) Ripping off your clothes. (16) Going in with rushin' hands and roamin' fingers. (17) Getting some. (18) Doing the wild thing. (19) Erotica maxima. (20) Going freestyle. (21) Getting raunchy. (22) 'Doing the shagnasty.' (23) 'Gotta getta hunka burnin' love.' (24) Sowing your wild oats. (25) Shaggin' on the run. (26) Doing a hit and run.*

> AVA GARDNER: *"It's a pity nobody believes in simple lust anymore."*
> JOHNNY MCGREW: *"Sometimes late at night your date's clothes look even better when they're thrown on the floor."*
> MARQUIS DE SADE: *"Lust's passion will be served; it demands, it militates, it tyrannizes."*
> THE DOORS: *"Light My Fire"* (Song)
> ARISTOPHANES/'LYSISTRATA': *"I'll make it short: they're dying to get laid."*
> JIMMY CARTER, NOBEL: *"I've looked on many women with lust. I've committed adultery in my heart many times. God knows I will do this and forgives me."*
> MATTHEW 26:41: *"The spirit indeed is willing, but the flesh is weak."*
> CHRISSIE HYNDE: *"In my experience lust only ever leads to misery. All the suspicion and jealousy and anguish it unleashes. I don't want those things in my life."*
> GERRY GOFFIN AND CAROLE KING: *"Will You Still Love Me Tomorrow"* (Song)
> DANIELLE STEEL: *"Lust is temporary, romance can be nice, but love is the most important thing of all."*
> D. EARL JOHNSTON: *"Lust is found in a young man's quandary, in an old man's memory, and in a woman's diary."*
> JOSEPH JOUBERT: *"What is true by lamplight is not always true by sunlight."*
> OSHO: *"In love the other person is important; in lust you are important."*
> BRIDGETT DEVOUE: *"Lust rushes but love waits."*

Similar: craving, desire, horniness, raunch, lewdness, carnality, eroticism, insatiability
Opposite: apathy, dislike, indifference, dislike, disenchantment

Lying. [See **Deception** and **Truth**]

Manifestation. How things appear or make themselves known. *Popular or Heart-Based Usage: (1) How things show up/show out. (2) Indications appearing. (3) Things coming to pass. (4) Making real your dreams. (5) 'Lo and behold.' (6) 'The proof's in the pudding.' (7) Your ship coming in. (8) 'You have arrived.' (9) Experiencing mind over matter. (10) Seeing signs and wonders. (11) Leaving no doubt. (12) Things writ large.*

WAYNE DYER: *"You'll see it when you believe it."*

SUNDAY ADELAJA: *"When you reach out in faith, God backs you up with manifestation."*

EDGAR CAYCE: *"What one thinks about continually, they become; what one cherishes in their heart and mind they make a part of the pulsation of their heart, through their own blood cells, and build in their own physical..."*

PAM GREGORY: *"Your abundance will be linked to the frequency of your heart."*

ROBERT COLLIER: *"Our subconscious minds have no sense of humor, play no jokes and cannot tell the difference between reality and an imagined thought or image. What we continually think about will eventually manifest in our lives."*

DAVID R. HAWKINS, MD, PHD: *"Guilt, so commonly used in our society to manipulate and punish, manifests itself in a variety of expressions, such as remorse, self-recrimination, masochism, and whole gamut of symptoms of victimhood."*

JOHN TRUDELL: *"What I view life like is about energy. Everything is about energy— everything. We physically are little units of electrical energy, and we vibrate and project electromagnetic thought."*

NIKOLA TESLA: *"I am trying to awake the energy contained in the air. These are the main sources of energy. What is considered as empty space is just a manifestation of matter that is not awakened."*

ALBERT EINSTEIN, PHD, NOBEL (attributed): *"Everything is energy and that's all there is to it. Match the frequency of the reality you want and you cannot help but get that reality. This is not philosophy. This is physics."*

DENISE LINN: *"Shift the focus from what you want to do, to how you want to be...how you want to feel."*

HELEN BROWN WILMANS: *"Men create wealth in the character of the thoughts they entertain."*

DR. JOE DISPENZA: *"To be happy with yourself in the present moment while maintaining a dream of your future is a grand recipe for manifestation."*

THE BEATITUDES: *"Blessed are the pure in heart; for they shall see God."*

OPRAH WINFREY: *"Follow your instincts. That's where true wisdom manifests itself."*

SAYING: *"If you want something in your life you've never had, you'll have to do something you've never done."*

Manifestation. *(continued)*

DAVID MOREHOUSE, PHD: *"You should dream your dreams, and then live your life in the moment so as to create the space for those dreams to manifest—and they will."*

PAM GREGORY: *"Your belief system will arrange and present your reality to you ... The universe is just a mirror."*

DR. JOE DISPENZA: *"Your brain does not know the difference between what you see physically and what you see mentally."*

ALAN MOORE: *"There is no coincidence. Only the illusion of coincidence."*

RALPH WALDO EMERSON: *"Once you make a decision, the universe conspires to make it happen."*

EARL NIGHTINGALE: *"Whatever we plant in our subconscious mind and nourish with repetition and emotion will one day become a reality."*

WALT DISNEY: *"If you can dream it, you can do it."*

DR. JOE DISPENZA: *"Feel it. Believe it. Become it."*

LYNNE MCTAGGART: *"Thoughts become things."*

Similar: exhibition, appearance, evidence, expression, revelation, embodiment

Opposite: obscured, suppressed, disguised, hidden, recessive, nondescript, vague

Marriage. The legally or socially recognized union of two people before God or a magistrate. *Popular or Heart-Based Usage: (1) Getting hitched. (2) Walking down the aisle. (3) Settling down. (4) Exchanging vows. (5) Making it legal. (6) Tying the knot. (7) Being equally yoked. (8) Not sweating the small stuff. (9) 2=1. (10) 'Two good forgivers.'*

PAUL TILLICH: *"The first duty of love is to listen."*

OVID: *"If thou wouldst marry wisely, marry thine equal."*

WILLIAM SHAKESPEARE: *"Love looks not with the eyes but with the mind."*

EMILY BRONTE: *"Whatever our souls are made of, his and mine are the same."*

FRANZ SCHUBERT: *"Happy is the man who finds a true friend, and far happier is he who finds that true friend is his wife."*

LAO TZU: *"Being deeply loved by someone gives you strength, while loving someone deeply gives you courage."*

RUTH GRAHAM: *"A happy marriage is the union of two good forgivers."*

RONALD REAGAN: *"There is no greater happiness for a man than approaching a door at the end of a day knowing that someone on the other side of the door is waiting for the sound of his footsteps."*

EDGAR CAYCE: *"Soul mates are brought together for a reason."*

MIGNON MCLAUGHLIN: *"A successful marriage requires falling in love many times, always with the same person."*

OSCAR WILDE: *"Ultimately the bond of all companionship, whether in marriage or in friendship, is conversation."*

H. JACKSON BROWN, JR.: *"Live so that when your children think of fairness, caring, and integrity, they think of you."*

DR. JOYCE BROTHERS: *"The best proof of love is trust."*

GOETHE: *"Love is an ideal thing, marriage is a real thing."*

RED SKELTON: *"All men make mistakes, but married men find out about them sooner."*

KAHLIL GIBRAN: *"Let there be spaces in your togetherness."*

SOCRATES: *"By all means marry. If you get a good wife, you'll become happy; if you get a bad one, you'll become a philosopher."*

BENJAMIN FRANKLIN: *"Keep your eyes wide open before marriage, half shut afterwards."*

OGDEN NASH: *"Whenever you're wrong, admit it; whenever you're right, shut up."*

DOUGLAS JOHNSTON: *"A woman may put on a bathing suit and never go near the water; another woman may put on a tennis dress and never set foot on a court. But friend, when a woman puts on a wedding dress, she means business."*

JON BON JOVI: *"As for (the) secret to staying married: 'My wife tells me that if I ever decide to leave, she is coming with me.'"*

Similar: coupling, wedding, matrimony, union, nuptials, bonding
Opposite: separation, divorce, disunion, dissolution

Meditation. [See also **Calm** and **Prayer**] (1) Taking control of your own mind. (2) Focusing attention on self-awareness and the training of your mental processes. *Popular or Heart-Based Usage: (1) Quieting your mind. (2) Unplugging. (3) Finding your center. (4) Going within. (5) Going Zen. (6) Stepping off the hamster wheel. (7) 'In it but not of it.' (8) Rediscovering your core stillness. (9) Tapping into your source. (10) Listening to your still small voice. (11) Creating inner spaciousness. (12) Repeating affirmations.*

CARL JUNG, MD: *"Who looks outside, dreams; who looks inside, awakes."*

ECKHART TOLLE: *"You are never more truly yourself than when you are still."*

DR. JOE DISPENZA: *"Meditation opens the door between the conscious and subconscious minds."*

JOSEPH NGUYEN: *"The moment we stop thinking is when our happiness begins."*

GAUTAMA BUDDHA: *"When you go into a space of nothingness, everything becomes known."*

EDGAR CAYCE: *"Through prayer we speak to God. In meditation, God speaks to us."*

BENJAMIN FRANKLIN: *"Reading makes a full man, meditation a profound man, discourse a clear man."*

DEEPAK CHOPRA: *"Meditation is not a way of making your mind quiet. It's a way of entering into the quiet that is already there—buried under the 50,000 thoughts the average person thinks every day."*

MADHAV GOYAL, MD, MPH: *"A lot of people have this idea that meditation means sitting down and doing nothing, but that's not true. Meditation is an active training of the mind to increase awareness."*

JOE ROGAN: *"The sensory deprivation chamber has been the most important tool that I've ever used for developing my mind."*

DANIEL GOLEMAN, PHD: *"Mindful meditation has been discovered to foster the ability to inhibit those very quick emotional impulses."*

JOHNS HOPKINS UNIVERSITY SCHOOL OF MEDICINE: *"In our study, meditation appeared to provide as much relief from some anxiety and depression symptoms as what other studies have found from anti-depressants…They also found no harm came from meditation."*

CAROLINE MYSS: *"The soul always knows what to do to heal itself. The challenge is to silence the mind."*

CONFUCIUS: *"The more man meditates upon good thoughts, the better will be his world and the world at large."*

PSALM 46:10: *"Be still, and know that I am God."*

JON STEWART: *"The enemy is noise. The goal is clarity."*

MA JAYA: *"Quiet the mind and the soul will speak."*

Similar: reflection, introspection, isolation, contemplation, reverie, deliberation

Opposite: disbelieve, disregard, carelessness, bypass, ignorance

Memory. Recalling a scene or information from the past. *Popular or Heart-Based Usage: (1) Picturing something in your mind. (2)* [Mannerism] *Looking up and to the right to recall. (3) What comes up. (4) Going to the Wayback Machine. (5) Having a flashback. (6) Sorting through yesterdays. (7) Connecting a name and face. (8) 'Total Recall' (9) Seeking what's familiar. (10) Having a favorite. (11) Tripping. (12) 'The first time I ever ...' (13) 'Think of a time when ...' (14) 'What was that?' (15) 'That rings a bell.'*

MARK TWAIN: *"A clear conscience is the sure sign of a bad memory."*

BENJAMIN FRANKLIN: *"Creditors have better memories than debtors."*

SIR NORMAN WISDOM: *"As you get older three things happen. The first is your memory goes, and I can't remember the other two."*

WILLIAM BOYD, CBE, FRSL: *"Memory is a dog that wants to please its master."*

PAT CONROY: *"Except for memory, time would have no meaning at all."*

SAMUEL JOHNSON: *"The true art of memory is the art of attention."*

WILLIAM GIBSON: *"Time moves in one direction, memory in another."*

D. EARL JOHNSTON: *"Every memory includes at least one dominant emotion."*

LINCOLN STOREY: *"In the educational processes of our fourth dimension, 'time-out' can be more like 'time-in.' Time (or linear cause-and-effect) + attention + emotion = memories. We reflect back in order to assess how to move forward."*

MICHEL DE MONTAIGNE: *"Nothing fixes a thing so intensely in the memory as the wish to forget it."*

ERIC KANDEL, MD, NOBEL: *"Memory is everything. Without it we are nothing."*

DR. JOE DISPENZA: *"Nerve cells that fire together, wire together. What syncs in the brain, links in the brain."*

VEDA AUSTIN: *"One of the reasons we have memory is so that we can learn."*

ECKHART TOLLE: *"People don't realize that now is all there ever is; there is no past or future except as memory or anticipation in your mind."*

ALBERT SCHWEITZER, BTH, MD, PHD, OM, NOBEL: *"Happiness is nothing more than good health and a bad memory."*

ABRAHAM LINCOLN: *"No man has a good enough memory to be a successful liar."*

GABRIEL GARCIA MARQUEZ: *"The heart's memory eliminates the bad and magnifies the good."*

DIETRICH BONHOEFFER: *"Gratitude changes the pangs of memory into a tranquil joy."*

JEAN-PAUL GUERLAIN: *"Perfume is the most intense form of memory."*

ROSA PARKS: *"Memories of our lives, of our works and deeds will continue in others."*

IRVING BERLIN: *"The Song is Ended (But the Melody Lingers On)"* (Song)

D. EARL JOHNSTON: *"Nostalgia revisits the past to lend hope to the present."*

Similar: reflection, retrospection, looking back, bookmarking, recall, yesterday, history

Opposite: erasure, blankness, amnesia, forgetfulness, comatose, now

Mentoring. [See **Coaching** and **Teaching**]

Mercy. (1) Showing compassion toward others. (2) Restraining yourself from punishing or harming others through the justifiable exercise of your power or position. (3) Choosing not to press an obvious advantage. *Popular or Heart-Based Usage: (1) Stepping back. (2) Being a lady or a gentleman. (3) Demonstrating goodwill. (4) Showing forbearance. (5) Standing down. (6) Granting someone a reprieve. (7) Laying down your sword. (8) Granting safe passage to another. (9) 'Kyrie Eleison!' (10) 'Do unto others as you would have them do unto you.' (11) Observing the Golden Rule. (12) 'Live and let live.' (13) 'What goes around, comes around.'*

> NELSON MANDELA, NOBEL: *"You will achieve more in this world through acts of mercy than through acts of retribution."*
> MUHAMMAD: *"If someone does not show mercy to people, then Allah will not show mercy to him."*
> HOSEA 6:6: *"For I desired mercy; and not sacrifice; and the knowledge of God more than burnt offerings."*
> AUGUSTINE OF HIPPO: *"Two works of mercy set a person free; forgive and you will be forgiven, and give and you will receive."*
> WILLIAM SHAKESPEARE: *"The quality of mercy is not strained; It droppeth as the gentle rain from Heaven upon the place beneath: It is twice-blessed, It blesseth him that gives and him that takes."*
> ROBERT E. LEE: *"The forbearing use of power does not only form a touchstone, but the manner in which an individual enjoys certain advantages over others is the test of a true gentleman."*
> PRAYER OF HUMBLE ACCESS: *"But thou art the same Lord, whose property is always to have mercy."*
> ABRAHAM LINCOLN: *"I've always found that mercy bears richer fruits than strict justice."*
> SIR EDWARD GEORGE BULWER-LYTTON: *"The pen is mightier than the sword."*
> MR. MISTER, RICHARD PAGE, STEVE GEORGE, JOHN LANG: *"Kyrie"* (Song)
> THOMAS AQUINAS: *"Justice without mercy is cruelty."*
> ADAM SMITH: *"Mercy to the guilty is cruelty to the innocent."*
> EDGAR ALLEN POE: *"Lord bless my poor soul."*
> JOYCE MEYER: *"Mercy is the stuff you give to people that don't deserve it."*
> ALEXANDER POPE: *"Teach me to feel another's woe, To hide the fault I see, That mercy I to others show, That mercy show to me."*
> JOHN BRADFORD: *"There but for the grace of God go I."*

Similar: leniency, forgiveness, clemency, forbearance, benevolence, tolerance, goodwill
Opposite: retribution, malevolence, meanness, cruelty, torture

Mindfulness. (1) Focusing awareness and attention on the present and your internal states. (2) Creating the ability to step back and look at your life. *Popular or Heart-Based Usage: (1) Observing yourself. (2) Pausing to see the bigger picture. (3) Being your own best friend. (4) Seeing what is. (5) Gaining consciousness. (6) Looking at your scene from 100,000 feet. (7) Having a God's-Eye view of your life. (8) 'It is what it is.' (9) 'Is this really right for me?' (10) 'Newsflash!' (11) Asking yourself: 'Hello?!?' (12) Waking up.*

ADAGE: *"The way you speak to yourself matters."*

HENRY DAVID THOREAU: *"It's not what you look at that matters, it's what you see."*

MOTHER TERESA, NOBEL: *"Be happy in the moment, that's enough. Each moment is all we need, not more."*

ECKHART TOLLE: *"In today's rush we all think too much, seek too much, want too much and forget about the joy of just Being."*

MICHAEL REARDEN: *"'Mindset' is looking at how you are looking at a situation."*

D. EARL JOHNSTON: *"Mindfulness is a level of awareness where we step back and observe not only what we are busily doing and thinking, but also how it makes us feel, and how we can also direct our attention to other things."*

OBSERVATION: *"What's wrong with this picture? I'm in it!"*

TARA BRACH, PHD: *"Mindfulness is a pause—the space between stimulus and response: that's where choice lies."*

BRACHA GOLDSMITH: *"Love is empowering. Fear is disempowering."*

THICH NHAT HANH: *"Mindfulness helps you go home to the present."*

PAM GREGORY: *"A wonderful exercise is writing sticky notes around the house where you can keep track of what you are thinking."*

JON KABAT-ZINN, PHD: *"Writing can be an incredible mindfulness practice."*

SHARON SALZBERG: *"Mindfulness isn't difficult, we just need to remember to do it."*

ECKHART TOLLE: *"Use your mind, don't let it use you."*

Similar: attention, focus, awareness, journaling, chronicling
Opposite: absent-mindedness, inattention, obliviousness, ignorance, careless

Miracle. (1) A surprising and beneficial event which is not readily explainable by natural laws. (2) An event outside the normal realm of cause-and-effect. (3) An occurrence many standard deviations outside the mean. (4) Attributing something unexpectedly good to the intervention of God. *Popular or Heart-Based Usage: (1) 'One in a million.' (2) A jaw-dropper. (3) 'Out of the clear blue sky.' (4) 'The Hand of God.' (5) 'God winks.' (6) 'Living on a prayer.' (7) Receiving a sign. (8) Getting touched by an angel. (9) Having an enemy become a friend. (10) The Passover. (11) The parting of the Red Sea. (12) Manna from Heaven. (13) The Burning Bush. (14) Turning water into wine. (15) Feeding the five thousand. (16) Walking on water. (17) Resurrection. (18) A supernatural event.*

PROVERB: *"A grateful heart is a magnet for miracles."*

ALBERT EINSTEIN, NOBEL: *"Don't wait for miracles, your whole life is a miracle."*

AUGUSTINE OF HIPPO: *"Miracles are not contrary to nature, only contrary to what we know about nature."*

HENRY DAVID THOREAU: *"When we bring what is within out into the world, miracles happen."*

SAYING: *"God winks are those unforgettable situations when God shows up."*

HEBREWS 13:1–3: *"Be not forgetful to entertain strangers: for thereby some have entertained angels unawares."*

HELEN STEINER RICE: *"The world's sweetest miracle, baby, is you."*

LEONARD NIMOY: *"The miracle is this: the more we share the more we have."*

JOEL OSTEEN: *"When you keep God in first place, He will take you places that you've never dreamed of."*

RUSSELL M. NELSON, MD, PHD: *"Obedience brings success; exact obedience brings miracles."*

SUSAN JEFFERS, PHD: *"By learning to trust your intuition, miracles seem to happen. Intuitive thoughts are gifts from the higher self."*

DR. PHIL MCGRAW: *"If you need a miracle, be a miracle."*

MENACHEM MENDEL SCHNEERSON: *"The philosopher, when he sees a miracle, looks for a natural explanation. The Jew, when he sees nature, looks for the miracle."*

THICH NHAT HANH: *"Every day we are engaged in a miracle which we don't even recognize; a blue sky, white clouds, green leaves, the black, curious eyes of a child—our own two eyes. All is a miracle."*

OSHO: *"Meditation makes you innocent, it makes you childlike. In that state, miracles are possible. That state is pure magic."*

WILLA CATHER, PULITZER: *"Where there is great love there are always miracles."*

EDWIN LOUIS COLE: *"Expectancy is the attitude for miracles."*

JEAN PAUL: *"The miracle on earth are the laws of heaven."*

Similar: phenomenon, marvel, wonder, revelation, portent, intervention
Opposite: normal, *status quo*, usual, regular, humdrum, routine

Mirroring. (1) Acknowledging and responding through duplication or imitation. (2) Reflecting or emulating the speech, content, or mannerisms of another person, whether consciously or subconsciously. *Popular or Heart-Based Usage: (1) Being a copy-cat. (2) 'Like kinds attract.' (3) 'When in Rome, do as the Romans do.' (4) 'Birds of a feather flock together.' (5) 'Monkey see, monkey do.' (6) Staying in step with the big boys. (7) 'I'll have what she's having.' (8) 'Money goes to money.' (9) Following the leader. (10) Adopting the corporate culture. (11) Buying in to the scene. (12) 'It takes one to know one.'*

ARISTOTLE: *"Friends hold a mirror up to each other; through that mirror they can see each other in ways that would not otherwise be accessible to them, and it is this mirroring that helps them improve themselves as persons."*

OSHO: *"If you love yourself, you love others. If you hate yourself, you hate others. Because in relationship with others … the other is a mirror."*

DUSTIN POIRIER: *"Karma is not a bitch, it's a mirror."*

BRACHA GOLDSMITH: *"The five people you interact with the most, they influence your energy."*

SOCRATES: *"The heart of the person before you is a mirror. See there your own form."*

CONFUCIUS: *"He who searches for evil, must first look at his own reflection."*

LOIS FARFEL STARK: *"We form a mental map, then that shape, shapes us."*

THE LAW OF ATTRACTION: *"Positive thoughts bring positive events into being, while negative thoughts bring negative events into being."*

ERNEST HOLMES: *"Life is a mirror and will reflect back to the thinker what he thinks into it."*

PAM GREGORY: *"Your belief system will arrange and present your reality to you … The universe is just a mirror."*

D. EARL JOHNSTON: *"Our beliefs project our world. To change what we will encounter in the future, we have to change what we are thinking right now."*

ADAGE: *"When things change inside you, things change around you."*

OSHO: *"Life is a mirror. It reflects your face. Be friendly. And all of life will reflect friendliness."*

THE GOLDEN RULE: *"Do unto others as you would have them do unto you."*

Similar: reflection, imitation, emulation, mimicking, projection
Opposite: disconnected, disinterested, careless, distorted, disjointed

Modesty. Having a predisposition toward the minimization of your own importance, accomplishments, or possessions as compared to others. *Popular or Heart-Based Usage: (1) Staying low key. (2) Standing in the shadows. (3) Giving the credit to others. (4) Letting actions speak louder than words. (5) Being chill. (6) Avoiding the limelight. (7) Being a team player. (8) Sharing the credit. (9) Being a servant leader. (10) Going low profile. (11) Keeping your head down. (12) 'Please, you go first.'*

WILLIAM SHAKESPEARE: *"The less you speak of your greatness the more I shall think of it."*

C. S. LEWIS: *"Humility is not thinking less of yourself, it is thinking of yourself less."*

WILL ROGERS: *"Never miss a good chance to shut up."*

DEMADES: *"Modesty is the citadel of beauty."*

COCO CHANEL: *"Modesty is the highest elegance."*

ARIANNA HUFFINGTON: *"Moving ourselves to the background and others to the foreground is evidence that the (spiritual) search is achieving its purpose."*

PAUL CEZANNE: *"The awareness of our own strength makes us modest."*

CONFUCIUS: *"He who speaks without modesty will find it difficult to make his words good."*

NAPOLEON HILL: *"Genuine wisdom is usually conspicuous through modesty and silence."*

DELPHINE DE GIRARDIN: *"Good taste is the modesty of the mind; that is why it cannot be either imitated or acquired."*

MAORI PROVERB: *"It would be better to let others praise."*

MAX BEERBOHM: *"The delicate balance between modesty and conceit is popularity."*

ALBERT EINSTEIN, PHD, NOBEL: *"Never underestimate your own ignorance."*

WILLIAM HAZLITT: *"No really great man ever thought himself so."*

EMILY DICKINSON: *"I'm nobody! Who are you?"*

JULES RENARD: *"Be modest! It is the kind of pride least likely to offend."*

Similar: deference, respectfulness, reserve, humility, self-abasement, demureness
Opposite: arrogance, boastfulness, narcissism, bragging, bumptiousness, conceit

Momentum. (1) Manifesting a shift in the magnitude and direction of energy. (2) The product of an object's mass and velocity. (3) Having and maintaining growth or success. (4) The expression of an emotion in vector terms of magnitude and direction. *Popular or Heart-Based Usage: (1) Seizing the day. (2) Gaining oomph. (3) Getting traction. (4) Picking up steam. (5) p=mv. (6) 'Mojo Risin'.'*

JOE ROGAN: *"Build confidence and momentum with each good decision you make from here on out and choose to be inspired."*

ANTHONY ROBBINS: *"Success comes from taking the initiative and following up…persisting…eloquently expressing the depth of your love. What simple action could you take today to produce a new momentum toward success in your life?"*

ANDREW GROVE: *"Most companies don't die because they are wrong; they die because they don't commit themselves. They fritter away their momentum and their valuable resources while attempting to make a decision. The greatest danger is standing still."*

LINCOLN STOREY: *"Let's clarify inertia and momentum. Inertia is about staying put in your chair, while momentum is more about climbing on the bandwagon."*

ANNE M. MULCAHY: *"When you have that window of opportunity called a crisis, move as quickly as you can, get as much done as you can. There's a momentum for change that's very compelling."*

SAM ALTMAN: *"Momentum and growth are the lifeblood of startups. This is probably in the top three secrets of executing well."*

TOM PETERS: *"Momentum is a fragile force. Its worst enemy: procrastination. Its best friend: a deadline."*

MARLON BRANDO: *"Never surrender to the momentum of mediocrity."*

AIMEE MULLINS, PHD: *"Believing in yourself is incredibly infectious. It generates momentum, the collective force of which far outweighs any kernel of self-doubt that may creep in."*

FRANCES E. WILLARD, MDIV: *"The world is wide, and I will not waste my life in friction when it could be turned into momentum."*

EARL WEAVER: *"Momentum? Momentum is the next day's starting pitcher."*

COACH CHIP KELLY: *"We talk about this all the time. In a game three things can happen—momentum swings, adversity, and random acts. If you're a competitor, you respond to it. If you're not a competitor, you react."*

TOM WATSON: *"Sometimes thinking too much can destroy your momentum."*

LILY TOMLIN: *"The road to success is always under construction."*

WILLIAM SHAKESPEARE: *"There is a tide in the affairs of men, which, if taken at the flood, leads on to fortune; Omitted, all the voyage of their life is bound in shallows and in miseries."*

Similar: power, thrust, impulse, drive, energy
Opposite: weakness, vulnerability, retreat, withdrawal, inactivity

Motivation. Having essential reasons or driving forces for your behavior. *Popular or Heart-Based Usage: (1) Being lit up. (2) Having your own motor. (3) Having something to prove. (4) Finding what makes your heart sing. (5) Being deeply moved by something. (6) Finding your mojo in any situation. (7) 'Having different reasons for different seasons.' (8) Focusing on who you really are.*

C. JOYBELL C.: *"The only way we can live, is if we grow."*

JIM ROHN: *"The more you care, the stronger you can be."*

ZIG ZIGLAR: *"It's not what you've got, it's what you use that makes a difference."*

JOHN WOODEN: *"Do not let what you cannot do interfere with what you can do."*

WAYNE DYER: *"Be miserable, or motivate yourself. Whatever has to be done, it's always your choice."*

LES BROWN: *"You need to make a commitment, and once you make it, life will give you some answers."*

ROBERT KIYOSAKI: *"People need to wake up and realize that life doesn't wait for you. If you want something, get up and go after it."*

ANTHONY ROBBINS: *"The only reason we really pursue goals is to cause ourselves to expand and grow. Achieving goals by themselves will never make us happy in the long term; it's who you become, as you overcome the obstacles necessary to achieve your goals, that can give you the deepest and most long-lasting sense of fulfillment."*

LAUREN FLESHMAN: *"Fear is replaced by excitement and a simple desire to see what you can do on the day."*

NAPOLEON HILL: *"Cherish your visions and your dreams, as they are the children of your soul; the blueprints of your ultimate achievements."*

ALBERT SCHWEITZER, BTH, MD, PHD, NOBEL: *"Success is not the key to happiness. Happiness is the key to success. If you love what you are doing, you will be successful."*

DALE CARNEGIE: *"People rarely succeed unless they have fun in what they are doing."*

ROBERT H. SCHULLER: *"Creative words create energy; negative words drain out energy."*

SIR BENJAMIN DISRAELI: *"Nurture your mind with great thoughts, for you will never go higher than you think."*

D. EARL JOHNSTON: *"Repetition is a life weapon. Both for you and against you."*

KAHLIL GIBRAN: *"Out of suffering have emerged the strongest souls; the most massive characters are seared with scars."*

HELEN KELLER: *"Look the world straight in the eye."*

CARL JUNG, MD: *"The privilege of a lifetime is to become who you truly are."*

Similar: reason, inspiration, stimulus, impetus, drive, ambition, inclination
Opposite: passivity, disinterest, apathy, neglect, lethargy, boredom

Music. Structuring instrumental, digital, vocal, beat, rhyme, and frequency elements into aesthetic or creative expressions of sound. *Popular or Heart-Based Usage: (1) Hearing it in your head. (2) Building it by heart. (3) Working the beatbox. (4) Creating ear candy. (5) Juke. (6) Vibes. (7) Bop. (8) Hip-hop. (9) Funk. (10) Riffing. (11) Jamming. (12) Grooving. (13) Refining the melody. (14) Finding the hook. (15) Matching the lyrics. (16) Creating the arrangements. (17) Laying down a track. (18) Working it all out.*

B. B. KING: *"I wanted to connect my guitar to human emotions."*

VICTOR HUGO: *"Music expresses that which cannot be put into words."*

MILES DAVIS: *"Man, sometimes it takes you a long time to sound like yourself."*

LUDWIG VAN BEETHOVEN: *"Music is a higher revelation than philosophy."*

WOLFGANG AMADEUS MOZART: *"Music is not in the notes, but in the silence between."*

CLAUDE DEBUSSY: *"Music is the arithmetic of sounds, as optics is the geometry of light."*

PYTHAGORAS: *"There is geometry in the humming of the strings. There is music in the placing of the spheres."*

PLATO: *"Rhythm and harmony find their way into the inward places of the soul. Music is moral law. It gives soul to the universe, wings to the mind, flight to the imagination, and charm and gaiety to life and to everything."*

JACO PASTORIUS: *"Music is the only thing keeping the planet together."*

CHARLES IVES: *"Maybe it is better to hope that music may always be transcendental language in the most extravagant sense."*

HERBERT SPENCER: *"Music must take rank as the highest of the fine arts—as the one which, more than any other, ministers to the human spirit."*

LINCOLN STOREY: *"Art shapes sound into music. It conveys the hint of a higher dimension beyond this world."*

BRYCE W. ANDERSON: *"I've found that no matter what life throws at me, music softens the blow."*

FRANK SINATRA: *"I never let my singing get in the way of my story-telling."*

HAL BLAINE: *"Once you've got it, you've got it. It will always be with you."*

MAURICE WHITE/EARTH WIND & FIRE: *"Most people can't see beauty or love. I see our music as medicine."*

HARLAN HOWARD: *"A country song is three chords and the truth."*

LOU REED: *"If it has more than three chords, it's jazz."*

MOLIÈRE: *"Of all the noises known to man, opera is the most expensive."*

IRVING BERLIN: *"The song is ended but the melody lingers on."*

LEO TOLSTOY: *"Music is the shorthand of emotion."*

LUDWIG BOERNE: *"Music is prayer."*

Similar: vibration, harmony, melody, art, tones, frequencies, expression
Opposite: noise, discord, cacophony, randomness

Narcissism. (1) Pursuing an exaggerated or relentless focus on your own concerns, often while belittling or dismissing others. (2) Engaging in excessive self-absorption, self-admiration, or self-promotion. *Popular or Heart-Based Usage: (1) Being full of yourself. (2) Putting yourself on a pedestal. (3) Making others wrong. (4) Controlling through micromanipulation. (5) Always feeling entitled. (6) Hogging the attention. (7) Holding court. (8) 'I'm far more "politically correct" than you.' (9) 'The world according to me.' (10) Surrounding yourself with flatterers. (11) Being a diva. (12) Making yourself the center of the story. (13) Being a drama queen/king. (14) 'You'll never understand my pain.' (15) Lacking self-awareness. (16) Being relentlessly critical. (17) Virtue signaling. (18) 'Can't be wrong.' (19) 'It's all about me.' (20) 'My issues always trump your issues.'*

GEORGE V. HIGGINS, MA, JD: *"Egotism is the art of seeing in yourself what others cannot see."*

TUCKER MAX, JD: *"The narcissistic act is not an act. I am actually a narcissist, very much so. My world revolves around me."*

DREW PINSKY, MD: *"I have to show you that I care more than you, and you don't care because I'm superior."*

SLOANE CROSLEY: *"New Yorkers have a delightfully narcissistic habit of assuming that if they're not conscious of a scene, it doesn't exist."*

KATYA ZAMOLODCHIKOVA: *"When you're a pathological narcissist, you have to fall in love with yourself every day."*

MASON COOLEY, PHD: *"Withhold admiration from a narcissist and be disliked. Give it and be treated with indifference."*

LINCOLN STOREY: *"A narcissist often excels at misdirection as a 'master of projection'—or accusing you of doing the very thing they are doing themselves."*

LACHLAN BROWN: *"A narcissist thrives on control and power ... Setting firm boundaries can help you regain control. It's about defining what is acceptable behavior and what is not, and then sticking to it."*

JORDAN PETERSON, PHD: *"Don't be a character in their story, be the author of yours ... It is about setting boundaries with language. ... (such as) ... 'I'm not interested in your opinion of me.' ... (or) ... 'I won't be spoken to that way.' ... (or) ... 'I'm on to you.' ... Respond with calm."*

SIGMUND FREUD, MD: *"Whoever loves becomes humble. Those who love have, so to speak, pawned a part of their narcissism."*

JENNY MCCARTHY: *"Having a child makes you realize the importance of life—narcissism goes out the window. Heaven on earth is looking at my little boy."*

VOLTAIRE: *"It is not love that should be depicted as blind, but self-love."*

BENJAMIN FRANKLIN: *"He who falls in love with himself will have no rivals."*

HUMORIST: *"Enough of me talking about me ... So what do you think of me?"*

Similar: egotism, self-love, conceit, self-centeredness, self-righteousness
Opposite: humility, self-effacement, reticence, introversion, unassumingness, inquiry

Nutrition. Consuming the necessary food, minerals, and liquids for health. *Popular or Heart-Based Usage: (1) Eating right. (2) Having a balanced diet. (3) Enjoying some soul food. (4) Getting what your body needs. (5) Covering the major food groups. (6) Getting nourishment that sticks to your ribs. (7) Having square meals. (8) Going healthy. (9) Avoiding toxins. (10) Eliminating junk. (11) Good Eats. (12) Home is where the hearth is.*

ROGER WILLIAMS: *"When in doubt, try nutrition first."*

VIRGINIA WOOLF: *"One cannot think well, love well, sleep well, if one has not dined well."*

THOMAS CARLYLE: *"He who has health, has hope; and he who has hope, has everything."*

HIPPOCRATES: *"Our food should be our medicine and our medicine should be our food."*

LINUS PAULING, MD, NOBEL (2X): *"You can trace every sickness, every disease, and every ailment to a mineral deficiency."*

T. COLIN CAMPBELL, PHD: *"Nutrition trumps genes."*

PETER THIEL, JD: *"The lowest-hanging fruit in preventative medicine is just to really focus on nutrition."*

JOEL FUHRMAN, MD: *"Medicines cannot drug away the cellular defects that develop in response to improper nutrition throughout life."*

MICHAEL TIERRA, L.AC, OMD: *"Diet is the essential key to all successful healing. Without a balanced diet, the effectiveness of herbal treatment is very limited."*

NATIONAL LIBRARY OF MEDICINE: *"Overall, the bulk of evidence suggests stress can affect micronutrient concentrations, often leading to micronutrient depletion."*

LINUS PAULING, MD, NOBEL (2X): *"Optimum nutrition is the medicine of tomorrow."*

ISAAC POHLMAN, MPH, RD: *"Stress depletes vitamins and minerals, making it more difficult to keep blood sugar in range."*

STEPHEN CURRY, NBA MVP (2X): *"The more years I go, the more experience I have, the more that nutrition and eating the right foods is important for recovery and things like that."*

RONNIE COLEMAN: *"Nutrition is 150% of the bodybuilding formula. It's that important."*

SCOTT EASTWOOD: *"You cannot out-train bad nutrition. It's impossible."*

KLEOVOULOS: *"It is best to do everything in moderation."*

APHORISM: *"Never take vitamins on an empty stomach."*

KELLY BARTON: *"Water is the most neglected item in your diet but one of the most vital."*

Similar: nourishment, foodstuff, cornucopia, victuals, diet, provender
Opposite: starvation, deprivation, malnutrition, neglect

Obedience. Yielding or deferring to the will or authority of another person, rule, or God. *Popular or Heart-Based Usage: (1) Respecting/Saluting your superiors. (2) Playing by the rules. (3) Toeing the line. (4) Keeping it all on the up-and-up. (5) Minding your p's and q's. (6) Following the chain of command. (7) Observing the rule of law. (8) Keeping it all between the lines. (9) Kissing someone's ring. (10) Sucking up. (11) Heeding a mission from God. (12) 'My way or the highway!' (13) 'Simon says!' (14) Playing 'Red light, Green light.' (15) 'Open, Sesame!' (16) 'Make it so.' (17) 'Roger that.' (18) 'Aye Aye!'*

L. FRANK BAUM/'THE WONDERFUL WIZARD OF OZ': *"Silence!...I am Oz, the Great and Terrible!"*

CAPT. JEAN-LUC PICARD: *"Make it so."*

PHARAOH RAMSES II: *"So let it be written. So let it be done."*

EZRA TAFT BENSON: *"The great test of life is obedience to God."*

CATHERINE OF SIENA: *"Obedience shows whether you are grateful."*

RUSSELL M. NELSON, MD, PHD: *"Obedience brings success; exact obedience brings miracles."*

DIETRICH BONHOEFFER: *"One act of obedience is better than one hundred sermons."*

ISLAM: *"Submission describes the state of mind of anyone who recognizes God's absolute authority, and who reaches a conviction that God alone has all authority."*

DEUTERONOMY 28:2: *"And all these blessings shall come on thee, and overtake thee, if thou shalt hearken unto the voice of the Lord thy God."*

JOEL OSTEEN: *"You cannot reach the fullness of your destiny without extra-mile obedience."*

THEODORE ROOSEVELT, NOBEL: *"Obedience of the law is demanded; not asked as a favor."*

SIMON BOLIVAR: *"If Nature is against us, we shall fight Nature and make it obey."*

ARISTOTLE: *"He who has never learned to obey cannot be a good commander."*

JEAN-JACQUES ROUSSEAU: *"Force does not constitute right...obedience is due only to legitimate powers."*

SUSAN B. ANTHONY: *"Resistance to tyranny is obedience to God."*

ROMANS 6:16: *"Ye are to whom ye obey."*

EXODUS 20:3: *"Thou shalt have no other gods before me."*

Similar: compliance, acquiescence, submission, abidance, agreeability, self-abasement, humility

Opposite: defiance, disobedience, contrariness, insolence, insurrection, rebellion

Obsession. [See also **OCD**] (1) Having an uncommon focus or fixation about something. (2) Having a dominant, intrusive, or recurring thought or impulse (good or bad) about a specific matter. *Popular or Heart-Based Usage: (1) Having a dominant preoccupation. (2) Maintaining a laser focus. (3) Getting zeroed in on one vision. (4) Losing the ability to change your views. (5) Getting stuck in a rut. (6) Having intrusive thoughts. (7) 'I can't stop thinking about it.' (8) Developing your own pet peeve(s). (9) Having a fetish. (10) Having a crush on someone. (11) Having a hang-up. (12) Having a burning desire.*

RICK WARREN: *"Passion drives perfection."*

BILL BUTLER: *"Passion is the oxygen of the soul."*

JOHN WATERS: *"Without obsession, life is nothing."*

VINCE LOMBARDI: *"Perfection is not attainable, but if we chase perfection we can catch excellence."*

CLAUDE MONET: *"Color is my daylong obsession, joy, and torment."*

CRISS JAMI: *"An over-indulgence of anything, even something as pure as water, can intoxicate."*

ALEXANDRA PAUL: *"Women have this obsession with shoes."*

DAX SHEPARD: *"I think all males from Detroit have an obsession with cars."*

UGO BETTI: *"'Mad' is a term we use to describe a man who is obsessed with one idea and nothing else."*

MARLENE DIETRICH: *"Sex: In America an obsession. In other parts of the world a fact."*

DAMON GALGUT: *"Real obsession needs an unconscious motivation behind it."*

JENNIFER SALAIZ: *"To have the beginning of a truly great story, you need to have a character you're completely and utterly obsessed with."*

BARBRA STREISAND: *"I've been called many names like perfectionist, difficult, and obsessive. I think it takes obsession, takes searching for the details for any artist to be good."*

BRUCE SPRINGSTEEN: *"Being an artist is this kind of occupation in which you have to make people care about your obsession."*

MERYL STREEP: *"Obsession is an attractive thing. People who are really, really interested and good at one thing and smart are attractive, if they're men."*

NAPOLEON HILL: *"Your ability to use the principle of autosuggestion will depend, very largely, upon your capacity to concentrate upon a given desire until that desire becomes a burning obsession."*

WALT DISNEY: *"To succeed, work hard, never give up and above all cherish a magnificent obsession."*

MASON COOLEY: *"Cure for an obsession: get another one."*

Similar: absorbed, preoccupied, immersed, fixated, captivated, infatuated, gripped
Opposite: easy-going, flexible, open-minded, indifferent, unconcerned

OCD or Obsessive-Compulsive Disorder. [See also **Obsession**] Having unwanted and intrusive recurring thoughts, worries, or fears which lead to compulsive behaviors. *Popular or Heart-Based Usage: (1) Having repetitive thoughts that won't go away. (2) Dealing with the bully in your head. (3) Finding refuge in ritual. (4) Feeling imprisoned by perfection. (5) Becoming a slave to ritual. (6) Reclaiming your inner spaciousness.*

TAMARA IRELAND STONE: *"Fighting OCD is like boxing. Each time you go against a thought, it's a punch to its strength."*

JEFFREY KLUGER, JD: *"People with anxiety disorders such as OCD know that nothing can be more paralyzing than having too many options. Go to a store to buy a sweater, find four that you like and the odds are pretty good that you'll stare and stare...and buy nothing at all."*

MARISA T. MAZZA, PSY.D: *"People with OCD often wear a mask. On the outside they appear so put together, but on the inside, they are falling apart."*

MAYO CLINIC: *"OCD obsessions are repeated, persistent, and unwanted thoughts, urges, or images that are intrusive and cause distress or anxiety."*

JOHNS HOPKINS MEDICINE: *"Obsessive-compulsive disorder (OCD) is a common anxiety disorder. It causes unreasonable thoughts, fears, or worries. A person with OCD tries to manage these thoughts through rituals."*

NATIONAL ALLIANCE ON MENTAL ILLNESS: *"Although people with OCD may know that their thoughts and behavior don't make sense, they are often unable to stop them."*

STANFORD MEDICINE: *"OCD symptoms: anxiety; preoccupation with dirt or germs or moral questions; and, fears of acting on unacceptable impulses."*

CLEVELAND CLINIC: *"Everyone experiences obsessions and compulsions at some point...But OCD is more extreme. It can take up hours of a person's day. It gets in the way of normal life and activities. Obsessions in OCD are unwanted, and people with OCD don't enjoy performing compulsive behaviors."*

HARVARD HEALTH PUBLISHING: *"OCD affects up to 3% of people worldwide. A childhood onset form can start around 10 years of age, more commonly in boys than girls. Most of the remainder of people with OCD have their first symptoms before they turn 25—in this group, women outnumber men. OCD symptoms usually don't develop after age 30."*

MAYO CLINIC: *"Cognitive Behavioral Therapy (CBT), a type of psychotherapy, is effective for many people with OCD. Exposure and response prevention (ERP), a part of CBT therapy, involves exposing you over time to a feared object or obsession, such as dirt. Then you learn ways not to do your compulsive rituals."*

ADAGE: *"OCD recovery doesn't just come to you. You have to make it happen."*

Disclaimer: No content on this page should be used as a substitute for competent medical or mental health advice from your doctor or qualified professional.

Optimism. Having a predisposition that present conditions are good and that future outcomes will be favorable. *Popular or Heart-Based Usage: (1) 'The glass is half-full.' (2) 'Thumbs up.' (3) 'Rise and shine!' (4) 'Can do!' (5) 'It's all good.' (6) Staying upbeat. (7) Looking on the bright side. (8) Giving it the benefit of the doubt. (9) Keeping a good attitude. (10) Making things happen. (11) Finding a way. (12) Being a problem solver. (13) Seeing doors opening in your mind. (14) Visualizing your desired outcomes. (15) Finding the silver lining. (16) Wearing rose-colored glasses. (17) Bright-eyed and bushy-tailed. (18) Trending with Pollyanna. (19) Being a perma-bull. (20) 'You betcha!' (21) Going with happy talk. (22) Being gung ho. (23) OFC! [Of Course!] (24) 'In it to win it.'*

DOLLY PARTON: *"The way I see it, if you want the rainbow, you gotta put up with the rain."*

PAUL HARVEY: *"Ever since I made tomorrow my favorite day, I've been uncomfortable looking back."*

HELEN KELLER: *"Optimism is the faith that leads to achievement. Nothing can be done without hope and confidence."*

MENACHEM MENDEL: *"Think good, and it will be good."*

RODGERS & HAMMERSTEIN: *"Oh, What a Beautiful Mornin'"* (Song)

APHORISM: *"Optimism leads us to new horizons. Pessimism keeps us under the covers."*

JOHN WOODEN: *"Things turn out best for people who make the best of the way things turn out."*

DANIEL KAHNEMAN, MD, NOBEL: *"It's a wonderful thing to be optimistic. It keeps you healthy and it keeps you resilient."*

MELINDA GATES: *"Optimism is not a passive expectation that things will get better. It is a conviction that we can make things better."*

ELON MUSK: *"We're going to make it happen. As God is my bloody witness, I'm hell-bent on making it work."*

ALBERT EINSTEIN, PHD, NOBEL: *"I'd rather be an optimist and a fool than a pessimist and right."*

MICHAEL JORDAN: *"Always turn a negative situation into a positive situation."*

JOSE ALTUVE: *"We all have that, we all have pros and cons, people who believe in you and people who don't believe in you. I'm not the only one. I like to prove people right, not wrong. I do it for the people who actually believe in me."*

PAUL HARVEY: *"Tomorrow has always been better than today, and it always will be."*

GEN. COLIN POWELL: *"Perpetual optimism is a force multiplier."*

LUKE 1:37: *"For with God nothing shall be impossible."*

THE BIBLE: *"Amen."*

Similar: positive, sanguine, bullish, hopeful, jovial, upbeat
Opposite: pessimistic, depressed, foreboding, fearful, bearish

Overwhelmed. [See **Stress** and **Trauma**]

Pain. Experiencing physical or emotional adversity, including related concerns about reduced capacity or function. *Popular or Heart-Based Usage: (1) 'This might sting a little.' (2) 'Yeow!' (3) 'Just make it stop!' (4) Finding out something the hard way. (5) Reaching for your meds. (6) 'It's something to work through.' (7) 'This is no picnic.' (8) 'Not a day at the beach.' (9) Experiencing discomfort and suffering. (10) 'Not fun at all.' (11) 'It's gonna hurt.'*

> HIPPOCRATES: *"Rest as soon as there is pain."*
> OVID: *"Be patient and tough; some day this pain will be useful to you."*
> SAYING: *"Don't resist your pain, just breathe through it."*
> PUBLILIUS SYRUS: *"The pain of the mind is worse than the pain of the body."*
> LORD BYRON: *"The great art of life is sensation, to feel we exist, even in pain."*
> BUDDHIST PROVERB: *"Pain is inevitable. Suffering is optional."*
> KAHLIL GIBRAN: *"Much of your pain is the bitter potion by which the physician within you heals your sick self."*
> CARL JUNG, MD: *"There is no coming to consciousness without pain."*
> AESCHYLUS: *"Nothing forces us to know what we do not want to know except pain."*
> BOB GOFF: *"We can't always see people's pain; they can always feel our love."*
> ERIC MANGINI: *"Each day you must choose, the pain of discipline or the pain of regret."*
> OPRAH WINFREY: *"Turn your wounds into wisdom."*
> JOHN PATRICK/'THE TEAHOUSE OF THE AUGUST MOON': *"Pain makes one think. Thought makes one wise. Wisdom makes life endurable."*
> SIMONE WEIL: *"Evil being the root of mystery, pain is the root of knowledge."*
> ARISTOTLE: *"We cannot learn without pain."*
> JIM MORRISON: *"You feel your strength in the experience of pain."*
> CHESTY PULLER, UNITED STATES MARINE: *"Pain is weakness leaving the body."*
> JOSEPH CAMPBELL: *"Find a place inside where there is joy, and the joy will burn out the pain."*
> GOOGLE GENERATIVE AI: *"For pain management, focusing on slow, deep breaths through the diaphragm is generally recommended as it promotes relaxation and can help alleviate pain."*
> KAHLIL GIBRAN: *"Your pain is the breaking of the shell that encloses your understanding."*
> PROVERB: *"The prettiest eyes have cried the most tears."*

Similar: suffering, affliction, torment, hurt, discomfort, writhing, convulsion
Opposite: peace, well-being, stability, serenity, relaxation, calm

Panic. (1) Reacting to a major threat by losing focus or abandoning coherent decision-making. (2) Becoming overstressed or overwhelmed. (3) Engaging in sudden erratic behavior. *Popular or Heart-Based Usage: (1) Things going haywire. (2) Getting swept up in hysteria. (3) Going to pieces. (4) Losing it (or losing control). (5) Freaking out. (6) Running around like a chicken with its head cut off. (7) Living in a total fire drill. (8) Breaking the glass. (9) Experiencing the sum of all fears. (10) Having things go south fast. (11) Having a cat and kittens too. (12) Redlining. (13) Flatlining. (14) Experiencing a 'Crash Team Entry Point.' (15) Having a really bad day at Black Rock. (16) Living in sudden max chaos. (17) 'Hell's Bells!' (18) 'Incoming!' (19) 'Every man for himself!' (20) 'Abandon ship!' (21) 'Kiss your rear end goodbye!' (22) Feeling a sudden paralyzing fear. (23) 'AHOOGA!'*

ANTHONY SCARAMUCCI: *"Panic implies that there is no rational thought taking place. That we are frozen and incapable of adjusting."*

STEPHEN KING: *"Panic is highly contagious, especially in situations when nothing is known and everything is in flux."*

SIMON SINEK: *"Panic causes tunnel vision. Calm acceptance of danger allows us to more easily assess the situation and see the options."*

CATHERINE TATE: *"Nothing prompts creativity like poverty, a feeling of hopelessness, and a bit of panic."*

JOHNNY MCGREW: *"When in confusion or panic, I can stay calm. It helps to know there's always one thing left that I can do, and do easily. Run like hell."*

ELIZABETH KENNY: *"Panic plays no part in the training of a nurse."*

SHAQUILLE O'NEAL: *"Generals don't panic; then the troops never panic."*

TERRY BRADSHAW: *"I would start with the most important thing a quarterback has to be: Poised. If you panic in that pocket, you are no good. I don't care what else is there; you have to be poised."*

SCOUTMASTER BILLY JIM VAUGHN: *"Leaders remain calm while others panic."*

BESSEL VAN DER KOLK, MD: *"We now know that panic symptoms are largely because the individual develops a fear of the bodily sensations with panic attacks. The attack may be triggered by something he or she knows is irrational, but fear of the sensations keeps them escalating into a full-body emergency."*

LINCOLN STOREY: *"When in panic, find the one thing that you know that is stable, that you must do. That is Step One. Then organize everything else around it."*

ANDREW WEIL, MD: *"Practicing regular, mindful breathing can be calming and energizing and can even help with stress-related health problems ranging from panic attacks to digestive disorders."*

SAYING: *"Order eventually emerges out of chaos."*

Similar: alarm, confusion, overwhelm, dread, pandemonium, distress, hysteria, calamity
Opposite: poise, calm, assurance, confidence, collectedness, centeredness

Paranoia. (1) Experiencing a concern, proven or unproven, that other people are systematically persecuting you or plotting harm against you. (2) Being hyper-vigilant about perceived threats. *Popular or Heart-Based Usage: (1) Feeling twitchy. (2) Getting antsy. (3) Looking over your shoulder. (4) Feeling spied on. (5) 'They're out to get me.' (6) 'No, they really **are** out to get me.'*

JOHN LENNON: *"Paranoia is just a heightened sense of awareness."*

PAUL BRODEUR: *"Paranoia is a social disease—you get it from screwing other people."*

JOHN MCAFEE: *"My well-discussed 'paranoia' urges me to believe that some tiny segment of the NSA's parsing algorithm is finely tuned to my voice."*

ARTHUR D. HLAVATY: *"Paranoia is the delusion that your enemies are organized."*

JOSEPH HELLER: *"Just because you're paranoid doesn't mean they aren't after you."*

PAULO COELHO: *"The more attention you pay an enemy, the stronger you make him. Be attentive, but don't be paranoid."*

CYNTHIA MCKINNEY: *"African-Americans have always known that a little bit of paranoia was healthy for us."*

ROBERT M. HUTCHINS: *"This is a do-it-yourself test for paranoia: you know you've got it when you can't think of anything that's your fault."*

ROB BREZSNY: *"Pronoia is the antidote for paranoia. It's the understanding that the universe is fundamentally friendly. It's a mode of training your senses and intellect so you're able to see the fact that life always gives you exactly what you need, exactly when you need it."*

MICHAEL LERNER: *"Energy always flows either toward hope, community, love, generosity, mutual recognition, and spiritual aliveness or it flows toward despair, cynicism, fear that there is not enough, paranoia about the intentions of others, and a desire to control."*

MAX LUCADO: *"The step between prudence and paranoia is short and steep. Prudence wears a seatbelt. Paranoia avoids cars. Prudence washes with soap. Paranoia avoids human contact. Prudence saves for old age. Paranoia hoards even trash. Prudence prepares and plans. Paranoia panics. Prudence calculates the risk and takes the plunge. Paranoia never enters the water."*

JORDAN PETERSON, PHD: *"You have to listen very closely and tell the truth if you are going to get a paranoid person to open up to you."*

WILLIAM S. BURROUGHS: *"Sometimes paranoia's just having all the facts."*

PHILIP K. DICK: *"Strange how paranoia can link up with reality now and then."*

ANDREW GROVE: *"Only the paranoid survive."*

GOLDA MEIR: *"Even paranoids have real enemies."*

Similar: hyper-vigilance, suspiciousness, wariness, distrust, skepticism, edginess
Opposite: confidence, trust, positivity, assuredness, expansiveness, calm

Parenting. Pursuing the care and proper development of children, especially your own. *Popular or Heart-Based Usage: (1) 'Being there' for your kids. (2) 'Bless this mess.' (3) Raising ankle-biters. (4) Arranging play dates and sleepovers. (5) Making birthday parties happen. (6) Knowing that sleep is a luxury. (7) Making it their home. (8) Keeping the peace. (9) Teaching them right and wrong. (10) Standing up for them. (11) Setting them straight. (12) Paying bills. (13) Keeping your promises. (14) Fueling their dreams.*

GALE SAYERS, 3X NFL MVP: *"The Lord is first, others are second, and I am third."*

GOV. JANE DEE HULL: *"At the end of the day, the most overwhelming key to a child's success is the positive involvement of parents."*

JIM VALVANO: *"My father gave me the greatest gift anyone could give another person: He believed in me."*

ROGER STAUBACH: *"One of my best memories growing up was when my parents talked to me and my father said: 'God gave us only one child, but He gave us a good one.'"*

ROBERT A. HEINLEIN: *"Don't handicap your children by making their lives easy."*

BESSEL VAN DER KOLK, MD: *"The parent-child connection is the most powerful mental health intervention known to mankind."*

HAROLD S. HULBURT, MD: *"Children need love, especially when they do not deserve it."*

JILL BOLTE TAYLOR, PHD: *"Just like children, emotions heal when they are heard and validated."*

CAROL S. DWECK, PHD: *"Children love this idea that their brain is like a muscle that gets stronger as they use it."*

DENNIS LAMBERT & BRIAN POTTER: *"Keeper of the Castle"* (Song)

ABIGAIL VAN BUREN: *"If you want your children to turn out well, spend twice as much time with them, and half as much money."*

FYODOR DOSTOEVSKY: *"The soul is healed by being with children."*

AHAD HA'AM: *"In disputes between parents and children, the children always get the upper hand."*

J. PITTMAN MCGEHEE, DD: *"God knows we need structure. We long for a father to establish limits, just as we long for a mother's nurturing."*

EILEEN KENNEDY-MOORE, PHD: *"By loving them for more than their abilities, we show our children that they are much more than the sum of their abilities."*

PETER USTINOV: *"Parents are the bones on which children cut their teeth."*

PEGGY O'MARA: *"The way we talk to our children becomes their inner voice."*

GOETHE: *"There are only two lasting bequests we can hope to give our children. One of these is roots, the other, wings."*

HEALTHYCHILDREN.ORG: *"The most powerful tool for effective discipline is attention—to reinforce good behaviors and discourage others."*

PROVERB: *"Sooner or later you have to grow up."*

ADAGE: *"A mother understands what a child does not say."*

Parenting. *(continued)*

PRINCESS DIANA: *"A mother's arms are more comforting than anyone else's."*

ARION C. GARRETTY: *"Mother's love is the fuel that enables a normal human being to do the impossible."*

RODNEY MIMS COOK, JR.: *"My life changed overnight when my mother turned to me and said, 'You have to talk. You can do anything you want in life.'"*

AMY VANDERBILT: *"Parents must get across the idea that I love you always, but sometimes I do not love your behavior."*

ADAGE: *"The essence of family is happy rituals and shared memories."*

ANNA QUINDLEN: *"Children should have enough freedom to be themselves—once they've learned the rules."*

STEVE LARGENT: *"When a child grows up without a father, there is an empty place where someone must stand, providing an example of character and confidence."*

CARL JUNG. MD: *"The greatest burden a child must bear is the unlived life of the parents."*

JOEL OSTEEN: *"You're in your Father's arms. He's holding you tightly."*

FREDERICK DOUGLASS: *"It is easier to build strong children than to repair broken men."*

SARAH PAYNE STUART: *"You are only as happy as your least happy child."*

APHORISM: *"Parenting is understanding that sleep is for sissies."*

BUMPER STICKER: *"Hire a teenager while they still know everything."*

NORA EPHRON: *"When your children are teenagers, it's important to have a dog around the house so that someone is happy to see you."*

ERMA BOMBECK: *"Never lend your car to anyone to whom you have given birth."*

D. EARL JOHNSTON: *"Parents of teenagers should be proficient in at least two languages—English and Sarcasm. Newcomers have also been known to dabble in Profanity during especially challenging moments."*

HUMORIST: *"Our son was finally graduating from college. He very thoughtfully reminded us he had learned that the origin of the word 'parent' actually came from combining the words 'pay' and 'rent.'"*

ERMA BOMBECK: *"I take a very practical view of raising children. I put a sign in each of their rooms: 'Checkout Time is 18 years.'"*

CAMRYN MANHEIM: *"Parents know how to push your buttons because, hey, they sewed them on."*

RUDYARD KIPLING, NOBEL: *"God could not be everywhere and therefore He made mothers."*

ABRAHAM LINCOLN: *"All that I am, or hope to be, I owe to my angel mother."*

JOSEPH JOUBERT: *"Children need models rather than critics."*

Similar: nurturing, fostering, influencing, arranging, engendering, supporting

Opposite: neglect, abandonment, disregard, disavowal, disengagement, absenteeism

Passion. Pursuing a personal goal or concept with intense purpose, focus, or enjoyment. *Popular or Heart-Based Usage: (1) Pursuing what is in your heart of hearts. (2) Having a burning desire for something. (3) Being all lit up about something. (4) Losing track of time. (5) Doing what you love. (6) What gets you revved up most. (7) Doing what you were built to do.*

E. M. FORSTER: *"One person with passion is better than forty people merely interested."*

GEN. FERDINAND FOCH: *"The most powerful weapon on earth is the human soul on fire."*

D. EARL JOHNSTON: *"When you keep getting so absorbed by something that you lose track of time, find a way to make a living from it. You've found the bullseye."*

RUMI: *"Let yourself be silently drawn by the same strange pull of what you really love. It will not lead you astray."*

MARIO ANDRETTI: *"I've always said, 'I didn't have a Plan B in life.' I was in pursuit of my dream from the very beginning. It's all about desire and passion. At all costs."*

DOMINIC: *"A man who governs his passions is master of his world. We must either command them or be enslaved by them. It is better to be a hammer than an anvil."*

RALPH WALDO EMERSON: *"Passion, though a bad regulator, is a powerful spring."*

DEEPAK CHOPRA: *"Always go with your passions. Never ask yourself if it's realistic or not."*

JOSEPH CAMPBELL: *"Passion will move men beyond themselves, beyond their shortcomings, beyond their failures."*

GAUTAMA BUDDHA: *"There is no fire like passion, there is no shark like hatred, there is no snare like folly, there is no torrent like greed."*

TONY HSIEH: *"The best businesses are really ones that can combine passion, profits and purpose."*

FRIEDRICH NIETZSCHE: *"He who has a why to live for can bear almost any how."*

ADAGE: *"If you can't stop thinking about it, take the risk."*

RICK WARREN: *"Passion drives perfection."*

BILL BUTLER: *"Passion is the oxygen of the soul."*

THE DOORS: *"Light My Fire"* (Song)

Similar: fervor, ardor, dedication, absorption, enchantment, captivation, enthrallment
Opposite: apathy, lethargy, indifference, boredom, disinterest

Passive-Aggressive. A behavioral pattern marked by outward displays of civility and compliance, but coupled with a tendency toward concealed resentment, hostility, or sabotage. *Popular or Heart-Based Usage: (1) Avoiding direct conflict. (2) Being deliberately vague. (3) Being covertly hostile. (4) Making a back-handed compliment. (5) Using praise as a vehicle for doubt. (6) Getting someone to second-guess themselves. (7) Setting someone up to fail. (8) Screwing things up behind the scenes. (9) Scheming in silence. (10) Lying in wait for someone. (11) Being a smiling back-stabber. (12) Making nice in public. (13) Playing the role of aggression's sneaky little cousin. (14) Having a hidden agenda. (15) Talking under your breath. (16) Being a 'silent assassin.' (17) Being a smiling cobra. (18) Forcing a smile. (19) Killing someone with faint praise. (20) Being a 'frenemy.' (21) Playing 'Spy vs. Spy.' (22) 'Just a friendly reminder!' (23) 'Silly me did I forget to tell you?' (24) 'A word to the wise.' (25) 'Who, me?'*

KAREN SALMANSOHN: *"I'd rather have an enemy who admits they hate than a friend who secretly puts me down."*

JOHNNY MCGREW: *"Just because someone smiles at you doesn't mean they're your friend."*

JIM ROHN: *"Every time we speak, we choose and use one of four basic communication styles: assertive, aggressive, passive, and passive-aggressive."*

CHARLOTTE HILTON ANDERSEN: *"Passive-aggressiveness is essentially fighting with someone else, but without directly inciting conflict."*

NINA VASAN, MD, MBA: *"It's a way to fight without admitting your feelings so you can blame the other person when they react."*

ANTON YELCHIN: *"I'm not passive aggressive. If something bothers me, I think about it, then I act on it. I express it."*

ROBERT GREENE: *"The passive aggressive arguer comes armed with tricky tactics. They cannot take the risk that they might be wrong: their self-esteem is too intertwined with their opinions. It is more important to affirm their rightness, and sense of superiority, than to arrive at the truth."*

ROBERT TEW: *"Don't let negative and toxic people rent space in your head. Raise the rent and kick them out."*

RICHELLE MEAD: *"You guys are so caught up in your polished images and your passive-aggressive comments that no one ever comes right out and says anything. Well, I'm going to."*

JENNA RYU: *"Ask for clarification. Call out the action, not the person."*

BERNARD BARUCH: *"Be who you are and say what you feel because those who mind don't matter and those who matter don't mind."*

BOB GOFF: *"Love difficult people. You're one of them."*

Similar: covertly hostile, resentful, back-handed, sulking, vengeful, frenemy, hidden
Opposite: direct, assertive, clear, unapologetic, forthright, confronting

Patience. Having to adjust to or deal with extended delay, trouble, or suffering. *Popular or Heart-Based Usage: (1) Being put on hold. (2) Waiting your turn. (3) Marking time. (4) Having to sit tight. (5) Cooling your heels. (6) Standing down. (7) Being stuck in Time Out. (8) Getting benched (or sidelined). (9) Taking a pause. (10) Holding the phone. (11) Holding your horses. (12) Having to sit for a spell. (13) Being stuck in turnaround. (14) Letting things unfold. (15) Letting the Earth spin. (16) Trusting and letting go. (17) Living in God's time. (18) Getting some seasoning. (19) 'Hurry up and wait.' (20) 'Wait for it.' (21) 'Not so fast!' (22) 'So you got an issue? Go to Helen Waite!'*

MARK TWAIN: *"All good things come unto them that wait—and don't die in the meantime."*

PROVERB: *"The watched pot never boils."*

D. EARL JOHNSTON: *"The problem with being patient is you have to wait."*

LAO TZU: *"I have just three things to teach: simplicity, patience, compassion. These three are your greatest treasures."*

ANDREW JOHNSTON: *"Be careful what you pray for. My prayer was for patience, and God blessed me with patience. I might have prayed for a solution."*

SAMUEL JOHNSON: *"Great works are performed not by strength but by perseverance."*

ECKHART TOLLE: *"When something gets in your way, it is still the way."*

ADAGE: *"If God is making you wait, then be prepared to receive more than you asked for."*

RUMI: *"Patience with small details makes perfect a large work, like the universe."*

RALPH WALDO EMERSON: *"Adopt the pace of nature; her secret is patience."*

ANDY WARHOL: *"The idea of waiting for something makes it more exciting."*

LEO TOLSTOY: *"The two most powerful warriors are patience and time."*

JEAN-JACQUES ROUSSEAU: *"Patience is bitter, but its fruit is sweet."*

AUGUSTINE OF HIPPO: *"Patience is the companion of wisdom."*

THOMAS F. FRIST, JR., MD: *"I am impatiently, very patient."*

MAHATMA GANDHI: *"To lose patience is to lose the battle."*

EPICTETUS: *"No great thing is created suddenly."*

SIR ISAAC NEWTON, FRS: *"Genius is patience."*

Similar: forbearance, perseverance, resolute, calm, tolerant, self-restrained, serenity, passivity

Opposite: agitation, intolerance, eruption, outburst, rebellion, activism

Peace. Having a state of mind characterized by acceptance and tranquility. *Popular or Heart-Based Usage: (1) Finding your center. (2) Being in the moment. (3) Finding 'time out of mind.' (4) Holding your sacred space. (5) Being fully present. (6) 'Om Shanti.' (7) 'Namaste.' (8) 'May the force be with you.' (9) 'Peace out.' (10) 'It's all good.' (11) Knowing sweet serenity.*

MOTHER TERESA, NOBEL: *"A smile is the beginning of peace."*

PROVERBS 14:30: *"A heart at peace gives life to the body."*

LAO TZU: *"If you are depressed you are living in the past, if you are anxious you are living in the future, if you are at peace you are living in the present."*

DALAI LAMA, NOBEL: *"Do not let the behavior of others destroy your inner peace."*

RONALD REAGAN: *"Peace is not absence of conflict, it is the ability to handle conflict by peaceful means."*

RALPH WALDO EMERSON: *"Nobody can bring you peace but yourself."*

ANCIENT ADAGE: *"As above, so below. As within, so without."*

JOSEPH CAMPBELL: *"The privilege of a lifetime is being who you are."*

THICH NHAT HANH: *"To live in the present moment is a miracle. The miracle is not to walk on water. The miracle is to walk on the green Earth in the present moment, to appreciate the peace and beauty that are available now."*

JILL BOLTE TAYLOR, PHD: *"My stroke of insight would be: peace is only a thought away, and all we have to do to access it is silence the voice of our dominating left mind."*

WILLIAM BLAKE: *"To see the world in a grain of sand and heaven in a wild flower, Hold infinity in the palm of your hand and eternity in an hour."*

JOSEPH CAMPBELL: *"Your sacred space is where you can find yourself again and again."*

ISAIAH 2:4: *"And they shall beat their swords into plowshares, and their spears into pruninghooks: nation shall not lift up sword against nation, neither shall they learn war anymore."*

PSALM 23:1–3: *"The Lord is my shepherd; I shall not want.*
> *He maketh me to lie down in green pastures;*
> *He leadeth me beside the still waters,*
> *He restoreth my soul."*

PHILIPPIANS 4:7: *"The peace of God, which passeth all understanding."*

ADAGE: *"When things change inside you, things change around you."*

Similar: serenity, calm, centeredness, contentedness, tranquility
Opposite: chaos, turmoil, disruption, calamity, unease

Perfectionism. Maintaining the urge or compulsion to achieve a desired result without error or flaw. *Popular or Heart-Based Usage: (1) Always going for a '10.' (2) Always going for straight A's. (3) Nailing it. (4) Hitting the bullseye. (5) Killing it. (6) Leaving no stone unturned. (7) 'No drips, no spills, no errors.' (8) Leaving 'no loose ends.' (9) Being a slave to yourself. (10) 'Nobody does it better.'*

STANLEY J. RANDALL: *"The closest to perfection a person ever comes is when he fills out a job application form."*

HUMORIST: *"Anyone can see that 'OCD' should be spelled 'CDO' once the letters are properly alphabetized."*

GEORGE ELIOT: *"The important work of moving the world forward does not wait to be done by perfect men."*

SALVADOR DALÍ: *"Have no fear of perfection, you'll never reach it."*

ANNE LAMOTT: *"Perfectionism is the voice of the oppressor."*

VINCE LOMBARDI: *"Perfection is not attainable, but if we chase perfection we can catch excellence."*

ARISTOTLE: *"Pleasure in the job puts perfection in the work."*

BRENE BROWN, MSW, PHD: *"Many people think of perfectionism as striving to be your best, but it is not about self-improvement; it's about earning approval and acceptance."*

EUGENE KENNEDY: *"There would be no need for love if perfection were possible. Love arises from our imperfection, from being different and always in need of the forgiveness, encouragement and that missing half of ourselves that we are searching for, as the Greek myth tells us, to complete ourselves."*

JOHNNY MCGREW: *"In marriage, you're not looking for someone who's perfect, maybe just perfect for you."*

BRENE BROWN, MSW, PHD: *"Let go of who you think you are supposed to be and embrace who you are."*

DESHAUN FOSTER: *"Sometimes authenticity resonates more deeply than perfection."*

SIR WINSTON CHURCHILL: *"They say that nobody is perfect. Then they tell you practice makes perfect. I wish they'd make up their minds."*

WILLIAM SHAKESPEARE: *"For there is nothing either good or bad, but thinking makes it so."*

SETH GODIN, BS, MBA: *"Your generosity is more important than your perfection."*

HENRY JAMES: *"Excellence does not require perfection."*

Similar: demanding, compulsive, obsessive, faultfinding, idealistic, doctrinaire
Opposite: easy-going, tolerant, relaxed, passive, disinterested

Perseverance. [See also **Determination**] Maintaining a course of action toward a goal despite risks, challenges, or delays. *Popular or Heart-Based Usage: (1) Having grit. (2) Having stick-to-it-iveness. (3) Gutting it out. (4) Shaking off disappointments. (5) Hanging in there. (6) Being built to last. (7) Doubling down (or redoubling your efforts). (8) Pressing on. (9) Pushing forward. (10) Plugging away. (11) Toughing it out. (12) Getting through it. (13) Working through the issues. (14) Going the distance. (15) 'Leaning in' to something. (16) 'Keeping on keeping on.' (17) Making it happen.*

THOMAS EDISON: *"When you have exhausted all possibilities, remember this—you haven't."*

GEN. GEORGE S. PATTON, JR.: *"In case of doubt, push on just a little further and then keep on pushing."*

TOM BRADY: *"I didn't come this far, only to come this far."*

ELON MUSK: *"For my part, I will never give up, and I mean never."*

CONFUCIUS: *"It does not matter how slowly you go, as long as you don't stop."*

DESMOND TUTU, NOBEL: *"There is only one way to eat an elephant; a bite at a time."*

SAMUEL JOHNSON: *"Great works are performed not by strength but by perseverance."*

CHARLES KETTERING: *"No one would have crossed the ocean if he could have gotten off the ship in the storm."*

ABRAHAM LINCOLN: *"When you come to the end of your rope, tie a knot and hang on."*

THEODORE ROOSEVELT, NOBEL: *"Courage is not having the strength to go on, it is going on."*

THOMAS PAINE: *"The harder the conflict, the more glorious the triumph."*

ANGELA LEE DUCKWORTH, PHD: *"Enthusiasm is common. Endurance is rare."*

PAULA ABDUL: *"Keep the faith, don't lose your perseverance, and always trust your gut instinct."*

ANDREA BOCELLI: *"Destiny has a lot to do with it, but so do you. You have to persevere, you have to insist."*

SIR WINSTON CHURCHILL: *"Success is not final, failure is not fatal: It is the courage to continue that counts."*

JOHN HEYWOOD: *"Rome was not built in a day."*

LOIS FARFEL STARK: *"We are what we build."*

EPICTETUS: *"No great thing was created suddenly."*

Similar: persistence, resolve, determination, stick-to-it-iveness
Opposite: apathy, abandonment, indifferent, scattered

Persuasion. Undertaking to influence or change someone's belief or viewpoint. *Popular or Heart-Based Usage: (1) Talking someone into something. (2) Having them try on an idea. (3) Gentle jawboning. (4) Smooth-talking. (5) Turning their hearts and minds. (6) Taking it one step at a time. (7) Piecing together your best arguments. (8) Emphasizing the benefits. (9) Whittling away resistance. (10) Getting to the decision-maker. (11) Laying it on thick. (12) Killing them with kindness. (13) Bringing them around to it. (14) Having them picture it in their mind. (15) Finally having someone's number.*

LUDWIG WITTGENSTEIN, PHD: *"At the end of reasons comes persuasion."*

PROVERB: *"You get more bees with honey."*

APHORISM: *"When you have the facts on your side, pound the facts. When you don't have the facts on your side, pound the table."*

ABRAHAM LINCOLN: *"If you wish to win a man over to your ideas, first make him your friend."*

BENJAMIN FRANKLIN: *"If you would persuade, you must appeal to interest rather than intellect."*

JANE AUSTEN: *"How quick come the reasons for approving what we like!"*

WILLIAM BERNBACH: *"Advertising is fundamentally about persuasion and persuasion happens to be not a science, but an art."*

CICERO: *"Nothing is so unbelievable that oratory cannot make it acceptable."*

GOETHE: *"Few persons are capable of being convinced the majority allow themselves to be persuaded."*

JOSH BILLINGS: *"The best way to convince a fool he is wrong is to let him have his own way."*

HONORE DE BALZAC: *"Men are so made that they can resist sound argument, and yet yield at a glance."*

LORD CHESTERFIELD: *"He makes people pleased with him by making them first pleased with themselves."*

SIR BENJAMIN DISRAELI: *"Everyone likes flattery. When it comes to Royalty you should lay it on with a trowel."*

ARISTOTLE: *"Character may almost be called the most effective means of persuasion."*

SUN TZU: *"Supreme excellence consists in breaking the enemy's resistance without fighting."*

ROY H. WILLIAMS: *"The first step in persuasion is to entice your target to imagine doing the thing you want them to do."*

JOSEPH JOUBERT: *"The aim of argument, or of discussion, should not be victory, but progress."*

WALT WHITMAN: *"We convince by our presence."*

Similar: convincing, oratory, rhetoric, debate, influencing, coaxing, cajoling
Opposite: disbelief, distrust, leeriness, apprehension, antagonism, rejection

Pessimism. Maintaining a focus on the least favorable aspects of things, or believing that the worst outcomes will prevail. *Popular or Heart-Based Usage: (1) 'The glass is half-empty.' (2) 'Thumbs down.' (3) 'Negative (or negatory) on that.' (4) Being a 'Debbie Downer.' (5) Pooh-poohing things. (6) Being a steady nay-sayer. (7) Casting shade. (8) Thinking dark thoughts. (9) Being bearish or being a 'perma-bear.' (10) 'It's all stupid. Why bother?' (11) Always playing the Bad Cop. (12) Being the Devil's Advocate. (13) 'Life stinks.' (14) Doomscrolling. (15) Having a negativity bias. (16) 'Nothing good ever happens to me.'*

OSCAR WILDE: *"A pessimist is someone who complains about the noise when opportunity knocks."*

ROBIN SHARMA: *"Better to be an optimist who gets disappointed than a pessimist who has no hope."*

LAURENCE J. PETER: *"An optimist expects his dreams to come true, a pessimist expects his nightmares to."*

GEORGE CARLIN: *"Some people see the glass half full. Others see it half empty. I see a glass that's twice as big as it needs to be."*

SAYING: *"About the glass being half-empty or half-full, it really kind of depends on whether you're drinkin' or pourin.'"*

PAUL HARVEY: *"I've never seen a monument erected to a pessimist. Every pessimist who ever lived has been buried in an unmarked grave."*

FYODOR DOSTOEVSKY: *"Man only likes to count his troubles, but he does not count his joys."*

WILLIAM JAMES, MD: *"Pessimism leads to weakness, optimism to power."*

GOLDA MEIR: *"Pessimism is a luxury that a Jew can never allow himself."*

WILLIAM ARTHUR WARD: *"The pessimist complains about the wind; the optimist expects it to change; the realist adjusts the sails."*

JOHN WOODEN: *"Do not let what you cannot do interfere with what you can do."*

TEACHING PROVERB: *"Can't never did."*

Similar: gloominess, defeatism, negativity, bleakness, discouragement, dark talk
Opposite: cheerfulness, excitement, optimism, sanguine, bullish

Pity. (1) Acknowledging the misfortunes and sufferings of others. (2) Suspending critical judgment and/or providing needed assistance to another. (3) A shame or disappointment. *Popular or Heart-Based Usage: (1) Feeling sorry for someone. (2) Giving someone a hand up. (3) Giving someone a lift. (4) Resetting yourself about someone in need. (5) Cutting someone a break. In the opposite, as self-pity: (6) Feeling sorry for yourself. (7) Having a pity party. (8) Going gardening to eat worms. (9) 'Self-pity goes nowhere.'*

WILLIAM BLAKE: *"Where mercy, love and pity dwell, there God is dwelling too."*

SAMUEL TAYLOR COLERIDGE: *"Pity is best taught by fellowship in woe."*

EMIL M. CIORAN: *"What is pity but the vice of kindness."*

LYMAN ABBOTT: *"It is easy to condemn, it is better to pity."*

MARTIN LUTHER KING, JR., NOBEL: *"Compassion does not just happen. Pity does, but compassion is not pity."*

BENJAMIN FRANKLIN: *"Pity and forbearance should characterize all acts of justice."*

HORACE MANN: *"To pity distress is but human; to relieve it is Godlike."*

D. EARL JOHNSTON: *"To take pity is to change your course to help someone who cannot help themself."*

FRIEDRICH NIETZSCHE: *"The deeper minds of all ages have had pity for animals."*

JOSE MARTI: *"Only those who spread treachery, fire, and death out of hatred for the prosperity of others are undeserving of pity."*

GEORGE ELIOT: *"Consequences are unpitying."*

OLIVER GOLDSMITH: *"Pity and friendship are two passions incompatible with each other."*

JOE FRAZIER: *"When I go out there, I have no pity on my brother. I'm out there to win."*

DALE CARNEGIE: *"Feeling sorry for yourself, and your present condition, is not only a waste of energy but the worst habit you could possibly have."*

ZIG ZIGLAR: *"The problem with pity parties is very few people come, and those who do don't bring presents."*

HELEN KELLER: *"Self-pity is our worst enemy and if we yield to it, we can never do anything wise in the world."*

Similar: compassion, mercy, commiseration, empathy, outpouring
Opposite: indifference, meanness, malevolence, abandonment

Poetry. A stylized form of literature which adds emotional impact through rhyme, meter, structure, imagery, comparisons, and vivid descriptions. *Popular or Heart-Based Usage: (1) Interpreting life. (2) Turning a phrase. (3) Capturing the essence. (4) Emotional shorthand. (5) Words of art from the heart. (6) Sculpting with words. (7) 'The rose of prose.' (8) Weaving words into wonder. (9) Words that take flight. (10) Life writ large.*

ROBERT FROST: *"Poetry is when an emotion has found its thought and the thought has found words."*

GWENDOLYN BROOKS: *"Poetry is life distilled."*

MURIEL RUKEYSER: *"Breathe-in experience, breathe-out poetry."*

PHILIBERT JOSEPH ROUX: *"Science is for those who learn; poetry, for those who know."*

SALMAN RUSHDIE: *"A poet's work is to name the unnameable, to point at frauds, to take sides, start arguments, shape the world, and stop it going to sleep."*

ALLEN GINSBERG: *"Poetry is not an expression of the party line. It's that time of night, lying in bed, thinking what you really think, making the private world public, that's what the poet does."*

JIM JARMUSCH: *"I think of poets as outlaw visionaries in a way."*

W. H. AUDEN: *"A poet must never make a statement simply because it sounds poetically exciting; he must also believe it to be true."*

LEONARDO DA VINCI: *"Painting is poetry that is seen rather than felt, and poetry is painting that is felt rather than seen."*

VOLTAIRE: *"Verses which do not teach men new and moving truths do not deserve to be read."*

SAMUEL TAYLOR COLERIDGE: *"I wish our young poets would remember my homely definitions of poetry; that is, prose = words in the best order; poetry = the best words in the best order."*

T. S. ELIOT: *"Genuine poetry can communicate before it is understood."*

NIELS BOHR, PHD, NOBEL: *"When it comes to atoms, language can be used only as poetry. The poet, too, is not nearly so concerned with describing facts as with creating images and establishing mental connections."*

WALLACE STEVENS: *"The poet is the priest of the invisible."*

DYLAN THOMAS: *"Do not go gentle into that good night, ... Rage, rage against the dying of the light."*

CARL SANDBURG, PULITZER: *"Poetry is an echo, asking a shadow to dance."*

WILLIAM BLAKE: *"Both read the Bible, day and night,*
   But thou readst black, where I read white."

DAME EDITH SITWELL: *"All great poetry is dipped in the dyes of the heart."*

ROBERT FROST: *"A poem begins in delight and ends in wisdom."*

Similar: verse, expression, rhetoric, outpouring, music, meter, rhyme
Opposite: prose, rote, droning, unthinkingness, lifelessness, blandness

Polite. (1) Demonstrating good manners. (2) Being respectful of others and intending to avoid creating offense. *Popular or Heart-Based Usage: (1) Being 'ladies and gentlemen.' (2) Exchanging pleasantries. (3) Chatting someone up. (4) Letting others go first. (5) Making (or playing) nice. (6) 'No offense intended.' (7) Being a Southern Belle or Southern Gentleman. (8) Minding your p's and q's. (9) Keeping your hands to yourself. (10) Dressing things up. (11) Sugar-coating unpleasant things. (12) Putting lipstick on a pig. (13) Loving someone to pieces. (14) Being a 'steel magnolia.' (15) Killing someone with kindness. (16) Being a simp. (17) Remembering always to say 'Yes, Sir,' 'Yes, Ma'am,' 'Please,' and 'Thank You.' (18) Making sure they know you were raised right. (19) Being on your best behavior. (20) Helping in the kitchen. (21) Smiling and nodding.*

TOMMY LEE JONES: *"Kindness and politeness are not overrated at all. They're underused."*

SIR BENJAMIN DISRAELI: *"Everyone likes flattery. When it comes to Royalty you should lay it on with a trowel."*

GUEST ROOM PLAQUE: *"To Our Weekend Guests: If we get to drinking on Sunday afternoon and start insisting that you stay over until Tuesday, please remember: **We Don't Mean It.**"*

JACKIE KENNEDY: *"I want minimum information given with maximum politeness."*

BURT REYNOLDS: *"Nowadays, instead of saying 'He's a prick,' I'll say 'He's complicated.'"*

THOMAS JEFFERSON: *"In truth, politeness is artificial good humor, it covers the natural want of it, and ends by rendering habitual a substitute nearly equivalent to the real virtue."*

F. DE LA ROCHEFOUCAULD: *"Politeness is the desire to be treated politely, and to be esteemed polite oneself."*

ARTHUR SCHOPENHAUER: *"Politeness is to human nature what warmth is to wax."*

AMY VANDERBILT: *"Good manners have much to do with the emotions. To make them ring true, one must feel them, not merely exhibit them."*

EMILY POST: *"Manners are a sensitive awareness of the feelings of others. If you have that awareness, you have good manners, no matter what fork you use."*

J. PAUL GETTY: *"In Japan, I was immensely impressed by the politeness, industrious nature, and conscientiousness of the Japanese people."*

JOSH BILLINGS: *"One of the greatest victories you can gain over someone is to beat him at politeness."*

PROVERB: *"You get more bees with honey."*

Similar: courtesy, respect, etiquette, mannerliness, civility, appropriateness, genteelness
Opposite: rudeness, inconsiderateness, discourtesy, disrespect, insolence

Politically Correct. (1) Conforming to social expectations. (2) Acting to minimize social offense. (3) Matching group behaviors. *Popular or Heart-Based Usage: (1) Being 'P.C.' (2) 'Keep between the lines!' (3) Heeding the dog whistle. (4) Not ruffling feathers. (5) 'Go with the flow.' (6) Staying off the radar. (7) Not standing out. (8) Not being an outlier. (9) Getting with the program. (10) Going woke. (11) Being on board. (12) 'In the fold.' (13) Being a social justice warrior. (14) Advocating safe spaces. (15) Asserting the moral high ground. (16) 'Offense to any is offense to all.' (17) Prioritizing social norms.*

> CHARLES OSGOOD: *"Being politically correct means always having to say you're sorry."*
>
> ROBERT KIYOSAKI: *"Being politically correct means saying what is polite rather than what is accurate. I'd rather be accurate."*
>
> LEE KWAN YEW: *"I tried always to be correct, not politically correct."*
>
> GEORGE CARLIN: *"Political correctness is America's newest form of intolerance."*
>
> BILLY GRAHAM: *"Our society strives to avoid any possibility of offending anyone— except God."*
>
> ROBERT GRIFFIN III: *"In the land of the free we are held hostage by the tyranny of political correctness."*
>
> RICHARD PETTY: *"Now they're getting so politically correct you can't even stick your tongue out at somebody."*
>
> SANDRA BERNHARD: *"I'm very much a humanist. I'm very much pro-choice. I'm very much politically correct."*
>
> JOHN LEGEND: *"Obviously, Kanye and I are very different in the way we express ourselves publicly. He's so passionate…about art, about culture, about creativity. And he's really good at it. And that honesty manifests itself in ways that are not politically correct, not socially acceptable sometimes."*
>
> ROLLO MAY, BDIV, PHD: *"The opposite of courage in our society is not cowardice, but conformity."*
>
> JOHN SUNUNU: *"Shakespeare would never have gone far in today's politically correct world."*
>
> DENNIS PRAGER: *"Political correctness is the inability to state certain truths because they may offend certain people."*
>
> TRACY MCGRADY: *"People are so scared to really voice who they are. They want to be politically correct. Just scared to see what other people's perceptions are."*
>
> CHARLTON HESTON: *"Why did political correctness originate on America's campuses? And why do you continue to tolerate it? Why do you, who're supposed to debate ideas, surrender to their oppression?"*
>
> GOLDA MEIR: *"One cannot and must not try to erase the past merely because it does not fit the present."*

Similar: evolved, conforming, highly-sensitive, socially conscious, deferential, sacrificing
Opposite: assertive, individualistic, expansive, challenging, courageous, unique

Popularity. (1) Being both widely known and favorably regarded. (2) Being well-liked. *Popular or Heart-Based Usage: (1) Having lots of supporters. (2) Being in vogue. (3) Being a hot ticket. (4) Being trendy. (5) Being known as cool. (6) Being a nice guy/great girl. (7) Hanging with the right crowd. (8) Being enamored by the group. (9) Having a big following. (10) 'Owning the place.' (11) Getting the votes. (12) Being in the majority. (13) Being an influencer. (14) Having pull. (15) Being recognized as a household name.*

JANE PENNYBACKER MOSBACHER: *"Approve of me or I'll scream."*

FREDDIE MERCURY: *"I won't be a rock star. I will be a legend."*

YOGI BERRA: *"Anyone who is popular is bound to be disliked."*

JULIUS IRVING: *"I firmly believe that respect is a lot more important, and a lot greater, than popularity."*

RICHARD PAUL EVANS: *"It is better to be loved by one person who knows your soul than millions who don't even know your phone number."*

WALT DISNEY: *"When people laugh at Mickey Mouse, it's because he's so human, and that is the secret of his popularity."*

PEARL NASH: *"9 Subtle Behaviors That Make People Instantly Like You More: 1. Active listening. 2. Being genuine. 3. Positive body language. 4. Showing appreciation. 5. Being reliable. 6. Being empathetic. 7. Humility. 8. Being respectful. 9. Being yourself."*

JOHNNY MCGREW: *"Ready to say goodbye to loneliness? Every time you enter a room, try smiling at people, and really mean it. Then watch the magic begin."*

ROBERT BREAULT: *"Charisma is not just saying hello. It's dropping what you're doing to say hello."*

MAX BEERBOHM: *"The delicate balance between modesty and conceit is popularity."*

GEORGE HENRY LEWES: *"To some men popularity is always suspicious."*

JEFFERSON FISHER: *"Not liking someone is no excuse for making yourself less likeable."*

IMMANUEL KANT: *"Seek not the favor of the multitude; it is seldom got by honest and lawful means. But seek the testimony of few; and number not voices, but weigh them."*

AUNG SAN SUU KYI, NOBEL: *"You may not think of politics, but politics think of you."*

MACHIAVELLI: *"Therefore the best fortress to be found is the love of the people, for although you may have fortresses they will not save you if you are hated by the people."*

COMMANDER RICHARD MARCINKO: *"Popularity is not leadership."*

PROVERB: *"Be yourself, no matter what they say."*

Similar: favor, admiration, approval, stylishness, renown, acclaim, charisma
Opposite: anonymity, loneliness, enmity, opposition, isolation, disfavor

Power. Having influence or control over others. *Popular or Heart-Based Usage: (1) Calling the shots. (2) Being a persuader. (3) Running with the alpha dogs. (4) Being a decider. (5) Having real pull. (6) Holding the cards. (7) Owning the room. (8) Pulling the strings. (9) Making it all happen. (10) Steepling your hands. (11) Sitting in the C-Suite. (12) Speaking last. (13) 'Got 'em by the short hairs.' (14) 'What I (we) say, goes.'*

HENRY KISSINGER, PHD, NOBEL: *"Power is the great aphrodisiac."*

WALTER ANNENBERG: *"The greatest power is not money power, but political power."*

MARGARET THATCHER: *"Power is like being a lady ... if you have to tell people you are, you aren't."*

THEODORE ROOSEVELT: *"Speak softly and carry a big stick; you will go far."*

RONALD REAGAN: *"When you can't make them see the light, make them feel the heat."*

WILLARD B. WAGNER: *"Everybody reports to somebody."*

MACHIAVELLI: *"Before all else, be armed."*

SAUL ALINSKY: *"Power is not only what you have, but what the enemy thinks you have."*

D. EARL JOHNSTON: *"When you give away your power of self-defense, you shouldn't be too surprised to find yourself a victim."*

PREAMBLE TO THE U.S. CONSTITUTION: *"We the People of the United States, in order to form a more perfect union, establish Justice, insure domestic Tranquility, provide for the common defense, promote the general welfare, and secure the blessings of Liberty to ourselves and our Posterity, do ordain and establish this Constitution ..."*

THOMAS JEFFERSON: *"Experience hath shewn, that even under the best forms of government those entrusted with power have, in time, and by slow operations, perverted it into tyranny."*

ROBERT GREENE/'THE 48 LAWS OF POWER': *"Everyone has a weakness, a gap in the castle wall. That weakness is usually an insecurity, an uncontrollable emotion or need; it can also be a small secret pleasure. Either way, it is a thumbscrew you can turn to your advantage."*

NAPOLEON BONAPARTE: *"Men are more easily governed through their vices than through their virtues."*

SIR JOHN DALBERG-ACTON: *"Power tends to corrupt, and absolute power corrupts absolutely."*

EDWIN LAND, FRS: *"The most important thing about power is to make sure you don't have to use it."*

FREDERICK DOUGLASS: *"Power concedes nothing without a demand."*

Similar: command, control, authority, dominion, influence, persuasion

Opposite: ineptitude, impotence, helplessness, weakness, void

Prayer. [See also **Calm** and **Meditation**] (1) Undertaking solemn communication with God, or invoking God. (2) Seeking a centering or focus according to your highest principles or aspirations. *Popular or Heart-Based Usage: (1) Getting on your knees. (2) Putting your hands together. (3) Seeking favor. (4) Pinging Heaven. (5) Coming clean with yourself. (6) Having moments in reverie. (7) Sharing your deepest confessions and hopes. (8) Baring your heart. (9) Going upstairs for help. (10) 'Is anyone up there listening?' (11) 'Can I get an Amen?' (12) 'Crystal Blue Persuasion.' (13) 'Thy will be done.'*

MATTHEW HENRY: *"Draw near to God and He will draw near to you."*

JOYCE MEYER: *"Prayer is simply talking to God like a friend."*

BOBBY LABONTE: *"If you're going to hope for change, you'd better start to pray for a change. If you're just hoping, you ain't going anywhere."*

MENACHEM MENDEL SCHNEERSON: *"God dwells where we let God in."*

ABRAHAM JOSHUA HESCHEL: *"Prayer begins at the edge of emptiness."*

SIR ISAAC NEWTON, FRS: *"All my discoveries have been made in answer to prayer."*

BILLY GRAHAM: *"You cannot pray for someone and hate them at the same time."*

DAVID WOLPE: *"Prayer is less about changing the world than it is about changing ourselves."*

MARIANNE WILLIAMSON: *"Prayer is the medium of miracles; in whatever way works for you, pray right now."*

MEISTER ECKHART: *"If the only prayer you ever say is thank you, it will be enough."*

ALFRED, LORD TENNYSON: *"More things are wrought by prayer than this world dreams of."*

SØREN KIERKEGAARD: *"Prayer does not change God, but it changes him who prays."*

D. EARL JOHNSTON: *"Many emotions can bring us to our knees: pain, sorrow, conflict, worry, loss, and also a vow. The wisdom of the ages teaches us that gratitude for what we already have helps build a fortress for future happiness."*

JOEL OSTEEN: *"God loves you too much to let you miss your purpose."*

PHILIPPIANS 4:13: *"I can do all things through Christ which strengtheneth me."*

MADALYN MURRAY O'HAIR: *"Two hands working can do more than a thousand clasped in prayer."*

DOMINIC: *"Arm yourself with prayer rather than a sword."*

WILLIAM JAMES, MD: *"The sovereign cure for worry is prayer."*

SCOTTISH PROVERB: *"Confession is good for the soul."*

YIDDISH PROVERB: *"If you pray for another, you will be helped yourself."*

AMIT RAY, PHD: *"The science of prayer is re-programming your unconscious mind and the art of prayer is connecting with the higher self."*

FRANK BUNKER GILBRETH, JR.: *"As long as there are final examinations in school, there will be prayers."*

TODD STOCKER: *"Starting a morning without prayer is like starting a car without gas."*

Prayer. *(continued)*

CHARLES R. MOORE: *"Do you believe in telepathy? No? Then what are you doing when you pray?"*

BILLY GRAHAM: *"It is not the body's posture, but the heart's attitude that counts when we pray."*

HO'OPONOPONO PRAYER: *"I'm sorry, please forgive me; thank you, I love you."*

A PRAYER: *"Thank you, God, for helping me to reassemble the broken elements of my life into a stronger vessel more suitable for Your will."*

DENNIS PRAGER: *"Prayer is not asking God to do something, it's asking God to help YOU do something."*

TODD STOCKER: *"A change of heart changes everything."*

A PRAYER: *"Lord, please open the right door and close the others."*

MEISTER ECKHART: *"God is nearer to me than I am to myself."*

ALBERT EINSTEIN, PHD, NOBEL: *"Coincidence is God's way of remaining anonymous."*

ANDREW MURRAY (attributed): *"We cannot enter the kingdom of God on our own."*

ALAN COHEN, MA: *"Appreciation is the highest form of prayer."*

QURAN: *"You alone we worship, and you alone we ask for help."*

IGNATIUS OF LOYOLA: *"Undertake nothing without consulting God."*

SHEMA YISRAEL: *"Hear, O Israel: The Lord is our God, the Lord is One."*

PSALM 46:10: *"Be still, and know that I am God."*

Similar: invoking, supplicating, beseeching, subservience, respect
Opposite: disdain, self-sufficiency, irreverence, disinterest, indifference

Prejudice. (1) Having a pre-established viewpoint about a topic, person, or group, and without concern for other relevant facts or details. (2) Having personal bias in a matter. *Popular or Heart-Based Usage: (1) Maintaining your own slant. (2) Always leaning the same way. (3) Having your foot on the scale. (4) Going with pre-set favorites. (5) Being narrow-minded. (6) Having confirmation bias. (7) Hanging on to legacy opinions.*

MAYA ANGELOU: *"Prejudice is a burden that confuses the past, threatens the future, and renders the present inaccessible."*

MOTHER TERESA, NOBEL: *"If you judge people, you have no time to love them."*

CHARLOTTE BRONTE: *"Prejudices, it is well known, are most difficult to eradicate from the heart whose soil has never been loosened or fertilized by education; they grow there, firm as weeds among stones."*

WILLIAM JAMES, MD: *"A great many people think they are thinking when they are merely rearranging their prejudices."*

VOLTAIRE: *"Prejudices are what fools use for reason."*

LEO TOLSTOY: *"Freethinkers are those who are willing to use their minds without prejudice and without fearing to understand things that clash with their own customs, privileges, or beliefs."*

VICTOR HUGO: *"Superstitions, bigotries, hypocrisies, prejudices, these phantoms, phantoms though they be, cling to life; they have teeth and nails in their shadowy substance, and we must grapple with them and make war on them."*

SAMUEL JOHNSON: *"There are in every age new errors to be rectified and new prejudices to be opposed."*

JAMEIS WINSTON: *"Judge me all you want, just keep the verdict to yourself."*

LINCOLN STOREY: *"The real answer to ending prejudice is contributing new solutions, and not wallowing in the trap of re-hashing old problems."*

TONI MORRISON, LITT.D, PULITZER, NOBEL: *"There is no time for despair, no place for self-pity, no need for silence, no room for fear. We speak, we write, we do language. That is how civilizations heal."*

OPRAH WINFREY: *"Excellence is the best deterrent to racism or sexism."*

RALPH WASHINGTON SOCKMAN: *"In overcoming prejudice, working together is even more effective than talking together."*

MARK TWAIN: *"Travel is fatal to prejudice, bigotry, and narrow-mindedness."*

ANDRE GIDE: *"There is no work of prejudice that the work of art does not finally overcome."*

LAURENCE J. PETER: *"Two things reduce prejudice: education and laughter."*

HENRY DAVID THOREAU: *"It is never too late to give up your prejudices."*

HARPER LEE: *"I think there's just one kind of folks. Folks."*

Similar: discrimination, ignorance, racism, sexism, ableism, ageism, genderism, bigotry
Opposite: acceptance, objectivity, impartiality, benevolence, inclusivity, friendship

Present. (1) Being focused on your current environment. (2) Paying attention to what is happening now. *Popular or Heart-Based Usage: (1) Being in the moment. (2) Being 'in the building.' (3) 'What's happening?' (4) 'What's going on?' (5) 'Right this second.' (6) 'Snap out of it!' (7) 'Be. Here. Now.' (8) Prodding someone with: 'Hello?!?' or 'Anyone there?' (9) Focusing on the Now. (10) In the spirit of the Zeitgeist. (11) Understanding what is really going on. (12) 'We the living.' (13) Staying in real time.*

ELEANOR ROOSEVELT: *"Yesterday is history. Tomorrow is a mystery. Today is a gift, that's why we call it 'the Present.'"*

DALAI LAMA, NOBEL: *"There are only two days in the year that nothing can be done. One is called yesterday and the other is called tomorrow, so today is the right day to love, believe, and mostly, live."*

ABRAHAM MASLOW, PHD: *"The ability to be in the present moment is a major component of wellness."*

MALCOLM FORBES: *"Presence is more than just being there."*

JAMES JOYCE: *"Absence, the highest form of presence."*

SCOUTMASTER BILLY JIM VAUGHN: *"All people are equal in time; we each have 24 hours per day. It's how we choose to spend them that's different."*

GAUTAMA BUDDHA: *"Do not dwell in the past, do not dream of the future, concentrate the mind on the present moment."*

ECKHART TOLLE: *"Realize deeply that the present moment is all you have. Make the Now the primary focus of your life."*

EDGAR CAYCE: *"Being present isn't something you do, it's something you are."*

MOTHER TERESA, NOBEL: *"Yesterday is gone, tomorrow has not yet come. We have only today, let us begin."*

LUDWIG WITTGENSTEIN, PHD: *"He who lives in the present lives in eternity."*

MENACHEM MENDEL SCHNEERSON: *"This is the key to time management—to see the value of every moment."*

RAM DASS: *"Be here now."*

BENEDICT OF NURSIA: *"Always we begin again."*

T. S. ELIOT: *"Every moment is a fresh beginning."*

EMILY DICKINSON: *"Forever is composed of nows."*

Similar: now, current, immediate, contemporary, aware
Opposite: absent, away, distracted, lost, stuck

Pride. (1) Feeling the achievement of standards from your actions and efforts. (2) Feeling well-prepared for life's coming challenges and successes. *Popular or Heart-Based Usage: (1) Meeting life's challenges head-on. (2) Feeling good about yourself. (3) Knowing you have what it takes. (4) Setting (or meeting) high standards. (5) Holding your head high. (6) Feeling second to none. (7) Respecting yourself. (8) Walking the walk. (9) Being proud as a peacock. (10) 'Good on ya.' (11) 'You done yourself right.'*

PROVERBS 16:18: *"Pride goes before destruction, and an haughty spirit before a fall."*

EZRA TAFT BENSON: *"With pride, there are many curses. With humility, there come many blessings."*

VOLTAIRE: *"We are rarely proud when we are alone."*

ABRAHAM LINCOLN: *"I like to see a man proud of the place in which he lives. I like to see a man live so that his place will be proud of him."*

ROBERT LOUIS STEVENSON: *"Of what shall a man be proud, if he is not proud of his friends?"*

BERNARD OF CLAIRVAUX: *"Pride only, the chief of all iniquities, can make us treat gifts as if they were rightful attributes of our nature, and, while receiving benefits, rob of Benefactor of His true glory."*

AUGUSTINE OF HIPPO: *"It was pride that changed angels into devils: It is humility that makes men into angels."*

GEORGES BERNANOS: *"It is a fine thing to rise above pride, but you must have pride in order to do so."*

DEMOCRITUS: *"The pride of youth is in strength and beauty, the pride of old age is in discretion."*

SAM WALTON: *"Outstanding leaders go out of their way to boost the self-esteem of their personnel. If people believe in themselves, it's amazing what they can accomplish."*

RONALD REAGAN: *"Some people wonder all their lives if they've made a difference. The Marines don't have that problem."*

DENZEL WASHINGTON: *"Don't stop until you're proud."*

UK TEAMS COMPETITION: *"There ain't no flies on us!*
There ain't no flies on us!
There might be flies on some of you guys;
But there ain't no flies on us!"

PROVERB: *"Be proud of who you are, not of what you have."*

Similar: self-satisfaction, gratification, self-esteem, bragging rights
Opposite: humility, shame, disgrace, inadequacy, pessimism, insecurity

Procrastination. Delaying or deferring needed action in the attempt to avoid drudgery, work, or unpleasant tasks. *Popular or Heart-Based Usage: (1) Putting something off. (2) Tabling something. (3) Putting a chore on hold. (4) Goofing off. (5) Dilly-dallying. (6) Hemming and hawing. (7) Back-sliding. (8) Stalling. (9) Pushing something to the bottom of the stack. (10) 'Stop bugging me about it!'*

OSCAR WILDE: *"Never put off until tomorrow what you can do the day after."*

JOHNNY MCGREW: *"Stayed in bed and got a ton of procrastination done today."*

JULES RENARD: *"Laziness is nothing more than the habit of resting before you get tired."*

WILLIAM JAMES, MD: *"Nothing is so fatiguing as the eternal hanging on of an uncompleted task."*

WILLIAM SHAKESPEARE: *"I wasted time, and now doth time waste me."*

NORMAN VINCENT PEALE: *"The really happy people are those who have broken the chains of procrastination, those who find satisfaction in doing the job at hand. They're full of eagerness, zest, productivity."*

MARIO ANDRETTI: *"If you wait, all that happens is that you get older."*

MASON COOLEY: *"Procrastination makes easy things hard, hard things harder."*

GABOR MATE, MD, CM: *"The attempt to escape from pain, is what creates more pain."*

DR. ROBIN YOUNGSON, MA, MBCHB: "Procrastination isn't laziness—it's trauma."

ALYCE CORNYN-SELBY: *"Procrastination is, hands down, our favorite form of self-sabotage."*

JOHNNY MCGREW: *"Procrastination is trying hard to hide from yourself."*

FRANCIS OF ASSISI: *"Start by doing what's necessary; then do what's possible; and suddenly you are doing the impossible."*

ADAGE: *"Where the challenge seems daunting, make the first step small."*

SHADE ZAHRAI, PHD: *"Action triggers motivation: 1) Do the quick things first. 2) Simulate a sense of urgency (set a timer). 3) (Do) stimulus control (eliminate the distractions)."*

GEN. GEORGE S. PATTON, JR.: *"A good plan violently executed now is better a perfect plan executed next week."*

SIMONE DE BEAUVOIR: *"Change your life today. Don't gamble on the future, act now, without delay."*

DESMOND TUTU, NOBEL: *"There is only one way to eat an elephant; a bite at a time."*

WALT DISNEY: *"The way to get started is to quit talking and begin doing."*

MARK TWAIN: *"The secret of getting ahead is getting started."*

SETH GODIN, BS, MBA: *"Keep starting until you finish."*

Similar: stalling, dawdling, delaying, dithering, hesitating, putting it off
Opposite: starting, completing, hastening, expediting, doing

Projection. (1) Assuming (or imagining) others will or should behave just as you would yourself. (2) Accusing other people of doing the very things you are doing. *Popular or Heart-Based Usage: (1) The pot calling the kettle black. (2) Emotional self-righteousness. (3) Pressing your own 'take' on something. (4) 'It takes one to know one.' (5) Virtue signaling. (6) 'They're all mini-me's.'*

MARK TWAIN: *"The Public is really a multiplied 'me.'"*
BILLY CORGAN: *"Compliments and criticism are all ultimately based on some form of projection."*
ELLIE GOULDING: *"America saw me as a projection of me that I always wanted. That is why I love going to America so much. I feel like I started off in America exactly how I wanted to start everywhere."*
ELLEN ULLMAN: *"A computer is not really like us. It is a projection of a small part of ourselves: that portion dedicated to logic, order, rule and clarity."*
D. EARL JOHNSTON: *"Projection can include sly misdirection. It can include finger-pointing at others when the real cause of the problem is the person pointing the finger."*
MERRIT MALLOY: *"Everything we say about other people is really about ourselves."*
WAYNE DYER: *"When you judge another, you do not define them, you define yourself."*
ECKHART TOLLE: *"The moment you interpret something, you are projecting."*
CARL JUNG, MD: *"The best political, social, and spiritual work we can do is to withdraw the projection of our shadow onto others."*
LOIS FARFEL STARK: *"We form a mental map, then that shape, shapes us."*
CONFUCIUS: *"He who searches for evil, must first look at his own reflection."*
WILLIAM SHAKESPEARE: *"Suspicion always haunts the guilty mind."*
LOIS FARFEL STARK: *"Our prism can become our prison."*
PROVERB: *"What goes around, comes around."*

Similar: coping, mirroring, narcissism, externalization, extrapolation, finger-pointing, defensiveness
Opposite: acceptance, acquiescence, obliviousness, introversion

Promise. Making a vow, pledge, or undertaking that something will be done. *Popular or Heart-Based Usage: (1) Giving your word. (2) Making an oath (or blood oath). (3) Keeping your word. (4) Swearing on a stack of Bibles. (5) 'No crosses count.' (6) 'Pinky swear.' (7) 'No fingers crossed.' (8) 'Cross my heart and hope to die, stick a needle in my eye.' (9) 'On my mother's grave.' (10) Remembering the rainbow. (11) 'This I swear.' (12) 'Honor Bright.' (13) 'On my honor.' (14) 'Forever and ever, Amen.' (15) Being bound by your heart.*

ROBERT W. SERVICE: *"A promise made is a debt unpaid."*

PUBLILIUS SYRUS: *"Never promise more than you can perform."*

SARAH DESSEN: *"True friendship is a promise you keep forever."*

JEAN-JACQUES ROUSSEAU: *"Those that are most slow in making a promise are the most faithful in the performance of it."*

ZIAD K. ABDELNOUR: *"Don't promise when you're happy, don't reply when you're angry, and don't decide when you're sad."*

NAPOLEON BONAPARTE: *"The best way to keep one's word is not to give it."*

BENJAMIN FRANKLIN: *"Tricks and treachery are the practice of fools, that don't have the brains enough to be honest."*

ROBERT FROST: *"The woods are lovely, dark and deep;*
        But I have promises to keep,
        And miles to go before I sleep;
        And miles to go before I sleep."

GENESIS 9:13: *"I do set my bow in the cloud, and it shall be for a token of a covenant between me and the earth."*

JEREMIAH 32:40: *"And I will make an everlasting covenant with them, that I will not turn away from them, to do them good; but I will put my fear into their hearts, that they shall not depart from me."*

SAYING: *"To be successful in life, it's better to under-promise and over-deliver."*

GEORGE STEPHANOPOULOS: *"The President has kept all the promises he intended to keep."*

CHILDREN'S POEM: *"Cross my heart and hope to die, stick a needle in my eye."*

D. EARL JOHNSTON: *"A promise of the heart, kept or broken, is never forgotten."*

PATRICIA RYAN: *"Deliver more than you promise."*

Similar: oath, commitment, guarantee, pledge, vow, bond, covenant
Opposite: renege, breach, welch, deceive, re-trade, undercut, take it back, abandon

Provocation. Initiating behavior which is reasonably expected to annoy, unbalance, or upset someone. *Popular or Heart-Based Usage: (1) Picking a fight. (2) Taunting someone. (3) Poking the bear. (4) Pissing someone off. (5) Borrowing trouble. (6) Stirring the pot. (7) Setting someone off. (8) Egging someone on. (9) Throwing the cat amongst the pigeons. (10) Being an agent provocateur. (11) Initiating a false flag operation. (12) Getting someone to take the bait. (13) 'But you/he/they started it!'*

PROVERB: *"Let sleeping dogs lie."*

CARL VON CLAUSEWITZ: *"All war presupposes human weakness and seeks to exploit it."*

OTTO VON BISMARCK: *"We live in a wondrous time, in which the strong is weak because of his scruples and the weak grows strong because of his audacity."*

THEODORE ROOSEVELT, NOBEL: *"A good Navy is not a provocation to war. It is the surest guarantee of peace."*

CICERO: *"Those wars are unjust which are undertaken without provocation. For only a war waged for revenge or defense can be just."*

MACHIAVELLI: *"There is nothing more difficult to take in hand, more perilous to conduct, or more uncertain in its success, than to take the lead in the introduction of a new order of things."*

MIKE DANIELS: *"The second guy always gets caught, and that's why you have to initiate it instead of retaliating."*

ROY COHN: *"I bring out the worst in my enemies and that's how I get them to defeat themselves."*

SAUL ALINSKY: *"The job of the organizer is to maneuver and bait the establishment so that it will publicly attack him as a 'dangerous enemy.'"*

JOHN TILLOTSON: *"To be able to bear provocation is an argument of great reason, and to forgive it of a great mind."*

THOMAS JEFFERSON: *"I have sworn upon the altar of God eternal hostility against every form of tyranny over the mind of man."*

ARTHUR CRAVAN: *"Every great artist has the sense of provocation."*

JACQUES CHIRAC: *"Anything that can hurt the convictions of another, particularly religious convictions, must be avoided. Freedom of expression must be exercised in a spirit of responsibility."*

RALPH WALDO EMERSON: *"What is indispensable to inspiration?...Sound sleep and the provocation of a good book or a companion."*

RUDYARD KIPLING, NOBEL: *"If—"* (Poem)

Similar: taunting, goading, audacity, instigation, baiting, prodding
Opposite: harmonizing, calming, pacifying, ameliorating, smoothing

Purpose. Having reasons, intentions, and objectives. *Popular or Heart-Based Usage: (1) 'What is the real driver?' (2) 'What's behind it?' (3) Finding the meaning. (4) Knowing the motivation. (5) Having your reasons. (6) Finding yourself. (7) Discovering the Way. (8) Heeding your Guardian Angel. (9) Making your appointment with the Universe. (10) 'All signal, no static.' (11) Having a calling. (12) Following through.*

OPRAH WINFREY: *"There is no greater gift you can give or receive than to honor your calling. It's why you were born. And how you become most truly alive."*

PABLO PICASSO: *"The meaning of life is to find your gift. The purpose of life is to give it away."*

DALAI LAMA, NOBEL: *"Our prime purpose in life is to help others. And if you can't help them, at least don't hurt them."*

GEORGE ELIOT: *"What do we live for, if not to make life less difficult for each other?"*

WASHINGTON IRVING: *"Great minds have purposes; others have wishes."*

MERYL STREEP: *"What makes you different or weird, that's your strength."*

D. EARL JOHNSTON: *"Finding your purpose is stripping away your ego and anything else that isn't really you."*

T. D. JAKES: *"If you can't find your purpose, figure out your passion. For your passion will lead you right into your purpose."*

GEN. FERDINAND FOCH: *"The most powerful weapon on earth is the human soul on fire."*

GEORGE WASHINGTON: *"But as it has been a kind of destiny, that has thrown me upon this service, I shall hope that my undertaking it is designed to answer some good purpose."*

ECCLESIASTES 3:1: *"To every thing there is a season, and a time to every purpose under heaven."*

LINCOLN STOREY: *"The more you are grateful for what you have, the closer you are to finding and knowing your true purpose."*

ALEXANDER HAMILTON: *"To answer the purpose of the adversaries of the Constitution, they ought to prove, not merely that particular provisions in it are not the best, which might have been imagined, but that the plan upon the whole is bad and pernicious."*

EDGAR CAYCE: *"The ultimate purpose of our life is to rejoin God in conscious participation of divinity."*

WAYNE DYER: *"If you want to feel connected to your own purpose, know this for certain; Your purpose will only be found in service to others, and in being connected to the something far greater than your mind/body/ego."*

JOEL OSTEEN: *"God loves you too much to let you miss your purpose."*

JOHNNY MCGREW: *"Do stuff that gives your Guardian Angel goosebumps."*

Similar: motive, intention, cause, resolve, determination, grounds, impetus, thrust
Opposite: chance, happenstance, coincidence, fluke

Quantum Physics. [See also **Electromagnetism, Frequency, Gravity,** and **Light**] (1) Recognizing how space, time, energy, and matter manifest and interact. (2) Studying the linkages between energy and particles at the sub-atomic or most fundamental level. *Popular or Heart-Based Usage: (1) 'Mind over matter.' (2) Where observation influences existence. (3) 'The Observer Effect.' (4) How time, cause, and effect may invert at the subatomic level. (5) Inconsistencies in sequential time. (6) 'In the fullness of time.' (7) Understanding retro-causality. (8) Quantum entanglement. (9) Understanding String Theory. (10) The underpinnings of the holographic universe. (11) 'Probability predicts the persistence of matter.' (12) 'Spooky action at a distance.' (13) Mind-bending stuff. (14) 'Ahead Warp Factor five, Mr. Sulu.'*

RICHARD FEYNMAN, PHD, NOBEL: *"I think I can safely say that nobody understands Quantum Mechanics."*

SIR LAWRENCE BRAGG, NOBEL: *"God runs electromagnetics on Monday, Wednesday, and Friday by the wave theory, and the devil runs it by quantum theory on Tuesday, Thursday, and Saturday."*

VICTOR FREDERICK WEISSKOPF, PHD: *"When things get tough, there are two things that make life worth living: Mozart, and quantum mechanics."*

NIELS BOHR, PHD, NOBEL: *"Everything we call real is made of things that cannot be regarded as real."*

ALBERT EINSTEIN, PHD, NOBEL: *"Reality is merely an illusion, albeit persistent one."*

JAMES LOVELOCK, PHD, CH, CBE, FRS: *"If you start any large theory, such as quantum mechanics, plate tectonics, evolution, it takes about 40 years for the mainstream science to come around."*

WERNER HEISENBERG, PHD, NOBEL: *"The atoms or elementary particles themselves are not real; they form a world of potentialities or possibilities rather than one of things or facts."*

EUGENE WIGNER, PHD, NOBEL: *"It was not possible to formulate the laws of quantum mechanics in a fully consistent way without reference to consciousness."*

MAX PLANCK, PHD, NOBEL: *"I regard consciousness as fundamental. I regard matter as derivative from consciousness."*

ALBERT SZENT-GYORGYI, PHD, NOBEL: *"Nature is one. It is not divided into physics, chemistry, quantum mechanics."*

AMIT GOSWAMI, PHD: *"Suppose that instead of everything being made of atoms, everything is made of consciousness. What then?"*

PAUL LEVY: *"Quantum Physics reveals to us that turning the gaze of our attention towards anything is a powerful creative act that alters, energizes, and potentiates whatever our gaze falls upon. Focus is food. Focusing our attention is an act of creation in and of itself."*

AMIT GOSWAMI, PHD: *"Consciousness, not matter, is fundamental."*

Quantum Physics. *(continued)*

GOOGLE GENERATIVE AI: *"The Large Hadron Collider allows us to study quantum entanglement at the highest energies ever achieved, giving us a unique window into the fundamental nature of the universe."*

NIELS BOHR, PHD, NOBEL: *"It is not possible to observe the phenomena of quantum mechanics without changing them."*

NIELS BOHR, PHD, NOBEL: *"Anyone who can contemplate quantum physics without getting dizzy hasn't understood it."*

DR. JOE DISPENZA: *"The quantum model asserts that we can signal the body emotionally and begin to alter a chain of genetic events without first having any actual physical experience that correlates to that emotion."*

LYNNE MCTAGGART: *"If consciousness operates at the quantum level, it would naturally operate outside space and time, and we would theoretically have access to information—'past' and 'future.'"*

Similar: observational, foundational, subatomic, trans-dimensional, warp factoring
Opposite: galactic, universal, classical, Newtonian, 3-dimensional

Racism. Prejudging or discriminating against another person or group because of their skin color, ethnicity, or biological and/or cultural backgrounds. *Popular or Heart-Based Usage: (1) Stereotyping others. (2) Calling people names. (3) Race-baiting. (4) Being mean-spirited. (5) Painting groups with a broad brush. (6) Making it about color and not character. (7) Focusing on differences not similarities. (8) Disrespecting others.*

MARTIN LUTHER KING, JR., NOBEL: *"I have a dream that my four little children will one day live in a nation where they will not be judged by the color of their skin, but by the content of their character."*

DESMOND TUTU, NOBEL: *"If you are neutral in situations of injustice, you have chosen the side of the oppressor. If an elephant has its foot on the tail of a mouse and you say that you are neutral, the mouse will not appreciate your neutrality."*

NELSON MANDELA, NOBEL: *"No one is born hating another person because of the color of his skin, or his background, or his religion. People must learn to hate, and if they can learn to hate, they can be taught to love, for love comes more naturally to the human heart than its opposite."*

OPRAH WINFREY: *"I was raised to believe that excellence is the best deterrent to racism or sexism. And that's how I operate my life."*

MUHAMMAD ALI: *"Hating people because of their color is wrong. And it doesn't matter which color does the hating. It's just plain wrong."*

MICHAEL JORDAN: *"I realize I'm black, but I like to be viewed as a person, and this is everybody's wish."*

MAYA ANGELOU: *"Prejudice is a burden that confuses the past, threatens the future and renders the present inaccessible."*

MALCOLM X: *"I believe in human beings, and that all human beings should be respected as such, regardless of their color."*

ELDRIDGE CLEAVER: *"You're either part of the solution or you're part of the problem."*

DECLARATION OF INDEPENDENCE: *"We hold these truths to be self-evident, that all men are created equal."*

ABRAHAM LINCOLN: *"Achievement has no color."*

JOHN F. KENNEDY: *"Every American ought to have the right to be treated as he would wish to be treated, as one would wish his children to be treated."*

RITA LEVI-MONTALCINI, MD, NOBEL: *"I should thank Mussolini for having declared me to be of inferior race."*

JUSTICE THURGOOD MARSHALL: *"I wish I could say that racism and prejudice were only distant memories... We must dissent from the indifference. We must dissent from the apathy. We must dissent from the fear, the hatred..."*

Similar: prejudice, intolerance, bigotry, apartheid, segregation, xenophobia, chauvinism
Opposite: welcoming, inclusion, tolerance, embracing, generosity, respect

Rage. Experiencing violent or uncontrolled anger. *Popular or Heart-Based Usage: (1) Comin' in hot. (2) Being boiling mad. (3) Being on the warpath. (4) Being beside yourself. (5) Flying off the handle. (6) Totally losing it. (7) Being uncontrollably triggered. (8) Throwing a fit. (9) Going crimson. (10) Going mental. (11) Going postal. (12) Road rage. (13) Going ballistic. (14) Throwing stuff. (15) Blowing up. (16) Achieving weapons-grade anger. (17) 'That's it! Bombs away!' (18) Going full thermonuclear. (19) 'Get. Out!'*

HOWARD BEALE: *"I'm mad as hell, and I'm not gonna take this anymore!"*

JAMES BALDWIN: *"To be a Negro in this country and to be relatively conscious is to be in a rage almost all the time."*

WILL ROGERS: *"People who fly into a rage always make a bad landing."*

PETER A. LEVINE, PHD: *"Flash rage — is an indication of trapped life force."*

RALPH WALDO EMERSON: *"A good indignation brings out all of one's powers."*

WILLIAM CONGREVE: *"Heaven has no rage like love to hatred turned, nor hell a fury like a woman scorned."*

PLUTARCH: *"No beast is more savage than man when possessed with power answerable to his rage."*

TUPAC SHAKUR: *"We live like caged beasts waiting for the day to let the rage free."*

KING SOLOMON: *"A soft answer breaks the rage, a tough answer encourages the fury."*

EDMUND BURKE: *"Rage and frenzy will pull down more in half an hour than prudence, deliberation, and foresight can build up in a hundred years."*

BENJAMIN FRANKLIN: *"If passion drives you, let reason hold the reins."*

KANYE WEST: *"It's rage, its creativity, it's pain, it's hurt, but it's the opportunity to still have my voice get out there through music."*

DYLAN THOMAS: *"Do not go gentle into that good night,... Rage, rage against the dying of the light."*

PIERRE CORNEILLE: *"Oh rage! Oh despair! Oh age, my enemy!"*

TINA BROWN: *"Servility always curdles into rage in the end."*

GEORGE SANTAYANA: *"Depression is rage spread thin."*

Similar: fury, outburst, apoplexy, bitterness, indignation, resentment, fulmination
Opposite: calm, serenity, peacefulness, contentment

Rational. Thinking and decision-making with appropriate emphasis on emotion, logic, and science. *Popular or Heart-Based Usage: (1) Having your head screwed on right. (2) Being cool, calm, and collected. (3) Working things out systematically. (4) Being the methodical voice. (5) Being a proud geek. (6) Acting like Mr. Spock. (7) Thinking it through. (8) Weighing all the facts and circumstances. (9) Getting to the right answers.*

ALBERT EINSTEIN, PHD, NOBEL: *"I never made one of my discoveries through the process of rational thinking."*

BESSEL VAN DER KOLK: MD: *"Our emotions assign value to experiences and thus are the foundation of reason."*

JONATHAN HAIDT, PHD: *"The human mind is a story processor, not a logic processor."*

NEIL DEGRASSE TYSON, PHD: *"Rational thoughts never drive people's creativity the way emotions do."*

JONATHAN HAIDT, PHD: *"It is only because our emotional brain works so well that our reasoning can work at all."*

FYODOR DOSTOEVSKY: *"If everything on earth were rational, nothing would happen."*

APHORISM: *"When you have the facts on your side, pound the facts. When you don't have the facts on your side, pound the table."*

ALBERT ELLIS, PHD: *"There's no evidence whatsoever that men are more rational than women. Both sexes seem to be equally irrational."*

WILL ROGERS: *"You can't legislate intelligence and common sense into people."*

STEPHEN HAWKING, CH, CBE, FRS, FRSA, PHD: *"To my mathematical brain, the numbers alone make thinking about aliens perfectly rational. The real challenge is to work out what aliens might actually be like."*

MR. SPOCK: *"May I say that I have not thoroughly enjoyed working with humans? I find their illogic and foolish emotions a constant irritant."*

MENACHEM BEGIN: *"He who threatens us will find us deaf to his threats. We are willing to listen only to rational arguments."*

NOAM CHOMSKY, PHD: *"Rational discussion is useful only where there is a significant base of shared assumptions."*

JEAN-JACQUES ROUSSEAU: *"Reason deceives us; conscience, never."*

ARISTOTLE: *"Why do I enjoy the company of beautiful women? You would have to be blind to ask."*

THOMAS AQUINAS: *"A man has free choice to the extent he is rational."*

JOHN DONNE: *"Reason is our soul's left hand, faith her right."*

ADAGE: *"Follow your heart. But take your brain with you."*

PYTHAGORAS: *"Reason is immortal, all else mortal."*

Similar: analytical, deliberate, enlightened, sensible, measured, balanced
Opposite: careless, confused, illogical, insane, crazy, inconsistent

Reaching Out. (1) Taking the initiative to establish a connection or dialogue with another person. (2) Either requesting or offering support or help. *Popular or Heart-Based Usage: (1) Making contact. (2) Opening up a conversation. (3) Being a friend. (4) Building a bridge. (5) Getting over yourself. (6) Breaking the ice. (7) Extending an olive branch. (8) Being there for someone else. (9) Showing up. (10) 'HMU' or 'HYU.' ['Hit Me Up' or 'Hit You Up.']*

GEORGE ELIOT: *"What do we live for, if not to make life less difficult for each other?"*

WINNIE THE POOH: *"You can't stand in your corner of the forest, waiting for others to come to you. You have to go to them sometimes."*

NORMAN B. RICE: *"Dare to reach out your hand into the darkness, to pull another hand into the light."*

CRAIG D. LOUNSBROUGH: *"Love is a choice to reach beyond myself not once but twice. First, I reach out to God to grant me the love I don't possess, and then I reach out to others to give them that love."*

WAYLON LEWIS: *"We are all struggling. Reach out. Be kind. Mean it."*

CHARLES DICKENS: *"No one is useless in this world who lightens the burdens of another."*

SUNDAY ADELAJA: *"When you reach out in faith, God backs you up with manifestation."*

ALBERT EINSTEIN: *"Our lives will be measured by what we do for others."*

BROOKE AXTELL: *"Please reach out for help, your voice will save you."*

LAILAH GIFTY AKITA: *"Reach out for the heavenly blessings!"*

MATTHEW 7:7–8: *"Ask, and it shall be given to you; seek, and ye shall find; Knock, and it shall be opened unto you: For every one that asketh receiveth; and he that seeketh findeth; And to him that knocketh it shall be opened."*

WALT WHITMAN: *"When one reaches out to another, he touches the face of God."*

BRIAN HOLLAND, LAMONT DOZIER, EDDIE HOLLAND: *"Reach Out I'll Be There"* (Song)

Similar: connecting, relating, collaborating, cooperating, respecting
Opposite: separating, disconnecting, dissociating, individuating, isolating

Reality. (1) Identifying what genuinely exists, as compared to what merely seems to exist. (2) Acknowledging the differences between absolute reality, objective reality, and subjective reality. (3) Recognizing what actually matters in a situation. *Popular or Heart-Based Usage: (1) Getting to the bottom of things. (2) 'It is what it is.' (3) Acknowledging the metadata. (4) 'Getting it.' (5) Knowing the score. (6) Accepting the birds and the bees. (7) Recognizing the truth about sausage-making. (8) Knowing 'how the cow ate the cabbage.'*

SIR ISAAC NEWTON, FRS: *"Gravity explains the motions of the planets, but it cannot explain who sets the planets in motion."*

NIKOLA TESLA: *"If you want to find the secrets of the universe, think in terms of energy, frequency and vibration."*

NIELS BOHR, PHD, NOBEL: *"Everything we call real is made of things that cannot be regarded as real."*

ALBERT EINSTEIN, PHD, NOBEL (attributed): *"Everything is energy and that's all there is to it. Match the frequency of the reality you want and you cannot help but get that reality. This is not philosophy. This is physics."*

RALPH WALDO EMERSON: *"Once you make a decision, the universe conspires to make it happen."*

EARL NIGHTINGALE: *"Whatever we plant in our subconscious mind and nourish with repetition and emotion will one day become a reality."*

D. EARL JOHNSTON: *"You create your coming reality by the nature of the thoughts you entertain."*

PAM GREGORY: *"Your belief system will arrange and present your reality to you ... The universe is just a mirror."*

ROBERT RINGER: *"Reality isn't the way you wish things to be nor the way they appear to be but the way they actually are."*

SALMAN RUSHDIE: *"Reality is a question of perspective."*

M. C. ESCHER: *"Are you really sure a floor can't also be a ceiling?"*

HERMANN HESSE: *"There is no reality except the one contained within us."*

PHILIP K. DICK: *"Reality is that which, when you stop believing in it, doesn't go."*

ALBERT EINSTEIN, PHD, NOBEL: *"Reality is merely an illusion, albeit a persistent one."*

GEORGE LUCAS: *"Always remember, your focus determines your reality."*

WILLIAM BLAKE: *"What is now proved was once only imagined."*

MARK TWAIN: *"Reality can be beaten with enough imagination."*

WAYNE DYER: *"Our intention creates our reality."*

WALT DISNEY: *"If you can dream it, you can do it."*

Similar: existence, truth, facts, verity, actuality
Opposite: fantasy, illusion, fiction, simulation

Redemption. (1) Restoring a clear standing by atoning for an error, making amends, or repaying a debt. (2) Being released from sin, evil, error, or hardship, often through the undertaking of sacrifice. (3) Experiencing a profound transformation of the heart. (4) Attaining forgiveness. *Popular or Heart-Based Usage: (1) Getting out of jail free. (2) Getting a 'do-over.' (3) Getting a fresh start. (4) Taking a mulligan. (5) Getting a hall pass. (6) Wiping the slate clean. (7) Being pardoned. (8) Paying your debts to society. (9) Personally cleaning house. (10) Recovering your life. (11) Having your sins blotted out. (12) Being born again (or second birth). (13) Undertaking a deep-down soul cleansing. (14) Experiencing profound grace. (15) Having a total change of heart. (16) Undertaking penitence and conversion. (17) 'Metanoia' (experiencing a life change from penitence or conversion). (18) 'All is forgiven.' (19) 'Olly olly oxen free.' (20) 'Free at last!'*

TODD STOCKER: *"A change of heart changes everything."*

MARTIN LUTHER KING, JR., NOBEL: *"Love has within it a redemptive power. And there is a power there that eventually transforms individuals."*

REBA MCENTIRE: *"Easter is very important to me, it's a second chance."*

STEPHEN KING/FRANK DARABONT: *"The Shawshank Redemption"* (Book/Film)

TENNESSEE WILLIAMS: *"Hell is yourself and the only redemption is when you put yourself aside to feel deeply for another person."*

C. S. LEWIS: *"Mere improvement is not redemption, though redemption always improves people."*

PABLO NERUDA: *"Give me life, for my life, all lives, give me all the pain of everyone, I'm going to turn it into hope."*

BETH MOORE: *"You cannot amputate your history from your destiny, because that is redemption."*

FRIEDRICH NIETZSCHE: *"There is something to pardon in everything, there is also something to condemn."*

MACHIAVELLI: *"A battle that you win cancels all of your mistakes."*

GEORGE ELIOT: *"The best happiness will be to escape the worst misery."*

MAHATMA GANDHI: *"No human being is so bad as to be beyond redemption."*

D. EARL JOHNSTON: *"Redemption is about finding yourself painfully lost, and then rediscovering the truth and who you really were all along."*

ISAIAH 44:22: *"I have blotted out, as a thick cloud, thy transgressions, and, as a cloud, thy sins; return unto me, for I have redeemed thee."*

LAMENTATIONS 3:58: *"Oh Lord, thou hast pleaded the causes of my soul; thou hast redeemed my life."*

ACTS 3:19: *"Repent ye therefore, and be converted, that your sins may be blotted out, when the times of refreshing may come from presence of the Lord."*

ADAGE: *"Redemption is God and sinners reconciled."*

Similar: restoration, exoneration, absolution, vindication, realization, rescue, release
Opposite: forfeiture, rejection, abandonment, deprivation, stagnation, damnation

Regret. (1) Focusing on a past failure or deficiency. (2) Yearning for an improved result after recognition of a missed opportunity or adverse outcome. *Popular or Heart-Based Usage: (1) Cringing about something. (2) Wanting to turn back time. (3) Wincing. (4) Wishing it was all different. (5) Backing off (or backing out). (6) Crawfishing about something. (7) Getting buyer's remorse. (8) Being on your heels. (9) Bailing out. (10) Pulling the plug. (11) Going low-profile. (12) Trying to un-do something. (13) Looking for a fixer. (14) Doing damage control. (15) Wanting a do-over. (16) Re-grouping. (17) Needing a reset. (18) Slipping out the back. (19) Walking something back. (20) Taking it all back. (21) Putting on the hair shirt. (22) Wearing sackcloth and ashes. (23) Harboring heartache. (24) 'Coulda woulda shoulda.' (25) 'Oops!' (26) 'Yikes!' (27) 'Dang.'*

WILL ROGERS: *"Don't let yesterday take up too much of today."*

VINCE LOMBARDI: *"Nobody who ever gave his best regretted it."*

SIR PAUL MCCARTNEY, JOHN LENNON: *"Yesterday"* (Song)

WILLIAM GEORGE PLUNKETT: *"Three things that never come back: the spent arrow; the spoken word; the lost opportunity."*

LUCILLE BALL: *"I'd rather regret the things I've done than regret the things I haven't done."*

REAR ADM. GRACE HOPPER, PHD: *"If it's a good idea, go ahead and do it. It's much easier to apologize than it is to get permission."*

MACHIAVELLI: *"It is better to act and repent than not to act and regret."*

HENRY DAVID THOREAU: *"Never look back unless you are planning to go that way."*

MARK TWAIN: *"Never regret anything that made you smile."*

NATHAN HALE: *"I only regret that I have but one life to give for my country."*

JACKIE JOYNER-KERSEE: *"It's better to look ahead and prepare, than to look back and regret."*

CHARLES DICKENS: *"Reflect upon your present blessings—of which every man has many—not on your past misfortunes, of which all men have some."*

ARMAND HAMMER: *"Regrets and recriminations only hurt your soul."*

RUMI: *"Why do you stay in prison when the door is so wide open?"*

LOUISE HAY: *"How empty of me to be so full of you."*

JENNIFER ANISTON: *"There are no regrets in life, just lessons."*

CHARLOTTE BRONTE: *"Remorse is the poison of life."*

MYRON HENDRICKS: *"Regret and fear are twin thieves. They rob you of today."*

Similar: remorse, sorrow, contrition, penitence, disappointment
Opposite: enthusiasm, confidence, satisfaction, unrepentance

Rejection. Getting refused, turned down, or denied (or denying/turning something down). *Popular or Heart-Based Usage: (1) Getting the cold shoulder. (2) Not making the cut. (3) Getting snubbed. (4) Getting passed over. (5) Getting the brush-off. (6) Getting a 'Dear John.' (7) Getting the hook. (8) Getting tossed. (9) Getting dumped. (10) Getting benched. (11) Getting a red card. (12) Getting blackballed. (13) Getting shot down. (14) Getting slapped in the face. (15) Getting kicked in the teeth. (16) Getting a thumbs down. (17) Going back to the drawing board. (18) 'Sorry, Charlie!'* Alternately, as the initiator: *(19) Kicking someone out. (20) Giving someone the finger. (21) Flipping someone off. (22) Blowing someone off. (23) Turning your back on someone. (24) Putting the kibosh on something. (25) Nixing something. (26) 'No stinkin' badges!' (27) 'That won't fly here.' (28) 'No dice.' (29) 'Forget about it.' (30) 'Give me a break.' (31) 'Nice try.' (32) 'You lost your mind?' (33) 'No room at the inn!' (34) 'Go soak your head!' (35) 'Go fly a kite!' (36) 'No chance!' (37) 'Game's locked.' (38) 'Kiss off!' (39) 'Ain't gonna happen!' (40) 'No Way!' (41) 'Get lost!' (42) 'Start packing!' (43) 'Good riddance!' (44) 'See ya!'*

TAVIS SMILEY, PHD: *"Sometimes rejection in life is really redirection."*

F. SCOTT FITZGERALD: *"Work like hell! I had 122 rejection slips before I sold a story."*

SYLVESTER STALLONE: *"I take rejection as someone blowing a bugle in my ear to wake me up and get going, rather than retreat."*

RAY BRADBURY: *"You have to learn to take rejection not as an indication of personal failing but as a wrong address."*

GROUCHO MARX: *"I refuse to join any club that would have me as a member."*

ANTHONY ROBBINS: *"You must learn how to handle rejection. To succeed, you must learn how to cope with a little word 'no,' learn how to strip that rejection of all its power. The best salesmen are those who are rejected most. They are the ones who can take away any 'no' and use it as a prod to go onto the next 'yes.'"*

LINCOLN STOREY: *"Your challenge is to be so good they just can't say no. So either show up with something that sells itself, or make friends with criticism and rejection. Success is all about adjustment."*

RALPH WALDO EMERSON: *"Don't waste yourself in rejection, nor bark against the bad, but chant the beauty of the good."*

RICK PITINO: *"Failure is good. It's fertilizer. Everything I've learned about coaching, I've learned from making mistakes."*

HENRI NOUWEN, DRS: *"The greatest trap in our life is not success, popularity, or power, but self-rejection."*

ELBERT HUBBARD: *"The final proof of greatness lies in being able to endure criticism without resentment."*

ZIG ZIGLAR: *"A clear rejection is always better than a fake promise."*

Similar: elimination, exclusion, rebuff, dismissal, scorn, termination, abandonment
Opposite: approval, acceptance, ratification, endorsement

Release. [See also **Catharsis**] (1) Feeling relief from solving a persistent problem. (2) Achieving clarity and uplift after sorting out a confusion or misunderstanding. *Popular or Heart-Based Usage: (1) Having an 'Aha' moment. (2) Getting a load off your mind. (3) Having a personal epiphany. (4) Untangling an old mess. (5) Getting a needed emotional reset. (6) Venting or blowing off steam. (7) Getting something out in the open. (8) Getting to the heart of a problem. (9) Getting out of jail free. (10) Coming out. (11) Letting something go. (12) Unburdening yourself. (13) Cutting loose a ball and chain. (14) Setting yourself free. (15) 'Eureka!' (16) 'OMG! Yes, that's IT!'*

ADAGE: *"Release your fears and you will unlock your growth."*

JOSEPH CAMPBELL: *"We must let go of the life we have planned, so as to accept the one that is waiting for us."*

WILFERD PETERSON: *"Release your problem to God with a prayer that the answer will come in its own good time and place."*

WILLIAM BLAKE: *"Mercy, pity, and peace, Are the world's release."*

RAY STEVENSON: *"Humor is a very important thing. It is a natural predilection. It is an emotional release."*

DOROTHY PARKER: *"Art is a form of catharsis emotional release, purging, cleansing, purifying."*

TYLER PERRY: *"I didn't have a catharsis for my childhood pain, most of us don't, and until I learned how to forgive those people and let it go, I was unhappy."*

JACK KORNFIELD: *"To let go is to release the images and emotions, the grudges and fears, the clingings and disappointments of the past that bind our spirit."*

OBSERVATION: *"Sometimes you don't feel the weight of something you've been carrying until you feel its release."*

PROVERB: *"If you love something, let it go. If it comes back to you, it's yours forever. If not, it was never yours."*

CHUCK PALAHNIUK: *"Unless we have that moment of chaos, followed by the emotional release of realization, nothing will be remembered."*

JAMES R. DOTY, MD: *"You can't let yourself out of prison until you realize you are in prison."*

DAPHNE ROSE KINGMA: *"Holding on is believing that there's a past; letting go is knowing that there's a future."*

LAO TZU: *"When I let go of what I am, I become what I want to be."*

ADAGE: *"Breathe and release anything that does not serve you."*

PAULO COELHO: *"If it's still in your mind, it is still in your heart."*

ADAGE: *"Letting go is not the same as giving up."*

H. HILL MCALISTER: *"Forgiveness is release."*

Similar: catharsis, epiphany, surrender, aha, freedom
Opposite: muddlement, resistance, overwhelmed, overburdened, embroiled, trapped

Reliable. [See **Trustworthy**]

Religion. (1) The organization of beliefs, practices, and behaviors in the reverence of God or an exalted leader. (2) The outward demonstration of an inward adherence to a set of teachings or beliefs. *Popular or Heart-Based Usage: (1) Going to services at church, temple, synagogue, mosque, or a retreat. (2) Observing a belief system. (3) Getting on your knees. (4) Getting right with God. (5) Adhering to the Ten Commandments. (6) Following the Golden Rule. (7) Memorizing the Quran. (8) Reciting the Shema. (9) Being 'born again.' (10) Abiding by the Word. (11) 'Obey Allah and obey the Messenger.' (12) Living your mantra. (13) Following your faith. (14) Walking your walk.*

ABRAHAM LINCOLN: *"When I do good, I feel good. When I do bad, I feel bad. That is my religion."*

PIERRE TEILHARD DE CHARDIN: *"We are not human beings having a spiritual experience. We are spiritual beings having a human experience."*

RALPH WALDO EMERSON: *"Religion is to do right. It is to love, it is to serve, it is to think, it is to be humble."*

WOODROW WILSON, PHD, NOBEL, PRESIDENT: *"There is no higher religion than human service. To work for the common good is the greatest creed."*

GEORGE BERNARD SHAW: *"There is only one religion, though there are a hundred versions of it."*

H. L. MENCKEN: *"Morality is doing what is right, no matter what you are told. Religion is doing what you are told, no matter what is right."*

KARL MARX: *"Religion is the sign of the oppressed creature, the heart of a heartless world, and the soul of soulless conditions. It is the opiate of the people."*

BLAISE PASCAL: *"Men never do evil so completely and cheerfully as when they do it from religious conviction."*

ALBERT EINSTEIN, PHD, NOBEL: *"Blind belief in authority is the greatest enemy of truth."*

CARL SAGAN, PHD: *"Science is not only compatible with spirituality; it is a profound source of spirituality."*

SIR ISAAC NEWTON, FRS: *"Gravity explains the motions of the planets, but it cannot explain who sets the planets in motion."*

SENECA: *"Religion is regarded by the common people as true, by the wise as false, and by rulers as useful."*

MARK TWAIN: *"Religion consists in a set of things which the average man thinks he believes, and wishes he was certain."*

DALAI LAMA, NOBEL: *"This is my simple religion. There is no need for temples; no need for complicated philosophy. Our own brain, our own heart is our temple; the philosophy is kindness."*

Religion. *(continued)*

CHARLES DARWIN: *"The question of whether there exists a Creator and Ruler of the Universe has been answered in the affirmative by some of the highest intellects that have ever existed."*

ALLYN FONTAINE: *"There are usually two basic camps of human behavior—the forces of love, creation, and expansion on the one hand, and the allies of fear, chaos, and contraction on the other. Religions and interest groups, often through flawed organizations, generally align with one side or the other."*

THOMAS NAGEL, PHD: *"Perhaps the belief in God is the belief that the universe is intelligible, but not to us."*

THOMAS JEFFERSON: *"I contemplate with sovereign reverence that act of the whole American people which declared that their legislature should 'make no law respecting an establishment of religion, or prohibiting the free exercise thereof,' thus building a wall of separation between Church & State."*

JOHN F. KENNEDY: *"Tolerance implies no lack of commitment to one's own beliefs. Rather it condemns the oppression or persecution of others."*

ISAAC BESHEVIS SINGER: *"Doubt is part of all religion. All the religious thinkers were doubters."*

NAPOLEON BONAPARTE: *"Religion is excellent stuff for keeping common people quiet."*

SIR FRANCIS BACON: *"A little philosophy inclineth man's mind to atheism, but depth in philosophy bringeth men's minds about to religion."*

MAX PLANCK, PHD, NOBEL: *"Both religion and science require a belief in God. For believers, God is in the beginning, and for physicists He is at the end of all considerations... To the former He is the foundation, to the latter, the crown of the edifice of every generalized world view."*

NIKOLA TESLA: *"Religion is simply an ideal. It is an ideal force that tends to free the human being from material bonds."*

R. BUCKMINSTER FULLER: *"God, to me, it seems, is a verb, not a noun, proper or improper."*

BLAISE PASCAL: *"There is a God-shaped vacuum in the heart of every man."*

D. EARL JOHNSTON: *"Religion is a system of beliefs and practices to enhance our lives. Take a look at what you really believe in, because your beliefs build your opinions and emotions, and your emotions drive all scenes."*

Similar: ritual, belief, worship, theology, creed, observance, denomination, practice, doctrine, orthodoxy

Opposite: atheism, unbelief, irreverence, cynicism, agnosticism, apostasy, solo

Repetition. Engaging in a series of identical actions in order to improve retention, comprehension, or command of a topic. *Popular or Heart-Based Usage: (1) 'Ditto.' (2) Pursuing 'do-overs.' (3) 'Practice makes perfect.' (4) 'Drill it until you kill it.' (5) Learning by rote. (6) Installing 'muscle memory.' (7) Making it all second nature. (8) Rehearsing until it is down pat. (9) Looping. (10) Visualizing it. (11) Practicing until you can do it in your sleep. (12) Affirming conscious habits. (13) Utilizing the suggestive power of your subconscious. (14) 'X times over the subject means certainty.' (15) 'Do it again!'*

JOHN WOODEN: *"The eight laws of learning are explanation, demonstration, limitation, repetition, repetition, repetition, repetition, repetition."*

ANTHONY ROBBINS: *"Repetition is the mother of skill."*

MUHAMMAD ALI: *"It's the repetition of affirmations that leads to belief. And once that belief becomes a deep conviction, things begin to happen."*

WILL DURANT: *"We are what we repeatedly do. Excellence, then, is not an act, but a habit."*

LINCOLN STOREY: *"Repetition is a life weapon. Both for you and against you."*

ANTHONY BOURDAIN: *"We learn as professionals by repetition, by getting it wrong, getting yelled at and doing it again."*

REGGIE JACKSON: *"A baseball swing is a very finely tuned instrument. It is repetition, and more repetition, and then a little more after that."*

JERRY RICE, NFL G.O.A.T.: *"Like I said, repetition in practice and hard work."*

JOHN ELIOT: *"Thinking is a habit, and like any other habit, it can be changed; it just takes effort and repetition."*

JOSEPH JOUBERT: *"To teach is to learn twice."*

THEATER DRESSING ROOM: *"An unrehearsed actor is the understudy's best friend."*

JILL BOLTE TAYLOR, PHD: *"Most of the circuits in our brains run on automatic. The more you think a thought, the more energy goes into that circuit. Eventually it gets enough energy to run the thought automatically without us needing to put more energy into it."*

DR. JOE DISPENZA: *"Nerve cells that fire together, wire together."*

D. EARL JOHNSTON: *"Our subconscious is very deeply influenced by repetition."*

W. CLEMENT STONE: *"You affect your subconscious mind by verbal repetition."*

EARL NIGHTINGALE: *"Whatever we plant in our subconscious mind and nourish with repetition and emotion will one day become a reality."*

DANIEL KAHNEMAN, MD, NOBEL: *"A reliable way to make people believe in falsehoods is frequent repetition, because familiarity is not easily distinguished from truth. Authoritarian institutions and marketers have always known this."*

FRANKLIN D. ROOSEVELT: *"Repetition does not transform a lie into a truth."*

JOHNNY MCGREW: *"A cliché is what happens when you beat an idea to death by over-repetition."*

Repetition. *(continued)*

SUSANNE RICEE: *"So, to sum up: the conscious mind is what we are actively think- ing about, the subconscious is what we've learned and stored in our brain, and the unconscious is what we're not aware of at all."*

CARL JUNG, MD: *"Man's task is to become conscious of the contents that press upward from the unconscious."*

JANE FONDA: *"We cannot always control our thoughts, but we can control our words, and repetition impresses the subconscious, and then we are master of the situation."*

EDGAR CAYCE: *"What one thinks about continually, they become; what one cher- ishes in their heart and mind they make a part of the pulsation of their heart, through their own blood cells, and build in their own physical..."*

ERIC KANDEL, MD, NOBEL: *"Memory is everything. Without it we are nothing."*

JOYCE BROTHERS, PHD: *"Success is a state of mind. If you want success, start thinking of yourself as a success."*

DR. JOE DISPENZA: *"A habit is a redundant set of automatic unconscious thoughts, behaviors, and emotions that are acquired through frequent repetition."*

JOHN ELIOT: *"Thinking is a habit, and like any other habit, it can be changed; it just takes effort and repetition."*

EDWARD DE BONO, MD, PHD: *"Intelligence is something we are born with. Thinking is a skill that must be learned."*

LINCOLN STOREY: *"Repetition enhances retention."*

PERIANDER: *"Practice is everything."*

Similar: practice, rehearsal, drill, duplication, replication, rote, habit-forming
Opposite: one-off, solo, original, first-time, debut, opening

Resentment. Harboring hostility (expressed or unexpressed) toward another for per-ceived bad behavior or unfair treatment. *Popular or Heart-Based Usage: (1) Feeling like you were done wrong. (2) Feeling held back. (3) Getting the shaft. (4) Gnashing your teeth. (5) Sucking hind tit. (6) Biting your lip. (7) Having a chip on your shoulder. (8) Hating your path. (9) Feeling abused. (10) Having major issues. (11) Feeling chained down. (12) Being disrespected. (13) Holding a grudge. (14) Wishing ill on people. (15) Being bitter. (16) Wanting payback. (17) 'I've had it.' (18) 'Fed up to here!' (19) 'Enough!'*

LADY NANCY ASTOR, CH: *"Sir, if you were my husband, I'd poison your tea."*
SIR WINSTON CHURCHILL: *"Madame, if you were my wife, I'd drink it!"*

SAYING: *"I don't get mad, I get even. Never forgive, never forget."*
ANN LANDERS: *"Hanging onto resentment is letting someone you despise live rent-free in your head."*
CATHERINE PONDER: *"When you hold resentment toward another, you are bound to that person or condition by an emotional link that is stronger than steel. Forgiveness is the only way to dissolve that link and get free."*
PAUL LEVY: *"Unexpressed creativity ... is poison to the human psyche."*
REV. NEAL S. MCGOWAN: *"Next to sexual sins, resentment is the most pleasurable of all vices. Humility and forgiveness trump resentment."*
LAWRENCE G. LOVASIK: *"Strength of character means the ability to overcome resentment against others, to hide hurt feelings, and to forgive quickly."*
ECKHART TOLLE: *"The ego's unconscious core feeling of 'not enough' causes it to react to someone else's success as if that success has been taken away from 'me.' But in order to attract success, you need to welcome it wherever you see it."*
LINCOLN STOREY: *"When a person insults you, slights you, leaves you out, or offends you, don't get trapped in it. Just ask yourself out loud: 'What kind of person does that?' Then take your answer and move ahead with your life."*
ARISTOTLE: *"The high-minded man does not bear grudges, for it is not the mark of a great soul to remember injuries, but to forget them."*
APHORISM: *"A strong person does not seek revenge. They move on and let karma do the dirty work."*
ABRAHAM LINCOLN: *"Never signed and never delivered."* (Lincoln's practice of handling resentment by writing a scathing 'venting' letter to his adversary, but never sending it.)
ELBERT HUBBARD: *"The final proof of greatness lies in being able to endure criti-cism without resentment."*
GREG GUTFELD: *"Behind every resentment is your role in it."*
PROVERB: *"If you don't like your boss, find a new one."*

Similar: hostility, bitterness, antagonism, animosity, indignation, seething
Opposite: tolerance, calm, acceptance, delight, sympathy, affection, support

Resistance. Maintaining a stance of noncooperation, defensiveness, and/or opposition about the advancement of someone or something. *Popular or Heart-Based Usage: (1) Not budging. (2) Pushing back. (3) Digging in. (4) Fending things off. (5) Hemming and hawing about something. (6) Slow-walking your response. (7) Holding the line. (8) Blowing the whistle. (9) Using counter-measures. (10) Building roadblocks. (11) Putting up walls. (12) Being a die-hard. (13) Making a pain in the ass of yourself. (14) Taking your ball and going home. (15) 'Talk to the hand.' (16) 'Not having it.' (17) 'No girls (boys) in the fort!' (18) 'This game is locked.' (19) 'NFW.' [No Freaking Way.] (20) 'Not on my watch.' (21) 'Not in our house.' (22) 'Noop!' (23) 'That will not be happening here.' (24) 'No can do.'*

> VICTOR HUGO: *"Armies can be resisted, but not an idea whose time has come."*
> LOUISE HAY: *"Resistance is the first step to change."*
> ELBERT HUBBARD: *"The path of least resistance is what makes rivers run crooked."*
> CONSTANCE FRIDAY: *"Resistance is a sign that shows you're going the right way."*
> MALCOLM X: *"If someone puts their hands on you make sure they never put their hands on anybody else again."*
> SUN TZU: *"To fight and conquer in all our battles is not supreme excellence; supreme excellence consists in breaking the enemy's resistance without fighting."*
> ECKHART TOLLE: *"It may look as if the situation is creating the suffering, but ultimately this is not so—your resistance is."*
> MICHAEL ALAN SINGER: *"If you are resisting something, you are feeding it. Any energy you fight, you are feeding. If you are pushing something away, you are inviting it to stay."*
> ECKHART TOLLE: *"Whatever you accept completely, you go beyond. If you fight it, you're stuck with it."*
> PAM GREGORY: *"The more you resist a situation, the stronger it becomes."*
> CARL JUNG, MD: *"What you resist not only persists, but will grow in size."*
> AARON DOUGHTY: *"If you fight it, you are feeding it."*
> APHORISM: *"That which you resist, you get."*

Similar: unwillingness, opposition, noncompliance, uncooperativeness, denial
Opposite: faithfulness, loyalty, support, enthusiasm, acceptance

Resonance. Having, matching, or seeking an appealing vibration, frequency, or form. *Popular or Heart-Based Usage: (1) Tuning in. (2) Being on the same wavelength. (3) Echoing something deep within. (4) 'Seems familiar.' (5) 'That is so ME!' (6) When something is ringing true.*

JOSE ARGUELLES, PHD: *"The essence of information…is not its content but its resonance."*

JOSEPH CAMPBELL: *"I think what we're seeking is an experience of being alive, so that our life experiences on the purely physical place will have resonance within out innermost being and reality, so that we actually feel the rapture of being alive."*

D. EARL JOHNSTON: *"We resonate with things already in our heart of hearts."*

BOB LEFSETZ, JD: *"Artists are tuning forks. Their goal is to create resonance in the audience."*

KARLHEINZ STOCKHAUSEN: *"When a certain piece of music penetrates a person, a resonance is set in motion and an inner voice says: 'I like this resonance. It elevates me. It develops hitherto unknown possibilities in me. I don't recognize myself. This is very interesting.'"*

ANDY GARCIA: *"I think if the movie has resonance and stimulates the viewer to talk about it, you can have as large an audience as you want."*

NANCY DUARTE: *"The only way to resonate at a level that persuades is to know who you are addressing…It's easy to persuade a friend, you need to think about your audience until you know them as a friend."*

RUSS KYLE: *"Our thoughts, imbued with intention and emotion, act as magnets, drawing us to people, situations, and experiences that resonate with our inner state."*

NIKOLA TESLA: *"If you want to find the secrets of the universe, think in terms of energy, frequency, and vibration."*

CARL SAGAN, PHD: *"I believe that in every person is a kind of circuit which resonates to intellectual discovery—and the idea is to make that resonance work."*

BETTY GRECO SHER: *"You know you are best friends when you can be totally happy doing nothing together."*

CAROL GILLIGAN, PHD: *"Both love and democracy depend on voice—having a voice and also the resonance that makes it possible to speak and be heard."*

JESSE JACKSON: *"If there are occasions when my grape turned into a raisin and my joy bell lost its resonance, please forgive me. Charge it to my head and not to my heart."*

ANNE RICE: *"It's an awful truth that suffering can deepen us, give a greater luster to our colors, a richer resonance to our words."*

Similar: matching, echoing, reverberating, duplicating, mirroring, identifying
Opposite: antiresonance, repulsion, gapping, disjunction, resistance

Respect. Acknowledging and supporting the existence, rights, and viewpoints of others and yourself. *Popular or Heart-Based Usage: (1) Giving someone their due. (2) Looking someone in the eye. (3) Giving someone their space. (4) Acknowledging with a firm handshake or embrace. (5) Giving it up for someone. (6) Giving someone a nod or applause. (7) Giving props to someone. (8) Giving a shout-out. (9) Paying respects. (10) Observing the protocols. (11) Bowing in acknowledgment. (12) Approaching someone with hat in hand. (13) Waiting your turn. (14) Going on bended knee. (15) Squaring your shoulders. (16) Kissing someone's ring. (17) Being a lady or gentleman. (18) Minding your manners. (19) Honoring your parents. (20) Visiting someone's grave. (21) Giving the Devil his due. (22) Treating someone as you would want to be treated. (23) 'You Da Man.' (24) 'Namaste.' (25) 'Saludos.' (26) Observing the Golden Rule.*

ROSA PARKS: *"I would like to be known as a person who is concerned about freedom and justice and equality and prosperity for all people."*

JACKIE ROBINSON: *"I am not concerned with your liking or disliking me…All I ask is that you respect me as a human being."*

KAREN SALMANSOHN: *"Once you know your worth, you will stop offering discounts."*

DON BLACK & MARK LONDON: *"To Sir, with Love"* (Song)

PHILIP JAMES BAILEY: *"Respect is what we owe."*

JANE ADDAMS: *"Civilization is a method of living, an attitude of equal respect for all men."*

MALCOLM X: *"I have more respect for a man who lets me know where he stands, even if he's wrong, than the one who comes up like an angel and is nothing but a devil."*

LAO TZU: *"When you are content to be simply yourself, and don't compare or compete, everybody will respect you."*

CLINT EASTWOOD: *"Respect your efforts, respect yourself. Self-respect leads to self-discipline. When you have both under your belt, that's real power."*

D. EARL JOHNSTON: *"Showing respect gets you more than halfway to making a new friend."*

APHORISM: *"A good first impression builds respect, but the last impression is the lasting impression."*

MATTHEW 15:27: *"And she said, 'Truth, Lord: yet the dogs eat of the crumbs which fall from their master's table.'"*

MIGUEL DE CERVANTES: *"Give the devil his due."*

APHORISM: *"Respect existence or expect resistance."*

Similar: appreciation, dignity, esteem, reverence, approval
Opposite: disdain, disregard, criticism, irreverence

Responsible. (1) Being in charge. (2) Being accountable or answerable for appropriate behavior, guidelines, or results. *Popular or Heart-Based Usage: (1) Leading the charge. (2) Setting the tone (direction). (3) Stepping up. (4) Wearing the mantle. (5) Taking the helm. (6) 'Owning' the situation. (7) Accepting (or suffering) the consequences. (8) Shouldering the load (or burden). (9) Facing the music. (10) Paying the piper. (11) Having the finger pointed at you. (12) Taking the blame. (13) Copping to something. (14) Taking the rap. (15) Being the grown-up (in the room). (16) Overriding the predicament. (17) Taking care of business. (18) 'The buck stops here.' (19) 'I've got this.'*

JOHN C. MAXWELL: *"The greatest day in your life and mine is when we take total responsibility for our attitudes. That is the day we truly grow up."*

GEN. BRUCE CLARKE: *"When things go wrong in your command, start searching in increasingly large circles around your own desk."*

GEORGE ELIOT: *"Consequences are unpitying."*

ECKHART TOLLE: *"If you find your here and now intolerable and it makes you unhappy, you have three options: remove yourself from the situation, change it, or accept it totally."*

JILL BOLTE TAYLOR, PHD: *"Take responsibility for the energy you bring."*

CARL ROGERS, PHD: *"The only person who cannot be helped is that person who blames others."*

ELDRIDGE CLEAVER: *"You are either part of the solution or you're part of the problem."*

BYRON DORGAN: *"You can delegate authority but you can't delegate responsibility."*

KAHLIL GIBRAN: *"Friendship is always a sweet responsibility, never an opportunity."*

JOAN DIDION, PULITZER: *"The willingness to accept responsibility for one's own life is the source from which self-respect springs."*

D. EARL JOHNSTON: *"It is a special moment, a magical moment, when we know that a child trusts us. It's a sacred moment."*

WINNIE MADIKIZELA-MANDELA: *"We have a shared destiny, a shared responsibility to save the world from those who attempt to destroy it."*

ECKHART TOLLE: *"Many people don't realize until they are on their deathbed and everything external falls away that no thing ever had anything to do with who they are. In either case, you can only go beyond it by taking responsibility for your inner state now."*

TODD STOCKER: *"You are responsible for your actions, not their responses."*

MAHARISHI MAHESH YOGI: *"Responsibility can never be given. It can only be taken."*

Similar: authority, burden, obligation, supervision, answerability, ownership
Opposite: immunity, self-interest, evasion, exemption, denial

Revenge. (1) Inflicting reciprocal or measured harm on another person in response to a prior aggression. (2) Retaliating. *Popular or Heart-Based Usage: (1) An eye for an eye. (2) Getting even. (3) Bringing an ass-kicking. (4) Bringing a big can of whoop-ass. (5) Settling an old score. (6) Returning the favor. (7) Making someone hurt bad. (8) Getting payback. (9) Doing wet work. (10) 'Two can play.' (11) 'Now it's my turn.' (12) 'Take that!'*

DANIEL CRAIG: *"Revenge doesn't stop."*

ADAGE: *"Revenge is a dish best served cold."*

PROVERB: *"What goes around, comes around."*

GAMAL ADBEL NASSER: *"What was taken by force, can only be restored by force."*

ARNAUD AMALRIC: *"Kill them all, for God knows which are his own."*

WILLIAM SHAKESPEARE: *"The time is out of joint: O cursed spite, That ever I was born to set it right."*

MACHIAVELLI: *"If you need to injure someone, do it in such a way that you do not have to fear their vengeance."*

VICTORIA AVEYARD: *"Kneel or Bleed."*

PROVERB: *"Taking an eye for an eye leaves everyone blind."*

RAHEEL FAROOQ: *"Revenge is possible only if you spare the enemy."*

PROVERB: *"A man who desires revenge should dig two graves."*

SPANISH PROVERB: *"No revenge is more honorable than the one not taken."*

SIR FRANCIS BACON: *"A man that studieth revenge keeps his own wounds green."*

ALBERT EINSTEIN, PHD, NOBEL: *"Weak people revenge, strong people forgive, intelligent people ignore."*

APHORISM: *"A strong person does not seek revenge. They move on and let karma do the dirty work."*

FRANK SINATRA: *"The best revenge is massive success."*

ROBERT LOUIS STEVENSON: *"Sooner or later, everyone sits down to a banquet of consequences."*

MARIANNE WILLIAMSON: *"May we not succumb to thoughts of violence and revenge today. But rather to thoughts of mercy and compassion. We are to love our enemies that they might be returned to their right minds."*

LEVITICUS 19:18: *"Thou shalt not avenge, nor bear any grudge against the children of thy people."*

IRISH PROVERB: *"May God turn the hearts of those that do not love us;*
    And if He will not turn their hearts;
    May He at least turn their ankles;
    So we may know them by their limp."

Similar: payback, retaliation, retribution, spite, gotcha
Opposite: forgiveness, clemency, grace, mercy, pardon, absolution

Risk. [See also **Vulnerability**] Undertaking a course of action which has exposure to danger or loss. *Popular or Heart-Based Usage: (1) Putting yourself out there. (2) Going out on a limb. (3) Having downside exposure. (4) Having skin in the game. (5) Having a dog in the fight. (6) Having your fat in the fryer. (7) Leading with your chin. (8) Taking the bull by the horns. (9) Winging it. (10) Heading off into the wild blue yonder. (11) Taking your life into your own hands. (12) Rolling the dice. (13) Betting on yourself. (14) Throwing your hat into the ring. (15) Being an entrepreneur. (16) Leaping without a net. (17) Stepping across the line. (18) Crossing the Rubicon. (19) 'Things could go south.' (20) 'No guarantees in life.' (21) 'You only live once.' (22) 'What the hell.' (23) 'It's now or never.' (24) 'Come what may.' (25) 'Wish me well.' (26) 'Here goes.'*

MARY SCHMICH, PULITZER: *"Do one thing every day that scares you."*

WILL ROGERS: *"Why not go out on a limb? That's where the fruit is."*

GEN. GEORGE S. PATTON, JR.: *"Take calculated risks. That is quite different from being rash."*

PETER F. DRUCKER: *"There is the risk you cannot afford to take, and there is the risk you cannot afford to take."*

JIM ROHN: *"If you are not willing to risk the unusual, you will have to settle for the ordinary."*

PABLO PICASSO: *"I am always doing that which I cannot do, in order that I may learn how to do it."*

E. E. CUMMINGS: *"Once we believe in ourselves, we can risk curiosity, wonder, spontaneous delight, or any experience that reveals the human spirit."*

NICK VUJICIC: *"Risk, then, is not just part of life. It is life. The place between your comfort zone and your dream is where life takes place. It's the high-anxiety zone, but it's also where you discover who you are."*

M. SCOTT PECK: *"There can be no vulnerability without risk; there can be no community without vulnerability."*

LEO BUSCAGLIA, PHD: *"The person who risks nothing, does nothing, has nothing, is nothing, and becomes nothing. He may avoid suffering and sorrow, but he simply cannot learn, feel, change, grow or love."*

JOYCE BROTHERS, PHD: *"Accept that all of us can be hurt, that all of us can and will surely at times fail. Other vulnerabilities like being embarrassed or risking love, can be terrifying, too. I think we should follow a simple rule: if we can take the worst, take the risk."*

JOE ROGAN: *"The universe rewards calculated risk and passion."*

ROBERT REDFORD: *"Not taking a risk is a risk. That's how I see it."*

JOSEPH JOUBERT: *"Chance generally favors the prudent."*

Similar: danger, uncertainty, gamble, chance, venture, probability, speculation
Opposite: certainty, stability, guarantee, security

Sabotage. (1) Orchestrating hidden destruction to gain surprise military, business, or personal/political advantage. (2) Setting up someone for failure through concealed action or inaction. *Popular or Heart-Based Usage: (1) Being underhanded with someone. (2) Being a false friend. (3) Setting someone up. (4) Messing someone up. (5) Stacking the deck. (6) Screwing someone over. (7) Doing someone in. (8) Booby-trapping something. (9) Doctoring a drink. (10) Creating a trickeration. (11) Back-stabbing someone. (12) Giving someone the shaft. (13) Putting in the fix. (14) Moving the goalposts. (15) Switching the rules. (16) Planting full-on misinformation. (17) Moving someone's cheese. (18) Withholding key facts. (19) Doing someone dirty. (20) Deep-sixing a deal. (21) Finishing someone off.*

NELSON MANDELA, NOBEL: *"I do not deny that I planned sabotage. I did not plan it in a spirit of recklessness nor because I have any love of violence. I planned it as a result of a calm and sober assessment of the political situation that had arisen after many years of tyranny, exploitation, and oppression of my people."*

MACHIAVELLI: *"Never do an enemy a small injury."*

KATHERINE GRAHAM: *"If we had failed to pursue the facts as far as they led, we would have denied the public knowledge of an unprecedented scheme of political surveillance and sabotage."*

MICHAEL BUBLE: *"I have a tendency to sabotage relationships; I have a tendency to sabotage everything. Fear of success, fear of failure, fear of being afraid. Useless, good-for-nothing thoughts."*

BRIE LARSON: *"Girls in this industry sabotage each other."*

JOHNNY MCGREW: *"Some people out there just aren't satisfied until they hold somebody else back or sabotage their happiness."*

PETER MCWILLIAMS: *"If you are not playing a big enough game, you'll screw up the game you're playing just to give yourself something to do."*

JOHN C. MAXWELL: *"Leaders who are kind of insecure or egocentric, they basically sabotage themselves."*

APHORISM: *"What you withhold from yourself, you withhold from others."*

Similar: subversion, subterfuge, undermining, underhandedness, treachery, treason
Opposite: fidelity, loyalty, devotion, faithfulness, support, benevolence

Sacrifice. (1) Enduring a hardship to facilitate a broader benefit for yourself or others. (2) Offering up something of great value in exchange for advantage, favor, or blessing. *Popular or Heart-Based Usage: (1) 'Short-term pain for long-term gain.' (2) Taking one for the team. (3) Drawing the short straw. (4) Falling on your sword. (5) Taking the fall for something/someone. (6) Giving up an organ transplant. (7) Biting the bullet. (8) Being the guinea pig. (9) Having a tough pill to swallow. (10) Volunteering for a suicide mission. (11) Making a deal with the Devil. (12) Giving blood, sweat, and tears for a cause. (13) Making really hard choices. (14) Being a bodhisattva. (15) Putting others first. (16) 'Grin and bear it.' (17) Biting the bullet. (18) Being willing to take the L.*

JOEL OSTEEN: *"What kind of blessings will your children and grandchildren have because you did the right thing, even when it was hard?"*

JUSTICE THURGOOD MARSHALL: *"I never worked hard until I got to Howard Law School and met Charlie Houston ... I saw this man's dedication, his vision, his willingness to sacrifice, and I told myself, 'You either shape up, or ship out.' When you are being challenged by a great human being, you know you can't ship out."*

SADHU VASWANI: *"True love is selfless. It is prepared to sacrifice."*

JOSEPH CAMPBELL: *"When you make the sacrifice in marriage, you are not sacrificing to each other but to unity in the relationship."*

JIM WEATHERLY: *"Midnight Train to Georgia"* (Song)

DAVID M. HENDRICKS: *"When you get to the end of a tight game, and the player opposite you is taking plays off because he just can't go anymore, you'll know it's all about your conditioning and sacrifice in practice."*

LOUIS ARMSTRONG: *"I was determined to play my horn against all odds, and I had to sacrifice a whole lot of pleasure to do so."*

WILLIAM FAULKNER: *"In writing, you must kill all your darlings."*

PELE: *"Success is no accident. It is hard work, perseverance, learning, studying, sacrifice and most of all, love of what you are doing or learning to do."*

CHESTY PULLER, UNITED STATES MARINE: *"Pain is weakness leaving the body."*

MAHATMA GANDHI: *"A man who was completely innocent, offered himself as a sacrifice for the good of others, including his enemies, and became the ransom for the world. It was the perfect act."*

AUNG SAN SUU KYI, NOBEL: *"People ask me about what sacrifices I've made. I always answer: I've made no sacrifices, I've made choices."*

WANGECHI MUTU: *"Motherhood is the ultimate call to sacrifice."*

Similar: offering, atonement, penance, repentance, forbearance, abstinence, self-denial
Opposite: greed, selfishness, narcissism, self-centeredness, addiction

Sadness. Experiencing exhaustion, disappointment, failure, or the absence of something cherished. *Popular or Heart-Based Usage: (1) Being down in the dumps. (2) Feeling blue/feeling spent. (3) Adjusting to a loss. (4) Feeling real heartache. (5) Being torn up. (6) Being in a funk. (7) Feeling washed out. (8) Having a hang-dog look. (9) Being down in the mouth. (10) Having a long face. (11) Feeling dejected. (12) Feeling achy breaky. (13) Feeling empty. (14) Just going through the motions of life. (15) Feeling plain butthurt.*

FRANK OCEAN: *"When you are happy you enjoy the music, but when you're sad you understand the lyrics."*

PAULO COELHO: *"Tears are words that need to be written."*

PAUL WILLIAMS AND ROGER NICHOLS: *"Rainy Days and Mondays"* (Song)

OSCAR WILDE: *"Where there is sorrow there is holy ground."*

HENRY WADSWORTH LONGFELLOW: *"Every man has his secret sorrows which the world knows not; and often times we call a man cold when he is only sad."*

FYODOR DOSTOEVSKY: *"Pain and suffering are always inevitable for a large intelligence and a deep heart. The really great men must, I think, have great sadness on earth."*

GABRIEL GARCIA MARQUEZ: *"Don't cry because it ended, smile because it happened."*

EMILE DURKHEIM: *"Sadness is a product of our own thought. We create it out of whole cloth."*

BILL BLASS: *"Red is the ultimate cure for sadness."*

ABRAHAM LINCOLN: *"To ease another's heartache is to forget one's own."*

AUNG SAN SUU KYI, NOBEL: *"When you feel helpless, help someone."*

MARK TWAIN: *"The source of all humor is not laughter, but sorrow."*

ANDRE GIDE: *"Sadness is almost never anything but a form of fatigue."*

PROVERB: *"Sometimes you just need a good cry."*

Similar: melancholy, depression, anguish, distress, regret, dysphoria, dejection
Opposite: cheer, delight, happiness, joy, exultation

Sandbagging. Deliberately managing the expectations and responses of others by means of calculated misstatement or underperformance. *Popular or Heart-Based Usage: (1) Putting someone on. (2) Getting someone to take the bait. (3) Trolling someone. (4) Saying it with a straight face. (5) Saying it tongue in cheek. (6) Pulling the wool over someone's eyes. (7) Giving someone a big head fake. (8) Gaslighting someone. (9) Manipulating someone. (10) Pushing misinformation. (11) Gaming the system. (12) Moving the goalposts. (13) Snookering someone. (14) Moving someone's cheese. (15) Getting someone to fall for a ruse. (16) Hoodwinking someone. (17) Deliberately getting it twisted for maximum effect.*

IRVING BERLIN: *"A Man Chases a Girl (Until She Catches Him)"* (Song)

JIM E. MORA: *"Playoffs? Don't talk about—playoffs? You kidding me? Playoffs? I just hope we can win a game!"*

DAVID S. WARD: *"The Sting"* (Film)

CHRIS TERRIO, ANTONIO J. MENDEZ, JOSHUAH BEARMAN: *"Argo"* (Film)

LARRY BEINHART, HILARY HENKIN, DAVID MAMET: *"Wag the Dog"* (Film)

JAMES M. CAIN, BILLY WILDER, RAYMOND CHANDLER: *"Double Indemnity"* (Film)

WARNING SIGN: *"Do not feed the trolls."*

CLEVER RABBIT: *"Oh, no! Please, please don't throw me in that thicket!"*

ROY COHN: *"I bring out the worst in my enemies and that's how I get them to defeat themselves."*

SAUL ALINSKY: *"The job of the organizer is to maneuver and bait the establishment so that it will publicly attack him as a 'dangerous enemy.'"*

D. EARL JOHNSTON: *"A con artist plays to our greatest vulnerabilities—probing for those blind spots of weakness where we can be ready, willing, and able to fall for some magical outcome."*

MARISHA PESSL: *"For every man there exists bait he cannot resist swallowing."*

MARK TWAIN/'THE ADVENTURES OF TOM SAWYER': *"Yes, she's awful particular about this fence; it's got to be done very careful; I reckon there ain't one boy in a thousand, maybe two thousand, that can do it the way it's got to be done."*

HELEN ROWLAND: *"A wise woman puts a grain of sugar into everything she says to a man, and takes a grain of salt with everything he says to her."*

PAMELA ANDERSON: *"It's great to be a blonde. With low expectations it's very easy to surprise people."*

MARILYN MONROE: *"It takes a smart brunette to play a dumb blonde."*

Similar: deceiving, enticing, tricking, downplaying, understating, fibbing, baiting
Opposite: bragging, boasting, blustering, overstating, embellishing

Sarcasm. (1) Saying the opposite of what you mean, for insulting or humorous effect. (2) Employing negative or ironic humor, often to undercut or to deride someone. *Popular or Heart-Based Usage: (1) Being snarky. (2) Being a wag. (3) Being a crank. (4) Cutting something (or someone) down. (5) Mocking someone. (6) Snapping back. (7) Being a wise guy. (8) Being a smart aleck/smartass. (9) Trolling and smirking. (10) Making the point to love someone 'to pieces.' (11) 'Go ahead. Make my day.' (12) 'Nice try, pal.'*

EXAMPLE: *"No coffee, no talkee."*
EXAMPLE: *"I've got a good heart. But this mouth…"*
EXAMPLE: *"Sorry for the mean, awful, accurate things I say."*
EXAMPLE: *"Sarcasm. Making the world a better place, one insult at a time."*
EXAMPLE: *"Living the Dream? Totally. Right here in my parents' basement."*
EXAMPLE: *"Want an Inspirational Quote of the Day? Don't be an ass."*
EXAMPLE: *"Just because I don't care doesn't mean I don't understand."*
EXAMPLE: *"Falling on your face. Simply brilliant."*
EXAMPLE: *"What was your first clue, Sherlock."*

PROVERB: *"Nobody likes a smartass."*
KRISTEN SCHAAL: *"Sarcasm doesn't read sarcastic in print."*
OXFORD ONLINE ENGLISH: *"Sarcasm is taken from the context."*
JOHNNY MCGREW: *"Sarcasm usually gets you two things—an initial laugh, and then fewer friends. Using it means you want to make something sting."*
PENNY MARSHALL: *"You had to learn at a certain age what sarcasm is, you know?"*
DANA PERINO: *"Sarcasm is like cheap wine—it leaves a terrible aftertaste."*
D. EARL JOHNSTON: *"Parents of teenagers should be proficient in at least two languages—English and Sarcasm. Newcomers have also been known to dabble in Profanity during especially challenging moments."*
THOMAS CARLYLE: *"Sarcasm I now see to be, in general, the language of the devil; for which reason I have long since as good as renounced it."*
COMEDY CLUB DRESSING ROOM: *"Sarcasm can dig and satire can bite, but self-deprecation will make it go right."*
LINCOLN STOREY: *"Sarcasm is like lust or greed—where only one person really expects to enjoy it."*
OSCAR WILDE: *"Sarcasm is the lowest form of wit but the highest form of intelligence."*
FRANCESCA GINO, PHD: *"Sarcasm expresses the poisonous sting of contempt, hurting others and harming relationships. As a form of communication, sarcasm takes on the debt of conflict."*
FORD FRICK: *"Avoid sarcasm. Don't insist on the last word."*

Similar: cynicism, contempt, satire, ridicule, derision, insult, scorn, mockery, disdain
Opposite: acclaim, praise, sincerity, candor, earnestness, support

Satisfaction. Feeling contented with your actions, possessions, or accomplishments. *Popular and Heart-Based Usage: (1) Being happy with your lot in life. (2) Getting what you called for. (3) Feeling quietly content. (4) 'All good.' (5) 'Copacetic.' (6) 'No worries.' (7) 'Done and dusted.' (8) 'No brag, just fact.' (9) 'How do you like them apples?'*

FRANCOIS RABELAIS: *"A bellyful is a bellyful."*

HENRY DAVID THOREAU: *"This life is not for complaint, but for satisfaction."*

LINUS PAULING, MD (2X NOBEL): *"Satisfaction of one's curiosity is one of the greatest sources of happiness in life."*

EPICTETUS: *"He is a wise man who does not grieve for the things which he has not, but rejoices for those which he has."*

WENTWORTH MILLER: *"You have to love what you do, and you have to need it like you need air. And there's nothing else that would give me the same degree of satisfaction as acting, which is why I can't walk away from it."*

ARTHUR SCHOPENHAUER: *"Satisfaction consists in freedom from pain, which is the positive element of life."*

GERARD WAY: *"One day your life will flash before your eyes. Make sure it's worth watching."*

GEORGE HORACE LATIMER: *"You've got to get up every morning with determination if you're going to go to bed with satisfaction."*

NORMAN VINCENT PEALE: *"The really happy people are those who have broken the chains of procrastination, those who find satisfaction in doing the job at hand. They're full of eagerness, zest, productivity."*

ANTHONY ROBBINS: *"Change happens when the pain of staying the same is greater than the pain of change."*

JOHN F. KENNEDY: *"We cannot be satisfied with things as they are. We cannot be satisfied to drift, to rest on our oars, to glide over a sea whose depths are shaken by subterranean upheavals."*

MADONNA: *"A lot of people are afraid to say what they want. That's why they don't get what they want."*

MAHATMA GANDHI: *"Earth provides enough to satisfy ever man's needs, but not every man's greed."*

JERRY LEWIS: *"I am probably the most selfish man you will ever meet in your life. No one gets the satisfaction or the joy that I get out of seeing kids realize there is hope."*

HOLLY BLACK: *"If curiosity killed the cat, it was satisfaction that brought it back."*

SALVADOR DALÍ: *"There are some days when I think I'm going to die from an overdose of satisfaction."*

BEN FRANKLIN: *"Well done is better than well said."*

Similar: contentment, pleasure, enjoyment, gratified
Opposite: displeasure, discontent, irritation, anxiety, unfulfilled

Self-Control. [See also **Control**] (1) Having command over your own impulses, actions, and emotions. (2) Having willpower. *Popular or Heart-Based Usage: (1) Behaving yourself. (2) Minding your manners/Minding your p's and q's. (3) Playing by the rules. (4) Being on top of your game. (5) Keeping between the lines. (6) Not taking the bait. (7) Earning/renewing your hall pass. (8) Controlling your demons. (9) Avoiding 'Double Secret Probation.' (10) Keeping it very 'P.C.' (11) 'Just say no!' (12) 'The lines are our friends.' (13) Conforming with norms.* Alternately, when losing self-control: *(14) Backsliding. (15) Splurging. (16) Bingeing. (17) Getting over-served. (18) Letting yourself go. (19) 'The Devil made me do it!' (20) Allowing yourself to get 'sucked in.'*

OSCAR WILDE: *"The only thing I cannot resist is temptation."*

KATHARINE HEPBURN: *"If you obey all the rules, you miss all the fun."*

JANE AUSTEN: *"I will be calm. I will be mistress of myself."*

ARISTOTLE: *"What lies in our power to do, it lies in our power not to do."*

BENJAMIN FRANKLIN: *"If passion drives you, let reason hold the reins."*

CRISS JAMI: *"Showing a lack of self-control is in the same vein granting authority to others: 'Perhaps I need someone else to control me.'"*

ANTHONY ROBBINS: *"Take control of your consistent emotions and begin to consciously and deliberately reshape your daily experience of life."*

MARK TWAIN: *"A habit cannot be tossed out the window; it must be coaxed down the stairs a step at a time."*

KELLY MCGONIGAL, PHD: *"There is a secret for greater self-control, the science points to one thing: The power of paying attention."*

WILLIAM SHAKESPEARE: *"Refrain to-night; And that shall lend a kind of easiness to the next abstinence, the next more easy."*

DR. JOE DISPENZA: *"If you want a new outcome, you will have to break the habit of being yourself, and reinvent a new self."*

D. EARL JOHNSTON: *"We become known both for what we repeatedly do, as well as for what we repeatedly do not do."*

FYODOR DOSTOEVSKY: *"If there is no God, everything is permitted."*

CONFUCIUS: *"He who conquers himself is the mightiest warrior."*

Similar: will-power, self-mastery, self-denial, self-discipline, restraint, command
Opposite: self-gratification, self-indulgence, capitulation, backsliding, bingeing

Selfish. [See also **Envy, Greed, Insecurity,** and **Jealousy**] (1) Showing a lack of concern or consideration for others. (2) Doing things that unduly benefit yourself over others. *Popular or Heart-Based Usage: (1) Being really pushy. (2) Always looking out for Number One. (3) Being a spoiled brat. (4) Being a jerk. (5) Being a mooch. (6) 'Get outta my way!' (7) 'My way or the highway!' (8) 'Me first!' (9) Getting stuck on yourself.*

DOMINIC: *"We must sow the seed, not hoard it."*

MOTHER TERESA, NOBEL: *"If you are kind, people may accuse you of selfish ulterior motives; be kind anyway."*

GEORGE ELIOT: *"What do we live for, if not to make life less difficult for others?"*

WILL ROGERS: *"Why there ain't nothing but one word wrong with everyone of us, and that's selfishness."*

GORDON B. HINCKLEY: *"We are all prone to be a little selfish, a little lazy."*

LORD BYRON: *"We are all selfish and I no more trust myself than others with a good motive."*

HERBERT SPENCER: *"What a cage is to a wild beast, the law is to a selfish man."*

ANDREW JACKSON: *"It is to be regretted that the rich and powerful too often bend the acts of government to their own selfish purposes."*

ADAM GRANT, PHD: *"Some people are called selfish in all their relationships. These people are called sociopaths."*

ANNE SULLIVAN: *"We imagine that we want to escape our selfish and commonplace existence, but we cling desperately to our chains."*

JANE AUSTEN: *"Selfishness must always be forgiven you know, because there is no hope of a cure."*

DR. PHIL MCGRAW: *"The truth is, I think we are a self-less society, not a selfish society. Because we are so busy now."*

ADAM SMITH: *"Individual ambition serves the common good."*

MANSUR AL-HALLAJ: *"Between me and You, there is only me. Take away the me, so only You remain."*

CAROL BURNETT: *"It's also selfish because it makes you feel good when you help others. I've been helped by acts of kindness from strangers. That's why we're here, after all, to help others."*

RITA LEVI-MONTALCINI, MD, NOBEL: *"I tell young people: Do not think of yourself, think of others. Think of the future that awaits you, think about what you can do and do not fear anything."*

RUMI: *"Once you conquer your selfish self, all your darkness will change to light."*

JERRY LEWIS: *"I am probably the most selfish man you will ever meet in your life. No one gets the satisfaction or the joy that I get out of seeing kids realize there is hope."*

Similar: greedy, egotistical, narcissistic, stingy, narrow, self-minded, self-absorbed
Opposite: generous, high-minded, liberal, magnanimous, considerate, accommodating

Sensitive. Relating to the speed of your reactions to other people, ideas, or issues. *Popular or Heart-Based Usage: (1) Having your antennae up. (2) Being vigilant/ hyper-vigilant. (3) Having thin skin. (4) Being easily triggered. (5) Being super-aware. (6) Getting easily emotional. (7) Being touchy. (8) Being a fussbudget. (9) Being needy. (10) Seeking safe spaces. (11) Wearing your heart on your sleeve. (12) Having a chip on your shoulder. (13) Feeling entitled. (14) Always playing the victim. (15) 'Poor me!' (16) Being a high-maintenance person. (17) Pointing out the micro-aggressions of others.*

JANE PENNYBACKER MOSBACHER: *"Approve of me or I'll scream."*

MIKE TYSON: *"My biggest weakness is my sensitivity. I am too sensitive a person."*

RUSSELL HORNSBY: *"As a black man, so often you grow up suppressing your emotions and sensitivity."*

ANG LEE: *"Sensitivity and money are like two parallel lines. They don't meet."*

CAMILLE PAGLIA: *"Manhood coerced into sensitivity is no manhood at all."*

VINEET RAJ KAPOOR: *"Sensitivity and resolve are opposites. You need good negotiation skills to retain both."*

LINCOLN STOREY: *"Sensitivity is a measure of how quickly and how deeply we respond to something new."*

NICOLE APPLETON: *"I find intelligence sexy. I find a sense of humor sexy. I find sensitivity sexy."*

KARYN HALL, PHD: *"Emotionally sensitive people in particular often feel controlled by their emotions."*

AUGUSTO CURY, MD: *"Sensitive people suffer more, but they love more and dream more."*

SIR WILLIAM OSLER, MD, FRS: *"The good physician treats the disease; the great physician treats the patient who has the disease."*

D. EARL JOHNSTON: *"A woman can often demonstrate steadfastness faster than a man can demonstrate sensitivity."*

YASMIN MOGAHED: *"Your beauty is in your sensitivity. Don't let anyone take it from you."*

Similar: reactive, touchy, impressionable, emotional, hyper-aware
Opposite: indifferent, callous, hard-hearted, neglectful, tone-deaf

Serenity. Experiencing a comfortable and joyous mindfulness or peace. *Popular or Heart-Based Usage: (1) Being comfortable in your own skin. (2) Having a peaceful, easy feeling. (3) Being really laid back. (4) Having a 'Kumbaya' experience. (5) Being at one with the universe. (6) 'Om Shanti.' (7) 'Oneness Song.' (8) Feeling true to your highest purposes. (9) Knowing who you are. (10) Allowing life to unfold.*

REINHOLD NIEBUHR: *"God grant me the serenity to accept the things I cannot change, the courage to change the things I can, and the wisdom to know the difference."*

GAUTAMA BUDDHA: *"Serenity comes when you trade expectations for acceptance."*

THICH NHAT HANH: *"Every breath we take, every step we make, can be filled with peace, joy, and serenity."*

HENRI MATISSE: *"What I dream of is an art of balance, of purity and serenity devoid of troubling or depressing subject matter—a soothing, calming influence on the mind, rather like a good armchair which provides relaxation from physical fatigue."*

ANNE MORROW LINDBERGH: *"For me the core, the inner spring, can best be refound through solitude."*

HAROLD W. BECKER: *"Serenity is the tranquil balance of heart and mind."*

RALPH WALDO EMERSON: *"Tomorrow is a new day. You shall begin it well and serenely."*

LAO TZU: *"Do your work, then step back. The only path to serenity."*

D. EARL JOHNSTON: *"Serenity is understanding what you are all about. Sometimes it takes a good while."*

PHILIPPIANS 4:7: *"And the peace of God, which passeth all understanding, shall keep your hearts and minds through Christ Jesus."*

PSALM 29:11: *"The Lord will give strength unto his people. The Lord will bless his people with peace."*

Similar: peace, calmness, tranquility, composure, quietude, acceptance
Opposite: agitation, disturbance, volatility, tempestuousness, chaos

Shame. (1) Reflecting with regret on your own perceived weaknesses or misdeeds. (2) Ridiculing or calling out someone as a means of modifying their behavior. *Popular or Heart-Based Usage: (1) Beating yourself up. (2) Wearing the hair shirt. (3) Wanting to climb out of your own skin.* Alternately, when projecting shame onto others: *(4) Belittling someone. (5) Publicly holding someone accountable for their alleged misdeeds or transgressions. (6) Deliberately making others feel remorse for their behavior. (7) Pointing out their micro-aggressions. (8) Tattling on someone. (9) Ratting someone out. (10) "Umm! I'm gonna tell!" (11) Guilt-tripping someone.*

WILL ROGERS: *"Eventually you stop lying about your age and start bragging about it."*

BRENE BROWN, MSW, PHD: *"Shame is the most powerful, master emotion. It's the fear we are not good enough."*

GEORGE CARLIN: *"Political correctness is America's newest form of intolerance."*

ANN PATCHETT: *"Shame should be reserved for the things we choose to do, not the circumstances that life puts upon us."*

JOHN GRISHAM: *"Addicts know no shame. You disgrace yourself so many times you become immune to it."*

WILLIAM FAULKNER: *"Unless you're ashamed of yourself now and then, you're not honest."*

D. EARL JOHNSTON: *"There is rarely a silence so loud as the silence after blame or an accusation proved wrong."*

PROVERB: *"Fool me once, shame on you; fool me twice, shame on me."*

ROBERT THURMAN: *"You should never be ashamed of the suffering you've been through."*

LEANN RIMES: *"I'm not gonna apologize for who I am and what I've gone through."*

NEIL DEGRASSE TYSON, PHD: *"There's no shame in admitting what you don't know. The only shame is pretending you know all the answers."*

MOKOKOMA MOKHONOANA: *"You cannot really shame a man who sincerely does not care what others think of him."*

BENJAMIN FRANKLIN: *"Being ignorant is not so much a shame, as being unwilling to learn."*

Similar: remorse, humiliation, ignominy, chagrin, embarrassment, tattling
Opposite: pride, praise, esteem, exuberance, ebullience, calm, self-assuredness

Sigh. (1) Exhaling upon the conclusion and acceptance of a matter. (2) Releasing concern about a resolved matter. *Popular or Heart-Based Usage: (1) Shrugging. (2) 'Whew.' (3) 'No further questions.' (4) 'Well, that's water under the bridge.' (5) 'That's done and dusted.' (6) 'Whatever.' (7) 'Oh well.' (8) 'Moving on.' (9) "Turning the page.' (10) 'That's that.'*

> ARNOLD HAULTAIN: *"A woman can say more in a sigh than a man can say in a sermon."*
>
> THOMAS SHADWELL: *"Words may be false and full of art; Sighs are the natural language of the heart."*
>
> ROBERT ORBEN: *"A sigh is an amplifier for those who suffer in silence."*
>
> SYDNEY J. HARRIS: *"When I hear somebody sigh, 'Life is hard,' I am always tempted to ask, 'Compared to what?'"*
>
> TROY SMITH: *"A game like this helps everybody. It was a sigh of relief. A great confidence boost."*
>
> JIMMY CARTER, NOBEL: *"We reached a high point in my opinion with the passage of civil rights legislation and Martin Luther King's success and the crusade of others. I think we kind of breathed a sigh of relief as if we had achieved the end of racial discrimination or white supremacy."*
>
> FRANK PERETTI: *"A good book or movie or screenplay should be emotionally satisfying. When they're done, you want people to breathe a deep sigh and say 'Wow.'"*
>
> OUIDA: *"There is a chord in every heart that has a sigh in it if touched right."*
>
> JOHNNY MCGREW: *"After hearing our troops had discovered a leaky septic tank buried under the base pumpkin patch, the Colonel pushed away his half-eaten Thanksgiving dessert with a sigh, 'Sergeant, you were right about the pie.'"*
>
> MINNA ANTRIM: *"The drama of life begins with a wail and ends with a sigh."*
>
> JAN GOSS: *"A sigh is the release of resistance."*

Similar: exhale, murmur, accept, whew, gasp, utterance, groan, suspire, breathe
Opposite: praise, endorse, favor, (or, alternately) reject, dislike, disagree

Silence. Deciding not to communicate. *Popular or Heart-Based Usage: (1) Going off the grid. (2) Going dark. (3) Going incommunicado. (4) Going radio silent. (5) Holding your hand over your mouth. (6) Clamming up. (7) Zipping it. (8) Being under a gag order. (9) Observing the Code/Omerta. (10) Shutting up. (11) 'Notta lotta yadda.' (12) 'Hear no evil, see no evil, speak no evil. No.' (13) 'Cat got your tongue?' (14) 'Pipe down!' (15) 'Hush!' (16) 'Nothing but crickets.' (17) Not making a peep. (18) Hearing a pin drop.*

LEONARDO DA VINCI: *"Nothing strengthens authority so much as silence."*

SIR WINSTON CHURCHILL: *"We are masters of the unsaid words, but slaves of those we let slip out."*

ALLY CARTER: *"Ooh. The silent treatment."*

WILL ROGERS: *"Never miss a good chance to shut up."*

CICERO: *"Silence is one of the great arts of conversation."*

MIGUEL DE CERVANTES: *"A closed mouth catches no flies."*

RUMI: *"Silence is the language of God. All else is poor translation."*

LAO TZU: *"He who knows does not speak, and he who speaks does not know."*

CHARLES DE GAULLE: *"Silence is the ultimate weapon of power."*

ADAGE: *"Silence is often misinterpreted but never misquoted."*

HENRY DAVID THOREAU: *"Silence is the universal refuge."*

PROVERB: *"Never mistake a woman's silence for ignorance."*

MARCEL ACHARD: *"Women like silent men. They think they are listening."*

EMILY DICKINSON: *"Saying nothing … sometimes says the most."*

CONFUCIUS: *"Silence is a true friend who never betrays."*

ADAGE: *"Heed the power of the unspoken word."*

EURIPIDES: *"Silence is true wisdom's best reply."*

JOSH BILLINGS: *"Men who have much to say use the fewest words."*

PROVERB: *"Silence is the hardest argument to refute."*

SIGMUND FREUD, MD: *"Unexpressed emotions will never die. They are buried alive and will come forward later in uglier ways."*

FEDERICO GARCIA LORCA: *"To burn with desire and keep quiet about it is the greatest punishment we can bring on ourselves."*

C. S. LEWIS: *"I have learned now that while those who speak about one's miseries usually hurt, those who keep silence hurt more."*

MARTIN LUTHER KING, JR., NOBEL: *"In the end, we will remember not the words of our enemies, but the silence of our friends."*

ADAGE: *"The most tragically broken hearts are caused by unspoken words."*

D. EARL JOHNSTON: *"We are sustained in life when we hear from those we love."*

Similar: reticence, reflection, quiet, secrecy, hesitance, hushing
Opposite: agitation, clamor, noise, cacophony, outburst

Sin. (1) Transgressing against a known code of moral or ethical behavior. (2) Reaching when you should withdraw or withdrawing when you should reach. *Popular or Heart-Based Usage: (1) Back-sliding. (2) Knowing it's wrong, but doing it anyway. (3) Getting your hops. (4) Sowing your oats. (5) Blowing off some steam. (6) Falling for the snares.*

BILL MAHER: *"Everything that used to be a sin is now a disease."*

COLLEGE STUDENT: *"Yes, I have my morals. I just choose to ignore them from time to time."*

MARTIN SCORSESE: *"You make a deal. You figure out how much sin you can live with."*

JOHNNY MCGREW: *"Sin is simple—it's doing something you know is wrong."*

ADM. HYMAN G. RICKOVER: *"If you are going to sin, sin against God, not the bureaucracy. God will forgive you, but the bureaucracy won't."*

OSCAR WILDE: *"The only difference between the saint and the sinner is that every saint has a past, and every sinner has a future."*

BLAISE PASCAL: *"There are only two kinds of men: the righteous who think they are sinners and the sinners who think they are righteous."*

MIGUEL DE CERVANTES: *"A private sin is not so prejudicial in this world, as a public indecency."*

HENRY WARD BEECHER: *"Compassion will cure more sins than condemnation."*

IBN QAYYIM AL-JAWZIYYA: *"Sins have many side-effects. One of them is that they steal knowledge from you."*

BILLY GRAHAM: *"I think that the Bible teaches that homosexuality is a sin, but the Bible also teaches that pride is a sin, jealousy is a sin, and hate is a sin; evil thoughts are a sin. So I don't think that homosexuality should be chosen as the overwhelming sin that we are doing today."*

JAMES L. NICODEM: *"Sin will take you where you didn't plan to go. It will keep you there longer than you planned to stay. And it will cost you more than you intended to pay."*

OLIVER WENDELL HOLMES, SR, MD: *"Sin has many tools, but a lie is the handle which fits them all."*

JUSTICE OLIVER WENDELL HOLMES, JR.: *"The character of every act depends on the circumstances in which it is done."*

WALT WHITMAN: *"I am as bad as the worst, but, thank God, I am as good as the best."*

LINCOLN STOREY: *"Sin is where the mind says 'Go!' but the heart says 'No!'"*

D. EARL JOHNSTON: *"The first seducers of Integrity have usually been either Cool, Cash, or Convenient."*

DANIEL DEFOE: *"'Tis no sin to cheat the devil.'"*

Similar: transgression, crime, immorality, lapse, trespass, offense, peccadillo, wrong
Opposite: good deed, blessing, kindness, virtue, benevolence

Sincere. (1) Behaving without guile or deception. (2) Being known for the truth and transparency of your intent. *Popular or Heart-Based Usage: (1) Keeping it real. (2) Having a heart-to-heart talk. (3) Keeping it on the level. (4) Being true blue. (5) Being a straight shooter. (6) Talking turkey. (7) Not speaking with a forked tongue.*

FRANKLIN D. ROOSEVELT: *"Be sincere; be brief; be seated."*

OSCAR WILDE: *"A little sincerity is a dangerous thing, and a great deal of it is absolutely fatal."*

ABRAHAM LINCOLN: *"If I were two-faced, would I be wearing this one?"*

WALTER INGLIS ANDERSON: *"The most sincere compliment we can pay is attention."*

GEORGE HENRY LEWES: *"Insincerity is always weakness; sincerity even in error is strength."*

PEGGY NOONAN: *"Sincerity and competence is a strong combination. In politics, it is everything."*

SHINTO SAYING: *"Sincerity is the single virtue that binds divinity and man into one."*

MATTHEW 15:18: *"Those things that proceed out of the mouth come from the heart."*

JOHN WOODEN: *"Sincerity may not help us make friends, but it will help us keep them."*

LEXI JOHNSTON: *"I would tell my younger self that God's grace is sufficient. That your greatest strength is honesty in weakness."*

JOHN COLTRANE: *"You can play a shoestring if you're sincere."*

HENRY WARD BEECHER: *"Sorrow makes men sincere."*

HENRY DAVID THOREAU: *"Any sincere thought is irresistible."*

OSCAR WILDE: *"Be yourself; everyone else is taken."*

CONFUCIUS: *"Sincerity is the way of heaven."*

Similar: honesty, forthrightness, clarity, candor, transparency
Opposite: dissembling, misleading, deception, lying, guile

Sorrow. Reflecting with profound distress about a bad ending, loss, mistake, or personal disappointment. *Popular or Heart-Based Usage: (1) Feeling heartache. (2) Being torn up about something. (3) Crying buckets. (4) Feeling broken-hearted. (5) Thinking how it used to be. (6) Saying farewell to a friend. (7) Wanting to turn back time. (8) Missing your old and favorite joys.*

OSCAR WILDE: *"Where there is sorrow there is holy ground."*

RALPH WALDO EMERSON: *"Sorrow looks back, worry looks around, faith looks up."*

HENRY WADSWORTH LONGFELLOW: *"Every man has his secret sorrows."*

RALPH WALDO EMERSON: *"Sorrow makes us all children again."*

KAHLIL GIBRAN: *"We choose our joys and sorrows long before we experience them."*

WILLIAM SHAKESPEARE: *"Parting is such sweet sorrow that I shall say goodnight till it be morrow."*

THOMAS AQUINAS: *"Sorrow can be alleviated by good sleep, a bath, and a glass of wine."*

ANN LANDERS: *"People who drink to drown their sorrows should be told that sorrow knows how to swim."*

KAHLIL GIBRAN: *"In truth you are weeping for that which has been your delight."*

RUMI: *"Sorrow prepares you for joy. It sweeps everything out of your house, so that new joy can find space to enter."*

HENRY WARD BEECHER: *"Sorrow makes men sincere."*

PROVERB: *"Earth holds no sorrow that heaven cannot heal."*

Similar: anguish, sadness, grief, regret, brooding, emptiness
Opposite: cheer, delight, joy, gaiety, fun

Sorry. Undertaking an apology, making amends, or acknowledging an imposition, slight, or failure toward others. *Popular or Heart-Based Usage: (1) Making polite excuses. (2) Trying to smooth things over. (3) Extending an olive branch. (4) Taking your meals in the doghouse. (5) Sleeping on the sofa. (6) Going to someone with hat in hand. (7) Kissing someone's rear end. (8) Taking the blame for a mistake. (9) 'Mea culpa.' (10) 'My bad.' (11) 'Please forgive me.' (12) 'My fault.' (13) 'I'll make it up to you.'*

MARK TWAIN: *"Let us so endeavor to live so that when we come to die that even the undertaker will be sorry."*

RUSH LIMBAUGH: *"Sorry to interrupt myself, but it's the only way I stop talking."*

TERRY BRADSHAW: *"If I could reach down in my heart, I would say I'm sorry for every unkind word and thought I ever had."*

SIR ELTON JOHN, BERNIE TAUPIN: *"Sorry Seems to Be the Hardest Word"* (Song)

MARTIN LUTHER: *"Let the wife make the husband happy to come home, and let him make her sorry to see him leave."*

AN APOLOGY: *"I am sorry from the bottom of my heart for hurting you. I was wrong. Please forgive me. I love you."*

BRUCE WILLIS: *"My wife heard me say I love you a thousand times, but she never once heard me say sorry."*

HARRY BELAFONTE: *"All too often, I'm sorry to say, I relegated my family to the cracks and margins."*

MIGNON MCLAUGHLIN: *"True remorse is never just a regret over consequence; it is a regret over motive."*

DALE CARNEGIE: *"Feeling sorry for yourself, and your present condition, is not only a waste of energy but the worst habit you could possibly have."*

PATRICIA HEATON: *"I have always believed that when you're feeling sorry for yourself, the best thing to do is help someone else."*

Similar: apologetic, contrite, regretful, distressed, penitent, humble
Opposite: unrepentant, heartened, unremorseful, disdainful

Spirit. (1) Regarding life's causal, defining, and non-physical essence. (2) Relating to the animating force or nature of a thing. *Popular or Heart-Based Usage: (1) What moves you. (2) Your heart of hearts. (3) Your fifth-dimensional self. (4) Metaphysical you. (5) Signature of being. (6) Out-of-body essence. (7) Soulful. (8) Pneuma. (9) 'It's driving the meatsuit.' (10) 'Bodies are soul cages.'/As God, or a Supreme Being: (11) YHWH (12) The Great 'I AM.' (13) Allah. (14) The Most High God. (15) The Holy Spirit. (16) The Holy Comforter. (17) The Prime Mover. (18) The Unmoved Mover. (19) Summum Bonum. (20) Source. (21) 'Mind of the Matrix.' (22) Your Higher Self. (23) Unity Consciousness.*

OXFORD LANGUAGES DICTIONARY: *"Spirit. The non-physical part of a person which is the seat of emotions and character; the soul."*

GENESIS 1:1–2: *"In the beginning God created the heaven and the earth. And the earth was without form, and void; and darkness was upon the face of the deep. And the Spirit of God moved upon the face of the deep."*

EXODUS 3:14: *"And God said unto Moses, I AM THAT I AM."*

JOHN 1:14: *"And the Word was made flesh, and dwelt among us."*

ARISTOTLE: *"There must be a first cause, an unmoved mover, that is the source of all change and motion while being itself unchanging and unmoving."*

SIR ISAAC NEWTON, FRS: *"Gravity explains the motions of the planets, but it cannot explain who sets the planets in motion."*

MAX PLANCK, PHD, NOBEL: *"As a man who has devoted his whole life to the most clearheaded science, to the study of matter, I can tell you as a result of my research about atoms this much: There is no matter as such. All matter originates and exists only by virtue of a force which brings the particle of an atom to vibration and holds this most minute solar system of the atom together. We must assume behind this force the existence of a conscious and intelligent spirit. This spirit is the matrix of all matter."*

HENRY FORD: *"I am in exact accord with the belief of Thomas Edison that spirit is immortal, that there is a continuing center of character in each personality."*

PAM GREGORY: *"The whole universe is one consciousness. We are fractals of that."*

JOHN D. CAPUTO, PHD: *"God does not exist, God insists."*

HENRY DAVID THOREAU: *"Every man casts a shadow; not his body only, but his imperfectly mingled spirit. This is his grief. Let him turn which way he will, it falls opposite to the sun; short at noon, long at eve. Did you never see it?"*

C. S. LEWIS: *"Humans are amphibians—half spirit and half animal. As spirits they belong to the eternal world, but as animals they inhabit time."*

STELLA ADLER: *"You act with your soul. That's why you all want to be actors, because your souls are not used up by life."*

ELIE WIESEL, NOBEL: *"There are victories of the soul and spirit. Sometimes, even if you lose, you win."*

Spirit. *(continued)*

PIERRE TEILHARD DE CHARDIN: *"We are not human beings having a spiritual experience. We are spiritual beings having a human experience."*

CHRISTOPHER REEVE: *"Your body is not who you are. The mind and spirit transcend the body."*

RITA LEVI-MONTALCINI, MD, NOBEL: *"The body does whatever it wants. I am not my body; I am my mind."*

STEPHEN HAWKING, CH, CBE, FRS, FRSA, PHD: *"My advice to other disabled people would be, concentrate on things your disability doesn't prevent you doing well, and don't regret the things it interferes with. Don't be disabled in spirit as well as physically."*

MARTHA GRAHAM: *"The body is a sacred garment. It's your first and last garment; it is what you enter life in and what you depart life with, and it should be treated with honor."*

ALBERT EINSTEIN, PHD, NOBEL (attributed): *"We are slowed down sound and light waves, a walking bundle of frequencies tuned in to the cosmos. We are souls dressed up in sacred biochemical garments and our bodies are the instruments though which our souls play their music."*

ECKHART TOLLE: *"Being spiritual has nothing to do with what you believe and everything to do with your state of consciousness."*

D. EARL JOHNSTON: *"Through the ages, Earth has been noted as a place where we rediscover ourselves as timeless hyper-dimensional souls lodged for a time in temporary four-dimensional bodies."*

AUNG SAN SUU KYI, NOBEL: *"It is part of the unceasing human endeavor to prove that the spirit of man can transcend the flaws of his own nature."*

LINCOLN STOREY: *"In the spirit universe, the highest intention trumps all."*

WALT WHITMAN: *"Let your soul stand cool and composed before a million universes."*

DEEPAK CHOPRA: *"Gratitude is one of the most effective ways of getting in touch with your soul."*

PAM GREGORY: *"We are essentially electromagnetic beings."*

HERBERT SPENCER: *"Music must take rank as the highest of the fine arts—as the one which, more than any other, ministers to the human spirit."*

RUMI: *"And so it is, that both the Devil and the angelic Spirit present us with objects of desire to awaken our power of choice."*

E. E. CUMMINGS: *"Once we believe in ourselves, we can risk curiosity, wonder, spontaneous delight, or any experience that reveals the human spirit."*

JOHN 18:36: *"My kingdom is not of this world."*

Similar: soul, essence, phantom, apparition, specter, poltergeist, ghost, revenant
Opposite: body, person, physique, flesh, meat body, soul cage

Stress. [See also **Trauma**] Experiencing an overload of competing demands, data, or challenges, and including related emotional and physiological effects. *Popular or Heart-Based Usage: (1) Feeling overwhelmed. (2) Being under the gun. (3) Struggling to cope. (4) Feeling slammed. (5) Choking on a project. (6) Squeezing ten pounds of problems into a five-pound sack. (7) Dealing with TMI. ['Too Much Information.'] (8) Going full-tilt boogie. (9) Being stuck in 'Deadline City.' (10) Needing some downtime. (11) Getting burned out. (12) Feeling maxed out. (13) Feeling fried. (14) Dealing with 'fight or flight.' (15) Nearing a snapping point. (16) Feeling like you are toast. (17) Experiencing battle fatigue. (18) Being in the Red Zone. (19) Struggling with PTSD ['Post-Traumatic Stress Disorder']. (20) Dealing with a chemical imbalance. (21) Working through it all.*

DAVID ALLEN: *"You can do anything but not everything."*

MAHATMA GANDHI: *"There is more to life than increasing its speed."*

NAV.AL: *"In mental terms, stress is an inability to decide what is important."*

ECKHART TOLLE: *"Stress is caused by being 'here' but wanting to be 'there.'"*

NATALIE GOLDBERG: *"Stress is an ignorant state. It believes that everything is an emergency."*

SAYING: *"Stress is like trying to stuff ten pounds of sand into a five-pound sack."*

ELIZABETH A. STANLEY, MD: *"Stress is our internal response to an experience that our brain perceives as threatening or challenging."*

DR. JOE DISPENZA: *"Every time we knock the body out of chemical balance, that is called 'stress.'"*

NATIONAL LIBRARY OF MEDICINE: *"Overall, the bulk of evidence suggests stress can affect micronutrient concentrations, often leading to micronutrient depletion."*

WILLIAM JAMES, MD: *"The greatest weapon against stress is our ability to choose one thought over another."*

ASTRID ALAUDA: *"Don't let your mind bully your body into believing it must carry the burden of its worries."*

MARILYN MANDLE DICK: *"Are you all stressed up with nowhere to go? Commandment #11 should have been 'Thou shalt not stress.'"*

KELLY CLARKSON: *"God will never give you anything you can't handle, so don't stress."*

NATALIE GOLDBERG: *"Stress is basically a disconnection from the earth, a forgetting of the breath."*

AMIT RAY, PHD: *"Conscious breathing is the best antidote to stress, anxiety and depression."*

CONFUCIUS: *"Life is really simple, but we insist on making it complicated."*

OVID: *"Take rest; a field that has rested gives a bountiful crop."*

Similar: overwhelmed, overworked, aggravated, conflicted, exhausted, burned-out
Opposite: relaxed, carefree, lighthearted, rested, happy-go-lucky, contented

Stubborn. Being steadily resistant to change or to altering your beliefs or views. *Popular or Heart-Based Usage: (1) Crossing your arms. (2) Not budging. (3) Digging in. (4) Sticking your fingers in your ears. (5) Being hardheaded. (6) Being a slow learner. (7) Not having it. (8) 'Not a chance.' (9) 'Talk to the hand.' (10) 'Go to Helen Waite!'*

MEREDITH WILLSON (*Iowa native*): *"We're so gosh-darned stubborn we can stand touchin' noses for a week at a time and never see eye-to-eye."*

JOHNNY MCGREW: *"People can use a polite word like 'stubborn' when they really mean something more like: 'Not happening. Try me when Hell freezes over.'"*

WILL ROGERS: *"Even if you're on the right track, you'll get run over if you just sit there."*

JOHN ADAMS: *"Facts are stubborn things."*

MARK TWAIN: *"Facts are stubborn, but statistics are more pliable."*

DAVID L. DONOHO, PHD, SHAW PRIZE, GAUSS MEDAL: *"You may not like what some statisticians do. You may feel they don't share your values. They may embarrass you. But that shouldn't lead us to abandon the term 'statistics.'"*

OLIVIA DE HAVILLAND: *"I loved France, although I initially thought they were stubborn for always speaking French."*

MELANIE MARTINEZ: *"I'm really stubborn, and I'm okay with that."*

CHRIS EVERT: *"To be a tennis champion, you have to be inflexible. You have to be stubborn. You have to be arrogant. You have to be selfish and self-absorbed. Kind of tunnel vision almost."*

PAT SUMMITT: *"Sometimes I'm more stubborn than I am smart."*

PAULO COELHO: *"The brave are always stubborn."*

OSHO: *"The less people know, the more stubbornly they know it."*

BARRY STERNLICHT: *"As the facts change, change your thesis. Don't be a stubborn mule, or you'll get killed."*

DREW SCOTT: *"Being stubborn is not an asset. You have to be able to see things through other people's eyes."*

WILLIE AAMES: *"Being stubborn can be a good thing. Being stubborn can be a bad thing. It just depends on how you use it."*

CHUCK NOLL: *"Being stubborn is a virtue when you're right; it's only a character flaw when you're wrong."*

ALBERT EINSTEIN, PHD, NOBEL: *"The distinction between the past, the present, and the future is only a stubbornly persistent illusion."*

FRIEDRICH NIETZSCHE: *"Many are stubborn in pursuit of the path they have chosen, few in pursuit of the goal."*

IMMANUEL KANT: *"The wise man can change his mind; the stubborn one, never."*

JEFF BEZOS: *"We are stubborn on vision. We are flexible on details."*

Similar: obstinate, resolute, unyielding, fixed, intolerant, obdurate, rigid, unshakeable
Opposite: flexible, yielding, open-minded, easy-going, free-wheeling, free-flowing

Subconscious. A part of your mind and memory which operates below or beneath your direct conscious awareness, but which can influence your current thoughts, emotions, and behavior. *Popular or Heart-Based Usage: (1) What's in the back of your mind. (2) Having a thought pop into your head. (3) Having blind spots. (4) The influence of 'hidden persuaders.' (5) What comes up when you restimulate a past injury or trauma. (6) 'Once bitten, twice shy.' (7) Understanding stimulus-response patterns. (8) Relating to the hidden power of the past. (9) Understanding auto-suggestion. (10) Being subject to subliminal stimuli. (11) 'What came over me?' (12) Experiencing intrusive thoughts. (13) Recognizing the mind-body connection. (14) Understanding the prioritizing power of repetition.*

WILLIAM JAMES, MD: *"The greatest discovery of the nineteenth century was not in the realm of the physical sciences, but the power of the subconscious mind…"*

ALBERT ELLIS, PHD: *"It is important to be mindful and aware of these unconscious thoughts and motives, as they can have a great impact on our behavior, decisions, and relationships with others."*

CARL JUNG, MD: *"Until you make the subconscious conscious it will direct your life and you will call it fate."*

JOSEPH MURPHY, PHD, DD: *"Your subconscious mind does not argue with you. It accepts what your conscious mind decrees."*

THOMAS EDISON: *"Never go to sleep without a request to your subconscious."*

EARL NIGHTINGALE: *"Whatever we plant in our subconscious mind and nourish with repetition and emotion will one day become a reality."*

W. CLEMENT STONE: *"You affect your subconscious mind by verbal repetition."*

JANE FONDA: *"We cannot always control our thoughts, but we can control our words, and repetition impresses the subconscious, and then we are master of the situation."*

ROBERT COLLIER: *"Our subconscious minds have no sense of humor, play no jokes, and cannot tell the difference between reality and an imagined thought or image. What we continually think about will eventually manifest in our lives."*

NORA EPHRON: *"When you are attracted to someone, it just means that your subconscious is attracted to their subconscious, subconsciously."*

ANDREW WYETH: *"I dream a lot. I do more painting when I'm not painting. It's in the subconscious."*

D. H. LAWRENCE: *"I can never decide whether my dreams are the result of my thoughts, or my thoughts the result of my dreams."*

NAPOLEON HILL: *"The possibilities of creative effort connected with the subconscious mind are stupendous and imponderable."*

RITA LEVI-MONTALCINI, MD, NOBEL: *"You've been thinking about something without willing to for a long time…Then, all of the sudden, the problem is opened to you in a flash and you suddenly see the answer."*

Subconscious. *(continued)*

CARL JUNG, MD: *"Man's task is to become conscious of the contents that press upward from the unconscious."*

ENLIGHTENEDSOLUTIONS.COM: *"Our subconscious is where we store all of our emotional information and memory, such as the emotions we associate with our traumas and hurts, our fears, anxieties and insecurities, our mistakes, wrongs, and regrets."*

SIGMUND FREUD, MD: *"Unexpressed emotions will never die. They are buried alive and will come forward later in uglier ways."*

APA DICTIONARY: *"Repetition compulsion: in psychoanalytic theory, an unconscious need to reenact early traumas in the attempt to overcome or master them."*

PSYCHCENTRAL.COM: *"Repetition compulsion is when you unconsciously desire to reenact earlier trauma…It occurs when you repeat traumatic behaviors from your past, even when you know it's not good for you."*

DR. JOE DISPENZA: *"The conscious mind may be in the present, but the subconscious mind-body is living in the past."*

MICHAEL T. MICHAEL, PHD: *"Unconscious emotions are of central importance to psychoanalysis."*

SUSANNE RICEE: *"So, to sum up: the conscious mind is what we are actively thinking about, the subconscious is what we've learned and stored in our brain, and the unconscious is what we're not aware of at all."*

D. EARL JOHNSTON: *"Emotions arise from the subconscious as default behavior patterns, and they can be transformed by awareness, conscious beliefs, and repetition."*

JOEL OSTEEN: *"When a negative thought comes, erase it and replace it."*

CANDACE BEEBE PERT, PHD: *"Your body and your mind are not separate, we cannot treat one without the other."*

HARVEY MACKAY: *"Give your subconscious a chance to work by turning your brain off from time to time. Don't focus on work on solving problems constantly."*

FRANCINE SHAPIRO, PHD: *"During REM sleep, the brain allows the appropriate neural connections to make needed associations. The memory is processed and shifted to a more adaptive, usable form. That's why you can go to bed worried about something but wake up feeling better or with a solution."*

DANIEL KAHNEMAN, NOBEL: *"You think with your body, not with your brain."*

ANTONIO DAMASIO, MD, PHD, HONDA PRIZE: *"We are not thinking machines that feel; rather, we are feeling machines that think."*

Similar: reactive, hidden, past, primordial, subliminal, occluded, reptilian
Opposite: analytical, conscious, outer, logical, linear, rational, creative, present

Submission. Yielding or deferring to the will or authority of another, or to God. *Popular or Heart-Based Usage: (1) Being obedient. (2) Accepting your role. (3) Bending the knee. (4) Paying your dues. (5) Being humble (or loyal). (6) Checking your ego at the door. (7) Being a team player. (8) Being a servant leader. (9) Deferring to the greater good. (10) Kowtowing to others. (11) Knowing when to suck up. (12) Bending over backwards for someone. (13) Bowing and scraping to someone. (14) Falling prostrate. (15) Kissing someone's ring. (16) 'Flattery can get you everywhere.' (17) Being a simp. (18) Being a toady. (19) Accepting full subservience. (20) Sucking in your breath. (21) Voluntarily stepping down or stepping back. (22) Lowering your eyes or staring at the floor.*

ISLAM: *"Submission describes the state of mind of anyone who recognizes God's absolute authority, and reaches a conviction that God alone has all authority."*

WILLIAM P. YOUNG: *"Submission is not about authority and it is not obedience; it is all about relationships of love and respect."*

REBECCA WEST: *"Submission to poverty is the unpardonable sin against the body. Submission to unhappiness is the unpardonable sin against the spirit."*

JUNE CARTER CASH: *"I stayed in submission to my husband, and he allowed me to do anything I wanted to. I felt like I was lucky to have that kind of romance."*

GLORIA STEINEM: *"I always say to audiences of men: 'Cooperation beats submission. Trust me.'"*

HENRY MILLER: *"True strength lies in submission which permits one to dedicate his life, through devotion, to something beyond himself."*

JEAN-JACQUES ROUSSEAU: *"Liberty is obedience to the law which one has laid down for oneself."*

SIR BENJAMIN DISRAELI: *"Everyone likes flattery. When it comes to Royalty you should lay it on with a trowel."*

LEO TOLSTOY: *"God cannot be understood by logical reasoning but only by submission."*

GAUTAMA BUDDHA: *"Better than worshiping gods is obedience to the laws of righteousness."*

ANDY STANLEY: *"Divine direction begins with unconditional submission."*

RUSSELL M. NELSON, MD, PHD: *"Obedience brings success; exact obedience brings miracles."*

MARTIN LUTHER: *"Obedience is the crown and honor of all virtue."*

Similar: acquiescence, yielding, obedience, surrender, abidance, agreeability
Opposite: defiance, disobedience, contrariness, insolence, insurrection, resistance

Success. Achieving or realizing a goal. *Popular or Heart-Based Usage: (1) Getting the hang of it. (2) Getting it done. (3) Getting the W. (4) Beating the odds. (5) Making it happen. (6) Lighting up the board. (7) Taking the checkered flag. (8) Having a box-office smash. (9) Taking no prisoners. (10) Crushing it. (11) Killing it. (12) Hitting it big. (13) A tour de force. (14) Having a 360 win. (15) 'It all worked out.' (16) 'With flying colors.'*

JONATHAN WINTERS: *"I couldn't wait for success, so I went ahead without it."*

WILL ROGERS: *"The road to success is dotted with many tempting parking spaces."*

JOYCE BROTHERS, PHD: *"Success is a state of mind. If you want success, start thinking of yourself as a success."*

JOHNNY CASH: *"Success is having to worry about every damn thing in the world, except money."*

GOLDA MEIR: *"To be successful, a woman has to be much better at her job than a man."*

CHARLES DARWIN: *"It is not the strongest of the species that survive, nor the most intelligent, but the one most responsive to change."*

ALBERT EINSTEIN, PHD, NOBEL: *"Success = 1 part work + 1 part play + 1 part keep your mouth shut."*

BRIAN TRACY: *"Winners make a habit of manufacturing their own positive experiences in advance of the event."*

MICHAEL JORDAN: *"I have missed more than 9,000 shots in my career. I've lost almost 300 games. 26 times I've been trusted to take the game winning shot and missed. I've failed over and over and over again in my life. And that is why I succeed."*

TOP COACHES AND ATHLETES: *"Success means keeping focus and a short memory during a game. You will be distracted if you dwell on your mistakes. The next play is happening now."*

SUMNER REDSTONE: *"Success is not built on success. It is built on failure. It is built on frustration. Sometimes it is built on catastrophe."*

WARREN BUFFETT: *"The difference between successful people and very successful people is that very successful people say 'no' to almost everything."*

JOHN G. MEDLIN, JR.: *"Be the first person someone else thinks of when they have a problem they cannot solve."*

JOAN RIVERS: *"I succeeded by saying what everyone else is thinking."*

MAHATMA GANDHI: *"First they ignore you, then they laugh at you, then they fight you, and then you win."*

RUSSIAN ADAGE: *"Success is finishing next-to-last in a two-person race."*

ALEXANDRE DUMAS: *"Nothing succeeds like success."*

BUDDY MELGES: *"Start first and increase your lead."*

Similar: accomplishment, achievement, triumph, victory, completion
Opposite: failure, defeat, dud, disappointment, disaster, ruin, catastrophe

Suffering. (1) Living with the painful or negative consequences of your decisions and circumstances. (2) Experiencing life's hardships. *Popular or Heart-Based Usage: (1) Being in the pits. (2) Being down in the dumps. (3) Finding yourself between a rock and a hard place. (4) Doing hard time. (5) Having a really tough go. (6) Finding out what you're made of. (7) Knowing real heartache. (8) Facing the loss of your dreams.*

OPRAH WINFREY: *"Where there is no struggle, there is no strength."*

GOLDA MEIR: *"You'll never find a better sparring partner than adversity."*

LORD BYRON: *"Adversity is the first path to truth."*

ELIZABETH ANN SETON: *"Afflictions are the steps to heaven."*

JEWISH PROVERB: *"God is closest to those with broken hearts."*

EPICTETUS: *"Difficulties are things that show a person what they are."*

FRIEDRICH NIETZSCHE: *"That which does not kill us makes us stronger."*

SENECA: *"A gem cannot be polished without friction, nor a man perfected without trials."*

DONALD TRUMP: *"Going through tough times is a wonderful thing, and everybody should try it. Once."*

JOHN PATRICK/'THE TEAHOUSE OF THE AUGUST MOON': *"Pain makes one think. Thought makes one wise. Wisdom makes life endurable."*

D. EARL JOHNSTON: *"Few in severe distress have arrived there without asking: 'Why me?' And nearby, hopeful angels have whispered back: 'Of course you. Of course now. Now is your time to show up and to shine.'"*

JOSEPH CAMPBELL: *"It is by going down into the abyss that we recover the treasures of life. Where you stumble, there lies your treasure."*

SUFI PROVERB: *"When the ego weeps for what it has lost, the spirit rejoices for what it has found."*

RABBI NACHMAN OF BRESLOV: *"There is nothing more whole than a broken heart."*

JOHNNY MCGREW: *"If suffering builds character, then for sure I gotta be one well-built character."*

JAMES HOLLIS: *"The 'gift' of tragedy is not destruction, but humility."*

SHANTIDEVA: *"The source of all misery in the world lies in thinking of yourself. The source of all happiness lies in thinking of others."*

NORMAN VINCENT PEALE: *"In every difficult situation is potential value. Believe this, and then begin looking for it."*

WALT WHITMAN: *"These are the days that must happen to you."*

ALBERT EINSTEIN, PHD, NOBEL: *"Adversity introduces a man to himself."*

RUMI: *"The wound is the place where the Light enters you."*

SONIA RUMZI: *"Suffering teaches joy."*

Similar: misery, agony, hardship, predicament, plight, sad state
Opposite: wisdom, pleasure, delight, joy, euphoria, release

Suppression. Placing repetitive limitations or restrictions on the success of something or someone. *Popular or Heart-Based Usage: (1) Keeping a lid on something. (2) Holding someone down. (3) Holding something back. (4) Not giving something a fair shake. (5) Playing favorites. (6) Playing people against each other. (7) Keeping a foot on the scales. (8) Tamping things down. (9) Slow-walking a matter. (10) Keeping someone under your thumb. (11) Sitting on someone. (12) Refusing to recognize someone. (13) Sandbagging someone. (14) Holding someone's head under water. (15) Piling on. (16) Heaping ridicule on an idea. (17) Shaming someone. (18) Bullying someone. (19) 'Who's your daddy?' (20) Dodging (or hiding from) available proof or facts. (21) Enforcing a glass ceiling. (22) Camping out on someone's doorstep. (23) Playing 'whack-a-mole' with someone.*

ALEXANDER MEIKLEJOHN: *"Suppression is always foolish. Freedom is always wise. That is the faith, the experimental faith, by which we Americans have undertaken to live."*

JUSTICE WILLIAM O. DOUGLAS: *"The dominant purpose of the First Amendment was to prohibit the widespread practice of government suppression of embarrassing information."*

ROBIN MORGAN: *"An indigenous feminism has been present in every culture in the world and in every period of history since the suppression of women began."*

SUSAN GLASPELL: *"It is through suppression that hells are formed in us."*

CAMILLE PAGLIA: *"We must take the best from the left and from the right to devise new strategies for the twenty-first century. The reluctance of liberal professors to speak out against the rampant abuses committed on their side (e.g., the suppression of free speech, the excesses of women's studies and French theory) has simply increased the power of the right."*

GILBERT S. MERRITT, JR.: *"I am sure that as soon as speech was invented, efforts to suppress and control it began, and that process of suppression continues unabated."*

JOHNNY MCGREW: *"Muffled euphoria can be a suitable emotional response when your mother-in-law announces she has postponed her visit by a year."*

LORD NORTHCLIFFE: *"News is what somebody somewhere wants to suppress; all the rest is advertising."*

LENNY BRUCE: *"It's the suppression of the word that gives it the power, the violence, the viciousness."*

MARK TWAIN: *"I know your race. It is made up of sheep. It is governed by minorities, seldom or never by majorities. It suppresses its feelings and its beliefs and follows the handful that makes the most noise."*

CARL SAGAN, PHD: *"The cure for a fallacious argument is a better argument, not the suppression of ideas."*

Similar: restricting, curtailing, denying, bullying, shaming, undermining, undercutting
Opposite: encouraging, touting, liberating, believing, supporting, releasing, freeing

Surprise. (1) Experiencing the sudden emergence of something new. (2) Recognizing (or initiating) new events, facts, or things. *Popular or Heart-Based Usage: (1) Not seeing it coming. (2) Raising eyebrows. (3) Being stunned. (4) Being dumbstruck. (5) Growing wide-eyed. (6) Caught flat-footed. (7) Gasping. (8) Being thrown a curveball. (9) Getting thrown for a loop. (10) 'Like a deer in headlights.' (11) Swearing out loud. (12) Jaw-drop wonder. (13) Getting a bolt from the blue. (14) Being blown away. (15) Jumping a foot. (16) Feeling gob-smacked. (17) Being flabbergasted. (18) Flipping the script. (19) 'Wow!' (20) 'Presto!' (21) 'Shazam!' (22) 'Newsflash!' (23) 'What a kick in the head!' (24) 'Yikes!' (25) 'Boo!' (26) 'Gotcha!' (27) 'Holy Smokes/Toledo/Cow!' (28) 'Hell's Bells!' (29) 'You don't say!' (30) 'Oopsy-daisy!' (31) 'Oh, snap!' (32) 'You kidding me?' (33) 'You serious?' (34) 'Damn, dude!' (35) 'Shock the world!' (36) 'Get out!' (37) 'Yowza!' (38) 'Oh My God!'*

ARISTOTLE: *"The secret to humor is surprise."*

BORIS PASTERNAK: *"Surprise is the greatest gift which life can grant us."*

JOSÉ ORTEGA Y GASSET: *"To be surprised, to wonder, is to begin to understand."*

CHARLES MORGAN: *"There is no surprise more magical than the surprise of being loved. It is God's finger on man's shoulder."*

DESMOND TUTU, NOBEL: *"We may be surprised at the people we find in heaven. God has a soft spot for sinners. His standards are quite low."*

HENRY FORD: *"One of the greatest discoveries a man makes, one of his greatest surprises, is to find he can do what he was afraid he couldn't do."*

JULIA CAMERON: *"Mystery is at the heart of creativity. That, and surprise."*

JOHN PAUL JONES: *"Whoever can surprise well must conquer."*

SUN TZU: *"Direct confrontation will lead to engagement, and surprise will lead to victory."*

DEVIL: *"Such a sweet surprise. They never see me coming."*

GEN. GEORGE S. PATTON, JR.: *"Never tell people how to do things. Tell them what to do and they will surprise you with their ingenuity."*

SIR FRANCIS BACON: *"A sudden bold and unexpected question doth many times surprise a man and lay him open."*

JANE AUSTEN: *"Surprises are foolish things. The pleasure is not enhanced, and the inconvenience is often considerable."*

WILLIAM S. BURROUGHS: *"If you weren't surprised by your life you wouldn't be alive. Life is surprise."*

JOHN AVERY: *"After a hard day, try to think of something good about it before you go to sleep—the result may surprise you."*

PAMELA ANDERSON: *"It's great to be a blonde. With low expectations it's very easy to surprise people."*

JOHNNY MCGREW: *"No matter what, act surprised on your birthday."*

Similar: amazement, revelation, shock, astoundment, thunderbolt
Opposite: calmness, composure, indifference, boredom, monotony, sameness

Surrender. (1) Conceding or relinquishing a position to an adversary. (2) Admitting defeat. (3) Abandoning an unsupportable viewpoint or belief. *Popular or Heart-Based Usage: (1) Giving up. (2) Giving in. (3) Waving a white flag. (4) Backing off. (5) Ducking out. (6) Bowing out. (7) Crawfishing. (8) Eating crow. (9) Throwing in the towel. (10) Doing a 180. (11) Throwing it in reverse. (12) Noting a schedule conflict. (13) Suddenly playing nice. (14) Making your apologies. (15) Slipping out the back. (16) Heading for the exits. (17) Punting. (18) Calling it quits. (19) Bailing out. (20) Subbing out. (21) Tapping out. (22) Folding your tent. (23) Falling on your sword. (24) Suing for peace. (25) Taking some time off. (26) Taking time to be with the family. (27) 'Lose your ego.' (28) Tossing in your cards. (29) Pulling the ripcord. (30) Going under. (31) Hearing the call of St. Peter. (32) Consulting with the Grim Reaper. (33) Giving up the ghost. (34) Eating a dirt sandwich. (35) Bending the knee. (36) Accepting what's coming to you. (37) Wearing the brown helmet. (38) Going down with the ship. (39) Begging for mercy. (40) Crying Uncle. (41) Crying for Mama. (42) Pleading 'No mas.'*

JOHN PAUL JONES: *"I have not yet begun to fight!"*

VINCE LOMBARDI: *"The harder you work, the harder it is to surrender."*

SIR WINSTON CHURCHILL: *"We shall defend our island, whatever the cost may be, we shall fight on the beaches, we shall fight on the landing grounds, we shall fight in the fields and in the streets, we shall fight in the hills: we shall never surrender."*

HERNANDO CORTEZ: *"Burn the ships. We will not leave here without victory."*

COLONEL WILLIAM BARRET TRAVIS: *"I shall never surrender nor retreat."*

KING LEONIDAS OF SPARTA: *"No retreat. No surrender. That is Spartan Law."*

WOMEN OF SPARTA: *"Come back with your shield—or on it."*

ECKHART TOLLE: *"Accept—then act. Whatever the present moment contains, accept it as if you had chosen it. Always work with it, not against it."*

MARIANNE WILLIAMSON: *"The moment of surrender is not when life is over. It's when it begins."*

DOROTHY PARKER: *"So I'm thinking of throwing the battle; would you kindly direct me to hell?"*

SRI CHINMOY: *"Surrender is a journey from outer turmoil to the inner peace."*

JIM CARREY: *"It is better to risk starving yourself than surrender. If you give up on your dreams, what's left?"*

LAURA PAUSINI: *"I have to admit, in the end, I like to surrender to someone; the person I love."*

RUMI: *"Try something different. Surrender."*

Similar: capitulation, concession, submission, abandonment, abdication, yielding

Opposite: fighting, hunkering down, resisting, withstanding, steadfastness

Suspicious. Having a concern or belief that questionable or inappropriate activity has taken place. *Popular or Heart-Based Usage: (1) Raising your eyebrows. (2) Feeling that something (or someone) is shady or sketchy. (3) Feeling that things don't add up. (4) Being on to someone. (5) Having second thoughts. (6) 'This smells fishy.' (7) 'Something ain't right.' (8) Having your antennae up. (9) Keeping tabs on someone. (10) Poking around about a matter. (11) Keeping an eye on it. (12) Putting someone under a watch. (13) Checking out the timeline. (14) Being troubled by the scene. (15) 'That's kinda sus.'*

WILLIAM SHAKESPEARE: *"Suspicion always haunts the guilty mind."*

JOHNNY MCGREW: *"After he organized two Ponzi schemes through six foreign accounts, the IRS finally got him on suspicion of impersonating a taxpayer."*

HOSEA BALLOU: *"Suspicion is far more apt to be wrong than right, more often unjust than just. It is no friend to virtue, and always an enemy to happiness."*

ROD SERLING: *"There are weapons that are simply thoughts. For the record, prejudices can kill and suspicion can destroy."*

THOMAS BECKET: *"Those who tread among serpents, and along a tortuous path, must use the cunning of the serpent."*

THOMAS PAINE: *"Suspicion is the companion of mean souls, and the bane of all good society."*

JOHNNY MCGREW: *"One of your jobs in life is to sharpen up your BS detector. Ten percent of everyone you meet will smile big and then steal your lunch money if you let them."*

PETRARCH: *"Suspicion is the cancer of friendship."*

FYODOR DOSTOEVSKY: *"A hundred suspicions don't make a proof."*

MAHATMA GANDHI: *"The moment there is suspicion about a person's motives, everything he does becomes tainted."*

D. EARL JOHNSTON: *"There is rarely a silence so loud as the silence after a suspicion proved wrong."*

MARK JAMES: *"Suspicious Minds"* (Song)

Similar: mistrustful, doubting, disconcerted, questionable, troubled, concerned, misgivings, having qualms, having reservations

Opposite: assurance, confidence, coming clean, credence, faithfulness

Tact. Communicating in a manner to minimize any offense taken by others, especially regarding unpleasant news. *Popular or Heart-Based Usage: (1) Being charming. (2) Winning people over. (3) Chatting someone up. (4) Sweet talking. (5) Sugar-coating something. (6) Hitting all the right notes. (7) Being glib. (8) Giving good PR. (9) Having good BS. (10) Hanging your jaw right. (11) Having kissed the Blarney Stone. (12) Being an amiable spokesperson. (13) Talking smooth as silk. (14) Mounting a charm offensive. (15) Dressing something up. (16) Knowing how to put lipstick on a pig. (17) Polishing a turd. (18) Being an iron fist in a velvet glove. (19) Being a 'steel magnolia.' (20) Wearing a Teflon suit. (21) Being a good gabber. (22) Being a smooth operator. (23) Accentuating the positives. (24) Killing them with kindness. (25) Being a first-class spin doctor.*

WILL ROGERS: *"Diplomacy is the art of saying 'Nice doggie' until you can find a rock."*

SIR WINSTON CHURCHILL: *"Tact is the ability to tell someone to go to hell in a way that they look forward to the trip."*

LEO BUSCAGLIA, PHD: *"Tact is rubbing out another's mistake instead of rubbing it in."*

ABRAHAM LINCOLN: *"Tact: the ability to describe others as they see themselves."*

SIR ISAAC NEWTON, FRS: *"Tact is the art of making your point without making an enemy."*

GAIUS POPILLIUS LAENAS: *"Before you step out of that circle give me a reply to lay before the Senate."*

WILSON MIZNER: *"In the battle of existence, Talent is the punch; Tact is the clever footwork."*

MILES DAVIS: *"It's the notes you don't play that make the difference."*

MARK TWAIN: *"A politician is not as narrow minded as he forces himself to be."*

ALFRED P. SLOAN: *"Bedside manners are no substitute for the right diagnosis."*

HENRY VAN DYKE: *"Tact is the unsaid part of what you think."*

ADAGE: *"Heed the power of the unspoken word."*

Similar: diplomacy, thoughtfulness, mannerliness, optimism, positivity, consideration
Opposite: pessimism, thoughtlessness, bluntness, ill-considered, brashness, disrespectfulness

Teaching. [See also **Coaching**] Providing facts, insights, and guidance to enable another to achieve their goals and objectives. *Popular or Heart-Based Usage: (1) Setting the agenda. (2) Marking the challenge. (3) Establishing the tone. (4) Getting buy-in. (5) Taking the role of expert / instructor / guru / master / mentor / sensei / priest / rabbi / mullah. (6) 'Show it, don't tell it.' (7) Making it fun. (8) Getting your points across. (9) Lighting the fire. (10) Opening minds. (11) Being the trusted 'go-to' person. (12) Always being there. (13) 'Repetition is the parent of certainty.'*

PROVERB: *"An average teacher tells. A better teacher explains. A good teacher demonstrates. A great teacher inspires."*

BENJAMIN FRANKLIN: *"Tell me and I forget. Teach me and I remember. Involve me and I learn."*

PHIL COLLINS: *"In learning you will teach, and in teaching you will learn."*

MAIMONIDES: *"Give a man a fish and you feed him for a day; teach a man to fish and you feed him for a lifetime."*

ALBERT EINSTEIN, PHD, NOBEL: *"Example isn't another way to teach, it is the only way to teach."*

GALILEO GALILEI: *"You cannot teach a man anything, you can only help him find it within himself."*

GOETHE: *"Correction does much, but encouragement does more."*

CHINESE PROVERB: *"Teachers open the door, but you must enter by yourself."*

DAVID M. HENDRICKS: *"Find your mentor. Learn from someone who wants you to be big."*

OPRAH WINFREY: *"I think mentors are important and I don't think anybody makes it in the world without some form of mentorship. Nobody makes it alone."*

DON BLACK & MARK LONDON: *"To Sir, with Love"* (Song/Film)

JOHN C. MAXWELL: *"Students don't care how much you know, until they know how much you care."*

ROBERT A. HEINLEIN: *"Don't handicap your children by making their lives easy."*

ALEXANDER THE GREAT: *"I am indebted to my father for living, but to my teacher for living well."*

MAYA ANGELOU: *"When you learn, teach, when you get, give."*

KEN VENTURI: *"I don't believe you have to be better than everyone else. You have to be better than you ever thought you could be."*

JAMES ALLEN: *"People seek guidance from him who is master of himself."*

ARISTOPHANES: *"The wise learn many things from their enemies."*

ANATOLE FRANCE, NOBEL: *"Nine tenths of education is encouragement."*

LOIS FARFEL STARK: *"A good mentor can birth a life force."*

PROVERB: *"When the student is ready, the teacher will appear."*

Similar: guiding, counseling, tutoring, mentoring, coaching, advising
Opposite: mis-informing, rivaling, mis-directing, distracting, sabotaging, undermining

Telepathy. Communicating thoughts by means other than spoken words or traditional physical processes. *Popular or Heart-Based Usage: (1) Mind-reading. (2) Utilizing a sixth sense. (3) Thought transference. (4) Knowing alpha-to-gamma brainwaves.*

C. D. BROAD: *"Telepathy, both simultaneous and cognitive, is now an experimentally established fact."*

DRASEN: *"When you match the frequency, you connect of influence the object or person. Telepathy works when two people are on the same frequency."*

CARL JUNG, MD: *"Another dream-determinant that deserves mention is telepathy. The authenticity of this phenomenon can no longer be disputed today."*

MARK ZUCKERBERG: *"You're going to be able to capture a thought in its ideal and perfect form in your head. You'll be able to share that with the world, in a format where they can get it."*

ALAN TURING, PHD, OBE, FRS: *"These disturbing phenomena [Extra Sensory Perception] seem to deny all our scientific ideas. How we should like to discredit them! Unfortunately the statistical evidence, at least for telepathy, is overwhelming."*

BRIAN JOSEPHSON, PHD, NOBEL: *"I think telepathy exists, and I think quantum physics will help us understand its basic properties."*

RUPERT SHELDRAKE, PHD: *"What you do, what you say and what you think can influence other people by morphic resonance."*

DAVID MOREHOUSE, PHD: *"Remote Viewing was created as a means of gathering information but it has proven to be much more."*

HANS BERGER, MD: *"We see in the electroencephalogram a concomitant phenomenon of the continuous nerve processes which take place in the brain, exactly as the electrocardiogram represents a concomitant phenomenon of contractions of the individual segments of the heart."*

EDGAR CAYCE: *"First begin between selves, set a definite time, and each at that time put down what the other is doing. Do this 20 days. You shall find you have the key to telepathy."*

DEAN RADIN, PHD: *"The universe looks less like a big machine than a big thought."*

CLINT EASTWOOD: *"I've had moments when I've thought about somebody, picked up the phone to call them and they are on the line already, and I think that maybe there's some vibration, some connection."*

CHARLES R. MOORE: *"Do you believe in telepathy? No? Then what are you doing when you pray?"*

RUMI: *"I closed my mouth and spoke to you in a hundred silent ways."*

Similar: clairvoyance, precognition, premonition, parapsychology, telesthesia
Opposite: ignorance, incomprehension, accident, dismissive, careless

Terror. (1) Experiencing a sudden existential threat of coercion or death from others. (2) Being a target of deliberate overwhelm, fear, or disruption. *Popular or Heart-Based Usage: (1) 'When someone wreaks chaos on your world.' (2) Having your heart in your throat. (3) Being white-knuckled. (4) Freaking out. (5) Screaming bloody murder. (6) Having your hair stand on end. (7) Being frightened to your core. (8) Knowing stark raving madness. (9) Fearing the worst. (10) Experiencing 'the heart of darkness.' (11) Fearing there is 'no way out.' (12) Panic to the max. (13) Having no control.*

KJELL MAGNE BONDEVIK: *"Terror is contempt for human dignity."*

ANTOINE DE SAINT-EXUPERY: *"Only the unknown frightens men. But once a man has faced the unknown, that terror becomes the known."*

ALFRED HITCHCOCK: *"There is no terror in the bang, only in the anticipation of it."*

MARIE ANTOINETTE: *"No one understands my ills, nor the terror that fills my breast, who does not know the heart of a mother."*

VICTORIA AVEYARD: *"Kneel or bleed."*

YASSER ARAFAT: *"We totally and absolutely renounce all forms of terrorism."*

YITZHAK SHAMIR: *"Even if there is peace with all the Arab states, I don't know if the terrorism against us will pass from this world."*

PATRICK J. KENNEDY: *"Terrorism is a psychological warfare. Terrorists try to manipulate us and change our behavior by creating fear, uncertainty, and division in society."*

RAND PAUL: *"I am ready to debate how we fight terrorism without giving up our liberty."*

SIR TONY BLAIR: *"The purpose of terrorism lies not just in the violent act itself. It is in producing terror. It sets out to inflame, to divide, to produce consequences which they then use to justify further terror."*

YASSER ARAFAT: *"Whoever stands for a just cause cannot possibly be called a terrorist."*

BARACK OBAMA, NOBEL: *"Where the stakes are highest, in the war on terror, we cannot possibly succeed without extraordinary international cooperation."*

Similar: dread, fright, chaos, disorder, mayhem, bloodshed, lynching, anarchy, disorientation, destruction

Opposite: calm, ease, composure, normalcy, civility, content

Thinking. Using your mind to consider or reason about something. *Popular or Heart-Based Usage: (1) Engaging in a topic. (2) Noodling on a thing. (3) Using your grey matter. (4) Internally referencing. (5) Processing words and symbols. (6) Paying attention.*

MARTIN LUTHER KING, JR., NOBEL: *"Rarely do we find men who willingly engage in hard, solid thinking. There is almost a universal request for easy answers and half-baked solutions."*

EDWARD DE BONO, MD, PHD: *"Intelligence is something we are born with. Thinking is a skill that must be learned."*

MAHATMA GANDHI: *"Keep your thoughts positive because your thoughts become your words. Keep your words positive because your words become your behavior. Keep your behavior positive because your behavior becomes your habits. Keep your habits positive because your habits become your values. Keep your values positive because your values become your destiny."*

JOHN ELIOT: *"Thinking is a habit, and like any other habit, it can be changed; it just takes effort and repetition."*

WILLIAM JAMES, MD: *"A great many people think they are thinking when they are merely rearranging their prejudices."*

WARREN BUFFETT: *"There is nothing like writing to force you to think and get your thoughts straight."*

ANNE MORROW LINDBERGH: *"I must write it all out, at any cost. Writing is thinking. It is more than living, it is being conscious of living."*

JOHN SPENCE: *"Sometimes you need to distance yourself to see things clearly."*

STEVE JOBS: *"Don't be trapped by dogma—which is living with the results of other people's thinking."*

PROVERBS 4:23: *"Keep thy heart with all diligence: for out of it are the issues of life."*

MARIANNE WILLIAMSON: *"The truth is you are responsible for what you think, because it is only at this level that you can exercise choice."*

LUTHER BURBANK: *"It is well for people who think, to change their minds occasionally in order to keep them clean."*

THOMAS EDISON: *"The best thinking has been done in solitude. The worst has been done in turmoil."*

CLARENCE DARROW: *"If you lose the power to laugh, you lose the power to think."*

HANS CHRISTIAN ANDERSEN: *"It is the power of thought that gives man power over nature."*

PLATO: *"Thinking is the soul talking with itself."*

Similar: reasoning, considering, reflecting, cogitating, deliberating
Opposite: vacuousness, unconsciousness, incapacitation, comatose, braindead

Time. (1) Measuring motion in the fourth dimension. (2) Experiencing past, present, and future. (3) An inherent principle in the cause-and-effect universe. *Popular or Heart-Based Usage: (1) Chronos. [or 'Linear Time.'] (2) Kairos. [or 'God's Time.'] (3) The Grim Reaper. (4) Knowing the Wheel in the Sky. (5) Taking laps around the sun. (6) 'Days are numbers.' (7) Punching the clock. (8) Living in 'Space-time.' (9) Holding back the years. (10) 'Hurry up and wait.' (11) 'A watched pot never boils.' (12) Being put in the penalty box. (13) Being in Time Out. (14) 'Time flies.' (15) 'Life begins.' (16) The Power of Now.*

ECKHART TOLLE: *"The more you are focused on time—past and future—the more you miss the Now, the most precious thing there is."*

FRIEDRICH NIETZSCHE: *"When one has a great deal to put into it, a day has a hundred pockets."*

ELEANOR ROOSEVELT: *"Yesterday is history. Tomorrow is a mystery. Today is a gift, that's why we call it 'the Present.'"*

DOGEN ZENJI: *"It is believed by most that time passes; in actual fact, it stays where it is."*

CHARLES BUXTON: *"You will never 'find' time for anything. If you want time, you must make it."*

MICHAEL ALTSHULER: *"The bad news is time flies. The good news is you're the pilot."*

ALBERT EINSTEIN, PHD, NOBEL: *"The only reason for time is so that everything doesn't happen at once."*

JOHN WOODEN: *"It takes time to create excellence. If it could be done quickly, more people would do it."*

WAYNE DYER: *"Stop acting as if life is a rehearsal. Live this day as if it were your last. The past is over and gone. The future is not guaranteed."*

WILLIAM SHAKESPEARE: *"I wasted time, and now doth time waste me."*

CARL JUNG, MD: *"The privilege of a lifetime is to become who you truly are."*

MILES DAVIS: *"Man, sometimes it takes you a long time to sound like yourself."*

BRUCE LEE: *"If you love life, don't waste time, for time is what life is made of."*

LEONARDO DA VINCI: *"Time stays long enough for anyone who will use it."*

THEOPHRASTUS: *"Time is the most valuable thing a man can spend."*

DANTE ALIGHIERI: *"The wisest are most annoyed at the loss of time."*

GEOFFREY CHAUCER: *"The lyf so short, the craft so long to lerne."*

PROVERB: *"Your time is the greatest gift you can give someone."*

PABLO PICASSO: *"It takes a very long time to become young."*

BENJAMIN FRANKLIN: *"You may delay, but time will not."*

MAX FRISCH: *"Time does not change us. It just unfolds us."*

JOAN DIDION: *"Time is the school in which we learn."*

Similar: chronology, period, interval, passage, duration, tenure, spell, stretch, era, epoch
Opposite: void, nothingness, instant, beginning, zero point, intention

Tolerant. (1) Granting respect and peaceful coexistence to others having different backgrounds or viewpoints. (2) Maintaining a willingness to listen and learn. *Popular or Heart-Based Usage: (1) Being open-minded. (2) Being accepting of others. (3) Taking a laissez-faire approach. (4) Being easy-going. (5) 'Kum-ba-yah' togetherness. (6) Being cool with other people. (7) 'No worries.' (8) 'I'm down with that.' (9) 'No biggie.' (10) 'The more the merrier.' (11) 'No problem.' (12) 'I'm OK, you're OK.' (13) 'Live and let live.'*

ROBERT GREEN INGERSOLL: *"Tolerance is giving to every other human being every right that you claim for yourself."*

PERVEZ MUSHARRAF: *"Islam teaches tolerance, not hatred; universal brotherhood, not enmity; peace, and not violence."*

HELEN KELLER: *"The highest result of education is tolerance."*

GEORGE ELIOT: *"The responsibility of tolerance lies with those who have the wider vision."*

SIMON WIESENTHAL, HON. PHD: *"Human rights is the only ideology that deserves to survive."*

JOHN F. KENNEDY: *"Tolerance implies no lack of commitment to one's own beliefs. Rather it condemns the oppression or persecution of others."*

MARTIN LUTHER KING, JR., NOBEL: *"We may have all come on different ships, but we're in the same boat now."*

JUSTICE LOUIS BRANDEIS: *"Neutrality is at times a graver sin than belligerence."*

PEW RESEARCH CENTER/THE HINDU: *"Also, for most Hindus, religious tolerance was not just a civic virtue but also a religious value, with 80% of them stating that respecting other religions was an integral aspect of 'being Hindu.'"*

NEAL A. MAXWELL: *"Today, in place of some traditionally shared values is a demanding conformity pushed, ironically, by those who will eventually not tolerate those who once tolerated them."*

MARY BAKER EDDY: *"I would no more quarrel with a man because of his religion than I would because of his art."*

SHAFI MUSADDIQUE: *"Toledo may be monolithic in its Catholic population but it retains its deep seated love affair with 'Convivencia,' loosely translated as coexistence and closely linked to the idea of living and learning together."*

MADALYN MURRAY O'HAIR: *"I feel that everyone who wants to say anything, do anything, should be able to say anything or do anything, within the limits of not hurting another person."*

GEORGE CARLIN: *"Political correctness is America's newest form of intolerance."*

MARCUS AURELIUS: *"Be tolerant with others and strict with yourself."*

EPICTETUS: *"All religions must be tolerated—for every man must get to heaven in his own way."*

Similar: accepting, granting, enduring, allowing, concurring, forbearing, patient
Opposite: resisting, prohibiting, proscribing, averse, rejecting, attacking

Trauma. [See also **Overwhelm, Stress, Subconscious**] (1) Experiencing a sudden or inescapably stressful event which overwhelms your ability to cope, either physically or emotionally. (2) Experiencing a partial or full shutdown of conscious mental processes. (3) Experiencing an incident of severe physical injury or emotional distress which may be unresolved long after the event. *Popular or Heart-Based Usage: (1) Sensory overload. (2) System shutdown. (3) Feeling gob-smacked. (4) Rendered speechless. (5) Being in shock. (6) Passing out. (7) Blacking out. (8) Going 'in and out.' (9) Not all there. (10) Whomped upside the head. (11) Hearing tweetie birds. (12) Having a concussion. (13) Getting your bell rung. (14) Getting crowned. (15) Seeing stars. (16) Going tilt. (17) All shook up. (18) Being assaulted. (19) Being a battered soul. (20) Being raped. (21) Feeling deeply betrayed. (22) Going numb. (23) Being stupefied. (24) Seeing your life pass before your eyes. (25) Short-circuiting/shorting out. (26) Being incapacitated. (27) Losing consciousness. (28) Experiencing PTSD. (29) Getting stuck in the (past) event. (30) Wanting to deny it happened. (31) 'Shock and denial.' (32) Trying to block it out. (33) Trying to compartmentalize. (34) Incomplete memories. (35) Having flashbacks.*

RICHARD PETTY: *"I closed my eyes, held my breath and then everything went black."*

LINCOLN STOREY: *"Trauma is an epic overwhelming event or situation, physical or emotional, which can result in a very harmful and continuing fixation of your attention. It is the continuing gap where words have not yet been found."*

ANNE GRANT, LCSW: *"Just as the body goes into shock after a physical trauma, so does the human psyche go into shock after the impact of a major loss."*

STEPHEN PORGES, PHD: *"Trauma compromises our ability to engage with others by replacing patterns of connection with patterns of protection."*

ELIZABETH A. STANLEY, PHD: *"Although our thinking brains tend to consider chronic stress, shock trauma, developmental trauma, and relational trauma to be different things, they all create the same effects in the mind-body system."*

BESSEL VAN DER KOLK, MD: *"As long as the trauma is not resolved, the stress hormones that the body secretes to protect itself keep circulating, and the defensive movements and emotional responses keep getting replayed."*

JUDITH L. HERMAN, MD: *"After a traumatic experience, the human system of self-preservation seems to go onto permanent alert, as if the danger might return at any moment."*

OSHO: *"Unless the original experience can be brought into the light, the pain will always return."*

JENNIFER ASHTON, MD: *"People who have gone through trauma need help with logistics in the short term."*

DREW PINSKY, MD: *"Trauma survivors have a deficiency in their capacity to regulate emotions—they're too prolonged and too intense and too negative."*

CARL JUNG, MD: *"Man's task is to become conscious of the contents that press upward from the unconscious."*

Trauma. *(continued)*

SIGMUND FREUD, MD: *"Unexpressed emotions will never die. They are buried alive and will come forward later in uglier ways."*

MARIA POPOVA: *"The very thing we come to dread after experiencing trauma—close contact with other people—is also the thing we most need to regain psycho-emotional solidity and begin healing."*

APA DICTIONARY: *"Repetition compulsion: in psychoanalytic theory, an unconscious need to reenact early traumas in the attempt to overcome or master them."*

PSYCHCENTRAL.COM: *"Repetition compulsion is when you unconsciously desire to reenact earlier trauma...It occurs when you repeat traumatic behaviors from your past, even when you know it's not good for you."*

DR. JOE DISPENZA: *"The conscious mind may be in the present, but the subconscious mind-body is living in the past."*

D. EARL JOHNSTON: *"Emotions arise from the subconscious as default behavior patterns, and they can be transformed by awareness, conscious beliefs, and repetition."*

HARVEY MACKAY: *"Give your subconscious a chance to work by turning your brain off from time to time. Don't focus on work on solving problems constantly."*

FRANCINE SHAPIRO, PHD (FOUNDER, EMDR): *"Unprocessed memories not only can intensify our sensations and emotional responses, they can also prevent us from feeling."*

CANDACE BEEBE PERT, PHD: *"Your body and your mind are not separate, and we cannot treat one without the other."*

DANIEL KAHNEMAN, MD, NOBEL: *"You think with your body, not with your brain."*

ANTONIO DAMASIO, MD, PHD, HONDA PRIZE: *"We are not thinking machines that feel; rather, we are feeling machines that think."*

BESSEL VAN DER KOLK, MD: *"Trauma victims cannot recover until they become familiar with and befriend the sensations in their bodies. Being frightened means that you live in a body that is always on guard."*

JILL BOLTE TAYLOR, PHD: *"Just like children, emotions heal when they are heard and validated."*

PETER A. LEVINE, PHD: *"The paradox of trauma is that it has both the power to destroy and also the power to transform and resurrect."*

Similar: injury, blow, shock, overwhelm, suffering, incapacitation, restimulation
Opposite: blessing, comfort, favor, reconsideration, reconsolidation, reintegration, ease

Trolling. Delivering a comment or question designed to provoke, insult, or create doubt. *Popular or Heart-Based Usage: (1) Baiting someone. (2) Messing with someone. (3) Jerking someone's chain. (4) Getting inside someone's head. (5) Drawing someone out. (6) Getting a rise out of someone. (7) Getting in a dig. (8) Triggering someone. (9) Striking a nerve. (10) Cutting someone to the quick. (11) Drawing blood with a remark. (12) 'So you're a little touchy about that, eh?'*

HENRIK IBSEN: *"To live is to war with trolls."*

OSCAR WILDE: *"Don't feed the trolls; nothing fuels them so much."*

PETER MCWILLIAMS: *"Keep your goals away from the trolls."*

ROB MANUEL: *"Trolling taps into people's desire to poke fun, make trouble and cause annoyance."*

GAEL GREENE: *"The ego is that ugly little troll that lives underneath the bridge your mind and your heart."*

TINA FEY: *"To say I'm an overrated troll, when you have never even seen me guard a bridge, is patently unfair."*

DANE COOK: *"Trolls look for reasons to hate but really what they are mad at is the fact they are not included in anything ever."*

KEVIN BIEGEL: *"I think my generation has grown up knowing that you don't pay attention to trolls because trollin's what they do."*

ANDIE MACDOWELL: *"I try not to respond to trolls. I've learned blocking. If anybody is truly mean to me, or says something arrogant—don't respond, you'll only empower them. If you give them anything! So I'll block 'em. Or, if someone's annoying, but yet I still kind of like them, I mute them. Because they don't know! So then, it still looks like we're connected, but I don't have to listen."*

JOHNNY MCGREW: *"A troll is a saboteur looking to hijack your train of thought and make it their own."*

J. K. ROWLING, OBE, CH: *"Anyone can speak Troll; all you have to do is point and grunt."*

MAXIME LEGACE: *"Your attention has value. Don't give it away."*

MARK TWAIN: *"It is better to keep your mouth closed and let people think you are a fool than to open it and remove all doubt."*

Similar: insulting, inflaming, provoking, digging, probing, criticism, sarcasm
Opposite: approving, endorsing, supporting, promoting, kind

Trustworthy. Serving reliably and responsibly in someone else's interests. *Popular or Heart-Based Usage: (1) Always being dependable. (2) Always having someone's back. (3) Being true blue. (4) Keeping a confidence. (5) Inspiring a gut feeling of certainty. (6) Being a stand-up person. (7) Being a true performer. (8) Being a 'go to' resource. (9) Doing what is right and responsible. (10) Always keeping your word. (11) Standing by your promises. (12) Keeping it all between the lines. (13) Having a solid inner compass. (14) 'Your word is good.' (15) Being 'a rock' for someone. (16) Always getting it done.*

PROVERB: *"Not everyone who smiles at you is your friend."*
WILLIAM SHAKESPEARE: *"Love all, trust few, do wrong to no one."*
SAYING: *"Always trust your gut. It knows what your head hasn't figured out yet."*
HARRY EMERSON FOSDICK: *"No virtue is more universally accepted as proof of good character than trustworthiness."*
D. EARL JOHNSTON: *"It is a special moment, a magical moment, when we know that a child trusts us. It is a sacred moment."*
PROVERB: *"Trust takes years to build, seconds to break, and forever to rebuild."*
WILLIAM BLAKE: *"A truth that's told with bad intent beats all the lies you can invent."*
STEPHEN KING: *"The trust of the innocent is the liar's most useful tool."*
GEORGE ELIOT: *"There are men whose presence infuses trust and reverence."*
CONFUCIUS: *"Be loyal and trustworthy. Do not befriend anyone who is lower than you in this regard."*
HENRY L. STIMSON: *"The only way to make a man trustworthy is to trust him."*
GISELE BUNDCHEN: *"The more you trust your intuition, the more empowered you become, the stronger you become, and the happier you become."*
DR. JOYCE BROTHERS: *"Trust your hunches. They're usually based on facts filed away just below the conscious level."*
GOETHE: *"As soon as you trust yourself, you will know how to live."*
JEAN-JACQUES ROUSSEAU: *"Trust your heart rather than your head."*
PROVERB: *"To be trusted is a greater compliment than to be loved."*
THE 12 SCOUT LAWS: *"#1. A Scout is trustworthy."*
SAYING: *"God has perfect timing. Trust Him."*

Similar: reliable, dependable, steady, faithful, accountable, responsible
Opposite: ingenuous, suspicious, shifty, compromised, corrupt, vacillating

Truth. Regarding the essential or material facts and relevance of a matter. *Popular or Heart-Based Usage: (1) Knowing what matters. (2) Finding out. (3) Getting to the bottom of it. (4) 'Just the facts, Ma'am.' (5) Coming clean about something. (6) Getting down to brass tacks. (7) Peeling back the layers of the onion. (8) Going beyond fact-checking. (9) Separating the wheat from the chaff. (10) Making sure the story holds water. (11) 'Does that really ring true?' (12) 'No crosses count!' (13) 'Inquiring minds want to know.' (14) Keeping it all on the level. (15) 'Unvarnished.' (16) Saying it straight.*

HARLAN HOWARD: *"A country song is three chords and the truth."*

CHARLES H. SPURGEON: *"A lie can travel halfway around the world and back while the truth is putting on its boots."*

WILL ROGERS: *"Income tax has made more liars out of the American people than golf has."*

ADLAI STEVENSON: *"I offer my opponents a bargain: if they will stop telling lies about us, I will stop telling the truth about them."*

MARK TWAIN: *"There are three kinds of lies: lies, damned lies, and statistics."*

BAYARD RUSTIN: *"To be afraid is to behave as if the truth were not true."*

HENRY DAVID THOREAU: *"Rather than love, than money, than fame, give me truth."*

THOMAS JEFFERSON: *"It is error alone which needs the support of government. Truth can stand by itself."*

ARTHUR SCHOPENHAUER: *"All truth passes through three stages. First, it is ridiculed. Second, it is violently opposed. Third, it is accepted as being self-evident."*

ELISABETH KUBLER-ROSS, MD: *"The truth does not need to be defended."*
Copyright: Elisabeth Kubler-Ross Family Limited Partnership

OPRAH WINFREY: *"What I know for sure is that speaking your truth is the most powerful weapon we all have."*

NAT RICH: *"I learned there is a difference between 'true' and 'truth.' True is what is provable by way of observation, and truth is your opinion of what you think happened."*

IGNATIUS OF LOYOLA: *"Truth always ends in victory; it is not unassailable, but invincible."*

OSHO: *"Truth is not something outside to be discovered, it is something inside to be realized."*

ROSSLYN CHAPEL: *"Wine is strong. The king is stronger. Women are stronger still, but Truth conquers all."*

DR. PHIL MCGRAW: *"There is no truth, only perception of it."*

ALBERT GORE, JR., NOBEL: *"Climate change is an inconvenient truth."*

WILL ROGERS: *"A remark generally hurts in proportion to its truth."*

ALFRED, LORD TENNYSON: *"A lie which is half a truth is ever the blackest of lies."*

AL PACINO (OLIVER STONE): *"The eyes, Chico, they never lie."*

Truth. *(continued)*

GEORGE CLOONEY: *"One thing you learn selling women's shoes is that all women lie about their shoe size. And I mean **all** women."*

MARK TWAIN (attributed): *"He did not lie, he forgot to tell the truth."*

JOHNNY MCGREW: *"If lying is pre-varication, then the cover-up should be called post-varication."*

JEAN-JACQUES ROUSSEAU: *"There are always four sides to a story: your side, their side, the truth, and what really happened."*

JOSH BILLINGS: *"As scarce as truth is, the supply has always been in excess of the demand."*

THOMAS SHADWELL: *"Words may be false and full of art; Sighs are the natural language of the heart."*

MARTHA GRAHAM: *"Movement never lies. It is a barometer telling the state of the soul's weather to all who can read it."*

NOAM CHOMSKY, PHD: *"Nobody is going to pour truth into your brain. It's something you have to find out for yourself."*

THOMAS HOBBES: *"Hell is truth seen too late."*

RENÉ DESCARTES: *"If you would be a real seeker after truth, it is necessary that at least once in your life you doubt, as far as possible, all things."*

LINCOLN STOREY: *"Having only a few important facts can miss the real story. The Truth demands it all."*

PAM GREGORY: *"Always drop into your heart to find your own truth."*

TODD STOCKER: *"You should have feelings based on truth but you should not have truth based on feelings."*

SIOUX PROVERB: *"Speak truth in humility to all people. Only then can you be a true man."*

MIGUEL DE CERVANTES: *"Truth will rise above falsehood, as oil above water."*

RUSSIAN PROVERB: *"When it happens to you, you'll know it's true."*

EDWARD ABBEY: *"Better a cruel truth than a comfortable delusion."*

HENRY DAVID THOREAU: *"Truths and roses have thorns about them."*

DOUGLAS JOHNSTON: *"The greatest gift you can possess is an inquiring mind."*

MAHATMA GANDHI: *"Truth never damages a cause that is just."*

PROVERB: *"The truth can be a whisper, while a lie has to yell."*

WILLIAM SHAKESPEARE: *"To thine own self be true."*

Similar: facts, authenticity, genuineness, correctness, exactitude, tautology, reality
Opposite: falsehood, misrepresentation, dishonesty, deception, misdirection

Victim. Being a targeted or harmed party in an accident, crime, situation, or event. *Popular or Heart-Based Usage: (1) Being a patsy. (2) Getting the short end. (3) Being the mark. (4) Getting pushed around. (5) Getting picked on. (6) Having a target on your back. (7) Getting played. (8) Carrying a chip on your shoulder. (9) Getting screwed over. (10) Wearing a chalk outline. (11) Feeling sorry for yourself. (12) 'Poor little me!' (13) 'Why me?' (14) Subconsciously seeking a perpetrator. (15) Constantly re-living the event.*

PETER MCWILLIAMS: *"Definition of a victim: a person to whom life happens."*

NORA EPHRON: *"Above all, be the heroine of your life, not the victim."*

TOM HIDDLESTON: *"When people don't like themselves very much, they have to make up for it. The classic bully was actually a victim first."*

LADY GAGA: *"There really is no difference between the bully and the victim."*

ECKHART TOLLE: *"When you complain, you make yourself into a victim."*

KENDRICK LAMAR: *"My moms always told me, 'How long you gonna play the victim?' I can say I'm mad and I hate everything, but nothing really changes until I change myself."*

MAYA ANGELOU: *"I've learned that you shouldn't go through life with a catcher's mitt on both hands; you need to be able to throw something back."*

PAM GREGORY: *"When we are in victim mode, we will always attract bullies; however, when we are in empowerment mode, it simply does not happen."*

FRANCIS OF ASSISI: *"No one is called to be an enemy, all are your benefactors, and no one does you harm. You have no enemy except yourselves."*

JOHNNY MCGREW: *"Conspiracies may be true or not true, but believing in them only makes us victims. Let others point fingers, just strengthen your game."*

D. EARL JOHNSTON: *"Few in severe distress have arrived there without asking: 'Why me?' And nearby, hopeful angels have whispered back: 'Of course you. Of course now. Now is your time to show up and to shine.'"*

LINCOLN STOREY: *"Victimhood ends with looking forward, not back. Victimhood ends with a new start and gratitude."*

R. BUCKMINSTER FULLER: *"We are called to be architects of the future, not its victims."*

RICHARD BACH: *"If it's never our fault, we can't take responsibility for it. If we can't take responsibility for it, we'll always be its victim."*

STEVE MARABOLI: *"Beware of perpetrators in disguise…Some people set fires wherever they go, and have mastered the art of playing the burn victim."*

PAM GREGORY: *"Life is NOT happening to us. It is happening FOR us."*

JOEL OSTEEN: *"Be a victor not a victim."*

Similar: prey, dupe, sufferer, target, mark, gopher, patsy
Opposite: sovereign, mastermind, cause, instigator, perpetrator, initiator

Vision. (1) Having insight about future outcomes despite current unknowns. (2) Having clarity about the foundations for success. *Popular or Heart-Based Usage: (1) Having a plan. (2) Seeing where something is going. (3) Having second sight. (4) Seeing around corners. (5) Knowing the way. (6) Going with your dreams. (7) Ignoring the noise. (8) Creating order out of chaos. (9) Having your own private blueprint. (10) Taking the longer view. (11) Seeing the bigger picture. (12) 'Vision before provision.' (13) 'Using a telescope not a microscope.' (14) Seeing several moves ahead. (15) Playing 5D chess.*

JONATHAN SWIFT: *"Vision is the art of seeing the invisible."*

RUMI: *"Everyone sees the unseen in proportion to the clarity of his heart."*

ANTOINE DE SAINT-EXUPERY: *"It is only with the heart that one can see rightly; what is essential is invisible to the eye."*

WOODROW WILSON, PHD, NOBEL, PRESIDENT: *"You are not here merely to make a living. You are here in order to enable the world to live more amply, with greater vision, with a finer spirit of hope and achievement. You are here to enrich the world, and you impoverish yourself if you forget the errand."*

MICHELANGELO: *"The greatest danger for most of us is not that our aim is too high and we miss it, but that it is too low and we reach it."*

THE BEATITUDES: *"Blessed are the pure in heart; for they shall see God."*

USHER: *"You've got to be willing to have vision and foresight that leads you to an incredible end."*

NAPOLEON HILL: *"Hold a picture of yourself long and steadily enough in your mind's eye, and you will be drawn toward it."*

DALAI LAMA: *"In order to carry a positive action we must develop here a positive vision."*

ARIANNA HUFFINGTON: *"Live life as if everything is rigged in your favor."*

PETER F. DRUCKER: *"They see the pattern, understand the order, experience the vision."*

WILLIAM BLAKE: *"What is now proved was once only imagined."*

THOMAS EDISON: *"Vision without execution is hallucination."*

PROVERB: *"'I see' said the blind man, who couldn't see at all."*

FRANK GAINES: *"Only he who can see the invisible can do the impossible."*

D. EARL JOHNSTON: *"A short list of invisible things which are part of our daily lives: Gravity, radio waves, X-rays, the past, the future, our emotions, our values, our next breath, and God."*

CARL JUNG, MD: *"Who looks outside, dreams; who looks inside, awakes."*

SETH GODIN, BS, MBA: *"Invisible doesn't mean unimportant."*

PAUL GAUGUIN: *"I shut my eyes in order to see."*

Similar: foresight, prescience, precognition, planning, anticipation
Opposite: shortsightedness, improvidence, indifference, blindness

Voice. (1) Articulating your message in thought, speech, and song. *Popular or Heart-Based Usage: (1) Listening to your thoughts/self-talk. (2) Hearing the soundtrack of your mind. (3) Thinking out loud. (4) Sharing your views. (5) Spreading the news. (6) Taking the mike, bullhorn, or podium. (7) Clearing your throat. (8) 'From your lips to God's ears.' (9) Being heard.*

JULIE ANDREWS: *"Your voice is your calling card. It's the first thing people hear, and it tells them everything about who you are."*

ECKHART TOLLE: *"The first glimpse of awareness is recognizing there is a voice in your head."*

SOPHIE SCOTT: *"Finding your voice, to speak up for yourself and others, is vital... The process of finding your voice begins with recognizing the beliefs you hold and how they impact your use of your voice today."*

MILES DAVIS: *"Man, sometimes it takes you a long time to sound like yourself."*

STEVE JOBS: *"Don't let the noise of others' opinions drown out your own inner voice."*

ROBIN SHARMA: *"Speak your truth, even if your voice shakes."*

JOHN 1:1: *"In the beginning was the Word, and the Word was with God, and the Word was God."*

DEUTERONOMY 28:2: *"And all these blessings shall come on thee, and overtake thee, if thou shalt hearken unto the voice of the Lord thy God."*

D. EARL JOHNSTON: *"She was the one from the moment I realized that the voice in my head and the calm in her words were one and the same."*

PEGGY O'MARA: *"The way we talk to our children becomes their inner voice."*

LLOYD BLANKFEIN: *"Ambition is your inner voice that tells you, you can, and should, strive to go beyond your circumstances in life."*

DR. JOHN: *"When the voice and the vision on the inside is more profound, and more clear than all the opinions on the outside, you've begun to master your life."*

ALLYN FONTAINE: *"Changes come along in life. When our voice drops an octave or two, people are silently drawn to our confidence and calm; and when it rises to a whine, people quickly sense there's a problem."*

BROOKE AXTELL: *"Please reach out for help, your voice will save you."*

SOGYAL RINPOCHE: *"Two people have been living in you all your life. One is the ego—garrulous, demanding, hysterical, calculating—the other is the hidden spiritual being, whose still voice of wisdom you have only rarely heard or attended to—you have uncovered in yourself your own wise guide."*

ALBERT EINSTEIN, PHD, NOBEL: *"Be a voice not an echo."*

PROVERB: *"Listen to the still small voice of God."*

SAYING: *"Be the voice of those who have none."*

Similar: speech, utterance, expression, tone, cadence, twang, accent, song
Opposite: silence, whisper, mouthing, mute, speechless, quiet

Vulnerability. [See also **Risk**] (1) Demonstrating a willingness to being looked upon unfavorably while in the pursuit of an interest. (2) Being exposed to embarrassment, harm, or a loss of control through a disregard for your defenses. *Popular or Heart-Based Usage: (1) Saying the quiet part out loud. (2) Being naïve. (3) Revealing your personal stuff. (4) Wearing your heart on your sleeve. (5) Setting yourself up as a patsy. (6) Having chinks in your armor. (7) Putting a target on your back. (8) Baring your heart. (9) Blurting out the truth. (10) Taking personal risks. (11) Acknowledging your flaws. (12) 'Come what may.' (13) Making your intentions known. (14) Putting yourself out there.*

ASHTON KUTCHER: *"Vulnerability is the essence of romance."*

BRENE BROWN, MSW, PHD: *"Through my research, I have found that vulnerability is the glue that holds relationships together. It's the magic sauce."*

JAMES REDFIELD: *"We have to transcend our own negativity and vulnerability and work from our own inner security."*

LINCOLN STOREY: *"There is both vulnerability and respect in turning to an old friend and asking: 'We've known each other for a long time, would you level with me?'"*

ERMA BOMBECK: *"It takes a lot of courage to show your dreams to someone else."*

AARON DOUGHTY: *"Vulnerability is the ability to go into the wound."*

M. SCOTT PECK: *"There can be no vulnerability without risk; there can be no community without vulnerability; there can be no peace, and ultimately no life, without community."*

STEVE JOBS: *"Remembering that you are going to die is the best way I know to avoid the trap of thinking you have something to lose."*

VICTORIA PRATT: *"You show your vulnerability through your relationships, and those feelings are your soft spot. You need to have a soft spot."*

SOPHIA LOREN: *"Mistakes are part of the dues one pays for a full life."*

SONIA SOTOMAYOR: *"I have ventured to write more intimately about my personal life than is customary for a member of the Supreme Court, and with that candor comes a measure of vulnerability."*

D. EARL JOHNSTON: *"We can be our most vulnerable when we want to believe."*

BRENE BROWN, MSW, PHD: *"Vulnerability is not weakness; it's our greatest measure of courage."*

AMIT GOSWAMI, PHD: *"When we are aware of our inner growth potential yet have no pretensions about ourselves, when we are vulnerable, then we can change."*

Similar: susceptibility, exposure, openness, gullibility, amenableness, predisposition
Opposite: indomitability, invulnerability, invincibility

Wisdom. Having the experience, discernment, and insight to know how best to live and to engage with others. *Popular or Heart-Based Usage: (1) Knowing what really matters. (2) Knowing what's best for everyone. (3) Looking at things from 100,000 feet. (4) Having been around the block a few times. (5) Seeing around corners. (6) Knowing the moral high ground. (7) Understanding people and motives. (8) Being on the right side of history. (9) Speaking with your true voice. (10) Having personal gravitas. (11) Having good judgment. (12) Choosing your words carefully. (13) Knowing what you're doing.*

SENECA: *"No man was ever wise by chance."*

OSHO: *"Wisdom is experience, not information."*

ADAGE: *"Once you stop chasing the wrong things, the right things catch you."*

WILLIAM JAMES, MD: *"The art of being wise is the art of knowing what to overlook."*

MAYA ANGELOU: *"I'm considered wise, and sometimes I see myself as knowing. Most of the time, I see myself as wanting to know. And I see myself as a very interested person. I've never been bored in my life."*

GEORGE ELIOT: *"What do we live for, if not to make life less difficult for others?"*

AFRICAN PROVERB: *"If you want to go fast, go alone. If you want to go far, go together."*

STEVEN WRIGHT: *"Experience is something you don't get until just after you need it."*

LYNN WYATT: *"A man should be sure of two things before he marries—that she has a good relationship with her father, plus a good hobby or interest all of her own."*

IMMANUEL KANT: *"Science is organized knowledge. Wisdom is organized life."*

MICHEL DE MONTAIGNE: *"The most certain sign of wisdom is cheerfulness."*

JOEL OSTEEN: *"Wisdom is the ability to discern and understand motives."*

ALFRED, LORD TENNYSON: *"Knowledge comes, but wisdom lingers."*

ARISTOPHANES: *"The wise learn many things from their enemies."*

PROVERBS 9:10: *"Fear of the Lord is the beginning of wisdom."*

OSHO: *"Wisdom comes from the heart, it is not of the intellect."*

LEO TOLSTOY: *"The sole meaning of life is to serve humanity."*

D. EARL JOHNSTON: *"God knows we are all sophomores."*

AUGUSTINE OF HIPPO: *"Doubt is the origin of wisdom."*

PROVERB: *"Forget the mistake. Remember the lesson."*

GOETHE: *"Common sense is the genius of humanity."*

TODD STOCKER: *"The wise pause; the foolish react."*

DAVYD FARRELL: *"5D consciousness is Heaven."*

SAYING: *"Listen to the still small voice of God."*

EURIPIDES: *"Cleverness is not wisdom."*

Similar: discernment, acumen, judgment, prudence, circumspection, awareness
Opposite: ignorance, imprudence, thoughtlessness, impetuousness, rashness

Wonder. Contemplating reasons, possibilities, and an understanding of new things. *Popular or Heart-Based Usage: (1) Trying to wrap your head around something. (2) Spit-balling. (3) Being a propeller-head. (4) Re-defining a problem. (5) Throwing out the textbooks. (6) Going back to the drawing board. (7) Thinking outside the box. (8) Putting your heads together. (9) Getting hypothetical. (10) Brainstorming. (11) Calling in a think tank. (12) Floating an idea. (13) Tapping your index finger against your cheek. (14) Gazing into the future. (15) Thinking about future 'what-ifs.' (16) 'Behold!'*

GREEK PROVERB: *"Wonder is the beginning of wisdom."*

WALT DISNEY: *"If you can dream it, you can do it."*

SOCRATES: *"All thinking begins with wondering."*

ALBERT EINSTEIN, PHD, NOBEL: *"The most beautiful thing we can experience is the mysterious. It is the source of all true art and science. He to whom the emotion is a stranger, who can no longer pause to wonder and stand wrapped in awe, is as good as dead; his eyes are closed."*

JOSÉ ORTEGA Y GASSET: *"To be surprised, to wonder, is to begin to understand."*

GERRY SPENCE: *"I would rather have a mind opened by wonder than one closed by belief."*

ALBERT EINSTEIN, PHD, NOBEL: *"Be a loner. That gives you time to wonder."*

LINUS PAULING, MD (2X NOBEL): *"Satisfaction of one's curiosity is one of the greatest sources of happiness in life."*

RITA LEVI-MONTALCINI, MD, NOBEL: *"Progress depends on our brain. The most important part of our brain, that which is neocortical, must be used to help others and not just to make discoveries."*

BILL MAHER: *"Curious people are interesting people. I wonder why that is."*

MARGARET MEAD: *"One of the oldest human needs is having someone to wonder where you are when you don't come home at night."*

RONALD REAGAN: *"Some people wonder all their lives if they've made a difference. The Marines don't have that problem."*

NEIL ARMSTRONG: *"Mystery creates wonder, and wonder is the basis of man's desire to understand."*

COLLEGE STUDENT: *"I wonder if a girl like Jane could ever fall for a guy like me."*

ROBERT FULGHUM: *"Be aware of wonder. Live a balanced life—learn some and think some and draw and paint and sing and dance and play and work every day some."*

SOCRATES: *"Wonder is the beginning of wisdom."*

Similar: curiosity, awe, fascination, engaging, inquisitiveness
Opposite: disinterest, disregard, dismissive, apathy, boredom

Worry. Experiencing agitation or distress about a pending outcome or result. *Popular or Heart-Based Usage: (1) Fretting. (2) Losing sleep. (3) Nail-biting. (4) Pacing back and forth. (5) Feeling unsettled. (6) Doing the Rosary. (7) Being on pins and needles. (8) 'Oif shpilkes.' (9) Having the agita. (10) Feeling angst. (11) 'But my concerns are much bigger than your concerns.' (12) Having someone rattle your cage. (13) Hearing someone drop a few nasty hints in your direction. (14) Focusing on nothing at all. (15) 'What you focus on expands.' (16) Borrowing trouble. (17) Trying to steer the future.*

> BENJAMIN FRANKLIN: *"Do not anticipate trouble, or worry about what may never happen. Keep in the sunlight."*
>
> SWEDISH PROVERB: *"Worry often gives a small thing a big shadow."*
>
> MARK TWAIN: *"Worrying is paying interest on a debt you might not even owe."*
>
> CORRIE TEN BOOM: *"Worry does not empty tomorrow of its sorrow, it empties today of its strength."*
>
> THOMAS LOCKE: *"What worries you, masters you."*
>
> ECKHART TOLLE: *"Worry means the mind is controlling you. Worry is always pointless. A solution never comes out of worry."*
>
> MYRON HENDRICKS: *"Regret and fear are twin thieves. They rob you of today."*
>
> GEORGE ELIOT: *"Trouble's made us kin."*
>
> MATTHEW 6:34: *"Sufficient unto the day is the evil thereof."*
>
> EPICTETUS: *"There is only one way to happiness and that is to cease worrying about things which are beyond the power of our will."*
>
> RALPH WALDO EMERSON: *"Sorrow looks back, worry looks around, faith looks up."*
>
> WILLIAM JAMES, MD: *"The sovereign cure for worry is prayer."*
>
> D. EARL JOHNSTON: *"Delegate your worries to someone else. Let God handle them."*
>
> SIR WINSTON CHURCHILL: *"Let our advance worrying become advance thinking and planning."*
>
> H. HILL MCALISTER: *"Ninety-five percent of the things you worry about never happen."*
>
> JOHNNY MCGREW: *"Worry never solved anything. Don't worry. Find something different to do. Get busy. Politicians do this all the time. They call it 'pivoting to pressing new issues.'"*
>
> EDGAR CAYCE: *"When you get to the place where you would worry, Stop and pray."*

Similar: apprehension, agitation, fretting, uneasiness, dread, fixation
Opposite: boldness, confidence, serenity, calm, peacefulness

Writing. Creating through the art and craft of printed words. *Popular or Heart-Based Usage: (1) Composing. (2) Combining words. (3) Honing and editing. (4) 'Writing is re-writing.' (5) Turning a phrase. (6) Creating new worlds. (7) Imagineering.*

WARREN BUFFETT: *"There is nothing like writing to force you to think and get your thoughts straight."*

ANNE MORROW LINDBERGH: *"I must write it all out, at any cost. Writing is thinking. It is more than living, it is being conscious of living."*

PEGGY NOONAN: *"It's all writing, and in a funny way, I don't think writers fully understand what they do, where it comes from. They just do it."*

GUSTAVE FLAUBERT: *"It's a delicious thing to write. To no longer be yourself but to move in an entire universe of your own creating."*

WILLIAM ZINSSER: *"Four basic premises of writing: clarity, brevity, simplicity, and humanity."*

ABRAHAM LINCOLN: *"Never signed and never delivered."* (Lincoln's practice of 'cooling off' in anger by writing a scathing letter to his adversary, but never sending it.)

DOUGLAS FAIRBANKS, JR.: *"Writing is 90 percent applying the seat of the pants to the seat of the chair."*

WILLIAM FAULKNER, PULITZER, NOBEL: *"In writing, you must kill all your darlings."*

HARPER LEE, PULITZER: *"Any writer worth his salt writes to please himself."*

ERNEST HEMINGWAY, PULITZER, NOBEL: *"No tears in the writer, no tears in the reader."*

JOSEPH JOUBERT: *"Music has seven letters, writing has twenty-six notes."*

PAT CONROY: *"One of the greatest gifts you can get as a writer is to be born into an unhappy family."*

R. BUCKMINSTER FULLER: *"There is nothing in a caterpillar that tells you it is going to be a butterfly."*

LINCOLN STOREY: *"Writing is sculpting with words, until there is no difference between the page and your mind's eye."*

ERNEST HEMINGWAY, PULITZER, NOBEL: *"There is nothing to writing. All you do is sit down at a typewriter and bleed."*

DARYL HALL: *"Songwriting is about making a very, very personal statement but yet saying it in a way that a lot of people can relate to it themselves. That's the secret of a good lyric. It's that universal intimacy."*

F. SCOTT FITZGERALD: *"Work like hell! I had 122 rejection slips before I sold a story."*

JOAN DIDION, PULITZER: *"There's a point where you go with what you've got. Or you don't go."*

Similar: penning, composing, scribbling, authoring
Opposite: hacking, cranking, grinding, blocking, doodling, AI

Yearning. Seeking a cherished goal of self-betterment. *Popular or Heart-Based Usage: (1) Going after your dreams. (2) Setting out on your path. (3) Lifting yourself up by the bootstraps. (4) Heeding your call. (5) Improving your lot in life. (6) Going for it.*

CHRISTOPHER MORLEY: *"There are three ingredients in the good life: learning, earning, and yearning."*

MARTIN LUTHER KING, JR., NOBEL: *"Oppressed people cannot remain oppressed forever. The yearning for freedom eventually manifests itself."*

MENACHEM MENDEL SCHNEERSON: *"When the soul is starved for nourishment, it lets us know with feelings of emptiness, anxiety, or yearning."*

JOHN OF THE CROSS, OCD: *"Yearning: It needs to hurt to be worthy of the word. Otherwise it is just wanting."*

MATT DAMON, BEN AFFLECK/'GOOD WILL HUNTING': *"I gotta go see about a girl."*

RODGERS & HAMMERSTEIN: *"Climb Ev'ry Mountain"* (Song)

STATUE OF LIBERTY: *"Give me your tired, your poor, Your huddled masses yearning to breathe free."*

JOSE ORTEGA Y GASSET: *"Life is a series of collisions with the future; it is not the sum of what we have been; it is what we yearn to be."*

CASEY KASEM: *"Keep your feet on the ground and keep reaching for the stars."*

Similar: longing, craving, hungering
Opposite: abhorrence, aversion, disinclination, goofing off, sloth

Zeal. Having conviction, energy, and enthusiasm in pursuit of a goal or belief. *Popular or Heart-Based Usage: (1) Climbing into the arena. (2) Grabbing the bull by the horns.*

PROVERB: *"The newest convert is often the greatest zealot."*

WILL ROGERS: *"A fanatic is always the fellow that is on the opposite side."*

SANTIAGO RAMON Y CAJAL: *"All outstanding work, in art as well as in science, results from immense zeal applied to a great idea."*

ARIANNA HUFFINGTON: *"Be a go-giver, not a go-getter."*

THEODORE ROOSEVELT, NOBEL: *"My hat's in the ring. The fight is on and I'm stripped to the buff."*

ALAN COHEN, MA: *"Teach yourself freedom with the same zeal that the world has taught you limits."*

GAUTAMA BUDDHA: *"Through zeal, knowledge is gotten; through lack of zeal, knowledge is lost."*

THOMAS FULLER: *"Zeal without knowledge is fire without light."*

CHARLES BUXTON: *"Experience shows that success is due less to ability than to zeal."*

Similar: enthusiasm, fervor, interest, conviction, focus, fanaticism
Opposite: boredom, disinterest, indifference, laziness, apathy

APPENDIX A
SELECTED MASTERS OF EMOTION

LAO TZU (b. ca. 571 BCE)
Ancient Chinese philosopher, writer, and founder of Taoism. A contemporary of Confucius, he is believed to have written the *Tao Te Ching*.

EPICTETUS (50 CE?–135 CE)
Born a slave and crippled by a slaveowner in western Turkey, he later found his way to Greece and Rome as a philosopher, and was granted his freedom during the reign of Emperor Nero as one of the premier Stoic philosophers.

RUMI (1207–73)
Persian poet, Islamic scholar, and Sufi mystic whose works have transcended national borders and multiple languages from Greece to Central Asia and India for over seven hundred years. His poetry has more recently attained best-selling status in the U.S.

LEONARDO DA VINCI (1452–1519)
Italian artist, architect, engineer, scientist, and inventor whose contributions across numerous fields helped to shape the Renaissance. He is regarded as one of the most capable and influential geniuses in history.

MIGUEL DE CERVANTES (1547–1616)
Soldier, novelist, and playwright who is widely revered as the greatest Spanish language writer in history. He is best known for *Don Quixote of La Mancha,* which continues to be heralded as one of the most impactful books ever written.

WILLIAM SHAKESPEARE (1564–1616)
English poet and playwright who is generally regarded as the finest writer and dramatist in history. His works and observations about life have been translated and performed in more languages than any other author.

JOHANN WOLFGANG VON GOETHE (1749–1832)
German-born poet, writer, scientist, and statesman who is widely regarded as one of the world's most-followed writers and observers of life.

SIMON BOLIVAR (1783–1830)
Born in Caracas, he led what are now Venezuela, Bolivia, Colombia, Ecuador, Peru, and Panama to independence from Spain. Known as *El Libertador*, he is remembered as an enduring continental icon across much of South America.

VICTOR HUGO (1802–85)

Prolific and beloved French writer and politician widely regarded as the finest novelist in French history, and leader of the Romantic Movement.

ABRAHAM LINCOLN (1809–65)

Pioneer, lawyer, politician, and statesman. His frontier challenges as a young man, his humility and humor, and his leadership during the difficult Civil War have endeared him to the world as among the greatest of American Presidents.

HENRY DAVID THOREAU (1817–62)

American poet, essayist, naturalist, and philosopher whose writings influenced generations of authors, artists, leaders, and public figures around the world.

WALT WHITMAN (1819–92)

Known as 'America's Poet' in the revered tradition of Homer, Virgil, Dante, and Shakespeare, his works have inspired many generations of writers and thinkers.

FYODOR DOSTOEVSKY (1821–81)

Russian writer, essayist, and journalist, his major works including *Crime and Punishment* and *The Brothers Karamazov* have been translated into more than 170 languages and have remained influential in philosophy and literature.

LEO TOLSTOY (1828–1910)

Russian writer nominated for nineteen Nobel Prizes; his novels include *War and Peace* and *Anna Karenina*. He is regarded as one of the greatest authors of all time.

MARK TWAIN (1835–1910)

Born in Missouri as Samuel Langhorne Clemens, he adopted his pen name as Mark Twain and is best known for *The Adventures of Tom Sawyer* and the *Adventures of Huckleberry Finn*. In expanding his international audience into Europe as a revered humorist and lecturer, he has been regarded as the 'Father of American Literature.'

MAHATMA GANDHI (1869–1948)

Hindu-born lawyer, civil rights activist, and nationalist who adopted non-violence in leading India to independence from British rule. He is revered as the 'Father of the Nation,' and a humanitarian rights legend.

SIR WINSTON CHURCHILL (1874–1965)

Soldier, writer, and statesman, he rose to lead Britain through World War II as one of the most influential world leaders of the twentieth century. He remains regarded by many as one of the most accomplished leaders in world history.

CARL JUNG, MD (1875–1961)

Swiss-born psychiatrist, a student of Sigmund Freud, and a prolific writer who is regarded as the founder of modern analytical psychology. His interests included major contributions in archaeology, literature, philosophy, and religious studies.

ALBERT EINSTEIN, PHD (1879–1955)

German-born developer of the theory of relativity. He won the Nobel Prize in 1921 and is widely acknowledged as one of the greatest physicists of all time. While known primarily as a scientist, he also contributed extensively as an observer of life and the human condition.

WILL ROGERS (1879–1935)

Born in modern-day Oklahoma as a Cherokee citizen, he self-educated as an entertainer, writer, and humorist. Appearing in over seventy films, hosting a weekly national radio show, and writing thousands of daily national newspaper columns for the *New York Times* over ten years, he became the first multi-media celebrity and one of the most beloved figures in American history.

HELEN KELLER (1880–1968)

Alabama-born author, political activist, and disability rights advocate who lost her sight at nineteen months. Through her teacher and tutor, Anne Sullivan, she developed a full ability to communicate and earned the first deaf-blind B.A. degree at Radcliffe College.

ELEANOR ROOSEVELT (1884–1962)

Political figure, public speaker, and civil rights activist, she served twelve years as First Lady of the United States, and significantly expanded, professionalized, and redefined the role during the World War II era. Her stature as unofficial 'First Lady of the World' extended long after her husband's death in 1945.

JOHN WOODEN (1910–2010)

Indiana native who became best known for coaching UCLA to a record ten NCAA basketball championships, he is revered as one of the most successful coaches in any sport. His guiding principles have been widely adopted in many walks of life.

MOTHER TERESA (1910–97)

North Macedonia-born nun and founder of the Missionaries of Charity operating in over 130 countries, she was awarded the 1979 Nobel Peace Prize.

ALBERT ELLIS, PHD (1913–2007)

A founder of both Rational Emotive Behavioral Therapy (REBT) and Cognitive Behavioral Therapy (CBT), he is widely regarded as one of the most influential psychotherapists of the twentieth century. His techniques and teachings continue in worldwide use.

NELSON MANDELA (1918–2013)

South African revolutionary and anti-apartheid activist. After being imprisoned for twenty-seven years, he became the first President of South Africa (1994–99) and the 'Father of the Country.' He was honored with the Nobel Peace Prize in 1993.

THICH NHAT HANH (1926–2022)

Vietnamese-born Buddhist monk, vegetarian, and peace activist who was exiled to France and the West for most of his adult life, including continuing studies at Princeton and Columbia. He published more than 130 books, including a hundred in English, regarding his observations on the human condition.

MAYA ANGELOU (1928–2014)

North Carolina-born African-American activist, writer, and entertainer who became known as an unofficial 'Poet Laureate' of America. Nominated for the Pulitzer Prize and a Tony Award, she also won three Grammy Awards.

MARTIN LUTHER KING, JR. (1929–68)

Georgia-born Baptist minister and foundational leader of the American civil rights movement whose extensive writings, speeches, and advocacy of non-violence earned him the Nobel Peace Prize in 1964 and the Presidential Medal of Freedom in 1977.

DESMOND TUTU (1931–2021)

South African-born cleric, theologian, and anti-apartheid civil rights activist who became the first black archbishop of Cape Town. An active writer, he earned over a hundred honorary degrees around the world and was awarded the 1984 Nobel Peace Prize.

DALAI LAMA (1940–present)

The fourteenth Dalai Lama is the exiled political leader of Tibet and is its continuing Buddhist spiritual leader. He was awarded the Nobel Peace Prize in 1989.

ECKHART TOLLE (1948–present)

German-born spiritual teacher and self-help author living in Canada. In distress at age twenty-nine, he experienced a spiritual transformation and began to write. Tolle's best-selling books, talks and videos are estimated to have reached over a hundred million people around the world.

OPRAH WINFREY (1954–present)

Mississippi-born actor, author, producer, talk show host, and media entrepreneur who became known as the "Queen of All Media" and as the best-known African-American of the twentieth century. A rare winner of all four major entertainment industry awards (Emmy, Grammy, Oscar, and Tony), she was also awarded the Presidential Medal of Freedom in 2013.

Noted Modern Professionals and Academics

BRENE BROWN, MSW, PHD: Professor, Researcher, Storyteller, and Podcast Host; Author of Six NY Times #1 Best-sellers

ANTONIO DAMASIO, MD, PHD: Professor of Neuroscience, Psychology, Neurology; Honda Prize

DANIEL GOLEMAN, PHD: Psychologist and New York Times Journalist; Author of NY Times Best-seller *Emotional Intelligence*

DANIEL KAHNEMAN, MD: Psychologist, Economist, and Author; Nobel Prize

STEVEN PINKER, PHD: Cognitive Psychologist, Educator, Author Foreign Policy Magazine *'100 Global Thinkers'*

STEPHEN W. PORGES, PHD: Psychologist, Neuroscientist; Professor of Psychiatry; Author of *Polyvagal Theory*

MARTIN SELIGMAN, PHD: Psychologist, Author, Educator; Lifetime Award, American Psychology Association

BESSEL VAN DER KOLK, MD: Psychiatrist, Harvard Professor, Trauma Specialist; Author of NY Times #1 Best-seller *The Body Keeps the Score*

APPENDIX B
"SAUSAGE-MAKING"

LEONARDO DA VINCI: *"All thoughts start with emotion."*
CARL JUNG, MD: *"Emotion is the chief source of consciousness."*

"What is an emotion?"

This has been our question, as famously phrased in 1884 by Harvard-trained physician William James, who is regarded by many as the father of American psychology. In this book we have revisited this question by examining over 250 emotions and emotional states as seen through the eyes of 1,800 of the world's thought leaders and described in four thousand expert quotes. As we have outlined, we can frame emotions from the viewpoints of both our head and our heart as part science, part humanities, part literature, and part entertainment, and our process has highlighted the observations of the highly experienced few over the anonymous clinical responses of the unnamed many. A journey of this scope, and in this systematic breadth and format, appears not to have been undertaken before. Our voyage has included concise *briefings* about each emotional condition, and we hope to have helped you navigate and expand toward your worthy personal destinations of *Wisdom* and *Joy*.

Two frequently-heard remarks about Emotion are: "Well, an emotion is how you react to a situation" and "An emotion is just how you feel about something." While these two answers are widely understood from daily experience, they can be unsatisfying. As we have seen in these pages, by researching emotions more fully as they are viewed by hundreds of successful professionals, we have identified some powerful insights which may be worth incorporating into your own understanding. Knowledge and daily usefulness, taken together, can produce powerful advances.

As so many experts reveal, we each possess an often-underused capacity to alter our standard default-type *reactions* and *feelings* when interpreting life situations, and to *choose* alternate emotions and paths of behavior. The observations here from all walks of life and across three thousand years of history amply underscore that emotions include not only how we react and defend ourselves, but they also reveal that we can in many cases decide and choose them, just as others have in advancing their own lives. Many of their personal commentaries may have deeply surprised and hopefully even empowered you in your own life. Some insights cross over expected boundaries between the arts and sciences, and still others have ventured into the realm of the invisible and even into the spiritual. Many are undeniably enlightening. Among them are several "rear-view" personal observations about the human condition as viewed by individuals who have already made major contributions to the world, including a noted quote from a celebrated Italian-American neurobiologist and humanitarian who lived to the age of 103:

> RITA LEVI-MONTALCINI, MD, NOBEL: *"The body does whatever it wants. I am not my body; I am my mind."*

Emotions and the Domains of the Head and the Heart

As supported in these pages, life and emotions can best be understood from the dual perspectives of both the head and the heart. Through our senses and multifaceted nervous system we analyze the measurable physical universe from the *domain of the head,* also known as the brain and mind. Separately, but in tandem, we also navigate a less-measurable, invisible (and even spiritual) universe which has also been regarded as the *domain of the heart.* At the intersection of these two universes emerges our very personal world of emotions. Both our head and heart are involved in processing emotions, which in many ways represent the most personal things we possess, and so making friends with our emotions, both good and not-so-good, can become a very powerful asset. It may be said that there is no meaningful communication between two people which does not begin or end with emotion.

But from childhood we learn there are subtle differences between these two domains of experience, and we may navigate conflicting signals: "Use your head!" and, alternately, "Follow your heart!" While science continues to share major advances in the objective understanding of how our heads and hearts each function and process emotions, the arts and literature have traditionally viewed emotions and life from a softer or less measurable *heart-based* viewpoint. As we have developed, together the head and heart each help us solve problems in different and complementary ways. While each domain looks at life with its own emphasis and criteria, in the end we are often happiest when our heads and hearts align in agreement. In the current reference literature, this beneficial alignment of thoughts and feelings has come to be known as *emotional coherence.* For most of us, a primary goal is to pursue *Joy* and to avoid *Heartache,* and so even in our technology-infused society, the less-measurable quality of what's in our heart often still rules at the end of the day.

Let's step back and look at the apparent differences between how the brain and heart each "see" and process emotions. After all, isn't it commonly understood that the brain rules thought and so it must govern emotions too? On the other hand, for millennia, literature and the arts have clearly regarded emotions as *affairs of the heart.* So wait. When someone talks about heartache, isn't that just a metaphor or interpretation in the head? Or is heartache really a true physical pain resulting from extended deep sadness? Similarly, is *Hunger* a purely physical or an emotional condition, or can it be both?

It might surprise you to learn that science has revealed that the head and the heart each contain neurons and each generates its own readily measurable electromagnetic or "EM" field. Remarkably, the EM field of the heart is many times more powerful than that of the brain or head. Science has also identified that the physical and energetic processes of the heart operate in concert with emotional processing associated with the left and right hemispheres, amygdala, basal ganglia, and other structures of the brain. Yet neither modern science nor the arts maintain that the head or heart operates in sole command of our emotional experiences. Instead, the heart and head are each widely acknowledged as providing a dual-system emotional check and balance on the other, and they serve both emotions and mental health together through the widely-recognized "heart-brain connection." Thus, we see that emotions rely on, and combine, the processes of both the head and heart. And as we shall also see, the heart is also quite commonly regarded as the "seat" of the human spirit. While some might question the very existence of an invisible and not-measurable "human spirit," the *Spirit* briefing (pp. 278–79) highlights rare insights as expressed by well-known thought leaders from many different perspectives. As has been noted by several readers, these observations may prompt a reconsideration of some core existing beliefs about spirit, life, and emotion.

While neither science nor the arts have insisted on specific jurisdictions between the domains attributed to the head and heart, scores of prominent thinkers, including Nobel physicists Albert Einstein and Max Planck, have shared their own insights about the distinctions between the head and heart (and spirit). As outlined here, the domains of the head and heart have most often been characterized, at least metaphorically, as:

Where the Head (Brain) Is the Seat	**Where the Heart Is the Seat**
Facts, Thoughts, and Knowledge	Love, Emotions, and Feelings
The Body	The Human Spirit or Soul
Science	Conscience
Intellect	Intuition
Presence	Transcendence
Accounting/Assessment	Entrepreneurship/Advancement
Belief	Faith
Words	Poetry

The Three Basic Conditions of Being, Doing, and Having: Emotions Represent the Human 'Operating System'

Across the centuries, wise sages have also traditionally recognized three basic conditions of human experience as: *to be*, *to do*, and *to have*: and they have usually been prioritized in this way. That is to say, our prospects for success in life have been considered enhanced by first deciding what we want *to be*, then what we want *to do* with our lives, and followed by what we hope *to have* as the outcome of our choices. (Shakespeare famously drew attention to this sequence in *Hamlet*: "*To be, or not to be, that is the question.*") Whether our reactions and decisions are driven by the head or heart, (or ideally, both), our emotions provide the core venue or platform—as the equivalent of a *human operating system*—for navigating our physical conditions and executing on our intentions and goals. It is through emotions and the combined workings of our central nervous system and our bodies that we transform our reactions, thoughts, intentions, and energies into physical behavior. Stated differently, in our workaday fourth-dimensional world of space and time here on Earth, it is through emotions that *human beings* can become *human doings.*

Emotions and Electromagnetism: A Brief Discussion

Numerous experts from neuroscience to philosophy have noted that humans are also *electromagnetic beings.* This may be a new concept to many, and a brief explanation of the underpinnings may help. To greatly simplify the background physics, space and time are intertwined (per Einstein's Theory of Relativity) and together they imply distance. Distance, in turn, implies that motion is involved in travelling across space, and motion requires an initial motivator or an *energetic* quality of motion. Whether this energy results in light travelling across the galaxy or a person slowly walking across a room, it is fundamental that energy drives motion. Space is not empty, and it is home to various forms of energy, many of which we cannot see. Visible light (and human life) operates within a narrow band of the electromagnetic (or 'EM') field energy spectrum including invisible radio waves, X-rays, and gamma rays. While Earth's magnetic field shields us from much harmful radiation from space, our own EM energy fields are measured daily in diagnostic medicine via PET, MRI, EEG, and EKG technology. EM-spectrum energy thus represents a base facilitator for life and *energy in motion,* and for our purposes here, *e-motion.* Through our emotions, we turn thought energy into physical behavior.

In brief summary, the thoughts and electromagnetic/electrical impulses in our brain produce brainwaves which can be measured as frequencies (such as via an EEG) before they are translated by the mind (brain) and body into emotion, and then into physical motion and behavior. Whether we travel physically through space or pursue our days on Earth joyfully, angrily, in fear, or sadly bored, emotions represent the inner electromagnetic, energetic, and qualitative *how* it is that we are going about experiencing our lives. In this sense, emotions serve to connect our "inner world" with our "outer world." Where we are outwardly and physically exchanging significant things or data, we are also expressing what we are developing inwardly as our emotions.

Our Emotions Are Continuously Evolving

On a day-to-day basis, we tend to consider emotions as merely occasional, sporadic, or episodic events, and we can often consider ourselves as "non-emotional." That is to say, we often recall only notable emotional highlights which stand out, such as *Bill was in a great mood yesterday,* or *I know you were upset last night,* and then we regard the other in-between times of relative calm as either normal or non-emotional. But on further examination it turns out that we are virtually *always* emoting and shifting/morphing from one emotional backdrop to the next. For example, in the space of an hour we may transition from feeling *bored* while watching TV, to realizing we are *hungry*, to feeling *curious* about what is in the kitchen, to being *interested* when we spot our favorite goodies, to getting *annoyed* by the interruption of a phone call, to feeling *satisfaction* when diving into our favorite snacks, to feeling *contented*, and then returning to *boredom* again. The point is that as long as we are conscious (and even also when we are dreaming, for example), we are essentially always interpreting and navigating our consciousness and surroundings through our ever-vigilant *operating system* of biomechanical body parts, chemicals, and evaluations which we summarize as our emotions. We are virtually constantly shifting our attention, reassessing our environment, and updating our emotional interpretations and behavior. In this way, emotions are continuous and not merely episodic.

Where emotions are energetic in nature, and since they exist and function within the much broader EM energy spectrum, they can be characterized as progressive and/or morphing *spectrum* energies and as behavioral phenomena which can be broadly observed as on a continuum—somewhat like the progressive colors of a rainbow. While the location of any emotion within the spectrum may be subject to adjustment, the concept of locating emotions on a continuous spectrum from *Death* up to *Joy* and *Serenity* can be a useful analytical tool in assessing our own behavior and the responses of people around us. As a simple example, hospital caregivers have long noted that when a very seriously ill patient begins to make minor complaints about the food that the patient is often improving and on the mend—and therefore moving up the emotional spectrum toward recovery and survival.

Emotions Represent the 'Gears of Life'

A major observation of this book has been to help recognize that emotions are more than merely *reactions.* As noted, they can especially represent *choices* (and thus tools) which are ideally under our conscious control, and which serve us as our effective *Gears of Life.* Optimal emotional choices normally precede optimal life experiences. Just as a cyclist may utilize any of fifteen gears to meet the circumstances of varying types of terrain, so too may a person utilize different emotions to respond to the environment and to execute different intentions and decisions. To extend the comparison, we can decide to use different gears to go fast or slow on flat or uneven terrain. We can downshift when starting up a steep slope, or we can sometimes overreact and select the wrong gear when distracted or triggered by a swerving truck. We can also choose an easier gear (or by comparison, a different emotion) to pursue a path that is less challenging or more optimal.

Awareness is key, and there is a major benefit to recognizing that we often can choose our emotional "gears" and thereby not fall victim to habitual default-pattern reactions where conditions and emotions seem to kick in on their own or at times to get away from us. Self-defense will always prompt the instinctive or default pattern of quickly withdrawing from touching a hot stove, but in many less-urgent situations we can choose our emotions. For example, retaliation in moments of provocation or aggression is something we can either engage in or choose to avoid. We can choose more measured responses, or choose simply to walk away. In the world of competitive sports, the importance of conscious emotional decision-making has been re-phrased by numerous successful athletes and coaches as: "Play with emotion, but don't let your emotions play with you."

The noted twentieth-century psychoanalysis pioneers Sigmund Freud and Carl Jung each dedicated major parts of their careers to assessing that many of our initial *default* or habitual emotional reactions to events emerge from hidden *subconscious* patterns which can be understood and addressed once we are aware of them. Whether our immediate reactions arise from instinct, habit, self-defense, subconscious impulses, or from patterned responses developed early in our lives (or other sources), we often respond either reflexively, and to one degree or another *without even thinking*. It is easy to get drawn into familiar or *default* patterned responses. Yet the lessons of hundreds of expert contributors in these pages help guide us to understanding the value of mentally stepping back, of choosing (and even rehearsing) better responses, and of selecting better emotional *gears* to enhance our outcomes. As these pages reveal, the three vital roles of *Awareness*, *Belief*, and *Repetition* provide proven keys to identifying harmful default reaction patterns, and to installing better alternatives. The overriding goal is to take the time to *choose how we respond,* and not merely to *react*. Three thousand years of history advise us that this can represent the difference between success and failure in emotional outcomes.

Building Better Definitions about Emotions: Adding Subjective Phrases and Broader Building Blocks

During the research for this book, and including a review of scores of books, references, and websites over several years, an evident truth emerged that understanding emotions can pose a few challenges where the goal is understanding and building both definitions and beliefs "from the ground up," and including from the dual perspectives of both the head and the heart. It can be readily observed in many bookstores and online vendors that available dictionaries and popular reference works often dismiss how we look at or express emotions *subjectively* in our day-to-day life. That is, published definitions almost universally emphasize shorter "factual" or objective *domain of the head* definitions of emotion, and they almost universally omit the subjective *domain of the heart* contexts. But what we are *feeling* is often different from what others *observe* when looking at us.

By *subjective* (or *heart-based*), we are describing how we actually experience and then verbalize our viewpoints, in both words and writing, to describe the emotions we are feeling. As an example, a proud father would very likely *not* discuss his son's eagerness to attend a professional basketball game in purely "dictionary-style" or *objective* terms such as "Well, recently my son has expressed a heightened level of interest about attending the NBA game. I noticed today he appears less able to focus on his schoolwork." Instead, the father would much more likely use *subjective* (or *heart-based*) emotional phrases like, "Wow, Tommy is really lit up about going to the big game. He just can't wait." Experiential, subjective, and heart-based phrases like these have been dismissed in most explanatory literature, likely because they can be considered as short-lived, "slang," or overly trendy, and yet they are at the very core of how most people understand and express their emotions. But "slang" need not be vulgar, and we do know that Shakespeare long ago proved the enduring impact of useful subjective phrases.

Heart-Based Phrases Resonate Best in Describing Emotions

Simply stated, heart-based subjective phrases often provide superior relevance in helping to describe emotions. They are most often how people really express themselves, and they are powerful because they *resonate*. The listener can more easily duplicate them and re-live the speaker's emotional context. As we have seen in using popular and heart-based phrases to help create the building blocks of over 250 separate emotional states, they need not be exhaustive in order to be enlightening. In everyday life, *subjective* phrases clearly *dwarf* the level of use of their classic *objective* counterparts. Given their wide use and relevance, they have earned their "place at the table" when describing emotional states.

As noted earlier, the route of specifically defining and describing emotions has been less-travelled—and it has clearly been more of a pathway than a highway. Freud, known as the founder of psychoanalysis, and who completed over 320 works during his career, was surprisingly vague about a number of psychological terms, including emotion. As psychologist Dr. Michael T. Michael observed, and as reproduced by the National Institutes of Health, "Freud appears ambivalent about emotion." A review of the lifetime concordances of Freud's works reveals a preference for far more generalized insights into his assessments about emotion:

> SIGMUND FREUD, MD: *"The essence of an emotion is that we should be aware of it, i.e., that it should become known to consciousness."* (Freud 1915/1957, 177)

Separately, the highly-revered and legendary Carl Jung, renowned globally as the pioneering founder of analytical psychology, and whose *Collected Works* span twenty volumes, also took a fairly poetic view of emotion with a unique and metaphorical description:

CARL JUNG, MD: *"Emotion is the alchemical fire whose warmth brings everything into existence...emotion is the moment when steel meets flint, and a spark is struck forth, for emotion is the chief source of consciousness. There is no change from darkness to light or from inertia to movement without emotion."*

The full reasons for these titans using such roundabout descriptions are unclear, but may reflect that emotions cover vast experiences which are too broad for a one-size-fits-all definition. Also, it is through the self-referencing lens of emotion that we even engage in examining our own lives, and so they may have felt professional caution about a feedback loop where they actually *use* emotion to help *explain* emotion. Or, as writer-observer Colin Newton has humorously remarked, "Studying emotion is like asking an eyeball to examine itself." In practice, we might start out bravely with: "Well, an emotion is simply just how you feel." But on undertaking a deeper effort to explain what it is we are really *feeling* (and why), explanations and definitions can quickly get more nuanced and complicated. So even for the legends in the study of the mind, the *objective* process of explaining emotions has not been easy. Expanded ways to explain emotions are in order.

So far we note that virtually none of the legendary pioneers in psychology and psychoanalysis such as James, Freud, Jung, Carl Rogers, and Albert Ellis have revealed a focused dedication on producing detailed definitions of emotions, either *objective* (what is observed) or *subjective* (what is experienced), or otherwise clarifying their viewpoints as originating from either the head or the heart. As pioneers, perhaps they felt that others would add in these specifics later. While these giants and many subsequent-generation researchers have shared vast critical research and contributions regarding emotional causes and issues, very few have yet cataloged specific definitions of the so-called building blocks of individual emotions. Stated simply, very little has been located in the commercial domain when it comes to defining emotions one-by-one.

On reflection, a fundamental issue may be that the *scientists* who might undertake the task of defining emotions may have been reluctant to venture across the professional aisle into the *humanities*, and vice-versa. And even within the sciences, for example, it seems predictable enough that a neuroscientist would not be inclined to make bold pronouncements applying to cardiology, or any other advanced specialty. There may also have been an inherent process issue where the scientific method prefers *objective* terminology (that is, using words which describe how an emotion can be observed or measured by others), while the arts have tended toward more subjective terms (again, how it actually *feels* to experience the emotion). To be sure, there have been numerous advances in recent decades toward addressing more of the subjective or heart-based descriptions of emotions, such as addressed in the well-regarded concepts in *Emotional Intelligence* as developed by noted psychologist Daniel Goleman in his long-running *New York Times* bestseller from 1995.

But even more recent popular psychology reference works including the many best-sellers of the brilliant Antonio Damasio, Steven Pinker, and Brene Brown (among several others) have been largely single-emotion studies, or they represent more focused single-author viewpoints. These more recent releases have not generally focused their attention on detailing the definitional building blocks of a broader range of emotions, or viewing them from many viewpoints and/or across multiple fields of study. On examination, this pattern holds true not only for the definition of *emotion* itself, but also for the sub-definitions of specific individual emotions. The reader is often simply *assumed* to understand what is meant by most emotions and academic/technical terms. Lay readers rarely see needed definitions.

In general, most well-qualified academic voices have been reluctant to define, explain, and catalog emotions and emotional conditions "from the ground up." Several notable substitute approaches have included the introduction of personal anecdotes, the shortening of some complex technical definitions, a preference for using summarized clinical studies, and the occasional use of simple substitute synonyms. In a few cases, emotional states have come to be described via circular references, such as where "drunk" is defined as "intoxicated," and "intoxicated" is defined as "drunk." And yet for practical purposes, the field of defining emotions, either taken *one-by-one* and/or by expert objective and subjective phenomenological analysis, has been very noticeably underserved.

This readily-observable pattern of *definitional brevity* notably extends well beyond the legends of psychology and prominent single-author viewpoints. Might you be surprised to learn that nearly a quarter of the over 250 common day-to-day emotions and emotional states which are defined and described in these pages are simply not found *at all* as baseline entries in two of the leading print-version dictionaries of psychology? For example, the following forty common emotions and emotional behaviors were not located among the many thousands of entries in either the largest desktop American dictionary of psychology or in a well-known British counterpart:

Admiration	Defiant	Intimidation	Retaliation	Sorry
Antagonism	Disappointment	Lying	Revenge	Stubborn
Apology	Encouragement	Patience	Sabotage	Surrender
Appreciation	Evil	Peace	Sacrifice	Trolling
Caution	Failure	Prayer	Sarcasm	Truth
Clarity	Greed	Procrastination	Silence	Wonder
Confidence	Heroism	Promise	Sin	Yearning
Contentment	Indignant	Redemption	Sincere	Zeal

For clarity, of the more than 250 emotions and emotional conditions which have been researched and included in this book, at least 65 (about 25 percent) were simply not located at all in either leading desk reference dictionary of psychology.

How does this even make sense? The full explanations for such an obvious gap in the omission of day-to-day emotional entries such as these from both leading specialty dictionaries and from other standard desk references are not clear, but they likely include:

- Emotions transcend all fields of human experience, and so professionals working in one specific field or sub-specialty may be reluctant to put forward definitions which may potentially conflict with definitions developed in an adjacent field.

- Emotions are subjective phenomena which vary from person to person, and thus may be influenced by many visible and invisible factors, so they yield less readily to meaningful objective lab testing and/or to cataloging under scientific methods.

- Similar or overlapping emotional entries might make a second entry redundant: for example, such as *Caution* and *Wariness*; however, neither of these two sample emotions were located as entries in either noted psychology reference work.

In addition, emotions can be difficult to unpack and to define because of layered under-stories, and as a result of multiple factors including a host of shadow influences. These fundamental, secondary, and/or indirect contributors to emotions can include *Belief, Nutrition, Hydration, Music, Ego,* the *Subconscious,* and a few more exotic and even fringe considerations such as *Telepathy* and *Astrology.* (Astrology has been consulted through the centuries as a probability model for predicting emotional influences, even though it is regarded by the vast majority of modern scientific professionals as mere pseudoscience.) Add that there are also a number of other accepted scientific preconditions which contribute to emotional states, such as *Gravity, Electromagnetism* and *Quantum Physics*, all of which are well beyond the scope of most emotional table references (but they are included here). On review, and to add a touch of humor, after the myriad of contributing factors are each considered, maybe we should step back from it after all. Don't we each already have an actual lifetime of experience with emotions from birth, so aren't we each essentially pre-qualified as *unofficial experts* in emotions?

Humor aside, detailed definitions of emotions appear to be significantly underserved (if not essentially dismissed) in the bulk of available explanatory and popular literature. Delving just a little further into self-help bookshelves, we note that a supplemental "Emotional Glossary" and/or "Appendix" format is also rarely seen in recent commercial literature, and it is the rare recent book that focuses on definitions or similar current usages at all. More often a substitute is simply to relate intriguing celebrity anecdotes which can be highly interesting, but which appeal more to sheer curiosity than to practical understanding. Clearly, the observed pattern of minimizing or even disregarding the definitions of emotions one-by-one does not serve the purposes of the arts, sciences, self-help, or the advancement of knowledge in general.

What is available in much of self-help literature might be considered as only a modest part of what we might really want to know about emotions. Assembling both scientific (objective) and non-scientific (subjective) definitions and viewpoints into one place may be asking too much of either the arts or sciences, but our objective here has been very much to contribute to this long-underserved joint "building blocks" project.

Taking a New Approach: Development of the 'Emotionary' Briefing Adding Subjective Phrases and Quotes to Help Define Subjective Emotions

So many of the world's most prominent thinkers—from Plato, Aristotle, Da Vinci, Galileo, Kepler, and Newton in centuries past, to Hume, Hobbes, Locke, Kant, Voltaire, Rousseau, Jefferson, Einstein, Kettering, Chomsky, and Pinker into the Enlightenment and modern Industrial eras—and even adding talk show commentator Jon Stewart more recently—have highlighted the importance of establishing clarity through definitions as the essential building blocks of understanding. With this in mind, we have also included here two foundational entries: *Clarity* and *Definition(s)*. While *Awareness, Belief,* and *Repetition* (along with several subject definitions in this book including *Hydration* and *Conscious Breathing*) are not traditionally considered as 'emotions,' we draw special attention to their inclusion here for the significant value they bring to our general emotional well-being when they are examined and better understood.

On inspection, where many recent reference works have bypassed specific definitions of emotions altogether, the few that have even attempted have often addressed them only in limited and impersonal *objective* words and terms. After all, this is what dictionaries and reference works have always done. However, as noted, emotions are at the very least a two-sided phenomenon involving the heart and the head. They represent *subjective* or experiential states which can often be far easier to *express and compare* than to *define or explain*. We highlight the long history, going back at least to Shakespeare, of using resonating *subjective* wording and phrases when people really want to connect about emotions. In *Choosing Emotions,* we focus on adding these subjective expressions, very possibly for the first time. We are also including, as an innovation, thousands of highly useful quotes and key observations from hundreds of the world's leaders and acknowledged experts, in order to advance the field of addressing emotions. We believe that a new paradigm and model for defining emotions by adding resonant subjective experiences has clearly emerged.

Summary and Conclusions

Here we are creating a more usable framework for understanding over 250 common emotional states by identifying resonant subjective experiences as evidenced by: (1) vibrant popular usage on the one hand, and (2) highly-qualified expert observations on the other. Our focus has been to start with classic third-party *objective* definitions of emotions (that is, as traditionally described or observed by others), and then to take an innovative step further by adding vital *subjective* phrases and quotes as heard and used in real life (that is, emotions actually experienced and expressed by an individual; *You*).

For centuries, classic definitions have relied almost exclusively on *objective* terms. We are expanding the traditional model to cast our net more broadly by including *subjective* and experiential heart-based terms as used daily in real dialogue, plus adding relevant quotes from true experts as a favored alternative to anonymous clinical studies. And, where the standard dictionary-based *proof of understanding* has traditionally been posed as, "Now can you use that word (or emotion) in a sentence?" our revised format has enhanced the process by demonstrating how up to twenty-five world-class experts (per each emotional state) have already observed it in their own lives. We note that *Awareness, Belief*, and *Repetition* have each dramatically enhanced and advanced the understanding and mastery of any topic, and by observation each of these can prove especially useful regarding emotions.

What has emerged from our process is that the traditional *definition* of an emotion as found in classic reference works has been transformed into a more useful and relevant layout (the *full concept briefing, or 'emotionary'* format) for over 250 emotions and emotional behaviors, where emotions are described from both objective and subjective perspectives. What has also emerged is that where the intention is to connect emotionally with another person, then using resonant, subjective, heart-based wording and phrases is often best.

Toward a New Model for Defining Emotions

Choosing Emotions provides a concise and highly relatable catalog of world-class expert responses to William James's seminal question: "What is an emotion?" We are not aware of any comparable book which includes even a third as many emotions, or even a tenth as many expert contributors. Additionally, we have innovated a new format by adding fun, vivid, idiomatic, and subjective popular phrases as used in everyday language to amplify the understanding of each subjective state of emotion, and by adding actual expert observations in place of summarized clinical studies. Following the expanded *full concept briefing* for each of over 250 emotions and emotional conditions, we conclude in Appendix C with our *Suggested Primary and Expanded Sub-Definitions of Emotion*. These are new baseline objective definitions to help advance that emotions may be better-served both by revised general definitions, as well as by the addition of sub-definitions across more narrowly-defined fields of human interest and behavior. We hope you will find there is not a faster, more useful, or more entertaining way to gain an elite personal orientation to over 250 primary emotional conditions, and to understanding *emotions*, than from these pages.

APPENDIX C
SUGGESTED PRIMARY AND EXPANDED SUB-DEFINITIONS OF EMOTION

Primary Definitions of Emotion

1. Emotions constitute the bridge between thought and behavior. An emotion is a feeling, response, or decision about behavior, whether involuntary or voluntary, and it manifests the most dominant survival-based inputs, considerations, and objectives of an individual, couple, and/or the group. Emotions can reflect changing priorities of belief, relevance, and personal experience. Emotions are navigational.

   EXAMPLE: *Sue was quietly engrossed reading the book until the lightning bolt hit, when she screamed.*

2. Emotions represent the continuously evolving summary expression of awareness, interpretation, and behavior, by or among an individual, couple, and/or a group. Separate emotions may occur simultaneously, they may each be recognized within a continuum of similar behaviors or on a spectrum of broader behaviors, and they may each reflect varying degrees of personal engagement. Emotions may reflect contagious social adoption phenomena and similar momentum-type characteristics.

   EXAMPLE: *The volunteers grew impatient and several began to collect their things to abandon the meeting until a single calm figure strode to the podium and took charge.*

3. *Popular or Heart-Based Usage* (a.k.a. '*The Gears of Life*'): Where thought includes analysis and interpretation, emotion further reflects prioritization, engagement, and resulting behavior. Emotions may take form in either *subjective* (felt by self) or *objective* (observed by others) states and behavioral manifestations which align thought and intention with responsive action. Optimal emotional selection facilitates optimal life experiences.

   EXAMPLE: *Just as a cyclist may utilize any of fifteen gears to meet the circumstances of varying types of terrain, so too may an individual adopt or utilize different emotions to respond to the environment and to execute on different considerations, intentions, and decisions.*

Expanded Sub-Definitions of Emotion

1. *(Psychology/Behavioral)* Emotions operate uniquely at the intersection of body, mind, and spirit, and they manifest the bridge between thought and behavior. Emotions represent a reaction or choice about behavior which reflects either: (1) unconscious, subconscious, instinctive, or default stimulus-response patterns, and/or (2) a conscious decision based on experience, reason, beliefs, opinion, training, sensory inputs, survival, supervision, constraints, physical condition, physical exercise, diet, hydration, health, rest, chemical balances, neurotransmitters, personal or group relationships, goals, insights, and/or objectives. Changes in any of these underlying factors may contribute to a corresponding shift in emotion(s).

2. *(Thought, Philosophy, and Epistemology)* (1) Among sentient life forms, emotion presents the necessary platform and precondition of awareness which facilitates evaluation, reason, logic, intuition, aesthetics, selection, response, and/or action. Human emotion facilitates logic and is therefore not inferior to logic. (Or, stated alternately, reason and logic are subsets within a broader range of human emotional capabilities.) (2) Human consciousness interprets a new situation, evaluates the scene in the context of goals and objectives, and then reacts or selects a response from an available emotional repertoire.

   The Cycle of Emotion is: Awareness > Interpretation > Emotional Selection > Response > Behavior.

   Emotions animate. Human behavior and action follow an emotional predicate or 'driver.'

   What is likely a newer point of attention is the observation that emotions are not merely episodic or sporadic. Instead, they represent instead a *continuously evolving index of consciousness.* Even when we are by outward appearances 'unemotional,' at rest, or dreaming, we are continuously evaluating our environment, thoughts, and decisions, and thus we are constantly interpreting available inputs and advancing our emotions. As such, emotions are continuous and developmental, and they represent the iterative, adaptive, and behavioral drivers of human experience and survival.

   COROLLARY 1: *Our capacity for emotion both precedes and facilitates logic.*

   COROLLARY 2: *Emotional impression precedes emotional expression.*

   COROLLARY 3: *Every thought, decision, intention, memory, or dream has an emotional element or component.*

REFERENCE 1: Carl Jung, MD: *"Emotion is the chief source of consciousness."*

REFERENCE 2: Antonio Damasio, MD, PhD, Honda Prize: *"We are not thinking machines that feel; rather, we are feeling machines that think."*

REFERENCE 3: Bessel van der Kolk, MD: *"I want to emphasize that emotions are not opposed to reason; our emotions assign value to experiences and thus are the foundation of reason."*

REFERENCE 4: Jonathan Haidt, PhD: *"It is only because our emotional brain works so well that our reasoning can work at all."*

Additional References and Observations Within the Sciences

(Physics and Geometry) Just as vectors of force, acceleration, and velocity exist in the energetic universe, so too may specific emotions and emotional intentions exhibit magnitude and direction.

(Biology: Command and Control) Emotions as the Human Operating System. Emotion approximates the biological 'operating system' of the physical body. That is, similar and in parallel to the operating system of a computer, emotions facilitate basic command functions including receiving inputs, processing, scheduling, and executing tasks and physical output (behavior). Emotions may be single, combined, or collective in their expression by an individual, a pairing of individuals, and/or among a group. Emotional decisions and commands may be facilitated in the body through various organs, processes, and sub-systems. Emotions are also facilitated by complex natural chemical compounds and hormones including through the endocrine system, such as evidenced by the near-instantaneous release of energy-enhancing adrenaline into the bloodstream in response to the perception of sudden and/or severe threat or danger.

(Biophysics) (1) 'Emotion' refers to the electromagnetic carrier wave platform or venue for human consciousness and experience. Specific emotions emanate as energetic wave phenomena and/or vibrational frequencies in a range or repertoire, and their expression is facilitated within the body through the central nervous system, autonomic nervous system, pneumogastric (vagus) nerve, hypothalamus, amygdalae, basal ganglia, limbic system, cardiovascular system, endocrine system, muscular system, and by neuropeptides and neurotransmitters. Emotions may serve to motivate, enhance, attract, repel, cancel, lessen, and/or modify other emotions and wave energies, and they may influence or impact matter, energy, space and/or time. (2) A specific emotional reaction, intention, or decision may be observed as a specific behavioral or energetic pattern, and its measurement may be undertaken with non-invasive EEG ('*brainwave*'), fMRI, and/or ECG ('*heartwave*') assistance.

Emerging research suggests that DNA's helical geometry may function as a coupling antenna for integrating EM signals at the cellular level and within the body.

> COROLLARY 1: Intention and navigation represent orienting pre-physical conditions for emotion. They are relational and functional, not energetic or field phenomena.

> COROLLARY 2: Electromagnetism and electromagnetic processes represent the predominant energetic media for the manifestation of observable experience and behavior in fourth-dimensional space and time.

(Astrophysics) As ancient cultures recognized that the proximity and angular energy influences of the Sun and Moon influenced experiences on Earth (including the tides, seasons, and plantings), so too has modern science acknowledged that other invisible energies and frequencies serve to shape modern experience and emotion.

> PROVERBS: ANCIENT: *"As above, so below. As within, so without."*
> MODERN: *"Matter responds to energy and frequency."*
> COROLLARY 1: Matter coalesces around energy.
> COROLLARY 2: Matter is slow-moving energy.

> REFERENCE: Albert Einstein, PhD, Nobel (an often-attributed quote which remains still unverified): *"We are slowed down sound and light waves, a walking bundle of frequencies tuned in to the cosmos. We are souls dressed up in sacred biochemical garments and our bodies are the instruments though which our souls play their music."*

(Metaphysics and Philosophy) (1) Emotions represent the interface between body, mind, and spirit.

> REFERENCE: Carl Jung, MD, *Psychological Aspects of the Mother Archetype* (par. 179): *"Emotion is the alchemical fire whose warmth brings everything into existence...emotion is the moment when steel meets flint, and a spark is struck forth, for emotion is the chief source of consciousness. There is no change from darkness to light or from inertia to movement without emotion."*

(2) Emotions represent a fourth-dimensional manifestation of fifth-dimensional (or higher) thought or intention.

REFERENCE: Pierre Teilhard de Chardin, SJ, Legion of Honor: *"We are not human beings having a spiritual existence. We are spiritual beings having a human experience."*

(Linguistics and Causality) Emotion provides the necessary 'adverbial driver' or predicate to action in the physical universe. That is, emotion represents 'how' a subject behaves or executes its decisions and actions; e.g., emotion is represented by the italicized adverb/adverbial modifier in:

Terry (or Terry's dog) *lazily* crossed the road toward the house.
Terry (or Terry's dog) *eagerly* crossed the road toward the house.
Terry (or Terry's dog) *cautiously* crossed the road toward the house.

COROLLARY 1: *Emotion is the motivator preceding and accompanying physical action.*

COROLLARY 2: *A being does not cross a road without an emotional motivator or subtext.*

Third-Party Definitions in Comparison/Critical Review

emotion: A complex reaction pattern, involving experiential, behavioral, and physiological elements by which an individual attempts to deal with a personally significant matter or event. The specific quality of the emotion (e.g., fear, shame) is determined by the significance of the event. For example, if the significance involves disapproval from another, shame is likely to be generated. Emotion typically involves feeling but differs from feeling in having an overt or implicit engagement with the world. (APA Dictionary of Psychology, 2020)

emotion: Emotions are complex, largely automated programs of *actions* concocted by evolution. The actions are complemented by a *cognitive* program that includes certain ideas and modes of cognition, but the world of emotions is largely one of actions carried out in our bodies, from facial expressions and postures to changes in viscera and internal milieu. (Antonio Damasio, MD, PhD, *Self Comes to Mind: Constructing the Conscious Brain*, Vintage, 2010)

emotion: Involves complex layers of processes that are in constant interaction with the environment. At a minimum, these interactions involve cognitive processes (such as appraisal or evaluation of meaning) and physical changes (such as endocrine, autonomic, and cardiovascular changes), which may reveal some repeated patterns over time. Emotion can be seen as involving neurobiological, experiential, and expressive components. ... Emotions can be thought of as the inner and interpersonal process that 'evokes motion' and shape how our body feels and how our mind is motivated to act.' (UCLA Psychiatrist and NY Times best-selling author Daniel J. Siegel, MD, "The Essential Power of Being Aware," via BHNN Podcast, December 11, 2018)

emotion: (1) A complex mental reaction (such as anger or fear) subjectively experienced as strong feeling directed toward a specific object and typically accompanied by physiological and behavioral changes in the body; (2) a state of feeling; (3) the affective aspect of consciousness. (Merriam-Webster, "Emotion," Merriam-Webster.com dictionary, accessed February 22, 2021, at https://www.merriam webster.com/dictionary/emotion)

REFERENCES

Ackerman, Angela, and Becca Puglisi. *The Emotion Thesaurus: A Writer's Guide to Character Expression*. Writers Helping Writers, 2019.

Ackroyd, Peter. *Blake*. Ballantine Books, 1997.

Adler, Stella, Marlon Brando, and Howard Kissel. *The Art of Acting*. Applause Books, 2000.

Athans, Catherine, and Marie-France Louvel. *The Heart Brain: Did You Know You Have 3 Brains?* Angels Island Press, 2018.

Austin, Veda. *The Living Language of Water*. Veda Austin, 2024.

Barber, Sarah. "Body Language Signs That Have a Hidden Meaning." *TravellerGazette*. January 15, 2024.

Barrett, Lisa Feldman, and Cassandra Campbell. *How emotions are made*. Findaway World, 2017.

Bartlett, John, and Geoffrey O'Brien. *Bartlett's Familiar Quotations*. Little, Brown, and Co., 2012.

Baum, L. Frank, and Shaun Pendergast. *The Wonderful Wizard of Oz: A Picture Book Adaptation*. Random House Children's Books, 2013.

Bible, King James Version. Bible House, 1976.

Bloch, Amy, and Susie Berneis. *The Power of Heart: When and How to Get Out of Your Brain*. CELA, 2020.

Bloomsbury Anthology of Quotations. Bloomsbury, 2002.

Bradbury, Malcolm. *Roget's Thesaurus*. Cengage Learning, 1987.

Brown, Brené. *Atlas of the Heart: Mapping Meaningful Connection and the Language of Human Experience*. Random House, 2021.

Brulé, Dan. *Just Breathe: Mastering Breathwork*. Atria/Enliven Books, 2020.

Childre, Doc Lew, Deborah Rozman, Howard Martin, and Rollin McCraty. *Heart Intelligence: Connecting with the Heart's Intuitive Guidance for Effective Choices and Solutions*. Waterside Productions, 2022.

Collins, Jonathan D., and Melissa Binder. *Why Emotions Matter: Recognize Your Body Signals, Grow in Emotional Intelligence, Discover an Embodied Spirituality*. Independently Published, 2019.

Colman, Andrew M. *A Dictionary of Psychology*. Oxford University Press, 2015.

D'Agostino, Ryan. *Esquire the Meaning of Life: Wisdom, Humor, and Damn Good Advice from 64 Extraordinary Lives*. Hearst Books, 2009.

Damasio, Antonio R. *Self Comes to Mind: Constructing the Conscious Brain*. Vintage Books, 2012.

Damasio, Antonio R. *The Feeling of What Happens: Body, Emotion and the Making of Consciousness*. Vintage, 2000.

Damasio, Antonio R., and Julian Morris. *Feeling & Knowing: Making Minds Conscious.* Random House, 2021.

Damasio, Antonio. *Descartes' Error.* Penguin, 2005.

Dangerfield, Rodney. *It's Not Easy Bein' Me: A Lifetime of No Respect but Plenty of Sex and Drugs.* HarperEntertainment, 2004.

Das, Bhagavan. *The Science of Emotions.* Theosophical Press, 1953.

David, Susan A. *Emotional Agility: Get Unstuck, Embrace Change, and Thrive in Work and Life.* Penguin Random House, 2016.

De Bono, Edward, and George Daulby. *The Greatest Thinkers: Diagrams.* Weidenfeld & Nicolson, 1976.

Dispenza, Joe, and Gregg Braden. *Becoming Supernatural: How Common People Are Doing the Uncommon.* Hay House, 2019.

Dispenza, Joe. *Breaking the Habit of Being Yourself: How to Lose Your Mind and Create a New One.* Hay House, 2018.

Duckworth, Angela. *Grit: The Power of Passion and Perseverance.* Scribner, 2016.

Ekman, Paul. *Emotional Awareness: Overcoming the Obstacles to Psychological Balance and Compassion: A Conversation between the Dalai Lama and Paul Ekman.* Henry Holt & Co., 2009.

Ellis, Albert, and Debbie Joffe-Ellis. *Rational Emotive Behavior Therapy.* American Psychological Association, 2019.

Freud, Sigmund, James Strachey, Anna Freud, and Mark Solms. *The Revised Standard Edition of the Complete Psychological Works of Sigmund Freud.* Rowman & Littlefield, 2024.

Fulcanelli. *Le mystère des cathédrales.* Brotherhood of Life, 1990.

Funk, Charles Earle, and Tom Funk. *Horse Feathers and Other Curious Words.* Quill, 2001.

Ganeri, Anita, trans. *The Quran.* Evans, 2002.

Gerber, Michael E. *The E-myth revisited.* HarperCollins, 2009.

Gober, Mark. *An End to Upside Down Thinking.* Waterside Publishing, 2023.

Goldstein, Barry. *The Secret Language of the Heart: How to Use Music, Sound, and Vibration as a Tool for Healing and Personal Transformation.* Hierophant Publishing, 2016.

Goleman, Daniel. *Emotional Intelligence.* Bantam Books, 1995.

Goswami, Amit, Richard E. Reed, and Maggie Goswami. *The Self-Aware Universe: How Consciousness Creates the Material World.* Putnam's Sons, 1995.

Greene, Robert, and Joost Elffers. *The 48 Laws of Power.* Penguin Books, 2000.

Gregory, Pam. *How to Co-create Using the Secret Language of the Universe.* Silverwood Books, 2023.

Groeschel, Craig. *Winning the War in Your Mind: Change Your Thinking, Change Your Life.* Zondervan Books, 2021.

Haidt, Jonathan. *The Righteous Mind: Why Good People Are Divided by Politics and Religion*. Vintage Books, 2013.

Hall, Manly P. *The Secret Teachings of All Ages*. Philosophical Research Society, 1988.

Hawkins, David R. *Power vs. Force*. Hay House, 2012.

Herman, Judith L. *Trauma and Recovery*. Basic Books, 1997.

Holiday, Ryan. *Ego Is the Enemy*. Profile Books, 2016.

Holiday, Ryan. *The Obstacle Is the Way: The Ancient Art of Turning Adversity to Advantage*. Profile Books, 2014.

James, William. *Principles of Psychology*. 2 vols. Pantianos Classics, 2018.

James, William. "What Is an Emotion?" In *The emotions,* vol. 1, 11–30, n.d. https://doi.org/10.1037/10735–001.

Johnston, D. Earl. *Emotional Shorthand: 2500 Greatest Self-Help Quotes and Life Insights: Anxiety, Depression, Grit, Love, Joy, and 180 Emotions*. Jones Media Publishing, 2022.

Jung, C. G., and R. F. C. Hull. *The Archetypes and the Collective Unconscious*. China Social Sciences Publishing House, 1999.

Jung, C. G., Gerhard Adler, Michael Fordham, Herbert Read, William McGuire, and R. F. C. Hull. *The Collected Works of C. G. Jung*. Princeton University Press, 2023.

Kahneman, Daniel. *Thinking, Fast and Slow*. Farrar, Straus and Giroux, 2015.

King, Basil. *The Conquest of Fear*. Perlego, 2006.

King, Jacob, and Gary Crane. *Master Your Emotions*. Jacob King, 2019.

Kobliner, Shirley, and Harold Kobliner. *So to Speak: 11,000 Expressions That'll Knock Your Socks Off*. Tiller, 2020.

Lipton, Bruce H. *The Biology of Belief: Unleashing the Power of Consciousness, Matter & Miracles*. Hay House, 2015.

Lloyd, John, and John Mitchinson. *Advanced Banter: The Qi Book of Quotations*. Faber and Faber, 2009.

Maggio, Rosalie. *How to Say It: Choice Words, Phrases, Sentences, and Paragraphs for Every Situation*. Prentice Hall Press, 2009.

McTaggart, Lynne. *The Field: The Quest for the Secret Force of the Universe*. Harper, 2008.

McTaggart, Lynne. *The Intention Experiment: Using Your Thoughts to Change Your Life and the World*. Atria Paperback, 2013.

Merriam Webster's Collegiate Dictionary. Merriam-Webster, 2006.

Michael, Michael T. "Unconscious Emotion and Free-Energy: A Philosophical and Neuroscientific Exploration." May 21, 2020. pmc.ncbi.nlm.nih.gov.

Millman, Dan. *The Life You Were Born to Live: A Guide to Finding Your Life Purpose*. H. J. Kramer, 1993.

Nelson, Charles A., Michelle De Haan, and Kathleen M. Thomas. *Neuroscience of Cognitive Development: The Role of Experience and the Developing Brain*. Wiley, 2010.

Neville. *The Power of Awareness (Tarcher Cornerstone Editions)*. Jeremy P. Tarcher, 2014.

Osho. *The Book of Wisdom: The Heart of Tibetan Buddhism*. OSHO International, 2014.

Osteen, Joel. *Empty Out the Negative: Make Room for More Joy, Greater Confidence, and New Levels of Influence*. FaithWords, 2021.

Pearce, Joseph Chilton. *The Heart-Mind Matrix: How the Heart Can Teach the Mind New Ways to Think*. Park Street Press, 2012.

Pearsall, Paul. *The Heart's Code: Tapping the Wisdom and Power of Our Heart Energy*. Broadway Books, 1999.

Pert, Candace Beebe. *Molecules of Emotion: Why You Feel the Way You Feel*. Scribner, 2003.

Phillips, Donald T. *The Clinton Charisma: A Legacy of Leadership*. Palgrave Macmillan, 2008.

Porchia, Antonio, and W. S. Merwin. *Voices*. Copper Canyon Press, 2003.

Porges, Stephen W. *The Polyvagal Theory: Neurophysiological Foundations of Emotions, Attachment, Communication, and Self-Regulation*. W. W. Norton, 2011.

Powell, Diane Hennacy. "Interview." Buddha at the Gas Pump. June 23, 2024. https://batgap.com/diane-hennacy-powell-transcript/.

Powell, Diane Hennacy. *The ESP Enigma: The Scientific Case for Psychic Phenomena*. Walker, 2010.

Ricee, Susanne. "Subconscious vs Unconscious: The Complete Comparison." February 16, 2023. www.diversity.social.

Rodale, Jerome Irving, Laurence Urdang, and Nancy LaRoche. *The Synonym Finder*. Time Warner Co., 2000.

Rogers, Carl R. *On Becoming a Person: A Therapist's View of Psychotherapy*. Constable, 2004.

Rooney, Kathy. *Anthology of Quotations: Over 12000 Quotations Arranged by Theme*. Bloomsbury, 2002.

Rudd, Richard. *The Gene Keys: Embracing Your Higher Purpose*. Watkins, 2015.

Rushman, Carol. *The Art of Predictive Astrology: Forecasting Your Life Events*. Llewellyn Publications, 2002.

Shakespeare, William. *The Complete Works of William Shakespeare*. Race Point Publishing, 2014.

Shapiro, Fred R., and Louis Menand. *The New Yale Book of Quotations*. Yale University Press, 2021.

Singh, Manhardeep. *12 Laws of Life*. Self-published, 2024.

Singh, Manhardeep. *The Book of Witty One Liners*. Self-published, n.d.

Stanley, Charles F. *Emotions: Confront the Lies, Conquer with Truth*. Howard Books, 2013.

Stanley, Elizabeth A., and Bessel A. Van der Kolk. *Widen the Window: Training Your Brain and Body to Thrive During Stress and Recover from Trauma*. Avery, 2019.

Stark, Lois Farfel, Kelly Ulcak Moss, and Holly Walrath. *The Telling Image: Shapes of Changing Times*. Greenleaf Book Group Press, 2018.

Tierno, Michael. *Aristotle's Poetics for Screenwriters: Storytelling Secrets from the Greatest Mind in Western Civilization*. Hachette Books, 2015.

"Understanding the Subconscious Mind to Heal Ourselves." Accessed October 16, 2023. enlightenedrecovery.com.

van der Kolk, Bessel A. *The Body Keeps the Score: Brain, Mind, and Body in the Healing of Trauma*. Penguin Books, 2015.

VandenBos, Gary R. *APA Dictionary of Psychology*. American Psychological Association, 2015.

Webster's New World College Dictionary. Houghton Mifflin Harcourt, 2014.

www.azquotes.com

www.brainyquotes.com

www.goodreads.com

www.google.com

www.quotefancy.com

www.wikipedia.com

www.youtube.com

ALPHABETICAL INDEX OF CONTRIBUTORS

ALPHABETICAL INDEX OF EMOTIONS AND EMOTIONAL CONDITIONS

ABOUT THE AUTHOR

D. Earl Johnston is a former corporate executive and world champion sailor with deep interests in emotions and motivation. His colleagues and career mentors have included: the founder and CEO of the largest private company in Los Angeles, an Olympic gold medalist and 12-time world champion athlete from the Midwest, one of the first female vice presidents in Texas business history, a revered high school coach and languages teacher from Wisconsin, and a North Carolina executive twice voted the most admired bank CEO in America.

Choosing Emotions is his expanded second book on 272 emotional conditions as viewed by insightful professionals from all walks of life. The book includes three times as many emotions, as supported by more than ten times as many expert quotes, as any comparable reference work. While researching the book he served as a volunteer speaker to dozens of high school Advanced Placement classes across Southern California, and was voted Speaker of the Year among over 1,000 speakers.